M000197681

CONTEMPORARY

EATALY

ITALIAN COOKING

EATALY

Φ

ANTIPASTI

10

SOUPS

48

FRESH PASTA

92

DRIED PASTA

154

RICE

154

SAVORY TARTS AND PIES

190

FISH AND SEAFOOD

220

OSCAR FARINETTI

Foreword

What is a recipe book if not an occasion to talk about pleasure, harmony, healthiness, and sustainability, or the awareness of our alimentary choices? The American farmer-philosopher Wendell Berry wrote "Eating is an agricultural act." The consumer decides what farmers will grow tomorrow: demand, in a healthy market, drives production. Sometimes it happens that what is offered educates demand. In both cases, whichever side begins has the responsibility of quality. Both cook and diner represent demand and provider and in this case it doesn't matter who starts—if it's the chef who proposes or the consumer who asks. What counts is that the process becomes virtuous, that it innovates and improves constantly. What we put in our body is important for our health and we need to dedicate our energies to our culinary choices, always and everywhere.

My words are not the ones of a health fanatic. For a human being, who has feelings, intelligence, and the knowledge of irony, the act itself of eating must represent a true enjoyment of the senses, involving body, heart, and mind.

The best choices are the ones that provide positive emotions: the moving memory of an old recipe from home, the thrilling discovery of a rare flavor, the beauty of a resplendent dish . . . but the pleasure is enhanced by the awareness of healthiness and sustainability of the ingredients.

Italian cuisine was born as home cooking, therefore replicable and linked to territory, and has created a rich tradition of recipes, unique in the world. If anybody thinks that "home cooking" is something already seen, already tried, already eaten, I would like to remind them with great pleasure that we Italians possess a rich agricultural heritage, which depends on the geologic formation of our country, on the Mediterranean sea, and on the winds that contribute in creating so many microclimates. We are surrounded by an incredible variety of edible vegetable and animal species, which are the raw materials of our cuisine. It's the richness of our biodiversity.

Evolution of civilization has transformed various agricultural and conservation processes, which themselves have taken advantage of climatic and geographical conditions. Geography and sociopolitical history have accompanied the story of our food like they have the story of our art.

The best chefs I have met in my life were mainly great connoisseurs of the raw materials they use: they appreciate, study, and research them with tireless passion and only when they are finally satisfied of their quality do they use and transform them to create their dishes, for the pleasure of those who enjoy them. Therefore, great raw materials, like musical instruments, need the intervention of a conductor to tease out their best contribution to the performance—the recipe that ends up on our tables that will satisfy our senses and feed our hunger for food, but also for traditions, culture, and beauty. Making a spectacle of the world of cuisine is a chance that we must take to bring our attention back to our culinary choices.

Food Unites Us All

"Good food brings us together and helps us to find a common point of view. We believe that one of the greatest sources of joy is what happens around the dinner table."

Those words, which are taken from the manifesto of the preeminent global Italian food brand, Eataly, encapsulate the Italian approach to food and cooking. Using the highest quality ingredients—and always cooking with love—improves both our own lives and those of the people we care for, too.

CONTEMPORARY ITALIAN COOKING

Italian cuisine is steeped in tradition and culture, but family recipes have always been interpreted and adapted to suit a more modern way of life. This book will show you how to eat like a modern Italian wherever you are in the world.

With fresh and seasonal locally sourced ingredients, supplemented with only the very best of preserved fruit and vegetables, cured meats, oils, and flavorings, the modern Italian cook puts together dishes that are often lighter and quicker to prepare than those of past years, but certainly no less flavorsome.

And although the recipes in this comprehensive guide to contemporary Italian cuisine are quick and easy to prepare, they also embrace the philosophy of the Slow Food movement (a movement close to Eataly's own heart), which was set up in 1989 by food activist Carlo Petrini, to counteract a "fast-food epidemic" that seemed to be sweeping across Italy. Slow Food aims to promote the healthy lifestyle that following local food traditions and eating quality artisanal products brings.

THE SECRET TO A GREAT QUALITY OF LIFE

Eating well is one of the greatest pleasures in life. And eating like a contemporary Italian will result in great food on your table. But it requires excellent judgment—both to pick the best quality ingredients but also to decide how to combine them into one delicious whole. *Eataly* will show you how, from its illustrated glossary of ingredients to the hundreds of easy-to-follow recipes that demonstrate how to create a delicious and exquisitely balanced meal every time.

But don't spend any more time reading this . . . *l'appetito vien mangiando!*

ANTIPASTI

○ Preparation time: 15 minutes, plus 10 minutes marinating
♀ Wine suggestion: Alto Adige Val Venosta Riesling

Carpaccio of Amberjack with Ginger, Lime, and Pomegranate

Serves 4

1 (1-inch/2.5-cm) piece fresh
  ginger, peeled and grated
4 tablespoons extra virgin
  olive oil
grated zest and juice of
  1 unwaxed lime
1 (1 lb 2-oz/500-g) amberjack
  fillet (or other medium-
  color oil-rich fish), gutted,
  cleaned, skinned, boned,
  and cut into very thin strips
seeds from 1 large
  pomegranate
1 head chicory (curly endive)
1 Granny Smith apple
8 radicchio leaves
salt
sprigs of wild fennel,
  to garnish

First make the marinade. Put the ginger into the middle of a square of cheese-cloth (muslin), gather up the edges, and squeeze over a small bowl to extract the juice. Add 3 tablespoons of the oil, the lime zest, and ½ teaspoon salt to the bowl and whisk together.

Spread out the strips of fish on a plate and dress with the marinade. Let marinate for 10 minutes.

Meanwhile, put the pomegranate seeds, lime juice, the remaining oil, and a pinch of salt into a bowl and mix well.

Core and chop the apple. Arrange a few leaves of chicory (curly endive) and radicchio on individual serving plates. Place strips of the marinated fish on top. Sprinkle over the pomegranate seeds and apple pieces. Garnish with some wild fennel.

🕓 Preparation time: 20 minutes

Cooking time: 10 minutes

🍷 Wine suggestion: Colli Orientali del Friuli Verduzzo

Apple, Radicchio, and Herbed Soft Cheese Salad

Serves 4

2 Granny Smith apples

1½ tablespoons (¾ oz/20 g) butter

pinch of ground nutmeg

1 small baguette, sliced and lightly toasted

2 tablespoons acacia honey

3 tablespoons extra virgin olive oil

1 tablespoon balsamic vinegar

½ teaspoon salt

7 oz/200 g red and green radicchio, leaves torn

a few leaves of chicory (curly endive), torn

9 oz/250 g mild herbed soft cheese (ideally caciottina cheese), cut into small pieces

⅓ cup (2¼ oz/60 g) peeled almonds, chopped

Peel and core 1 of the apples and slice it into rings. Melt the butter in a skillet (frying pan), add the sliced apple and nutmeg, and cook over medium heat for 1 minute on each side, or until the apple has browned.

Heat the broiler (grill) to high. Spread the sliced bread in a single layer on a baking sheet, arrange the browned apples on top, drizzle with the honey, and broil (grill) for a few minutes until heated through.

To make a dressing, whisk together the oil, balsamic vinegar, and salt in a bowl.

Core and chop the remaining apple. Put the chopped apple into a bowl with the radicchio, chicory (curly endive), cheese, and almonds, pour over the dressing, and toss thoroughly.

Serve the salad with the toasted bread and apples.

TIP For a tasty variation on this dish, try substituting pears and a mature goat cheese for the apples and caciottina cheese. Choose two Kaiser pears, which have a firm flesh and a pleasant aroma. Peel the pears, cut them in half crosswise, and remove the seeds (pips). Then follow the method above, preparing and cooking the pears in the same way as for the apples.

Preparation time: 10 minutes

Cooking time: 40 minutes

Wine suggestion: Dolcetto d'Alba

Fried Polenta with Lardo and Truffle

Serves 4

1½ tablespoons (¾ oz/20 g)
  butter
pinch of salt
1½ cups (7 oz/200 g) coarse
  cornmeal
sunflower oil, for frying
7 oz/200 g lardo (ideally Lardo
  di Colonnata), sliced
1 black truffle

Pour generous 2 cups (15 fl oz/500 ml) water into a large pan, add the butter and salt, and bring to a boil. Gradually sprinkle in the cornmeal, stirring all the time with a wooden spoon to prevent lumps forming, and cook over medium–low heat for about 30 minutes until uniform and compact. As soon as the polenta is the right consistency, pour it into a dish, even it out so that it forms a layer about ½ inch/1 cm thick, and let cool.

Once the polenta has firmed up, cut it into 2 x 2-inch/5 x 5-cm squares. Pour enough oil into a deep skillet (frying pan) so that it is about 1¼ inches/3 cm deep. Heat the oil to 340°F/170°C, then add the polenta squares and cook over medium–high heat for about 5 minutes, turning halfway through the cooking time, until they are golden on both sides. You may need to do this in batches. Remove with a slotted spoon and drain on paper towels.

Put a few slices of lardo on each polenta square, shave over the truffle, and serve immediately.

NOTE Lardo di Colonnata is a pork product that has PGI (Protected Geographical Indication) status. It is made only in the mountain town of Colonnata, in the area of Carrara in Italy. The particular characteristic of this product is that it is aged in basins made of Carrara marble. The lardo is put into the basins in layers, alternating with layers of seasoning that include salt, pepper, cinnamon, cloves, coriander, sage, and rosemary.

Preparation time: 30 minutes, plus cooling
Cooking time: 1 hour
Wine suggestion: Cinque Terre

Octopus Salad with Potato and Olive Purée

Serves 4

1 (2¼-lb/1-kg) octopus, cleaned
1 lb 5 oz/ 600 g potatoes, unpeeled
⅓ cup (1¼ oz/30 g) pitted (stoned) black olives (ideally Taggiasca olives), chopped
a few basil leaves, shredded
4 tablespoons extra virgin olive oil, plus extra for drizzling
juice of ½ lemon
a few mixed salad leaves (greens)
salt

To garnish (optional)
thinly sliced raw vegetables
cooked shrimp (prawns)

Cook the octopus in a large pan of water over low heat for 1 hour. Alternatively, use a pressure cooker and reduce the cooking time to about 30 minutes. Let the octopus cool in its cooking water.

Meanwhile, cook the potatoes in a large pan of boiling salted water for 20–25 minutes, or until they are cooked through, then drain and let cool. Peel the potatoes and mash them coarsley with a fork. Transfer the mashed potatoes to a bowl, add the olives, basil, salt to season, and 2 tablespoons of the oil, and mix well.

Rinse the octopus under cold running water and then cut it into ¾–1¼-inch/ 2–3-cm pieces. Transfer to a bowl, add the remaining oil and the lemon juice, and toss well to coat.

To serve, place a large metal ring or cookie cutter in the center of each serving plate, arrange a layer of the potato and olive purée on the bottom, followed by a layer of octopus. Carefully remove the rings or cutters, top with some mixed salad leaves (greens), drizzle over a little extra oil, and sprinkle with salt. For an extra touch, if liked, garnish with some sliced raw vegetables and a few shrimps (prawns).

Preparation time: 15 minutes

Cooking time: 6 minutes

Wine suggestion: Conegliano Valdobbiadene
Superiore di Cartizze

Olivier Salad

Serves 6

4 potatoes, peeled and diced

4 carrots, peeled and diced

2 cups (11 oz/300 g) shelled
  fresh peas

3½ oz/100 g canned tuna,
  drained and mashed

salt

sliced raw carrot and wild
  fennel or quartered hard-
  cooked (hardboiled) eggs,
  to garnish

For the mayonnaise

1 egg

1 egg yolk

juice of ½ lemon

pinch of salt

¾ cup plus 1 tablespoon
  (7 fl oz/200 ml) sunflower oil

Bring a large pan of salted water to a boil. Meanwhile, fill a large bowl with iced water and set it beside the stove. Drop the potatoes and carrots into the boiling water and leave for 6 minutes, adding the peas 3 minutes before the end of the cooking time. Drain, plunge into the iced water, then drain again thoroughly.

Make the mayonnaise. Put the egg, egg yolk, lemon juice, and salt into a food processor. Blend on medium speed, adding the oil in a thin stream until the mayonnaise is thick and smooth.

Transfer the mayonnaise to a bowl and stir in the tuna, potatoes, carrots, and peas.

Garnish the salad with raw carrot and wild fennel salad or quarters of hard-cooked (hardboiled) egg.

Preparation time: 15 minutes

Cooking time: 5 minutes

Wine suggestion: Gutturnio Frizzante

Crostini with Sausage and Soft Cheese

Serves 4

9 oz/250 g creamy soft cheese
(ideally stracchino cheese)
9 oz/250 g Tuscan sausage,
finely chopped
14 oz/400 g rustic bread
(ideally Tuscan bread), cut
into ⅝ -inch/1.5-cm slices
salt and pepper
a few sage leaves, to garnish

Preheat the oven to 425°F/220°C/Gas mark 7.

Put the cheese and sausage into a bowl and mix together. Season with salt and pepper. Spread the sausage and cheese mixture on top of the sliced bread.

Arrange the crostini on a baking sheet and bake in the oven for 4–5 minutes until toasted and the sausage is cooked.

To serve, sprinkle the crostini with a little pepper and garnish with a few sage leaves.

NOTE Tuscan bread, also known as "pane sciocco" (silly bread) because it has no salt, is made from just type 0 flour, water, and natural yeast. Since 2004, a consortium of producers has safeguarded the heritage of this bread. The variety made at Altopascio, in the Lucca area of Italy, with its rectangular or longer shape, soft crumb, and crisp light golden crust, is highly regarded.

ANTIPASTO

ETIQUETTE

Antipasto is like a handshake, through which you understand the personality of the meal you are about to enjoy. For this reason, the first rule to follow in its preparation is to "love it". This starts with the choice of ingredients, which will need to complement not only each other but also the entire menu. Antipasto, as the word itself suggests, is the anticipation of the main course, so it needs to follow the same "theme": if the meal is going to be based on meat, the entrée cannot be fish, and vice versa. The only exceptions are vegetables, which are a good match for both meat and fish.

HOW TO SERVE ANTIPASTO

For formal dinners, a plate of entrées is served to each guest. If the choice of antipasto is a series of appetizers, current trends suggest that no more than five flavors should be combined, ranging from the most delicate to the strongest, and ensuring good visual presentation: the dish must be harmonious in terms of visual appeal as well as in terms of taste.

For mixed appetizers, the rule for presentation as well as taste is to follow a simple sequence of flavors and scents. Starting with salumi (sliced cured meats), uncooked or broiled (grilled) vegetables follow, leaving fish to the end. The same order is followed when helping yourself from a tray, which will be offered to the ladies first and then to the men, starting with the most important person at the table. Hot appetizers are served before cold ones so as not to affect the flavor of the various courses.

Dinners with friends are more informal. Even if the basic rules remain—coherence of courses and sequence of service—small trays can be left on the table, from which guests can help themselves as they wish, rather than serving out the appetizers to individual guests.

Etiquette requires entrées to be offered twice, but only after the tray has been taken back to the kitchen to be rearranged.

CUTLERY AND TABLE SETTING

To serve a perfect antipasto, classic table settings include both fork and knife but good manners require entrées, including mozzarella, to be eaten using only the fork. The knife is used almost exclusively as a support, with the exception of sardines, cured meats, and fish, in which case a knife and fork are essential.

Only fingers can be used to eat crostini, little tarts, small pizzas, or bruschetta. Bread must not be cut with a knife either. It is permitted to break bread into smaller chunks using a knife, but they must then be eaten with fingers.

Hard cheeses, on the other hand, are cut with a knife. To eat them, they are taken to the mouth on a bit of bread.

Olives must not be touched with fingers or cut with a knife, but are consumed speared with a fork or a toothpick, which is also used to return the stone to the plate.

The antipasto plate, unlike all other individually served dishes in later courses, is served from the left and not from the right. At the end of the course, the plate is again removed from the left, like all empty plates.

ACCOMPANYING WINE

Wine is served after the first round of entrées. To accompany the first few courses of a meal it is best to choose fresh and light wines, white or rosé, or young red wines or, depending on what is to be served, a sparkling wine.

⊙ Preparation time: 15 minutes

♀ Wine suggestion: Conegliano Valdobbiadene Prosecco Superiore

Corn Salad, Strawberries, and Fresh Goat Cheese

Serves 4

7 oz/200 g fresh, soft goat cheese (ideally caprino cheese), crumbled

3–4 basil leaves, cut into strips, plus extra basil leaves to garnish

5 tablespoons extra virgin olive oil

2 pieces crisp flatbread (ideally pane carasau from Sardinia)

5 cups (9 oz/250 g) corn salad (lamb's lettuce)

1²/₃ cups (9 oz/250 g) sliced strawberries

1 tablespoon balsamic vinegar

1 teaspoon honey (ideally acacia honey)

salt and white pepper

In a bowl, mix together the cheese and basil.

In a separate bowl, mix together 3 tablespoons of the oil with a pinch each of salt and white pepper. Break up the flatbread and brush it with the seasoned oil.

Arrange a few pieces of flatbread in individual bowls, then add the corn salad (lamb's lettuce) and a few sliced strawberries. Top with spoonfuls of the cheese and basil mixture, followed by the remaining flatbread, strawberries, and cheese.

In a small bowl, whisk together the remaining oil, balsamic vinegar, honey, and a pinch each of salt and pepper. Pour the dressing over the salad, and serve.

NOTE The scientific name for corn salad (lamb's lettuce) is *Valerianella olitoria* but it has many different common names in Italy, depending on the region, including valeriana, formentino, songino, soncino, gallinella, dolcetta, or valerianella. Corn salad has small heads of long, roundish, deep green leaves. It is eaten in salad and is often served together with other vegetables or fruit, such as scallions (spring onions), radishes, oranges, mandarins, or strawberries.

Preparation time: 15 minutes
Cooking time: 30 minutes
Wine suggestion: Castel del Monte Rosato

Mini Cocottes with Radicchio and Ricotta Cheese

Serves 4

extra virgin olive oil
12 oz/350 g radicchio (ideally
  Radicchio di Treviso)
1/2 shallot, chopped
2 tablespoons pine nuts
1 cup (9 oz/250 g) ricotta
  cheese
2 tablespoons grated
  Parmesan cheese
2 eggs, beaten
salt and pepper

Preheat the oven to 350°F/180°C/Gas mark 4. Grease four ovenproof mini cocotte dishes with oil and line with a few radicchio leaves. Cut the remaining radicchio into strips.

Heat 1 tablespoon oil in a skillet (frying pan), add the shallot, and cook over low heat for 3–4 minutes until soft. Add the strips of radicchio and cook for a few minutes more until the leaves darken.

Heat a separate dry skillet, add the pine nuts and cook over low heat for 5–6 minutes until they start to color.

Transfer the shallot and radicchio mixture to a bowl, stir in the ricotta and Parmesan, followed by the eggs and half the toasted pine nuts. Taste to check the seasoning and add salt and pepper if necessary. Spoon the mixture into the prepared cocottes, pressing down gently with the back of a spoon to ensure the filling is compact.

Place the cocottes in a baking pan and add boiling water to come halfway up the cocottes. Bake in the oven for 25 minutes. Serve immediately, garnished with the remaining pine nuts.

NOTE The Radicchio di Treviso used in this recipe is the early variety, which has a long head, white midrib, and deep red leaves. The superb late variety, known as a "winter flower", is a unique variety, developed from a complex local method of cultivation. Radicchio di Treviso has Protected Geographical Indication (PGI) status, and is delicious, tender, and crisp, with a pleasantly mild/bitter taste.

◷   Preparation time: 10 minutes

♉   Wine suggestion: Oltrepò Pavese Barbera Frizzante

Crostini with Salami, Goat Cheese, and Walnuts

Serves 4

7 oz/200 g soft goat cheese (ideally robiola cheese)

²/₃ cup (3 oz/80 g) chopped walnuts

2 thyme sprigs, leaves only, chopped, plus extra to garnish

1 small baguette, sliced

8 slices salami (ideally Felino), cut into thin strips

In a bowl, mix together the robiola with the walnuts and thyme. Spread the mixture onto the slices of bread. Arrange the salami on top of the cheese and garnish with a little extra thyme.

N O T E   Making salami was one of the first methods invented by man to preserve meat. Felino salami is an Italian specialty that comes from the town of Felino in the Parma area, where it is made using only top-quality coarse pork meat and cured for at least 25 days in controlled-temperature rooms. The salami has a compact texture, deep red color, delicate aroma, and mild taste.

Preparation time: 15 minutes
Wine suggestion: Capri Bianco

Classic Caprese Salad

Serves 4

1 lb 2 oz/500 g buffalo
  mozzarella cheese, cut into
  thick slices
4 tomatoes (about 1 lb
  2 oz/500 g), cut into thick
  slices
4 tablespoons extra virgin
  olive oil
1 teaspoon dried oregano
pinch of salt
5–6 basil leaves, to garnish

Stack alternating slices of tomato and mozzarella on individual serving plates. Drizzle over the oil and sprinkle with the oregano and salt. Serve the salad as soon as it is ready, garnished with basil.

NOTE Buffalo mozzarella cheese has been made in the Italian region of Campania for centuries. Buffalo have been bred on the coastal plains between Volturno and Sele since early medieval times, and buffalo milk is highly regarded. Documents from the twelfth century recount that the monks of San Lorenzo di Capua would offer a cheese called "mozza" or "provatura", with a piece of bread to pilgrims.

🕐 Preparation time: 35 minutes, plus desalting
Cooking time: 30 minutes
🍷 Wine suggestion: Colli Orientali del Friuli Malvasia

Salt Cod Balls

Serves 6

1 (1 lb 8½-oz/700-g) salt cod,
 desalted (see tip)
2⅔ cups (4 oz/120 g) fresh
 breadcrumbs
⅔ cup (2¼ oz/60 g) chopped
 almonds
pinch of salt
pinch of ground cinnamon
2 egg whites
3 tablespoons extra virgin
 olive oil
1 clove garlic, chopped
1 thyme sprig, leaves only,
 chopped
1 marjoram sprig, leaves only,
 chopped
1 lemon, cut into wedges, to
 serve

Preheat the oven to 400°F/200°C/Gas mark 6. Line a baking sheet with parchment (baking) paper.

Cook the salt cod in a large pan of boiling water for 10 minutes. Drain the cod, remove any bones, and chop finely. Transfer the fish to a bowl, add the breadcrumbs, almonds, salt, and cinnamon, and mix well.

In a large spotlessly clean bowl, whisk the egg whites until they form stiff peaks. Using a rubber spatula, gently fold the egg whites into the fish mixture. Using your hands, shape the mixture into 1¼–1½-inch/3–4-cm balls and place them on the prepared baking sheet.

In a small bowl, mix together the oil, garlic, and herbs. Drizzle the mixture over the fish balls and bake in the oven for 20 minutes, or until golden. Serve with wedges of lemon to squeeze over.

TIP   Salt cod is cod fillet preserved in salt. Before using, the salt needs to be thoroughly eliminated from the fish. To desalt salt cod: first rinse under cold running water, then cut the fish into pieces, put into a large bowl of cold water, and let stand in the refrigerator or a cool place for 48 hours, changing the water every 6 hours. Drain and dry the fish, remove the skin and bones, and cook as required.

Preparation time: 20 minutes
Cooking time: 35 minutes
Wine suggestion: Bianco di Custoza

Cornmeal Cakes with Pancetta

Serves 4

5 tablespoons extra virgin
olive oil

2 red onions, sliced

2 tablespoons cane sugar

1 tablespoon balsamic
vinegar

2 teaspoons butter, plus extra
for greasing

2/3 cup (4 oz/120 g) fine
cornmeal or cornflour, sifted

1/4 cup (1 1/4 oz/30 g) type 00
flour, sifted

1 egg

2/3 cup (5 fl oz/150 ml) milk

1 1/4 teaspoons baking powder

pinch of salt

4 slices smoked pancetta or
bacon, cut into small pieces

4–5 chives, chopped, to
garnish

First make the caramelized onion. Heat 1 tablespoon of the oil in a skillet (frying pan), add half the onions and 2 tablespoons water, and cook over medium heat for 5 minutes, or until the water is absorbed. Add the sugar and cook for 4–5 minutes until the onion has caramelized, then add the vinegar and cook for 2 minutes until the vinegar has evaporated. Remove from the heat.

Preheat the oven to 350°F/180°C/Gas mark 4. Grease four tall soufflé ramekins, each about 2 1/2 inches/6 cm, high and 2 1/2 inches/6 cm in diameter, with butter.

Melt the butter in a separate skillet, add the remaining onion, and cook over medium heat for 4–5 minutes until soft, then remove from the heat.

Mix together the flours, egg, milk, baking powder, and salt in a bowl. Stir in half the pancetta or bacon, the fried onion, and the remaining oil. Pour the mixture into the prepared ramekins, place them on a baking sheet and bake in the oven for 25 minutes until firm. Remove from the oven.

Garnish the cornmeal cakes with the caramelized onion, the remaining pancetta, and the chives. Serve warm.

NOTE Because of its high fat content, pancetta has always been considered a nourishing food. The meat comes from the pig's belly and the fatty muscular sides covering the pig's ribs. There are various types of pancetta—the most common in Italy is flat or rolled pancetta, while smoked pancetta has a characteristic flavor.

CHEF
Lorenza Alcantara

⊙ Preparation time: 30 minutes
Cooking time: 15 minutes

Potato and Saffron Bake with Poached Eggs

Serves 4

butter, for greasing
2 boiled potatoes
1 cup (8 fl oz/250 ml)
   whipping cream
6 extra-large (large) eggs
½ pinch saffron powder (or
   3 saffron threads)
¼ teaspoon ground nutmeg
white wine vinegar
salt and pepper

For the sauce
⅓ cup plus 1 tablespoon
   (3½ fl oz/100 ml) vegetable
   broth (stock)
3½ tablespoons whipping
   cream
1¾ cups (5 oz/150 g) grated
   Parmesan cheese

To garnish
Parmesan crisps
herb and baby salad leaves

Preheat the oven to 350°F/180°C/Gas mark 4. Grease a 7 x 6-inch/18 x 15-cm ovenproof dish with butter.

Mash the potatoes in a bowl. Transfer to a food processor, add the cream, two eggs, saffron and nutmeg, season with salt and pepper, and process until well combined.

Spoon the potato mixture into the prepared ovenproof dish. Place the dish in a baking pan and add boiling water to come halfway up the dish. Bake in the oven for 15 minutes, or until it is set.

Meanwhile, make the sauce. Pour the vegetable broth (stock) and cream into a pan and bring to a boil, then whisk in the Parmesan and season to taste with salt and pepper. Keep warm.

Bring a large pan of water to a boil, adding ¼ oz/10 g salt and 1 tablespoon vinegar per 4¼ cups (34 fl oz/1 liter) water. Break the remaining eggs into the pan and cook, keeping the water at 200°F/95°C, for 3 minutes, making sure the whites solidify and the yolks do not break. Remove the poached eggs with a slotted spoon and drain on paper towels.

Remove the potato bake from the oven and cut it into four rectangles. Spoon the sauce onto individual serving plates, place a rectangle of potato bake in the center of each plate, and top with a poached egg. Garnish with Parmesan crisps and herb and baby salad leaves.

♀ **WINE SUGGESTION** Dolcetto wine is an understated, composed, and convivial wine that should be drunk young without too much ceremony. Dolcetto has a magical fragrant note from the fermented grape must. Here this superb wine is perfectly matched with saffron, a combination that will both delight and amaze.

Preparation time: 15 minutes, plus cooling
Cooking time: 55 minutes
Wine suggestion: Alto Adige Lago di Caldaro Classico

Polenta Gratin with Speck Ham and Parmesan Cheese Sauce

Serves 4

7 tablespoons (3½ oz/100 g)
   butter
4 cups (1 lb 2 oz/500 g)
   polenta (ideally taragna,
   a blend of coarse cornmeal
   and buckwheat flour)
12 slices speck ham (about
   5 oz/150 g in total)
salt
a few mint leaves, to garnish

For the sauce
¾ cup plus 1 tablespoon
   (7 fl oz/200 ml) whipping
   cream
pinch of ground nutmeg
1½ cups (4½ oz/130 g)
   grated Parmesan cheese

Line a baking pan with parchment (greaseproof) paper.

Bring 8½ cups (68 fl oz/ 2 liters) salted water to a boil in a heavy pan. Add half the butter and stir until it has melted, then gradually sprinkle in the polenta, whisking all the time to prevents lumps forming—the mixture should be smooth and creamy. Cook over low heat for 40 minutes, stirring every so often with a wooden spoon.

Pour the polenta into the prepared baking pan and let it cool a little. Roll the polenta up from the short edge, lifting the parchment paper to help you—just as you would roll up a Swiss roll. Let cool in the refrigerator until cold.

Make the sauce. Pour the cream into a small pan, add the nutmeg, and bring to a boil. Stir in the Parmesan and cook over low heat, stirring all the time, for 10 minutes. Keep warm.

Cut the polenta roll into ¼-inch/5-mm slices. Melt the remaining butter in a skillet (frying pan), add the slices of polenta and cook over medium heat for 2 minutes on each side, or until golden.

To serve, pour the sauce into the middle of the serving plates, place a stack of polenta slices in the center of each plate, and arrange the speck ham on top. Garnish with mint leaves.

⊙ Preparation time: 35 minutes, plus rising and cooling

Cooking time: 30 minutes

♀ Wine suggestion: Valdobbiadene Superiore di Cartizze Extra Dry

Muffins with Mortadella, Cheese Sauce, and Balsamic Vinegar Cubes

Makes 12 muffins

4 cups (1 lb 2 oz/500 g)
  type 0 flour, sifted, plus
  extra for dusting
3²/₃ cups (1 lb 2 oz/500 g)
  whole wheat (wholemeal)
  flour (ideally buratto flour),
  sifted
2³/₄ teaspoons crumbled
  brewer's yeast or 1
  teaspoon instant yeast
4 teaspoons salt
extra virgin olive oil, for
  greasing
12 slices mortadella (ideally
  Bologna mortadella)

For the sauce
³/₄ cup plus 1 tablespoon
  (7 fl oz/200 ml) whipping
  cream
1¹/₂ cups (4¹/₂ oz/130 g)
  grated Parmesan cheese

**For the balsamic vinegar
  cubes**
1¹/₃ gelatin sheets (leaves,
  about ¹/₈ oz/4 g)
²/₃ cup (5 fl oz/150 ml)
  balsamic vinegar

Put the flours, yeast, and generous 2 cups (17 fl oz/500 ml) warm water into a large bowl and mix together, then transfer to a floured countertop and knead until the dough is smooth and elastic. Add the salt and ²/₃ cup (5 fl oz/150 ml) warm water and continue to knead until the salt has dissolved. Transfer the dough to an oiled bowl, cover with a damp dish towel, and let rise at room temperature for 3 hours, or until doubled in size.

Make the sauce. Pour the cream into a small pan and bring to a boil. Stir in the Parmesan and cook over low heat, stirring all the time, for 10 minutes. Let cool and then spoon the sauce into a pastry (piping) bag fitted with a ½-inch/1-cm tip (nozzle) and chill in the refrigerator for a couple of hours.

Preheat the oven to 350°F/180°C/Gas mark 4. Line a couple of baking sheets with parchment (baking) paper.

Divide the dough into 12 portions, shape them into balls, then flatten them a little to make muffins. Place the muffins on the prepared baking sheets, cover with dish towels, and let rise at room temperature for 20 minutes. Bake in the oven for 20 minutes, or until golden brown. Let the muffins cool on the baking sheets.

Make the gelatin (jelly). Soak the gelatin sheets (leaves) in a bowl of cold water for 10 minutes, then squeeze dry.

Pour the vinegar into a small pan and bring to a boil, then add the gelatin and cook over medium heat for 2 minutes, stirring continuously, until the gelatin has dissolved. Transfer to a bowl and let cool in the refrigerator until the gelatin has set. Cut the gelatin into cubes.

Cut the muffins in half. Spread, or pipe, a layer of the sauce onto the bottom of each muffin, top with the mortadella and some balsamic gelatin cubes, and then close with the top half of each roll.

○ Preparation time: 25 minutes
Cooking time: 30 minutes
♀ Wine suggestion: Gattinar

Pancetta, Chicken, and Sausage Rolls

Serves 4

11 oz/300 g skinless chicken
  breast, cut into 4 thin slices
2 thyme sprigs, leaves only
7 oz/200 g long sausage (you
  can use whichever type of
  sausage you prefer, but it
  is best to use one without
  herbs or seasoning)
12 thin slices pancetta or
  bacon
2 zucchini (courgettes), cut
  lengthwise into thin slices
5 tablespoons extra virgin
  olive oil
3/4 cup plus 1 tablespoon
  (7 fl oz/200 ml) white wine
1 clove garlic
3 sage leaves
salt and pepper
seasonal salad, to serve

Arrange the slices of chicken breast on the countertop and gently flatten with a rolling pin. Season the chicken with salt and pepper and sprinkle over half the thyme. Cut the sausage into pieces about the same width as the flattened chicken breast slices.

Lay out the slices of pancetta or bacon in groups of three overlapping, on the countertop. Put the slices of zucchini (courgettes) on top of the pancetta, followed by slices of chicken, and finish with a piece of sausage. Roll up each slice of pancetta with its fillings and secure the rolls with cocktail sticks (toothpicks).

Heat the oil in a pan, add the meat rolls and cook over medium heat for 15 minutes, or until brown all over. Pour over the wine, add the whole garlic clove, sage, and remaining thyme, cover, and cook for an additional 15 minutes, or until cooked through, checking the pan from time to time and adding a little water if necessary. Serve the meat rolls with a seasonal salad.

TIP   If you would like to try a lighter version of this delicious dish, replace the pancetta or bacon with slices of lean ham and add some champignon mushrooms that have been pan-fried in a little oil, 1 clove garlic, and some finely chopped flat-leaf parsley.

WHAT ARE SALUMI?

In Italy there are hundreds of different varieties of salumi (cured meats), most of which have ancient origins; each region, each valley, and each village produces its own specialties, often in small quantities.

"SALUMEN"

Salumi are the product of curing. The word "salume" derives from the Latin salumen, which means a product preserved in salt. Salt is the most commonly used natural preservative since ancient times. The term is generally used to refer to pork-based products, but beef and boar, horse, duck, and even fish can all be used.

The practice of salting as a conservation method started in Roman times: salt not only dehydrates meat tissues and inhibits the growth of harmful microorganisms, but also helps the aging process and improves the flavor of the finished product.

The first distinction between types of salumi is based on whether whole cuts of meat or mixes of ground (minced) and encased meat are used; the second is the distinction between uncooked and cooked salumi. Uncooked salumi can be whole seasoned pieces of meat (such as uncooked ham), or fresh encased products that need to be used quickly (some types of sausage), or encased and seasoned products (such as salami). Cooking can be used for both encased products such as mortadella, or whole pieces, as in the case of cooked ham. Salami can also be smoked, according to a typically Northern (Germanic and Mitteleuropean) tradition, as is the case with speck ham, for example.

THE CHOICE OF MEAT AND SPICES

Considering the numerous variables involved in processing salumi, it is very difficult to pinpoint a typical production process. However, the choice of meat is essential because each cut is processed according to the type of salumi required: the pig's front limbs are used to make zampone, the neck for coppa and capocollo, the thigh for hams, culatello for speck ham, the cheek for some types of salami, and so on. No part of the pig is wasted: even the blood is used to make blood puddings.

The chosen meat is salted, spiced, and aged. The stages of processing are essential and particularly delicate in the case of uncooked salumi.

Spices and flavors are created using natural substances, either locally sourced or more exotic varieties. The use of spices and flavors can strongly characterize the aroma and taste of salumi and can be quite varied. In addition to pepper, chili powder (widely used in particular in Southern regions), wild fennel, garlic, cloves, nutmeg, cinnamon, and even pine nuts can all be used.

CASINGS

The casing is what gives shape to salumi and allows the meat to age. Furthermore, the casing also protects the meat from air and light and, when natural casings are used, it allows the product to breathe. This helps the aging process and is essential for products destined for long-term aging.

Casings can be natural or synthetic. Synthetic casing is made with animal collagen, cellulose, or plastic materials. Natural casings are more delicate and are of bovine, suine, or ovine origin: cows' bladders (traditionally used for mortadella), pork rind (for zampone), or parts of the intestine. In this latter case, the intestinal tract gives its name to the casing and occasionally to the product, as in the case of gentile salami, which is always encased in the end part of the rectal intestine of the pig and which shares its name, or of mariola salami, a large pork salami that takes its name from the cecum used for its casing.

CHEF
Lucio Pompili

Preparation time: 30 minutes
Cooking time: 10 minutes

Langoustines with Pancetta and Panzanella Bread Salad

Serves 4

¹⁄₃ cup plus 1 tablespoon (3¹⁄₂ fl oz/100 ml) sunflower oil
a handful of basil leaves
5 oz/150 g pancetta or bacon (ideally guanciale), sliced
12 raw langoustines (Dublin Bay prawns), each about 3¹⁄₄–4³⁄₄ inches/8–12 cm long, peeled and deveined

For the panzanella bread salad
7 slices (7 oz/200 g) white bread
1 tablespoon white wine vinegar
extra virgin olive oil
1 onion, cut into thin strips
6 plum tomatoes, quartered
salt and pepper

First make the salad. Put the bread into a bowl with ¾ cup plus 1 tablespoon (7 fl oz/200 ml) water and the vinegar and let soak for 10 minutes. Remove the bread and squeeze out any excess liquid, and tear the bread into pieces.

Heat a little olive oil in a pan, add the onion, and cook over low heat for 3–4 minutes until soft and translucent. Add the tomatoes and soaked bread, season with salt and pepper to taste, and stir well. Let cool.

Heat the sunflower oil in a small pan, add a few basil leaves to the hot oil at a time and cook over high heat for just a few seconds until crisp. Remove with a slotted spoon and drain on paper towels. Repeat with the remaining basil leaves.

Wrap the pancetta or bacon slices around the langoustines (Dublin Bay prawns). Heat a little olive oil in a nonstick skillet (frying pan), add the wrapped langoustines, and cook over high heat for 2 minutes, or until the langoustines turn pink and are cooked through.

Serve the langoustines on top of the salad, garnished with fried basil leaves and drizzled with a little olive oil.

WINE SUGGESTION Otello Spumante Rosé Extra Dry is made from Pinot Nero and Lambrusco grapes. It has a bright color and an intense bouquet—the aromas of early-harvested Pinot Nero mingle with the classic Lambrusco. The fresh taste and softness of the slight sugar residue that balances the wine are offset by the acid note of the tomato and the mild flavors of langoustine and guanciale in this dish.

⏲ Preparation time: 35 minutes

Cooking time: 15 minutes

🍷 Wine suggestion: Penisola Sorrentina Lettere Frizzante

Soft Cheese, Salumi, and Semi-dried Cherry Tomato Pizza

Serves 6–8

4 cups (1 lb 2 oz/500 g)
   type 0 flour, sifted, plus
   extra for dusting
3²/₃ cups (1 lb 2 oz/500 g)
   whole wheat (wholemeal)
   flour (ideally buratto flour),
   sifted
2 teaspoons crumbled
   brewer's yeast or
   ³/₄ teaspoon instant yeast
4 teaspoons salt
extra virgin olive oil, for
   greasing

For the topping
1 lb 2 oz/500 g soft,
   stretched-curd cheese
   (ideally stracciatella cheese)
11 oz/300 g salumi (ideally
   capocollo), sliced
5 oz/150 g semi-dried cherry
   tomatoes (about 35), halved
a few basil leaves

Put the flours, yeast, and generous 2 cups (17 fl oz/500 ml) warm water into a large bowl and mix together, then transfer to a floured countertop and knead until the dough is smooth and elastic. Add the salt and ²/₃ cup (5 fl oz/150 ml) water and continue to knead until the salt has dissolved. Transfer the dough to an oiled bowl, cover with a damp dish towel, and let rise at room temperature for 3 hours, or until doubled in size.

Preheat the oven to 425°F/220°C/Gas mark 7. Grease a baking sheet with oil.

Stretch the dough to fit the prepared sheet and bake in the oven for 10–15 minutes until the crust is golden brown. Arrange the cheese in the middle of the pizza, surround it with the salumi, and sprinkle over the tomatoes and basil.

TIP   You could replace the capocollo with some thick-cut slices of bazzone ham, which is made in the mountain areas of the Serchio Valley in Garfagnana and is promoted by a Slow Food Presidium recognizing its quality. With its mild, rosy-colored fat, predominantly vegetable aroma, and aromatic taste, it is a perfect match for the stracciatella cheese on this pizza.

Preparation time: 15 minutes
Cooking time: 15 minutes
Beer suggestion: Weizenbock beer

Cheese with Speck Ham and Grilled Vegetables

Serves 4

1 zucchini (courgette), thinly
  sliced
1 eggplant (aubergine), thinly
  sliced
1 red bell pepper, cored,
  seeded, and cut into strips
extra virgin olive oil, for
  greasing
8 slices speck ham
4 soft, creamy rinded cheeses
  (ideally tomino cheeses)
salt

Lightly grease a cast-iron griddle pan with oil and heat until very hot. Add the vegetables and cook over medium heat for 1–2 minutes on each side until just cooked. Transfer the vegetables to a plate and season with salt.

Wrap 2 slices of speck ham around each cooking cheese and cook in the griddle pan for 2 minutes on each side.

Arrange the cheese and griddled vegetables on plates and serve immediately.

NOTE   Speck ham from Alto Adige is a boned cured ham that has been trimmed, dry-cured, slightly smoked with wood with a low resin content, and then left to air dry. It is made in the province of Bolzano, and particularly in the Val Venosta area. Speck ham is unique because of both the particular climate of the Alpine valleys and the traditional production method, which has been handed down from generation to generation. The mix of spices used to season the ham is a well-kept family secret.

⊙ Preparation time: 20 minutes
   Cooking time: 40 minutes
♀ Wine suggestion: Alto Adige Müller Thurgau

Potato and Speck Ham Salad

Serves 4

4 potatoes, unpeeled
2 tablespoons extra virgin
   olive oil
1 (5-oz/150-g) slice speck
   ham, diced
3½ cups (3½ oz/100 g) mixed
   baby leaf greens (salad)
⅓ cup (1½ oz/40 g) cashew
   nuts, coarsely chopped and
   toasted
1 red onion, thinly sliced into
   rings

For the salad dressing
½ cup (3¾ oz/115 g) plain
   yogurt
2 tablespoons horseradish
   sauce
3 tablespoons extra virgin
   olive oil
salt and pepper

Put the potatoes into a large pan of cold water, bring to a boil, and cook over medium heat for 40 minutes (including the time it takes for the water to come to a boil), or until a knife inserted into the potatoes comes out easily. Let cool and then peel and dice the potatoes. Transfer the potatoes to a bowl, pour over the oil, and gently toss to coat.

Meanwhile, heat a dry nonstick skillet (frying pan), add the speck ham, and cook over medium heat for 3–4 minutes until brown. Let cool, then add to the bowl with the potatoes and stir together.

Make the dressing. Put the yogurt, horseradish sauce, oil, and a pinch each of salt and pepper into a small bowl and beat until well combined.

To serve, divide the mixed baby leaf salad among serving plates, then add the potato and speck ham. Sprinkle over the cashew nuts and onion and drizzle with the dressing.

N O T E   You can easily make horseradish sauce at home. Put ¾ cup (2 oz/50 g) grated horseradish into a food processor, add 2 tablespoons superfine (caster) sugar, 4 tablespoons white wine vinegar, and a pinch of salt, and blend to a smooth and creamy consistency. The sauce can also be served with cotechino sausage or zampone (stuffed pig's trotter).

Preparation time: 25 minutes
Wine suggestion: Alto Adige Santa Maddalena

Speck Ham, Walnut, and Champignon Mushroom Salad

Serves 4

juice of 1/2 lemon
4 tablespoons extra virgin
   olive oil
11 oz/300 g speck ham, sliced
1/2 cup (21/4 oz/60 g) chopped
   walnuts
31/2 oz/100 g champignon
   mushrooms, sliced
31/2 cups (31/2 oz/100 g) salad
   greens (leaves), torn
salt and white pepper

First make the dressing. Put the lemon juice, oil, and a pinch each of salt and white pepper into a small bowl and whisk together.

Arrange the speck ham on a serving platter and sprinkle over the walnuts. Drizzle over the dressing, then add the mushrooms and salad greens (leaves), and serve.

NOTE   You can choose whichever salad greens (leaves) you prefer for this recipe. Why not try early Radicchio di Treviso? Its thick, dark red leaves with large white midribs will add a colorful touch to the dish, while its mild, very distinctive flavor goes perfectly with walnuts and mushrooms. You could also try using fresh cep mushrooms when they are in season.

Preparation time: 15 minutes

Cooking time: 15 minutes

Wine suggestion: Alto Adige Lagrein Kretzer

Sole and Speck Ham Rolls

Serves 4

4 (2-oz/50-g) thin slices speck
ham
4 (5-oz/150-g) sole fillets
2 tablespoons (1¼ oz/30 g)
butter
20 scallions (spring onions,
about 11 oz/300 g), three-
quarters of the green parts
removed, chopped
⅓ cup plus 1 tablespoon (3½
fl oz/100 ml) white wine
2 tablespoons balsamic
vinegar
salt and pepper

Put the slices of speck ham on the countertop and place a sole fillet on top of each slice. Season with salt and pepper, then roll up the speck ham and its filling and secure with a cocktail stick (toothpick).

Melt the butter in a heavy pan, then add the scallions (spring onions), season with salt and pepper, and pour over the wine. Cover and cook over medium heat for 5 minutes. Remove the lid, add the sole and speck ham rolls, and pour over the vinegar. Cover and cook for 10 minutes more, turning the rolls halfway through the cooking time. Serve immediately.

NOTE One of the latest trends in cooking is to prepare dishes with fish and cured meat products, for example shellfish (particularly crawfish/crayfish or scampi) with flat pancetta or bacon. There are many other recipes that match the mild, delicate flavor of fish with the stronger, fuller taste of the fat from cured meats.

⊙   Preparation time: 20 minutes

Cooking time: 3–5 minutes

♀   Wine suggestion: Colli Bolognesi Pignoletto Frizzante

Mortadella Mousse

Serves 4

1 (9-oz/250-g) slice
   mortadella, diced and
   grains of pepper removed
³/₄ cup (7 oz/200 g) ricotta
   cheese
juice of ¹/₂ lemon
¹/₂ baguette, sliced
unsalted shelled pistachios,
   finely chopped
salt and pepper

Put the mortadella, ricotta, and lemon juice into a food processor and blend well. Season with salt and pepper and blend again, stopping every so often and stirring the mixture with a spoon, until you have a smooth mixture.

Heat the broiler (grill) to medium–high. Arrange the bread slices in a single layer on a baking sheet and broil (grill) for a few minutes until golden brown.

Spread the mortadella mousse onto the toasted bread, sprinkle over the pistachios, and serve.

NOTE A classic ingredient of Bolognese cooking, mortadella is often simply called "la Bologna", which just shows how much of a local tradition it is. Made from pork, salt and pepper, spices, and pistachios, mortadella is a very popular cured meat, and it is an essential ingredient to make the stuffing for tortellini of Bologna.

SOUPS

Preparation time: 15 minutes

Cooking time: 20 minutes

Wine suggestion: Alto Adige Gewürztraminer

Fresh Pea Soup with Smoked Ham

Serves 4

extra virgin olive oil

2 potatoes, peeled and diced

1 shallot, chopped

3 1/3 cups (27 fl oz/800 ml) hot
  vegetable broth (stock)

3 1/2 cups (1 lb 2 oz/500 g)
  shelled fresh peas

1 small bunch basil, leaves
  chopped

piece of butter

4 oz/120 g smoked ham,
  cut into small strips

salt and pepper

a few mint leaves, to garnish
  (optional)

toasted bread, cubed,
  to serve (optional)

Heat a drizzle of oil in a large pan, add the potatoes and shallot, and cook over low heat for 5 minutes, or until soft but not browned. Pour over the broth (stock) and cook over medium heat for 10 minutes, then add the peas (retaining a few to garnish) and basil, adjust the seasoning if necessary, and cook for 5 minutes more. Use an immersion blender to blend the soup until smooth and homogenous.

Melt the butter in a skillet (frying pan), add the ham, and gently fry over medium heat for 3–4 minutes until crisp. Drain on kitchen paper.

Garnish the soup with the crisp ham, peas, and a few mint leaves, if liked, and serve with toasted bread, if liked.

NOTE Smoked ham is obtained by flavoring a fresh pork leg with spices and aromatic herbs, steaming it slowly, and then smoking it over wood, typically beech or juniper. This flavorful ham lends itself well to being used in many recipes, and it is also good served on slices of whole wheat (wholemeal) or rye bread.

○ Preparation time: 5 minutes

Cooking time: 50 minutes

♀ Wine suggestion: Leverano Bianco

Vegetable Minestrone

Serves 4

extra virgin olive oil

1 onion, sliced

1 celery stalk, thinly sliced

2 carrots, finely diced

2 zucchini (courgettes), finely
diced

2 potatoes, peeled and finely
diced

½ head broccoli, broken into
florets

½ cauliflower, broken into
florets

1 cup (3½ oz/100 g) green
beans, topped and tailed
and cut into short lengths

salt

8 cherry tomatoes, halved, to
garnish (optional)

Heat a little oil in a large pan, add the onion, celery, and carrots, and cook over medium heat for 5–6 minutes until they begin to brown. Add the zucchini (courgettes) and potatoes and cook, gradually adding 8½ cups (68 fl oz/2 liters) hot water a ladleful at a time, for about 40 minutes until the vegetables are soft, adding the broccoli, cauliflower, and green beans 15 minutes before the end of the cooking time. Taste to check the seasoning and add salt if necessary.

Serve the minestrone garnished with cherry tomatoes, if using.

NOTE There are many variations on minestrone: every Italian family has its own recipe, which can change depending on the season so as to use the freshest vegetables. To flavor this dish or make it more aromatic, add 1 tablespoon homemade Genoese pesto (made with basil, grated Parmesan and pecorino cheeses, extra virgin olive oil, and pine nuts) at the end of the cooking time.

⊙　　Preparation time: 30 minutes, plus 8–12 hours soaking

　　　Cooking time: 1¾ hours

♀　　Wine suggestion: Cerveteri Rosso

Pasta and Bean Soup

Serves 4

1 cup (7 oz/200 g) dried
　cranberry (borlotti) beans
extra virgin olive oil
1 onion, thinly sliced
3½ oz/100 g piece fatback
　(pork fat), thinly sliced
2 potatoes, peeled and cut
　into pieces
4¼ cups (34 fl oz/1 liter) hot
　vegetable broth (stock)
7 oz/200 g short egg pasta
　(ideally fresh)
rosemary sprigs, to garnish

Soak the beans in a bowl filled with cold water for 8–12 hours. Drain and rinse.

Heat a drizzle of oil in a very large pan, add the onion and pork fat, and cook over low heat for 4–5 minutes until browned. Add the potatoes and drained beans and cook for a few minutes over low heat, then add a ladleful of broth (stock) and cook, gradually adding the remaining broth a ladleful at a time, for about 1½ hours, until the beans are cooked.

Transfer half the soup to a food processor and blend until creamy. Add the pasta to the pan with the remaining soup and cook over low heat for 7 minutes or until pasta is cooked. Return the blended soup to the pan, stir well, and cook until heated through. Taste to check the seasoning and add salt if necessary.

Serve the soup garnished with rosemary, if liked, and a drizzle of oil.

NOTE Cranberry (borlotti) beans are one of the best known and most widely used vegetables in the Italian gastronomic tradition: they are part of the so-called peasant cuisine because they are cheap but also full of flavor and important nutritional substances. This soup can also be made with Casalbuono beans, which have been grown near Salerno in Italy since the thirteenth century, and are now protected by the Slow Food Presidia label. Every year the people of the village of Casalbuono, which nestles among the hills of the Diano valley, celebrate this vegetable with the *sagra dei fasul scucchiulariedde* (beans that are to be threshed and shelled festival).

Preparation time: 15 minutes

Cooking time: 40 minutes

Wine suggestion: Trentino Müller Thurgau

Pumpkin Soup with Saffron Croutons

Serves 4

extra virgin olive oil
piece of butter
1 onion, thinly sliced
4 cups (1 lb 5 oz/600 g)
    pumpkin flesh chunks
2 thyme sprigs
4¼ cups (34 fl oz/1 liter) hot
    vegetable broth (stock)
120 mg saffron threads
½ loaf slightly stale bread,
    cut into cubes

Heat a drizzle of oil and the butter in a large pan, add the onion, and cook over low heat for 5–6 minutes until soft and transparent. Add the pumpkin and thyme (retaining some thyme leaves for garnish) and cook for a few minutes more, then pour over the broth (stock), cover, and cook for 30 minutes, or until the pumpkin is tender. Use an immersion blender to blend the soup until smooth and homogenous.

Meanwhile, make the croutons. Put the saffron in a small bowl with 1¾ fl oz/ 50 ml warm water and let soak for 10 minutes. Lightly dip the bread cubes into the saffron water. Heat a dry nonstick skillet (frying pan) until very hot, then add the croutons and cook over medium heat for 7–8 minutes until crisp.

Serve the soup with the croutons and scatter with thyme leaves.

NOTE The king of spices, saffron is sometimes called red gold because it is necessary to pick 150,000 crocus flowers (*Crocus sativus*) and process them by hand in order to obtain 2¼ lb/1 kg of saffron. Used since ancient times, both as a natural dye and to flavor dishes with its unmistakeable taste, saffron is high in carotenoids that reduce the damage caused by free radicals. Saffron is an indispensable ingredient in Risotto alla Milanese (see page 182).

THE CORNERSTONES
OF ITALIAN CUISINE

In international cuisine, the cornerstones of Italian cuisine are generally called potage, a term that includes a variety of soups based on broth (stock), meat, fish, and vegetables, cooked in a pan and served in deep plates or bowls.

Zuppa, minestra, crema, and vellutata are all part of a large family of soups and are often confused with one another because they are prepared in very similar ways. Cooking them at home is an ancient and firmly rooted tradition in all regions of Italy.

THE CLASSIC DEFINITION: CLEAR AND THICKENED SOUPS

Classic cuisine essentially differentiates two types of potage or soup: "clear" soups, based on broth made with meat, fish, vegetables, shellfish, or poultry, which can be garnished, and consommé (clear broth served in a special two-handled bowl); and "thickened" soups, to which cream, butter, egg yolk, or starch have been added, which include crema and vellutata.

Starting from these two basic preparations, it is possible to create numerous dishes: from invigorating legume (pulses) soups to delicate asparagus *vellutata*, through to soups with rice and vegetables.

SPOONFULS OF DELIGHT:
ZUPPA, MINESTRA, CREMA, AND VELLUTATA

Zuppa and *minestra*, *crema* and *vellutata* are considered the cornerstones of Italian cuisine–popular, familiar dishes that reflect the seasons and bring to the table the most ancient regional traditions. Hot or cold, they have the captivating charm of comfort food: but what differentiates them?

Zuppa started as a poor man's substantial dish, prepared with what was readily available: offal and giblets, leftovers, low value fish, and vegetables from the garden. Simple and wholesome, it contains various chopped (not puréed) ingredients and is cooked with a liquid, which can be water or broth. The name derives from the Germanic term "*soppa*" which means "a slice of bread that has been soaked". Zuppa is traditionally poured over a slice of bread in the bottom of a bowl, which soaks up the liquid, making the dish drier, but sometimes the bread, normally *crostini* (toasted bread) is served separately. There is usually no pasta or rice in zuppa.

The name *minestra* comes from the Latin "*ministrare*", meaning "administer", indicating a dish that was brought to the table by the person who managed the household. Minestra has more broth and can also contain fresh pasta and rice, as well as vegetables, cereals, and even a beaten egg.

Vellutata takes its name from its smooth appearance and creamy consistency, which is achieved by adding starchy ingredients, such as wheat, potato starch, rice, or cornstarch (cornflour), to give the broth body and structure. The most common preparation technique starts with a roux of melted butter and flour mixed together in equal proportions (the same process is used for béchamel sauce), diluted with a hot liquid, to which vegetables, fish, meat, or shellfish are then added. When these are cooked, the ingredients are blended in a food processor or puréed and strained, and bound with an egg yolk, cream, or butter. If pure starches are used as thickeners, it is necessary to blend them with a little water first and then add them very slowly to hot preparations, and then continue cooking until the desired thickness is reached. The final garnish can be made with the same ingredients used to make the vellutata.

Finally *crema*, though similar to *vellutata* both in appearance and in its soft, silky consistency, is generally prepared with a single ingredient, strained, or processed in a food processor and flavored with cream. It can be made a little thicker by adding a pinch of rice flour or a few spoonfuls of milk.

Preparation time: 30 minutes, plus soaking

Cooking time: 1 hour

Wine suggestion: Langhe Bianco

Ginger Potato Soup with Bean Salad

Serves 4

½ cup (3½ oz/100 g) dried
  cranberry (borlotti) beans
1 bay leaf
3⅓ cups (27 fl oz/800 ml) hot
  vegetable broth (stock)
5 potatoes (about 1 lb 5oz/
  600 g), peeled and diced
1 (¾-inch/2-cm) piece fresh
  ginger, peeled and grated
11 oz/300 g fresh fava (broad)
  beans in their pods, shelled
  (⅔ cup prepared)
11 oz/300 g fresh peas in
  their pods, shelled (⅔ cup
  prepared)
extra virgin olive oil
2 celery stalks, cut into small
  pieces
1 carrot, cut into small pieces
salt and pepper
a few fronds of wild or
  cultivated fennel, to garnish

Soak the cranberry (borlotti) beans in a large bowl of cold water overnight. The next day, drain the beans and then cook them in a pan of boiling water with the bay leaf for at least 1 hour until tender and soft. Drain well.

Meanwhile, 30 minutes before the end of the cranberry bean cooking time, pour the stock (broth) into a pan and bring to a boil, add the potatoes, bring the stock back to a boil, and boil the potatoes for 10 minutes, or until very soft. Add the ginger, season with a pinch each of salt and pepper, and use an immersion blender to blend the soup to a purée.

Meanwhile, cook the fava (broad) beans and peas in a pan of boiling salted water for a few minutes until tender, then drain well. Transfer to a large bowl, add the drained cranberry beans, drizzle over a little oil, add a pinch of salt, and mix well.

Heat a little oil in a skillet (frying pan), add the celery and carrot, and cook over medium heat for 2–3 minutes until the vegetables just start to soften but still retain their bite.

Ladle the potato soup into the bottom of each serving bowl, arrange a little of the celery and carrot mixture on top, and finish with the bean salad. Garnish with a few fronds of fennel and serve immediately.

Preparation time: 20 minutes

Cooking time: 40 minutes

Wine suggestion: Nuragus di Cagliari

Fennel Soup with Croutons

Serves 4

2 tablespoons (1¼ oz/30 g)
   butter
1 shallot, chopped
2 potatoes, peeled and diced
2 fennel bulbs (about 1 lb
   5 oz/600 g), cut into pieces
   and fronds reserved
4¼ cups (34 fl oz/1 liter) hot
   vegetable broth (stock)
⅓ cup plus 1 tablespoon
   (3½ fl oz/100 ml) light
   (single) cream
2 dill sprigs, chopped
2 thick slices rustic bread
   (ideally Tuscan bread), cut
   into small cubes
2 tablespoons extra virgin
   olive oil, plus extra
   for drizzling
pinch of nutmeg
salt

Melt the butter in a large pan, add the shallot, and cook over medium heat for 4–5 minutes until soft and transparent but not browned. Add the potatoes and fennel and cook for a few minutes to let them absorb the flavor, then pour over the broth (stock) and cook for about 30 minutes until the vegetables are soft and almost melted. Use an immersion blender to blend the soup until smooth and homogenous. Stir in the cream and dill and cook for 5 minutes more. Taste to check the seasoning and add salt if necessary.

Meanwhile, make the croutons. Preheat the oven to 350°F/180°C/Gas mark 4. Spread the bread cubes in a single layer on a baking sheet, drizzle over the oil, and bake in the oven for 5 minutes or until golden brown and crisp. Transfer to a paper bag with a pinch of salt and the nutmeg and shake to coat.

Serve the soup hot, topped with the toasted croutons and reserved fennel fronds, and drizzled with a little extra oil.

NOTE   The best fennel to use for this soup is the Tarquinia variety, which is characterized by an excellent flavor and is ready to harvest after a fairly short growing period. This variety of fennel is cultivated in Tarquinia and Montalto di Castro, near Viterbo, and is recognizable by its wide leaves and yellow flowers.

Chickpea Soup with Carrots, Grains, and Cavolo Nero

Serves 4

1²/₃ cups (11 oz/300 g) dried chickpeas
extra virgin olive oil
1 cup (5 oz/150 g) diced carrots (ideally Polignano carrots)
1 red onion diced
²/₃ cup (2 oz/50 g) diced celery root (celeriac)
1 cup (1¼ oz/30 g) rosemary, leaves chopped
¹/₃ cup (½ oz/15 g) thyme, chopped
4¼ cups (34 fl oz/1 liter) hot vegetable broth (stock)
¾ cup (5 oz/150 g) sorghum grains
7 oz/200 g cavolo nero (Tuscan black cabbage)
1 clove garlic, crushed
salt

Soak the chickpeas in a large bowl of cold water overnight.

The next day, rinse the chickpeas under cold running water and drain well.

Heat ¾ cup (5 fl oz/150 ml) oil in a pan, add the carrots, red onion, celery root (celeriac), and herbs, and cook over medium heat for 5–6 minutes until soft. Stir in the drained chickpeas, then pour over the broth (stock) and cook for at least 2 hours until the chickpeas are soft.

Meanwhile, cook the sorghum grains in a large pan of boiling salted water for about 40 minutes until soft but still intact. Drain well.

Bring a large pan of water to a boil. Drop the cavolo nero (Tuscan black cabbage) into the boiling water and leave for 3 minutes. Drain well and then chop coarsely.

Heat a drizzle of oil in a skillet (frying pan), add the cavolo nero and garlic, and cook over medium heat for 3 minutes.

When the chickpeas are cooked, transfer three-quarters of the soup to a food processor and blend to a purée, then return to the pan with the remaining soup and mix well. Stir in the drained sorghum grains and cook over medium heat for 5–10 minutes until heated through. Serve the soup drizzled with a little oil and topped with the cavolo nero.

♀ **WINE SUGGESTION** Masseria Tamburi Primitivo, one of the best wines of the Salento region, is second only to Nero d'Avola in strength and depth. This wine reveals aromas of plums and blackberries in harmony with the spices and tobacco leaves. It complements the chickpea soup perfectly.

Preparation time: 20 minutes
Cooking time: 45 minutes
Wine suggestion: Morellino di Scansano

Acquacotta

Serves 4

extra virgin olive oil
1 clove garlic, chopped
2 onions, chopped
3 carrots, chopped
2 celery stalks, chopped
2 medium-sized potatoes,
   peeled and diced
1/2 red chile, chopped
2 1/4 lb/1 kg Swiss chard,
   coarsely chopped
3/4 cup (7 oz/200 g) puréed
   canned tomatoes (passata)
salt and pepper
4 slices toasted rustic bread,
   to serve

Heat a drizzle of oil in a very large pan, add the garlic clove and onions, and cook over low heat for 5 minutes, or until golden brown. Add the carrots, celery, and potatoes and pour over enough water to cover the vegetables. Season with salt and pepper, add the chile, then bring to a boil and cook for 10 minutes. Add the spinach beet or chard and the tomato purée and cook over low heat for 30 minutes, topping up with hot water if the soup gets too dry—the finished soup should be fairly liquid.

To serve, place a piece of toasted bread into each soup plate, pour over the Acquacotta, and drizzle over a little oil.

NOTE Acquacotta is one of the traditional soups of the Bassa Maremma region of Italy, between Grosseto and Viterbo. This soup would have been a typical lunch for the herdsmen who tended the cattle herds, so it is a peasant dish that is made to varying recipes depending on the availability of ingredients, all of which came from the countryside where the Tuscan herdsmen worked. You can enrich the soup by adding animal fats, such as fatback (porkfat) or bacon fat.

⊙ Preparation time: 20 minutes, plus soaking
Cooking time: 1 hour 15 minutes
♀ Wine suggestion: Capalbio Bianco

Spicy Black Bean and Pumpkin Soup

Serves 4

¼ cup (2 oz/50 g) dried
  black beans
extra virgin olive oil
1 yellow onion, thinly sliced
2⅔ cups (14 oz/400 g) diced
  pumpkin flesh
generous 2 cups (17 fl oz/
  500 ml) hot vegetable
  broth (stock)
1 red chile, cut into rings
salt and pepper

To serve
1 flat-leaf parsley sprig,
  chopped
4 tablespoons plain
  (natural) yogurt

Soak the black beans in a bowl of cold water overnight.

The next day, drain the beans and then cook them in a pan of boiling water for 40 minutes, or until tender but still firm. Drain well.

Heat a little oil in a large pan, add the onion, and cook over low heat for 5–6 minutes until soft and transparent. Add the pumpkin, pour over the broth (stock), and season with salt and pepper if necessary. Cover with a lid and cook for 5 minutes, then add the drained beans and chile and cook, uncovered, for 20 minutes until the pumpkin is soft, adding a little extra broth if necessary so that the soup does not reduce too much.

Spoon the soup into serving bowls, sprinkle with parsley, and serve with 1 tablespoon yogurt in a small bowl on the side for each person.

N O T E   Black beans are typical vegetables of Central America, particularly Mexico, where they are used chiefly in soups that are flavored generously with chiles. Once cooked, black beans have a much creamier consistency than other beans and thus lend themselves well to puréeing as an accompaniment to other dishes or as a topping for toasted bread.

Preparation time: 15 minutes

Cooking time: 10 minutes

Wine suggestion: Colli Bolognesi Classico Pignoletto

Spinach Noodles in Broth

Serves 4

3½ cups (3½ oz/100 g)
   spinach
1¼ cups (3½ oz/100 g)
   grated Parmesan cheese
2 eggs
pinch of ground nutmeg
grated zest of 1 unwaxed
   lemon
2 cups (3½ oz/100 g) fresh
   breadcrumbs
all-purpose (plain) flour,
   for dusting
8½ cups (68 fl oz/2 liters)
   vegetable broth (stock)

Put the spinach, Parmesan, eggs, nutmeg, and lemon zest into a food processor and process, gradually adding the breadcrumbs, until you have a fairly thick paste. Using your hands, shape the mixture into fist-size balls and lay these on a lightly floured countertop.

To make the noodles, pass the balls of spinach mixture through a food mill fitted with a coarse disc.

Bring the broth (stock) to a boil in a large pan. Drop the noodles into the boiling broth, then remove from the heat and let stand for 2–3 minutes until the noodles bob up to the surface. Serve hot.

TIP   If you don't have a food-mill disc with large holes you can use a potato ricer to make the noodles. To do this, make the spinach mixture as above, processing until you have a soft paste that can pass through the narrower holes of the potato ricer with ease. Hold the ricer over the pan of boiling broth (stock) and let the noodles drop directly into the broth, using a knife to cut off the noodles to the desired length as they emerge from the ricer.

⊙ Preparation time: 25 minutes
Cooking time: 35 minutes
♀ Wine suggestion: Cinque Terre

Mushroom, Potato, and Monkfish Soup

Serves 4

4 tablespoons extra virgin
 olive oil
1 small onion, chopped
2 potatoes, peeled and diced
1 bay leaf
11 oz/300 g mixed
 mushrooms, such as oyster,
 button, honey, and porcini
 mushrooms, the larger ones
 cut into small pieces
31/3 cups (27 fl oz/800 ml)
 hot vegetable broth (stock)
14 oz/400 g monkfish,
 cleaned, filleted, and cut
 into small pieces (see
 page 228)
salt and pepper
a few marjoram leaves,
 to garnish
toasted bread, to serve
 (optional)

Heat 2 tablespoons of the oil in a large pan, add the onion, and cook over low heat for 5 minutes, or until transparent. Add the potatoes, bay leaf, mushrooms, and broth (stock) and cook over medium heat for 25 minutes.

Heat 1 tablespoon of the oil in a nonstick skillet (frying pan), add the fish, and cook over medium heat for 5 minutes. Taste to check the seasoning and add salt and pepper if necessary. Add the monkfish to the soup and cook for an additional 5 minutes.

Serve the soup hot, drizzled with the remaining oil and garnished with marjoram leaves. If liked, accompany with slices of toasted bread.

NOTE   Monkfish is a sea fish whose meat is reminiscent of lobster, and it lends itself well to sauces. Its massive head is covered in bones and spines, so for this reason monkfish is usually sold without the head. Once the fish is skinned, with the central spine removed, you are left with two fillets that are very suitable for recipes such as this one.

⊙ Preparation time: 15 minutes, plus soaking
Cooking time: 1 hour 10 minutes

♀ Wine suggestion: Alto Adige Lago di Caldaro

Oat and Chickpea Soup

Serves 4

1½ cups (9 oz/250 g) polished whole oats
1⅓ cups (9 oz/250 g) dried chickpeas
4 tablespoons extra virgin olive oil
1 white onion, finely chopped
4 carrots, chopped
3 sage leaves, chopped, plus extra to garnish
4¼ cups (34 fl oz/1 liter) hot vegetable broth (stock)

Soak the oats and chickpeas in two separate containers filled with cold water for at least 12 hours, changing the water in both containers every 3–4 hours.

Heat 2 tablespoons of the oil in a large pan, add the onion, and cook over medium heat for 5 minutes, or until transparent. Add the carrot and sage and cook for a few minutes more.

Drain the oats and chickpeas and rinse well, then add them to the pan with the vegetables. Pour over the broth (stock) to cover the cereals and vegetables, cover, and cook for 1 hour, or until the oats and chickpeas are cooked through, adding a little more broth when necessary to keep the cereals and vegetables covered.

Serve the soup garnished with a few extra sage leaves and drizzled with the remaining oil.

NOTE Oats are a cereal crop that has excellent nutritional and energy-giving properties. They are recommended as a breakfast food because they are so rich in proteins and linoleic acid, and they are used widely in soups. This recipe uses polished oats, which have had their fibrous husks removed.

Preparation time: 15 minutes, plus soaking
Cooking time: 40 minutes
Wine suggestion: Garda Classico Chiaretto

Spelt Soup with Potatoes and Onions

Serves 4

¾ cup (6¼ oz/180 g) spelt
4 tablespoons extra virgin
  olive oil
1 large white onion, finely
  chopped
1 celery stalk, finely chopped
2 tomatoes, skinned, seeded,
  and crushed with a fork
4¼ cups (34 fl oz/1 liter) hot
  vegetable broth (stock) or
  boiling water
2 small potatoes, peeled
  and diced
1 small dried chile, chopped
a few sprigs flat-leaf parsley,
  chopped, to garnish
  (optional)

Rinse the spelt under cold running water then soak it in a large bowl of cold water for at least 2 hours. Drain and rinse.

Heat 2 tablespoons of the oil in a large pan, add the onion, celery, and tomatoes, and cook over medium heat for 5 minutes, then pour over the broth (stock) or boiling water, add the potatoes, and bring to a boil. Once the liquid comes to a boil, add the drained spelt, partially cover the pan, and cook over low heat for about 30 minutes, stirring frequently, until the spelt is cooked and the soup is thick. Just before the cooking time is up, add the chile and stir thoroughly.

Serve the soup drizzled with the remaining oil and garnish with a few parsley leaves, if liked.

NOTE   The tradition in central Italy, particularly in Tuscany and Umbria, is to cook cereal and bean soups in earthenware cooking pots. Terracotta is an insulating material that heats up more slowly than metal and yields the heat it has absorbed more slowly, thus keeping food hot for longer. Try using an earthenware pan to cook this soup or any other recipes that call for low heat without sudden changes in temperature.

⊙   Preparation time: 20 minutes
Cooking time: 50 minutes
🍷   Wine suggestion: Reggiano Lambrusco

Pumpkin, Chestnut, and Prosciutto Soup

Serves 4

extra virgin olive oil
1 shallot, finely chopped
2 rosemary sprigs
1 bay leaf
3$\frac{1}{3}$ cups (14 oz/400 g) small
   pumpkin flesh cubes
2 potatoes, peeled and cut
   into small cubes
1$\frac{1}{3}$ cups (7 oz/200 g) cooked
   and peeled chestnuts
3 oz/80 g ham rind
4$\frac{1}{4}$ cups (34 fl oz/1 liter) hot
   meat broth (stock)
piece of butter
3$\frac{1}{2}$ oz/100 g prosciutto
   (Parma ham), cut into thin
   strips

To garnish ·
piece of butter
4 sage leaves

Heat a drizzle of oil in a large pan, add the shallot, rosemary, and bay leaf, and cook over low heat for 2–3 minutes until sizzling. Add the pumpkin and potatoes and cook over high heat for 4 minutes, then add the chestnuts and cook for 5 minutes more. Add the ham rind, pour over the broth (stock), and cook over medium heat for 30–35 minutes until the vegetables are soft but still hold their shape.

Just before the soup is cooked, melt the butter in a skillet (frying pan), add the prosciutto (Parma ham), and cook over medium heat for 2–3 minutes until crisp. Remove the prosciutto and drain on paper towels.

To make the garnish, melt the butter in the same skillet you used to cook the prosciutto, add the sage leaves, and cook over medium heat for 1–2 minutes until crisp.

Remove the rosemary sprigs and bay leaf from the soup.

To serve, divide the soup among bowls, sprinkle over the crisp prosciutto, then garnish with the fried sage leaves.

⊙ Preparation time: 25 minutes, plus degorging

Cooking time: 30 minutes

♀ Wine suggestion: Garda Classico Chiaretto

Seafood Soup

Serves 4

1 lb 2 oz/500 g small ridged
  clams (ideally carpetshell
  clams)
1 lb 2 oz/500 g smooth clams
1 lb 2 oz/500 g mussels
2 tablespoons extra virgin
  olive oil
2 cloves garlic, central shoots
  discarded and cloves finely
  chopped
2 flat-leaf parsley sprigs,
  coarsely chopped
2 cups (11 oz/300 g) cherry
  tomatoes, quartered
1¼ cups (11 oz/ 300 g)
  puréed canned
  tomatoes (passata)
salt and pepper
toasted bread, to serve
  (optional)

Plunge the clams into a bowl of cold water and let them degorge for 1 hour to get rid of any sand.

Carefully clean the mussels with a small metal brush, then use tweezers to pull off the beards (the brown fibrous threads hanging from the shells) and rinse thoroughly.

Heat the oil in a very large pan, add the garlic and parsley, and cook over medium heat for 2 minutes, or until the garlic browns. Add the cherry tomatoes and cook for 5 minutes, then add the mussels and both types of clam, cover, and cook for 4–5 minutes until all the shells have opened. Discard any that do not open. Taste to check the seasoning and add salt and pepper if necessary. Pour over the puréed canned tomatoes (passata) and cook for 5 minutes more until the sauce has reduced.

Serve the soup drizzled with some oil and accompanied with toasted bread, if liked.

Preparation time: 20 minutes

Cooking time: 20 minutes

Wine suggestion: Colli del Trasimeno Bianco

Zucchini Soup with Croutons

Serves 4

4 tablespoons extra virgin
  olive oil, plus extra
  for drizzling
1 yellow onion, chopped
4 cups (1 lb 2 oz/500 g) diced
  zucchini (courgettes)
1 slightly stale pan (tin)
  loaf, thickly sliced, crusts
  removed, and cut into
  small cubes
1 thyme sprig, leaves only
salt and pepper
grated Parmesan cheese,
  to garnish (optional)

Heat the oil in a skillet (frying pan), add the onion, and cook over medium heat for 5 minutes, or until soft. Add the zucchini (courgettes) and cook over high heat for 2 minutes, stirring continuously. Lower the heat, season with salt, add a little hot water, and cook, covered, for 20 minutes, stirring occasionally, or until the courgettes are tender. Add a little more hot water if necessary—the soup should have the consistency of broth. Season with salt and pepper.

Meanwhile, make the croutons. Preheat the oven to 400°F/200°C/Gas mark 6. Spread the bread cubes in a single layer on a baking sheet, drizzle over a little oil, and sprinkle with the thyme. Bake in the oven for 7–8 minutes until golden.

Serve the soup topped with the croutons and garnished with a little Parmesan, if liked.

TIP   If you want to vary this recipe, you can replace the croutons with slices of rustic bread that have been fried with oil or butter. The slices of bread will be even more flavorful if you rub them lightly with a halved garlic clove before frying them.

⊙   Preparation time: 30 minutes, plus soaking

Cooking time: 45 minutes

♀   Wine suggestion: Orvieto Classico

White Cannellini Bean Soup with Romanesco Broccoli

Serves 4

1½ cups (11 oz/300 g) dried white cannellini beans
2 celery stalks, diced
1 carrot, diced
1 shallot, diced
1 small bunch flat-leaf parsley, chopped
1 bay leaf
2 cups (5 oz/150 g) romanesco broccoli florets
4 tablespoons extra virgin olive oil
1 clove garlic, crushed
1 small thyme sprig, leaves only
salt and pepper

To serve
5 oz/150 g blue goat cheese, cut into small cubes
rosemary oil, for drizzling

Soak the beans in a large bowl of cold water overnight.

The next day, rinse the beans under cold running water, then cook them in a pressure cooker for about 30 minutes until tender, using unsalted water to prevent the beans' skins from hardening. Alternatively, cook the beans in a pan of water over medium heat for 1 hour, or until tender. Drain and set aside.

Meanwhile, make the broth (stock). Put the celery, carrot, shallot, parsley, and bay leaf in a large pan, cover with 4¼ cups (34 fl oz/1 liter) water, and cook over low heat for 30 minutes.

Bring a large pan of water to a boil. Fill a large bowl with iced water and set it beside the stove. Drop the broccoli into the boiling water and leave for 8 minutes. Drain, plunge into the iced water, then drain again thoroughly. Transfer to a bowl, add 2 tablespoons of the olive oil and a pinch of salt, and stir to coat.

Heat the remaining olive oil in a large pan, add the garlic and thyme, and cook over low heat for 2 minutes, then add the drained beans and let them cook for a few minutes. Add a ladleful of the broth (the remaining broth can be stored in the refrigerator for 2 days or in the freezer for up to 2 months) and cook for a few minutes to allow the flavors to blend. Taste to check the seasoning and add salt and pepper if necessary. Use an immersion blender to blend the soup until smooth, add more broth, if needed, to achieve your desired consistency.

To serve, divide the soup among bowls, sprinkle over the blue goat cheese and broccoli florets, and drizzle with a little rosemary oil.

Preparation time: 15 minutes
Cooking time: 25–30 minutes
Wine suggestion: Curtefranca Bianco

Rice, Pea, and Pumpkin Soup

Serves 4

extra virgin olive oil
1 clove garlic, crushed
6 sage leaves, plus extra
  to garnish
1 cup (7 oz/200 g) risotto rice
  (ideally Ribe rice)
1³/₄ cups (7 oz/200 g) diced
  pumpkin flesh
²/₃ cup (3¹/₂ oz/100 g) shelled
  fresh peas
6¹/₄ cups (50 fl oz/1.5 liters)
  vegetable broth (stock)
grated Parmesan cheese,
  to sprinkle
salt and pepper

Heat a little oil in a large pan, add the garlic and sage leaves, and cook over low heat for 2 minutes, or until brown. Add the rice and toast for a few minutes, stirring with a wooden spoon, then add the pumpkin, peas, and broth (stock) and cook for 15–20 minutes until the rice is tender. Season with salt and pepper.

Serve the soup hot, sprinkled with some Parmesan and garnished with a few extra sage leaves.

TIP For a more colorful and tasty soup, serve it with some fried sage leaves. In a small bowl, beat 1 egg yolk with a pinch of salt, 2³/₄ fl oz/80 ml milk, and 1 tablespoon all-purpose (plain) flour to make a liquid batter. Let rest for 1 hour. In a separate spotlessly clean bowl, whisk an egg white until it forms stiff peaks, then gently fold the egg white into the batter. Heat plenty of sunflower oil in a small deep pan to 340°F/170°C. Dip the sage leaves into the batter and then carefully add them to the pan with the hot oil and cook for 1–2 minutes until golden.

Preparation time: 15 minutes

Cooking time: 40 minutes

Wine suggestion: Bardolino Chiaretto

Millet and Cauliflower Soup

Serves 4

1 cup (6¼ oz/180 g) millet
4¼ cups (34 fl oz/1 liter) hot
   vegetable broth (stock)
½ head cauliflower (about
   9 oz/250 g), cut into
   small cubes
extra virgin olive oil,
   for drizzling
1 small flat-leaf parsley sprig,
   finely chopped

Rinse the millet thoroughly under cold running water, drain well. Put the millet into a pan over medium heat and toast the millet for 5–6 minutes, stirring continuously, until light golden. Remove from the heat and let cool a little.

Pour 3⅓ cups (27 fl oz/800 ml) broth (stock) into the pan with the millet and stir. Put the pan back on the heat, bring to a boil, and cook for 15 minutes. Add the cauliflower, cover, and cook over low heat for 20 minutes, adding more broth if necessary. Stir in the parsley and drizzle with oil just before serving.

TIP   If you want to prepare a more filling soup that can be served as a single course in the winter, make the soup as above, replacing the cauliflower with Savoy cabbage cut into thin strips. Heat some oil in a nonstick skillet (frying pan), add 4 oz/120 g sausages, cut in half lengthwise, and cook over medium heat until brown. Once cooked, remove the sausages from the pan, leaving the fat behind, chop the sausage into pieces, and add them to the soup 5 minutes before the end of the cooking time.

Bean Soup with Wild Fennel, Octopus, and Onion

Serves 4

2 cups (11 oz/300 g) dried
  cicerchia beans (also known
  as grass peas or chickling
  vetch) or chickpeas

1 red onion (ideally an
  Acquaviva red onion),
  peeled and left whole

extra virgin olive oil

1 strip unwaxed orange zest

5 black peppercorns

1 clove

1 (1 lb-5 oz–1³⁄₄-lb/
  600–800-g) octopus,
  cleaned

²⁄₃ cup (3¹⁄₂ oz/100 g) diced
  carrots

¹⁄₂ red onion, diced

¹⁄₃ cup (2 oz/50 g) diced
  kohlrabi

¹⁄₃ cup (1¹⁄₄ oz/30 g) peeled
  and diced fresh ginger

1 clove garlic, diced

³⁄₄ cup (1¹⁄₄ oz/30 g) sliced
  mint (cut into strips)

2 oz/50 g kombu seaweed,
  cut into strips

¹⁄₂ cup (2 oz/50 g) chopped
  wild fennel

¹⁄₃ cup (¹⁄₂ oz/15 g) chopped
  thyme leaves

3¹⁄₄ tablespoons grated
  unwaxed lemon zest

salt

Soak the cicerchia beans in a large bowl of cold water for 12–18 hours. Drain well, and rinse.

Preheat the oven to 350°F/180°C/Gas mark 4.

Brush the whole peeled onion with a little oil. Place it in the center of a large piece of aluminum foil, add the orange zest, peppercorns, and clove, then wrap up the foil to form a parcel. Place the parcel on a baking sheet and bake in the oven for 1¹⁄₂ hours. Let cool, then cut the onion into strips. Set aside.

Meanwhile, pour 8¹⁄₂ cups (68 fl oz/2 liters) water into a large pan and bring to a boil. Add the octopus and cook for 15 minutes, then turn off the heat, cover, and let the octopus cool in the cooking liquid. Drain, reserving the cooking liquid. Cut the octopus into large slices and set aside.

Heat ²⁄₃ cup (5 fl oz/150 ml) oil in a large pan, add the carrots, red onion, kohlrabi, ginger, garlic, mint, kombu, fennel, and thyme, and cook over medium heat for 6–7 minutes until soft. Add the drained cicerchia beans and cook for a few minutes, then pour over the reserved octopus cooking liquid and cook for 2 hours. Transfer one-third of the mixture to a food processor and blend to a purée, then return to the pan and mix well. Taste to check the seasoning and add salt if necessary. Finish by stirring in the lemon zest.

Just before you are ready to serve, heat a dry nonstick skillet (frying pan), add the sliced octopus and baked onion strips, and cook over medium heat for 4–5 minutes until crisp on the outside.

Serve the octopus and onion with the cicerchia bean soup.

WINE SUGGESTION   Grillo Antica is a pearl among Sicilian wines. Benefitting from modern winemaking methods, and grown at high altitudes, it has recently found favor again. This wine offers citrus and Mediterranean fruit aromas combined with an elegant silkiness and marked mineral notes. It is excellent with this soup.

Preparation time: 20 minutes

Cooking time: 1 hour

Wine suggestion: Roero Arneis

Onion Soup
with Pecorino Cheese Toasts

Serves 4

extra virgin olive oil

13 yellow onions (about 3¼
lb/1.5 kg), thinly sliced

6⅓ cups (50 fl oz/1.5 liters)
hot vegetable broth (stock)

1 small bunch thyme,
leaves only

1 loaf rustic bread, cut into
½-inch/1-cm slices

1¼ cups (3½ oz/100 g) grated
pecorino cheese

salt

Heat a little oil in a large pan, add the onions, and cook over medium heat for about 10 minutes until soft and transparent but not browned, stirring frequently. Pour over the broth (stock), cover, and cook for about 30 minutes. Remove the lid and cook for 20 minutes more, stirring now and then, to let the soup reduce and thicken. At the end of the cooking time, add the thyme, taste to check the seasoning, and add salt if necessary.

Meanwhile, make the cheese toasts. Preheat the oven to 350°F/180°C/ Gas mark 4. Spread the slices of bread in a single layer on a baking sheet and bake in the oven for 5 minutes. Sprinkle over the pecorino, return to the oven, and bake for an additional 3 minutes.

Serve the soup with the cheese toasts.

NOTE   Onion soup is a typical French peasant dish that has become very popular, thanks to the ready availability of its ingredients and its full-bodied flavor. The original recipe calls for Gruyère cheese toasts, whereas this version substitutes pecorino cheese and rustic bread to make a totally Italian and extremely flavorful dish.

BROTH IN SOUP.
BUT WHICH BROTH?

In Italian tradition, "broth" (stock) is essentially a meat broth that is required by many recipes, such as those for *anolini*, *cappelletti*, *marubini*, *tortellini*, *passatelli*, and *pasta reale*. While it is true that these tasty first courses require a broth able to enhance their characteristics—and a meat broth performs this task very well—in practice there are various types of meat broth. There are also dishes that require a vegetable or fish broth, and "broth" is also a term used for several liquid or semi-liquid preparations that are considered to be soups in their own right, like consommé.

"GOOD BROTH"

The ingredients for the preparation of a good broth are quality lean beef, bones with marrow, possibly a piece of chicken, carrots, celery, and onion (with one or two cloves stuck in it) and, to taste, a few tomatoes and a small bunch of aromatic herbs.

Ingredients are immersed in cold water, to which a small quantity of coarse salt is also added. It is preferable to add more salt at the end of cooking rather than a larger quantity at the start, because when the broth is reduced it could prove to be salty enough. Slowly bring the water to a boil, then simmer for 2–3 hours. It is important to start with the ingredients in cold water to ensure that the meat slowly releases its nutrients.

If the purpose is to obtain a tasty piece of boiled meat rather than a good broth, it is necessary to immerse the meat in boiling water to ensure its surface is immediately seared, forming a protective film that prevents the nutrients from leaching into the broth. In this case, choose a better quality cut of meat, such as fiocco, pancia, piccione, biancostato, or codone. The resulting broth will be less tasty but it can still be used, for example, for preparing a risotto.

Meat broth is not necessarily dark, which is the case when it is prepared with red meat, it can also be a "light" broth when made with chicken, which is often the sort of broth required for tortellini.

There are also broths made with particular types of meat, for example with capon, a cockerel that has been castrated and whose meat is very flavorsome, which is used at

Christmas in the Emilian tradition. There is also a three-meat broth, *di terza* (made with capon, beef, and pork ribs) and a four-meat broth, *di quarta* (made with chicken, beef from both a de-sexed bullock and an adult bull, and pork chops) and there are also recipes based on broth made with pork bones.

A dish in its own right, rather than a base, consommé is a reduced beef or veal broth obtained by adding ground (minced) meat and chopped vegetables, then reducing and straining the broth. It can also be scented by adding a little sherry.

OTHER TYPES OF BROTH

Fish broths, or fumets, are suitable for shellfish risotto and some types of soup. They are prepared with chunks of lean white-fleshed fish (including fish bones and heads, but without the gills or dark parts) and herbs and spices. They are cooked for a much shorter time than meat broths (boil for 10 minutes for each 1 lb 2 oz/500 g of fish). Shellfish heads can be added to make the broth sweeter. It is best to avoid oily fish, like salmon, which are likely to make the broth bitter.

Vegetable broths are lighter than those made with fish and meat, and can be used to dilute some preparations, such as soup bases or delicate risottos, and for stracciatella soup (adding beaten eggs and Parmesan cheese to the boiling broth). They are prepared by simmering selected chopped vegetables—excellent choices are leek, celery, carrot, onion, and some tomatoes, or a turnip and one or two potatoes—possibly some aromatic herbs, and salt. The vegetables can then be used as a side dish or puréed. As this broth is completely fat free, it is ideal for very low calorie diets.

⊙ Preparation time: 20 minutes

Cooking time: 25 minutes

♀ Wine suggestion: Friuli Grave Refosco dal Peduncolo Rosso

Barley and Cavolo Nero Soup

Serves 4

⁷/₈ cup (6¹/₄ oz/180 g)
  pearled barley
6¹/₃ cups (50 fl oz/1.5 liters)
  vegetable broth (stock)
extra virgin olive oil
¹/₂ white onion, chopped
3¹/₂ oz/100 g salted and cured
  pork salami, cut into
  thin strips
3³/₄ cups (9 oz/250 g)
  chopped cavolo nero
  (Tuscan black cabbage)
salt and pepper

Rinse the pearled barley under cold running water, then put it into a very large pan with the vegetable stock (broth). Bring to a boil, then cook over medium heat for 20 minutes.

Meanwhile, heat a drizzle of oil in a separate pan, add the onion, and cook over low heat for 5 minutes, or until soft. Add the salami and cook for a few minutes, then add the cavolo nero (Tuscan black cabbage) and cook gently for about 15 minutes, stirring occasionally, until the cavolo nero is soft and almost falling apart.

Transfer the cavolo nero mixture to the pan with the pearled barley and cook for 5 minutes more. If the soup is too dry, pour in some extra vegetable broth (stock) until the desired consistency is reached. Season the soup with salt and serve with a generous grinding of pepper.

NOTE Cavolo nero (Tuscan black cabbage) is an indispensable ingredient in the traditional Tuscan ribollita soup. It is characterized by its large dark-green leaves whose surfaces are covered in "bubbles", which is why it is also called *riccio* (curl) in Italy.

CHEF

Alberto Bettini

⊙ Preparation time: 20 minutes

Cooking time: 30 minutes

Pumpkin Soup with Balsamic Vinegar

Serves 4

$1/2$ cup (4 fl oz/120 ml) extra
  virgin olive oil
1 tablespoon chopped shallot
7 cups ($1^3/4$ lb/800 g) diced
  pumpkin flesh
$3/4$ cup plus 1 tablespoon
  (7 fl oz/200 ml)
  carbonated water
$3/4$ cup ($3^1/2$ oz/100 g) type
  00 flour
12 small sage leaves
salt and pepper

To serve
1 tablespoon balsamic
  vinegar (ideally balsamic
  vinegar of Modena)
$1/3$ cup ($3^1/2$ oz/100 g) goat
  yogurt

Heat 3 tablespoons of the oil in a large pan, add the shallot, and cook over medium heat for 3–4 minutes until golden brown. Add the pumpkin and a pinch of salt and cook for 6 minutes, then pour over $1^2/3$ cups (14 fl oz/400 ml) hot water and cook for an additional 20–25 minutes until the pumpkin is very tender. Transfer the soup to a food processor and blend until the soup is creamy and homogenous. Taste to check the seasoning and add salt and pepper if necessary.

Meanwhile, make a batter by mixing the carbonated water and flour together in a small bowl to form a fairly thick mixture. Heat 3 tablespoons of the oil in a skillet (frying pan). Plunge the sage leaves into the batter, then carefully add them to the skillet and fry over high heat for 2–3 minutes until golden brown. Drain on paper towels.

Serve the soup with drops of balsamic vinegar, dollops of goat yogurt, and drizzles of the remaining oil, and garnish with the fried sage leaves.

♀ **WINE SUGGESTION** Manzoni Bianco goes well with the sweet, distinctive aroma of this soup. The sweetness of the soup's pumpkin, shallot, and yogurt is counterbalanced by the vinegar, but is reinforced by the sweetness of balsamic vinegar, while the battered sage adds more aroma and provides texture. The wine's alcohol content contrasts with the succulence and smoothness of the dish.

Vegetable Soup with Homemade Tagliatelle Pasta Squares

Serves 4

3 red-skinned potatoes, unpeeled
3 tablespoons extra virgin olive oil
1 yellow onion, chopped
¾ cup (3½ oz/100 g) chopped white celery
2 small carrots, chopped
2 oz/50 g mature pancetta or bacon, cut into ¼-inch/ 7-mm squares
⅓ cup (3½ oz/100 g) puréed canned tomatoes (passata)
4¼ cups (34 fl oz/1 liter) hot vegetable broth (stock)
salt and pepper

For the pasta
2⅓ cups (11 oz/300 g) type 00 flour, plus extra for dusting
3 eggs

To serve
5 tablespoons grated Parmesan cheese (ideally 36-month-aged Parmesan cheese)
1 flat-leaf parsley sprig, chopped

First make the pasta. Put the flour into a mound on the countertop, make a well in the center, and put the eggs into this. Using your hands, start by gradually mixing everything together, then knead until you obtain a smooth dough. Shape the dough into a ball, wrap in plastic wrap (clingfilm), and chill in the refrigerator for 1 hour.

Roll out the dough very thinly (about 1 mm thick) on a lightly floured work surface with a rolling pin or put it through a pasta machine. Let the pasta dry for a short while, then roll it up and cut across the roll at ¼-inch/7-mm intervals, then cut in the opposite direction to make small squares.

Cook the potatoes in a large pan of boiling water for 40 minutes, or until a knife inserted into them comes out easily.

Meanwhile, heat the oil in a large pan, add the pancetta or bacon, then add the onion, celery, and carrots, and cook over medium heat for 5–6 minutes until golden brown. Add the puréed canned tomatoes (passata) and cook over low heat for about 10 minutes until the sauce is thick.

Drain the potatoes, peel off the skins, then pass them through a potato ricer. While still very hot, add the riced potato to the pan with the vegetables, pour over the broth (stock), add 4 oz/120 g of tagliatelle squares, and cook for 5–6 minutes until the pasta is cooked. Taste to check the seasoning and add salt if necessary.

Serve the soup hot, sprinkled with Parmesan, chopped parsley, and a grinding of pepper.

🍷 **WINE SUGGESTION** This thick and extremely tasty soup, with its delicate vegetable flavors, is complemented perfectly by the freshness of Sauvignon Blanc. This white wine combines subtle vegetable and refined mineral notes with a soft background taste.

CHEF

Alberto Bettini

Preparation time: 1¼ hours, plus chilling

Cooking time: 5½ hours

Wine suggestion: Cabernet "I Vitigni"

Tortellini in Broth

Serves 4

For the broth

1 lb 2 oz/500 g stewing beef (shin or flank)

1 piece marrow bone

¼ chicken

1 carrot, chopped

1 celery stalk, chopped

1 small yellow onion, chopped

1 tablespoon coarse salt

For the filling

5¼ oz/165 g lean pork, cut into ¾-inch/2-cm slices

3 oz/85 g mortadella, finely chopped

1¼ oz/35 g Parma ham, preferably the small tapered end of a prosciutto (Parma ham), finely chopped

5 tablespoons grated Parmesan cheese (ideally 24-month-aged Parmesan cheese)

1 egg yolk

grated nutmeg

salt

For the pasta

2⅓ cups (11 oz/300 g) type 00 flour, plus extra for dusting

3 eggs

First, make the broth. Put all the ingredients into a stock pot (stew pan) and pour over 204 fl oz/6 liters cold water. Bring to a boil and cook over low heat for at least 5 hours, skimming the surface occasionally. Taste to check the seasoning and add more salt if necessary, then strain the broth through a fine-mesh strainer (sieve). Set aside.

To prepare the filling, heat a dry skillet (frying pan), then add the pork and cook over medium heat for 2–3 minutes on each side until cooked but still pink in the center. Let cool, then finely chop the pork. Transfer the chopped pork to a large bowl with all the remaining filling ingredients and stir thoroughly. Pass the mixture through a grinder (mincer) until you have a thin and homogenous mixture, then put the filling into a clean bowl and set aside.

Make the pasta. Put the flour into a mound on the countertop, make a well in the center, and put the eggs into this. Using your hands, start by gradually mixing everything together, then knead until you obtain a smooth dough. Shape the dough into a ball, wrap in plastic wrap (clingfilm), and chill in the refrigerator for 1 hour.

Roll out the dough thinly on a lightly floured countertop with a rolling pin or put it through a pasta machine. Cut the pasta into 1-inch/2.5-cm squares. Place a small amount of filling (roughly equal to the weight of the pasta) in the center of each square.

Fold the pasta squares in half to make triangles that enclose the filling and press the edges together. Shape the tortellini by bringing the tips of two corners of each pasta triangle together and pinching gently to seal.

Pour half the broth into a large pan and bring to a boil (the remaining broth can be stored in the refrigerator for 2 days or in the freezer for up to 1 month). Add the tortellini, bring the broth back to a boil, and cook for 1 minute or until the pasta bobs up to the surface. Serve immediately.

FRESH PASTA

Preparation time: 30 minutes

Cooking time: 15 minutes

Wine suggestion: Alto Adige Chardonnay

Tagliatelle Pasta with Runner Beans and Shrimp

Serves 4

16 raw shrimp (prawns)
  in their shells
1½ cups (5¼ oz/ 160 g)
  runner beans or
  green beans
extra virgin olive oil
1 carrot, chopped
1 celery stalk, chopped
1 scallion (spring onion),
  chopped
1 cup (5 oz/150 g) cherry
  tomatoes, halved
⅓ cup plus 1 tablespoon
  (3½ fl oz/100 ml) white wine
1 teaspoon tomato
  purée (paste)
11 oz/300 g egg tagliatelle
  pasta
grated zest of 1
  unwaxed lemon
salt and pepper

First prepare the shrimp (prawns). Rinse the shrimp under cold running water. Remove the heads (reserve these) and shells, keeping the tails intact. Using a sharp knife, cut through the back of each shrimp and remove and discard the intestine, being careful not to break it.

Bring a large pan of water to a boil. Meanwhile, fill a large bowl with iced water and set it beside the stove. Drop the runner beans into the boiling water and leave for 3 minutes. Drain, plunge into the iced water, then drain again thoroughly. Cut the beans into slices.

Heat a drizzle of oil in a skillet (frying pan), add the carrot, celery, and scallion (spring onion), and cook over medium heat for 4–5 minutes until golden brown. Add the shrimp heads and half the cherry tomatoes, pour over the wine, add the tomato purée (paste), and cook for 6–7 minutes until the sauce has thickened. Pass the sauce through a strainer (sieve) into a bowl and discard the vegetables and prawn heads. Keep warm.

Heat 2 tablespoons oil in a large nonstick skillet, add the remaining cherry tomatoes and the shelled shrimp, and cook over medium heat for 3–4 minutes until golden brown.

Meanwhile, cook the pasta in a large pan of boiling salted water according to the package directions until al dente, then drain well.

Transfer the drained pasta to the skillet with the shelled shrimp, then stir in the sliced beans. Taste to check the seasoning and add salt and pepper if necessary. Stir in the prepared sauce and lemon zest and cook over medium heat for 2 minutes until well mixed and heated through.

HOW TO STORE
FRESH PASTA

When we talk about shelf life, we mean the length of time a food product retains its sensory and nutritional characteristics and can be considered to be hygienically safe for consumption.

In Italy, labels must indicate the expiration date of food products or their durability term. The expiration date, or the "use by" date, indicates the time when the population of microorganisms in the food product is contained within safe limits. Every food product, in fact, can "host" bacteria, yeast, or molds that are present in minimal quantities initially, but which will multiply over time until they become harmful to health. The minimum durability time, or "best before" date, on the other hand, indicates the quality of the product: aroma, consistency, color, and taste. In fact, this can be affected even before the integrity of the product is compromised from a health and hygiene point of view.

FRESH PASTA OR PASTA WITH EXTENDED SHELF LIFE?

"Use by" and "best before" dates apply only if basic storage rules and environmental specifications are respected at every stage: from the time of purchase to when the product is consumed. Even at home, therefore, it is essential to control those variables that may have an impact on the conservation of purchased products, such as temperature, humidity, exposure to light and heat sources, as indicated on the product's label.

As far as fresh pasta is concerned, it is necessary to clarify an ambiguity: sometimes this expression is used to refer to egg pasta that is also available in dry form, and therefore has an extended shelf life. Vice versa, there are types of fresh pasta, with a rather short shelf life, that are not types of egg pasta (for example bigoli). Conservation of dried fresh pasta is not dissimilar from that of pasta made with durum wheat, as the humidity content of both is such as to ensure a long shelf life. When made at industrial level, fresh pasta that has not been dried is pasteurized and can therefore be kept in the refrigerator for several months.

Furthermore, there are types of fresh pasta that have been frozen and have, therefore, a very long shelf life.

STORAGE OF HOMEMADE PASTA

It is possible to store homemade pasta by drying it, or by keeping it in the refrigerator, or freezing it. Pasta that has not been filled can easily be dried by placing it on a floured countertop, where it will need to rest for several hours before being stored in a container. The time needed for drying, as well as storage time, depends on the ambient humidity and therefore also on the season. At the time of consumption, it is best to ensure that there are no stains on the pasta that may indicate the proliferation of molds, in which case it will be necessary to dispose of all the pasta in the same container and not only the pieces that appear to be contaminated.

Filled pasta, on the other hand, can only be dried in an industrial setting, and it is also difficult to store in the refrigerator because the filling will dampen the pasta, which could then develop holes or break up during cooking. In this case, therefore, it is best to store it by freezing it.

It is necessary to ensure that pasta pieces do not stick together, both in the case of filled and non-filled pasta. Long pasta, such as tagliatelle, tagliolini, etc. needs to be gathered in nests and dried briefly, then placed on a floured baking sheet and put in the freezer. In the same way, ravioli, tortelli, etc. must be frozen, ensuring that there is no contact between the individual pieces. Only once the pasta is frozen is it possible to place all the pieces together in a plastic bag or, even better, a plastic container.

Storage times vary depending on the type of pasta, ranging from 24–36 hours for non-filled egg pasta, stored in a refrigerator, to 2–3 months for frozen pasta.

⊙ Preparation time: 30 minutes, plus chilling
Cooking time: 1 hour 40 minutes
♀ Wine suggestion: Bolgheri Rosé

Maltagliati Pasta with Octopus Sauce

Serves 4

For the sauce
1 octopus, cleaned
extra virgin olive oil
2 celery stalks, finely chopped
3 carrots, finely chopped
1 onion, finely chopped
2 anchovy fillets preserved in
   oil, drained and well rinsed
3/4 cup (3 1/2 oz/100 g) drained
   and well rinsed capers
   preserved in oil
2 cups (1 lb 2 oz/500 g)
   puréed plum tomatoes
a few basil leaves, chopped
salt and pepper

For the pasta*
2 1/3 cups (11 oz/300 g) type 00
   flour, plus extra for dusting
3 eggs
2 tablespoons extra virgin
   olive oil

*dried pasta works
   equally well

Cook the octopus in a large pan of boiling salted water for 1 1/2 hours, then let it cool in its cooking water.

Meanwhile, make the pasta. Sift the flour into a mound on the countertop, make a well in the center, and put the eggs and oil into this. Using your hands, start by gradually mixing everything together, adding a little water if necessary, then knead the dough vigorously until you have a homogenous mixture. Shape the dough into a ball, wrap in plastic wrap (clingfilm), and chill in the refrigerator for at least 45 minutes.

Roll out the dough very thinly on a lightly floured countertop with a rolling pin or put it through a pasta machine. Cut the pasta into 1 1/2-inch/4-cm strips, then cut those strips into lozenges.

Heat a drizzle of oil in a large pan, add the celery, carrots, onion, anchovies, and capers and cook over medium heat for 5 minutes, or until soft and golden brown. Add the tomatoes, adjust the seasoning if necessary, and cook for about 25 minutes until the sauce has thickened.

Cut the octopus into 5/8-inch/1.5-cm pieces. Stir them into the tomato sauce and cook for 5 minutes more to let the flavors combine.

Meanwhile, cook the pasta in a large pan of boiling salted water for 3 minutes, or according to the cooking instructions if using dried pasta, then drain well.

Transfer the drained pasta to the pan with the octopus sauce, add the basil, gently mix together, and serve.

○ Preparation time: 1 hour, plus chilling

Cooking time: 1 hour

♀ Wine suggestion: Verdicchio dei Castelli di Jesi Classico Riserva

Pappardelle Pasta with Rabbit

Serves 4

For the pasta

2¹⁄₃ cups (11 oz/300 g) type 00 flour, plus extra for dusting

3 eggs

2 tablespoons extra virgin olive oil

For the sauce

extra virgin olive oil

1 celery stalk, finely chopped

1 carrot, finely chopped

2 cups (3¹⁄₂ oz/100 g) chopped flat-leaf parsley

1 rabbit, boned and the meat finely chopped

¹⁄₃ cup plus 1 tablespoon (3¹⁄₂ fl oz/100 ml) white wine

³⁄₄ cup plus 1 tablespoon (7 fl oz/200 ml) hot meat broth (stock)

salt and pepper

4 tablespoons grated aged pecorino cheese, to serve

First make the pasta. Sift the flour into a mound on the countertop, make a well in the center, and put the eggs and oil into this. Using your hands, start by gradually mixing everything together, adding a little water if necessary, then knead the dough vigorously until you have a homogenous mixture. Shape the dough into a ball, wrap in plastic wrap (clingfilm), and chill in the refrigerator for at least 45 minutes.

Roll out the dough very thinly on a lightly floured countertop with a rolling pin or put it through a pasta machine. Cut the pasta into rectangles about 12–14 inches/30–35 cm wide, roll them up, then cut the rolls into ⁵⁄₈-inch/1.5-cm slices. Unravel the strips of pasta and shape into nests.

Heat a drizzle of oil in a large pan, add the celery, carrot, and parsley, and cook over medium heat for 5 minutes, or until golden brown. Add the rabbit meat and fry briefly, then pour over the wine and broth (stock) and cook for about 45 minutes until the sauce is thick. Season with salt and pepper.

Meanwhile, cook the pasta in a large pan of boiling salted water for 3–4 minutes, then drain well.

Transfer the drained pasta to the pan with the rabbit sauce and cook over medium heat for 3–4 minutes until well mixed and heated through. Serve sprinkled generously with grated pecorino.

FRESH EGG PASTA AND THE LEGEND OF THE SFOGLINE

While it is true that pasta is the most typical of Italian dishes, both in the North and the South, in practice "pasta" can be everything or nothing. The best form of pasta is "fresh" pasta that is homemade. Egg pasta, the crown jewel of the Emilia Romagna region's culinary achievements, has an undoubted place of honor among all the available varieties. Its flavor is due to the compulsory combination of flour and eggs, but its forms are numerous and varied. When the pasta is simply cut into strips, it becomes tagliatelle, pappardelle, or tagliolini, depending on the width and shape of the strip. The possibilities are multiplied when it is used for the countless variants of filled pasta, or cut into sheets used to make lasagna and cannelloni.

THE CUSTODIANS OF TRADITION

Custodians par excellence of the egg pasta tradition are the so-called *sfogline*. In the past, these were the family's older women, whose task it was to prepare the dough and make the pasta. Today the *sfogline* are increasingly sought-after professionals.

They are so valued that in 2009 they become the objective of a bill of law designed "to bring value and promote handmade egg pasta from Emilia Romagna and the practice of its relative profession". This bill, as well as approving the "original recipe" of the real handmade egg pasta, suggests the "institution of the professional role of the *sfoglina* or *sfoglino* (female or male) to ensure the profession, which has always been undervalued in the past by being considered a domestic skill, is officially recognized."

Independently from its legal ratification, the last few years have seen an inspiring renaissance of this ancient skill and the success of numerous cooking schools set up in Bologna and its vicinity, with the task of training people who did not have a grand-mother to teach them the skill. Furthermore, excellence in this field is rewarded with various competitions, such as the Mattarello d'oro (the Golden Rolling Pin) and the Sfoglino d'oro (the Golden Sfoglino).

PREPARING THE DOUGH

The very existence of the sfoglina is an indication that fresh pasta must absolutely be stretched by hand, to ensure a rough surface able to absorb the sauce. Stretching the dough might not be the easiest thing in the world, especially for the younger generations who often don't have the manual dexterity which used to be common with housewives in the older times and who don't have role models to learn from, but the actual recipe for egg pasta is impossible to forget: 1 egg for every 3½ oz/100 g of flour. The egg must be of average size (around 2¼ oz/60 g) and the flour must be soft wheat. Some people add a pinch of salt but the Emilia Romagna tradition does not require it.

To make the pasta, it is necessary to have a countertop and a rolling pin. First of all, sift the flour onto the countertop and make a small "well" or dip in the center, then break the eggs into the well. Beat the eggs with a fork, then start to incorporate the flour using your fingertips, starting with the flour at the edge of the well. Mix well. When all the flour has been incorporated, start to knead the dough, using the palm of your hands in particular, sprinkling the countertop with more flour if the dough becomes sticky. Use a rubber spatula, or the edge of a knife, to scrape any dough left behind and incorporate these scraps back into the dough. After about ten minutes the dough should be smooth and compact. It is now time to let the dough rest in the refrigerator to let the ingredients blend well together.

When the dough has rested for a short time, sprinkle the countertop with flour, make a ball with the dough, then flatten it with your hands to create an even circle. Now it is time to start using the rolling pin to stretch it, turning it upside down frequently, to ensure a large, thin, and uniform disc.

⊙ Preparation time: 55 minutes, plus degorging
Cooking time: 25 minutes
🍷 Wine suggestion: Ostuni Bianco

Gnocchi with Broccoli Rabe, Mussels, and Clams

Serves 6

For the sauce
1 lb 2 oz/500 g clams
2¼ lb/1 kg broccoli rabe
 (cima di rapa)
extra virgin olive oil
2 cloves garlic, crushed
½ red chile, finely chopped
2¼ lb/1 kg mussels
1 sprig flat-leaf parsley
⅓ cup plus 1 tablespoon
 (3½ fl oz/100 ml) white wine
salt

For the gnocchi
13 floury potatoes (about 3¼
 lb/1.5 kg), peeled and cut
 into chunks
2⅓ cups (11 oz/300 g) type
 00 flour
1 egg
pinch of ground nutmeg
1 tablespoon salt

Plunge the clams into a bowl of cold water and let them degorge for 1 hour.

Meanwhile, make the gnocchi. Cook the potatoes in a large pan of boiling salted water for 20–25 minutes until a knife inserted into them comes out easily. Drain, then pass through a potato ricer into a bowl and let cool to lukewarm. Transfer to a countertop, add the flour, egg, nutmeg, and salt, and very quickly mix together and shape into a ball. Divide the mixture into four pieces and, using your hands, roll each piece into a long cylinder. Cut the cylinders into ¾-inch/2-cm pieces, then press each piece on the tines of a fork to give it the classic gnocchi shape.

Bring a large pan of water to a boil. Fill a large bowl with iced water and set it beside the stove. Drop the broccoli rabe (cima di rapa) into the boiling water and leave for a couple of minutes. Drain, plunge into the iced water, then drain again thoroughly.

Heat a drizzle of oil in a skillet (frying pan), add half the garlic, half the chile and the broccoli rabe and sauté over medium heat for 4 minutes to let the flavors develop. Remove from the heat and set aside.

Carefully clean the mussels with a small metal brush, then use tweezers to pull off the beards (the brown fibrous threads hanging from the shells). Rinse thoroughly.

Heat a drizzle of oil in a large pan, add the remaining garlic and chile, and the parsley, mussels and clams, and cook over high heat for 2 minutes, then pour over the wine, cover with a lid, and cook for 3–4 minutes until all the shells have opened. Discard any that do not open. Strain the mussels through a strainer (sieve) lined with a dishcloth and reserve the cooking liquor.

Meanwhile, cook the gnocchi in a large pan of boiling salted water until they rise to the surface, then drain well.

Transfer the gnocchi to the skillet with the clam and mussel sauce, adding 5 fl oz/150 ml of the mussel cooking water and the broccoli rabe, stir well, and sauté over medium heat for 2 minutes until well mixed and heated through. Serve very hot.

THE FUN OF COLORED

FRESH PASTA

Those making pasta at home can improvise by adding natural colors and flavors to the dough.

Green tagliatelle and lasagna made with spinach are quite common and easy to find commercially. Durum wheat pasta shapes can also be found in shops in various colors, but when making pasta at home it is possible to give free rein to the imagination.

Generally speaking, vegetable purées and finely chopped herbs are used to color egg pasta, but powders (such as cacao and saffron) or liquids (like squid ink) can be used too. Powders and other spices are easier to incorporate as they are dry and therefore do not have a significant impact on the consistency of the dough. Vegetable purées, however, must be measured carefully, as they have a high water content. As a rule of thumb, 3–3¼ oz/80–90 g of purée correspond to 1 egg which will need to be omitted from the starting recipe. This is an approximation and depends on the type of vegetable, its freshness, and the cooking method used. Flour can be added during kneading, if necessary, to adjust the moisture content of the dough.

DIFFERENT HUES

It is possible to choose from a range of different natural colors depending on personal taste and level of experience. Bright green can be made using spinach, nettles, or borage. The plants need to be stewed in a little oil to release as much liquid as possible, then squeezed, finely chopped, and added to the dough. For a softer green, use uncooked finely chopped fresh basil, mint, or sage. Red can be made using tomato purée (paste). Use beet (beetroot) for a purply red, and pumpkin or carrot can be used for orange. These vegetables need to be cooked first—preferably steamed or baked, to avoid the absorption of water during cooking—and then puréed.

Saffron and cacao will color the dough bright yellow and brown respectively, while using drops of squid ink will create various shades from grey to black.

DIFFERENT SHAPES

In addition to the classic lasagna and tagliatelle, and the traditional Tyrolean spaetzle, it is possible to use colored dough to make practically all fresh and filled pasta shapes: tagliolini, quadratini for soup, ravioli, tortelli, caramelle, and rosette, to name the most common ones. With a bit of practice it's easy to experiment with multicolored dough. For example, it is possible to create egg pasta sheets with green, yellow, and red stripes. Prepare one green, one yellow, and one red ball of dough. Roll each ball of dough into squares about 2 mm thick. Lay the squares on top of each other, dampening the surface slightly so they stick together, creating up to 15–20 layers. With a sharp knife, cut the loaf transversally, to create striped sheets 4–5 mm thick. These can then be stretched into thin sheets, either by hand or using a pasta machine.

DIFFERENT NUTRIENTS

The use of colored pasta not only improves the appearance of a dish but also enriches daily diets, since the vegetables and herbs contribute specific nutritional elements.

The color of vegetables, in fact, depends largely on the presence of polyphenols, which have an antioxidant effect on those who consume them. Furthermore, adding beet, nettle, and borage means including foods in our diet that are little used and yet are rich in valuable nutrients. Beets, for example, have a high mineral content, including iron and B vitamins, while nettles—also rich in iron—ensure a good intake of vitamins and calcium.

Preparation time: 1 hour, plus chilling

Cooking time: 10 minutes

Wine suggestion: Dolcetto d'Asti

Plin Pasta with Borage and Blue Cheese Fondue

Serves 6

For the filling

3½ cups (12 oz/350 g) borage

¾ cup (7 oz/200 g) cow milk
  ricotta cheese

salt and pepper

For the pasta

2⅓ cups (11 oz/300 g) type
  00 flour, plus extra for
  dusting

6 egg yolks

2 tablespoons extra virgin
  olive oil

For the fondue

2 cups (7 oz/200 g) grated
  semi-hard blue cheese
  (ideally Castelmagno
  cheese)

1½ cups (12 fl oz/350 ml)
  whole milk

First make the filling. Cook the borage in a large pan of boiling salted water for 4 minutes. Drain well, squeeze out any excess water, then finely chop the borage. Put the chopped borage into a large bowl, add the ricotta, and mix well. Taste to check the seasoning and add salt and pepper if necessary.

Make the pasta dough. Sift the flour into a mound on the countertop, make a well in the center, and put the eggs and oil into this. Using your hands, start by gradually mixing everything together, adding a little water if necessary, then knead the dough vigorously until you have a homogenous mixture. Shape the dough into a ball, wrap in plastic wrap (clingfilm), and chill in the refrigerator for at least 45 minutes.

Roll out the dough very thinly on a lightly floured countertop with a rolling pin or put it through a pasta machine.

Spoon the filling into a pastry (piping) bag. Pipe out a row of ½-inch/1-cm balls along the pasta, spacing them ½ inch/1 cm apart. Fold the pasta over to enclose the filling, then pinch around each ball of filling to seal and use a cookie cutter to cut between each piece to make squares of filled pasta measuring about ¾ inch/2 cm on each side.

Melt most of the blue cheese (reserving a handful to garnish the finished dish) with the milk in a double boiler or in a heatproof bowl set over a pan of gently simmering water and stir until the cheese has completely melted and the fondue is smooth.

Meanwhile, cook the plin pasta in a large pan of boiling salted water for 3 minutes, then drain well.

To serve, pour the blue cheese fondue over the pasta and sprinkle with the reserved blue cheese.

CHEF
Luca Zecchin

Preparation time: 50 minutes, plus resting
Cooking time: 2³/₄ hours
Wine suggestion: Dolcetto d'Asti

Lidia's Agnolotti Pasta

Serves 6–8

For the filling

¹/₃ cup (2³/₄ fl oz/80 ml) extra
   virgin olive oil
7 oz/200 g veal shoulder
1 rosemary sprig
1 slice of garlic
¹/₃ cup plus 1 tablespoon (3¹/₂
   fl oz/100 ml) white wine
1 carrot, finely diced
1 onion, finely diced
5 oz/150 g pork sausage meat
7 oz/200 g rabbit meat, diced
7 cups (7 oz/200 g) chicory
   (green curly endive)
3¹/₂ cups (3¹/₂ oz/100 g)
   spinach, coarsely chopped
4 eggs
¹/₂ cup (2 oz/50 g) grated
   Parmesan cheese
1¹/₂ tablespoons (³/₄ oz/20 g)
   butter
salt and pepper

For the pasta

4 cups (1 lb 2 oz/500 g) type
   00 flour, plus extra for
   dusting
1 egg, plus 11 egg yolks

First cook the veal shoulder. Heat 2 tablespoons of the oil in a large pan, add the veal shoulder, rosemary, and garlic, and cook over medium heat for 5 minutes on each side. Pour over the wine, cover, and cook for 20–25 minutes until the meat is tender. Remove the meat from the pan and set aside, reserving the cooking juices.

Heat the remaining oil in a large pan, add the carrot and onion, and cook over medium heat for 5–6 minutes until golden brown. Add the pork sausage meat and rabbit and cook over high heat for 5 minutes, or until just starting to brown. Cover, lower the heat, and cook for 2 hours, adding the roasted veal shoulder, chicory (curly endive), and spinach halfway through the cooking time. Let cool, then finely chop everything and place in a large bowl. Stir in the eggs and Parmesan. Taste to check the seasoning and add salt and pepper if necessary.

Strain the veal cooking juices into a pan and cook over high heat for about 5 minutes until reduced by about one third.

Sift the flour into a mound on the countertop, make a well in the center, and put the egg, 11 egg yolks, and 5–7 tablespoons cold water into this. Using your hands, vigorously mix everything together, knead to form and smooth dough, then cover with a damp dish towel and let the dough rest for 30 minutes.

Roll out the dough very thinly on a lightly floured countertop with a rolling pin or put it through a pasta machine. Put hazelnut-sized mounds of filling in a line on the pasta, spacing them ³/₄–1¹/₄ inches/2–3 cm apart. Fold the pasta over to enclose the filling, making sure it adheres well, and use a fluted cookie cutter to cut between each piece to make squares of filled pasta measuring about ³/₄ inch/2 cm on each side.

Cook the agnolotti pasta in a large pan of boiling salted water for about 1¹/₂ minutes, then drain well.

Meanwhile, reheat the veal cooking juices. Transfer the drained pasta to the pan with the meat sauce, add the butter, and gently stir together.

⊙ Preparation time: 30 minutes, plus soaking and resting
Cooking time: 20 minutes
Ⴓ Wine suggestion: Alto Adige Santa Maddalena

Canederli with Speck Ham

Serves 4

²/₃ cup (5 fl oz/150 ml) milk
2 eggs
a pinch of ground nutmeg
a pinch of pepper
9 oz/250 g stale bread, cut
   into chunks (about 5 cups)
2¹/₂ tablespoons (1¹/₄ oz/
   35 g) butter
1 onion, chopped
1 (3¹/₂ -oz/100-g) slice speck
   ham, chopped
¹/₃ cup (1¹/₂ oz/40 g) type 00
   flour
1 teaspoon chopped
   flat-leaf parsley
1 tablespoon chopped chives
8¹/₂ cups (68 fl oz/2 liters)
   meat broth (stock)

Mix the milk with the eggs, nutmeg, and pepper in a large bowl, then add the bread and let soak for 1 hour, stirring occasionally.

Heat the butter in a skillet (frying pan), add the onion and ham, and cook over low heat for 5 minutes, or until golden brown.

Add the flour, parsley, chives, and the fried ham and onion to the soaked bread, mix well, and then let rest for 20 minutes at room temperature. Shape the mixture into small balls, about 2³/₄–3¹/₄-inches/7–8 cm in diameter.

Pour the broth (stock) into a large pan and bring to a boil. Add the canederli to the broth and cook over low heat for about 15 minutes until cooked through. Serve immediately with the broth.

NOTE Canederli are large gnocchi made with stale bread and enriched with other ingredients such as speck ham, ordinary ham, or cheese, and scented with plenty of parsley. They can be served in broth (stock) or just as they are, with butter and sage. Canederli are one of the typical dishes of the Alto Adige and Trentino regions of Italy, but they are also widespread in the Friuli and upper Veneto regions, that is to say in all the regions that came under the dominion of the Austro-Hungarian Empire. Indeed, their name, *knödel* in German, derives from *knot* (meaning knot or lump) and bears witness unequivocally to their Germanic origin.

⊙ Preparation time: 20 minutes

Cooking time: 20 minutes

♀ Wine suggestion: Cirò Rosé

Garganelli Pasta with Sausage and Zucchini

Serves 4

4 pork sausages

1¼ cups (10 fl oz/300 ml) white wine

extra virgin olive oil

1 red onion, finely chopped

11¼ oz/320 g garganelli pasta (or other short, tubular pasta)

2 zucchini (courgettes), sliced

salt

Skin the sausages and crumble the sausage meat into a bowl. Pour over 5 fl oz/150 ml of the wine and mix well.

Heat a drizzle of oil in a skillet (frying pan), add the onion, and cook over medium heat for 5–6 minutes until golden brown. Pour over the remaining white wine, add the sausage meat, and cook for 10 minutes, or until well cooked and golden brown.

Meanwhile, cook the pasta in a large pan of boiling salted water according to the package directions until al dente, adding the zucchini (courgettes) 3 minutes before the end of the cooking time. Drain well.

Transfer the drained pasta and zucchini to the skillet with the sausage meat and cook over medium heat for 4–5 minutes until well mixed and heated through. Serve very hot.

TIP   For a more pronounced flavor, use artichokes instead of zucchini (courgettes). Trim the artichokes, discarding the inner chokes, the tougher outermost leaves, and their spiny tips. Cut the artichokes into pieces and add them to the skillet (frying pan) with the sausage meat. You could also replace the red onion with 2 scallions (spring onions) as scallions taste much better with the artichokes.

DRIED
PASTA

◷   Preparation time: 15 minutes

        Cooking time: 20 minutes

♀   Wine suggestion: Verdicchio dei Castelli di Jesi
        Classico Riserva

Mezzi Paccheri Pasta with Cheese Sauce and Artichokes

Serves 4

4 artichokes
extra virgin olive oil
1 clove garlic, crushed
1 cup (8 fl oz/250 ml)
   whipping cream
1¾ cups (5 oz/150 g) grated
   sweet and spicy hard cheese
   (ideally fossa cheese)
1½ tablespoons (¾ oz/20 g)
   butter, melted
12½ oz/360 g mezzi paccheri
   pasta (or other short,
   tubular pasta)
salt and pepper
a few chives, to garnish
   (optional)

Trim the artichokes, discarding the inner chokes, the tougher outermost leaves, and their spiny tips. Cut into even chunks.

Heat a little oil in a skillet (frying pan), add the artichokes and garlic, and season with salt and pepper. Cook over medium heat for 3–4 minutes, stirring occasionally, until the artichokes start to brown, then add a few tablespoons of water and cook for 5 minutes more, or until the artichokes are soft.

Meanwhile, heat the cream in a small pan, being careful not to let it boil. Remove from the heat, add the cheese and the melted butter, and use an immersion blender to blend until you have a soft creamy sauce. Keep warm.

Cook the pasta in a large pan of boiling lightly salted water (the cheese is already quite salty) according to the package directions until al dente, then drain well.

Transfer the drained pasta to the skillet with the artichokes and whisk in the cheese sauce. Serve immediately, garnished with a few chives, if liked.

⊙ Preparation time: 15 minutes

Cooking time: 10 minutes

♀ Wine suggestion: Cirò Bianco

Fusilli Pasta with Summer Vegetables, 'Nduja, and Salted Ricotta Cheese

Serves 4

4 asparagus spears
extra virgin olive oil
2 onions, sliced
10 cherry tomatoes, halved
1 yellow bell pepper, cored,
   seeded, and diced
1 carrot, diced
1 small eggplant
   (aubergine), diced
1 zucchini (courgette), diced
12 oz/350 g fusilli pasta
1 1/4 oz/30 g spicy sausage
   (ideally 'nduja), crumbled
a few basil leaves, chopped
2/3 cup (5 oz/150 g) coarsely
   grated salted ricotta cheese
salt

Break off the tough part at the base of the asparagus spears and discard. Cut the asparagus into slices about 1/4 inch/5 mm thick.

Heat a drizzle of oil in a large skillet (frying pan), add the onions, tomatoes, bell pepper, carrot, eggplant (aubergine), and zucchini (courgette), and cook over medium heat for 5–6 minutes until the vegetables are cooked through.

Meanwhile, cook the pasta in a large pan of boiling salted water according to the package directions until al dente, then drain well.

Transfer the drained pasta to the skillet with the vegetables. Add the asparagus, 'nduja, and a drizzle of oil and cook over medium heat for 2–3 minutes until heated through. Gently stir in the basil and ricotta. Serve.

NOTE 'Nduja is one of the most famous products in the Calabria region and it originates in Spilingo, in the Vibo Valentia region. It is a soft pork charcuterie product that is spreadable, and is very spicy thanks to the large quantity of chiles used in making it. It is the chiles that give it its characteristic bright red color.

⊙ Preparation time: 20 minutes

Cooking time: 15 minutes

Υ Wine suggestion: Langhe Bianco

Sedani Pasta with Rabbit and Mushrooms

Serves 4

extra virgin olive oil
11 oz/300 g lean rabbit
  meat, diced
1 thyme sprig, plus extra
  to garnish (optional)
1 bay leaf
1 rosemary sprig, plus extra
  to garnish (optional)
1/3 cup plus 1 tablespoon
  (3 1/2 oz/100 ml) white wine
1 celery stalk, cut into very
  small dice
1 carrot, cut into very
  small dice
1 shallot, cut into very
  small dice
4 cups (9 oz/250 g) coarsely
  chopped pioppini
  mushrooms (or you could
  use cremini (chestnut)
  mushrooms)
12 1/2 oz/360 g sedani
  pasta (or other short,
  tubular pasta)
1 flat-leaf parsley sprig,
  chopped
salt and pepper

Heat a drizzle of oil in a skillet (frying pan), add the rabbit meat and aromatic herbs, and cook over medium–low heat for 15 minutes, or until the meat is tender. Pour over the white wine and cook over medium heat for 3–4 minutes until the wine has evaporated. Add the celery, carrot, shallot, and mushrooms to the meat, then taste to check the seasoning and add salt and pepper if necessary.

Meanwhile, cook the pasta in a large pan of boiling salted water according to the package directions until al dente, then drain well. Let cool.

Transfer the drained pasta to the skillet with the meat sauce. Add the parsley and extra thyme and rosemary, if liked, and mix well. Serve.

TIP   Rabbit is often used instead of beef in Italy, because it contains a high level of protein, few fats, and little cholesterol. It can happen that rabbit tastes bad because the animal has not been properly fed; more than other animals, rabbits tend to transfer the taste of the food they eat to their own meat. To get rid of too intense a gamey aroma, soak the rabbit in water and vinegar for 1 hour before cooking.

⊙ Preparation time: 20 minutes

Cooking time: 15 minutes

Ⴓ Wine suggestion: Alto Adige Chardonnay

Pappardelle Pasta with Cheese, Pancetta, and Fava Beans

Serves 4

11 oz/300 g fresh fava (broad)
  beans in their pods, shelled
  (²/₃ cup prepared)
11¼ oz/320 g egg
  pappardelle pasta
3 cups (9 oz/250 g) grated
  aged pecorino cheese
²/₃ cup (2 oz/50 g) grated
  Parmesan cheese
2 tablespoons (1¼ oz/30 g)
  butter
4 slices pancetta or bacon,
  cut into thin strips
¹/₃ cup (2 oz/50 g) pine nuts
a few thyme leaves
salt and pepper

Cook the fava (broad) beans in a large pan of boiling water for about 15 minutes until tender.

Meanwhile, cook the pasta in a large pan of boiling lightly salted water according to the package directions until al dente.

While the pasta is cooking, put the pecorino and Parmesan into a large bowl, add the butter and a generous grinding of pepper.

Heat a dry nonstick skillet (frying pan), add the pancetta or bacon, and cook over medium heat for 2–3 minutes until crisp.

Heat a separate dry nonstick skillet, add the pine nuts, and toast over low heat for 5–6 minutes until they start to color.

To drain the pasta, twist portions of the pappardelle around a large fork and place them in the bowl of a large ladle, then tip the contents of the ladle into the bowl with the cheeses—a small amount of pasta cooking water will be caught in the ladle and this will combine with the cheeses to form a sauce. Repeat until all the pasta has been drained and added to the bowl, then mix the pasta vigorously with the cheeses. Add the fava beans and thyme and mix again.

Divide the pasta among serving plates, top with the crisp pancetta and the pine nuts, and serve immediately.

NOTE   Of all the vast variety of legumes, the large Leonforte variety of fava (broad) bean, grown in the Italian province of Enna, requires only a short cooking time, and does not need to be soaked. In Italy the beans are traditionally eaten as soon as they are picked, served simply with salt and pecorino cheese, or fried with oil, pancetta or bacon, and onions to make *frittedda*. Dried fava beans are used in Sicily to make other traditional recipes, and when browned in the oven they become "favi caliati", which are nibbled as a snack.

Preparation time: 10 minutes
Cooking time: 12 minutes
Wine suggestion: Roero Arneis

Caserecce Pasta with Sage and Pancetta

Serves 4

10–12 sage leaves
1/2 cup (2 1/4 oz/60 g) hazelnuts, toasted and coarsely chopped
1/3 cup (1 1/4 oz/30 g) grated aged pecorino cheese
5 tablespoons extra virgin olive oil
4 oz/120 g slices sweet pancetta or bacon
11 1/4 oz/320 g caserecce pasta (or other short, rolled pasta)
salt and white pepper

Put the sage leaves, half the hazelnuts, the pecorino, and oil into a food processor and process until the mixture is smooth and homogenous.

Heat a dry nonstick skillet (frying pan), add the pancetta or bacon, and fry over medium–high heat for 2–3 minutes until crisp. Drain the fried pancetta on paper towels and then cut into strips.

Meanwhile, cook the pasta in a large pan of boiling salted water according to the package directions until al dente, then drain well, reserving a little of the cooking water.

Dilute the sage sauce with a small ladleful of the reserved pasta cooking water—the sauce need to have a fairly liquid and creamy consistency.

Toss the drained pasta with the sage sauce and the pancetta and serve sprinked with the remaining hazelnuts and a dusting of white pepper.

N O T E   Sage is one of the most common aromatic herbs often used in Mediterranean cuisine. The most widespread variety, among the thousands that are known, is *Salvia officinalis maxima*. It can be used to flavor food and it makes fatty meats more digestible, pork in particular. The taste of sage marries perfectly with butter, giving rise to a rich sauce that can be used with pastas, such as caserecce or tagliatelle.

Preparation time: 15 minutes
Cooking time: 40 minutes
Wine suggestion: Barbera d'Alba

Reginette Pasta with Meat Ragu

Serves 4

2 tablespoons
  (1¼ oz/30 g) butter
2 tablespoons extra virgin
  olive oil, plus extra
  for drizzling
1 celery stalk, chopped
1 small carrot, chopped
¼ cup (1½ oz/40 g) chopped
  onion
11 oz/300 g ground (minced)
  meat (ideally a mixture
  of beef and pork)
½ glass red wine
⅓ cup (3½ oz/100 g) puréed
  canned tomatoes (passata)
1 tablespoon tomato
  paste (purée)
1 bay leaf
12 oz/350 g reginette
  pasta (or other ribbon-
  shaped pasta)
salt and pepper

To garnish
grated Parmesan cheese
  (optional)
a few thyme leaves (optional)

Heat the butter and oil in a large skillet (frying pan), add the vegetables, and fry over medium heat for 5 minutes. Add the meat and cook for 5 minutes, or until it starts to brown, then pour over the wine and cook over high heat for 5 minutes more, or until the wine has evaporated. Add the puréed canned tomatoes (passata), tomate purée (paste), ⅔ cup (5 fl oz/150 ml) water, and the bay leaf, then season with salt and cook over low heat for 25 minutes. Keep warm.

Cook the pasta in a large pan of boiling salted water according to the package directions until al dente, then drain well.

Transfer the drained pasta to the skillet with the meat ragu and gently mix together, adding a drizzle of oil and a sprinkling of pepper. Serve garnished with Parmesan and a few thyme leaves, if liked.

NOTE Reginette is a type of long pasta that originated in ancient Neapolitan times. The people of Naples dedicated the pasta to Princess Mafalda of Savoy because its wavy edges were reminiscent of the lace that was embroidered on royal clothes, and it was also known as mafaldine. Reginette lends itself to a variety of dishes, and it is particularly good when combined with weighty, dense sauces such as meat ragu.

⊙ Preparation time: 10 minutes
Cooking time: 15 minutes
♉ Wine suggestion: Scavigna Bianco

Ridged Penne Pasta
with Tomato, Tuna, and Olive Sauce

Serves 4

3 tablespoons extra virgin
  olive oil
1 clove garlic, crushed
2 anchovy fillets preserved in
  oil, drained
1 cup (3¹/₂ oz/100 g) pitted
  (stoned) green olives,
  coarsely chopped
1 cup (3¹/₂ oz/100 g) pitted
  (stoned) black olives,
  coarsely chopped
¹/₄ cup (1¹/₄ oz/30 g) capers
  preserved in salt, well rinsed
5 oz/150 g tuna preserved
  in oil, drained
2 cups (1 lb 2 oz/500 g)
  puréed canned tomatoes
  (passata)
2 oregano sprigs
11¹/₄ oz/320 g ridged
  penne pasta
3 tablespoons grated
  pecorino cheese
salt and pepper

Heat the oil in a large skillet (frying pan), add the garlic and anchovies, and cook over low heat for 2–3 minutes until the anchovies have dissolved. Add the olives, capers, and tuna and cook for a few minutes more, then add the puréed canned tomatoes (passata) and oregano, and season with salt and pepper. Cook over medium heat for about 10 minutes or until the sauce begins to thicken.

Meanwhile, cook the pasta in a large pan of boiling lightly salted water according to the package directions until al dente, then drain well.

Transfer the drained pasta to the skillet with the sauce and gently mix together. Sprinkle over the pecorino and serve.

NOTE Ready-pitted (-stoned) olives will save you time, but whole olives are preferable as they keep their flavor and consistency, though they do require a bit more patience.

⊙ Preparation time: 10 minutes

Cooking time: 20 minutes

♀ Wine suggestion: Franciacorta

Calamarata Pasta with Swordfish and Peas

Serves 4

4 ripe tomatoes
(about 14 oz/400 g)
5 tablespoons extra virgin
olive oil, plus extra
for drizzling
1 clove garlic, crushed
1 (7-oz/200-g) swordfish
fillet, diced
1¹/₃ cups (7 oz/200 g)
peas, cooked
a few mint leaves, chopped
pinch of chili powder
12 oz/350 g calamarata
pasta (or other short,
tubular pasta)
salt
¹/₄ cup (2¹/₄ oz/60 g) grated
salted ricotta cheese,
to serve

Bring a large pan of water to a boil. Meanwhile, lightly score a cross into the skin of each tomato. Drop the tomatoes into the boiling water and leave them for 30 seconds. Drain the tomatoes, then carefully peel off the skins and coarsely chop the tomato flesh.

Heat the oil with the garlic in a skillet (frying pan), add the fish, and cook over medium heat for 2 minutes until browned. Add the chopped tomatoes and the peas, pour in ¾ cup plus 1 tablespoon (7 fl oz/200 ml) water, and cook for 5 minutes over high heat until the tomatoes begin to fall apart. Turn off the heat, stir in the mint and chili powder, and season with salt.

Meanwhile, cook the pasta in a large pan of boiling salted water according to the package directions until al dente, then drain well. Let cool.

Transfer the drained pasta to the skillet with the sauce and gently stir to combine. Serve with a sprinkling of salted ricotta and a drizzle of oil.

NOTE   Calamarata is a short pasta typical of southern Italy. Its origin is contested between Naples and Sicily, and it gets its name from its ring shape, which is like a cut squid. This pasta lends itself well to being served with squid or other fish.

COOKING PASTA

To make a perfect pasta dish keep in mind a few tricks: the choice of pasta, the combination of shape and sauce, and the cooking method. Pasta is rich in starch, which is partly dispersed in the cooking water. Cooking for too long, or too aggressively, risks altering the sensory properties of the pasta and can ruin both consistency and flavor.

BOILING

This would seem to be the simplest cooking method but there are precise rules to follow, starting with quantities: 4¼ cups (34 fl oz/1 liter) of water is needed for every 3½ oz/100 g of pasta. Salt is only added when the water reaches boiling point: ½ oz/10 g for every 4¼ cups (34 fl oz/1 liter) of water. As soon as the water is boiling, "throw" the pasta in, stirring gently during the entire cooking time. Once the pasta is al dente, pour a glass of cold water into the pan to stop the pasta cooking and then drain.

TOSSING

Tossing the pasta in a large skillet (frying pan) with the chosen sauce is the best way to blend all the ingredients together and take full advantage of the binding qualities of starch. The sauce must be hot and the pasta al dente to ensure it does not overcook. While tossing the pasta and sauce on a high heat with firm wrist movements, add grated Parmesan cheese or pecorino cheese and a drizzle of extra virgin olive oil. If necessary, a little of the cooking water can be added to help bind the ingredients.

RISOTTO-STYLE

This method, widely used in professional kitchens, allows the pasta to retain more starch so that it feels creamier and achieves a subtler flavor.

The secret lies in the temperature of the ingredients. The broth (stock) or water must be boiling when added to the pasta. First prepare a cooking base, such as the classic soffritto: 1 onion, 1 carrot, and 1 celery stalk, chopped and sautéed in olive oil. Next, toast the pasta in a skillet for a couple of minutes. Add the sauce, vegetables, or fish. It is best to parboil these first to ensure the pasta does not overcook. Leave the pasta to absorb the flavors for 2–3 minutes before gradually adding the broth.

The time needed for the pasta to cook al dente varies with this method, compared with boiling, so it is necessary to add the broth very slowly and check often if the pasta is ready. If, for example, Sardinian gnocchetti cooks in 12–13 minutes, it is advisable to check if the pasta is cooked after ten minutes, and not add any more broth until the liquid in the skillet has completely evaporated.

As is the case with risotto, when using this method the pasta needs to be "cosseted and looked after". It is therefore essential to stir often to ensure the pasta becomes creamy, the starch is retained, and the flavors are well blended.

Serve the pasta when it is creamy and hot. The shapes most suitable for this type of cooking are those that are short and flat—farfalle, gnocchetti, penne, and orecchiette—which are easier to cook in this way and are more easily coated with the sauce.

BAKING OR AU-GRATIN

Timbales, pasta bakes, lasagne. Every type of baked preparation has its own secrets and tricks: with or without béchamel sauce, a drier or softer texture, with a crispy top or with a creamy and appetizing surface. There are, however, some general rules to follow to create the best baked dishes.

The pasta will be cooked twice so it is advisable to undercook it slightly when boiling it first. The more substantial shapes, such as lumaconi, conchiglioni, paccheri, and calamarata, are the most suitable because they collect the sauce well and they can also be filled to make the dish even tastier.

Once the pasta has been drained and coated with the chosen sauce, arrange it in a buttered dish and sprinkle the top with Parmesan cheese or with a beaten egg before baking.

Pasta bakes made with béchamel sauce need to be left to rest for a few minutes before serving to ensure the sauce reaches the right consistency.

⊙ Preparation time: 15 minutes

Cooking time: 10 minutes

♀ Wine suggestion: Alto Adige Sauvignon

Saffron Tagliolini Pasta with Zucchini and Prosciutto

Serves 4

3–4 tablespoons extra virgin olive oil

2 zucchini (courgettes), trimmed, cut in half lengthwise, and cut into rounds

1/2 leek, trimmed, cut in half, and cut into strips

3 1/2 oz/100 g prosciutto (Parma ham), thinly sliced

12 oz/350 g saffron tagliolini pasta

salt and pepper

Heat the oil in a skillet (frying pan), add the vegetables, and sauté over low heat for about 5 minutes until soft. Add the prosciutto (Parma ham), taste to check the seasoning, and add salt and pepper if necessary.

Meanwhile, cook the pasta in a large pan of boiling salted water according to the package directions until al dente, then drain well. Let cool.

Transfer the drained pasta to the skillet with the vegetables and prosciutto and cook over low heat for 2 minutes until heated through. Serve very hot.

NOTE Saffron tagliolini is characterized by its intense aroma and by the unmistakeable color given to it by this precious and elegant ancient spice. Try serving saffron tagliolini with light vegetable sauces, which will bring out its natural aroma and create a pleasant interplay of color on the plate.

⊙   Preparation time: 30 minutes, plus degorging

Cooking time: 20 minutes

♀   Wine suggestion: Bolgheri Rosé

Spaghetti Pasta with Mussels, Clams, Jumbo Shrimp, and Bell Pepper Purée

Serves 4

11 oz/300 g clams

2 red bell peppers

extra virgin olive oil

2 onions, chopped

11 oz/300 g mussels

5–6 cherry tomatoes, quartered

12½ oz/360 g spaghetti pasta

8 cooked, peeled, and deveined jumbo shrimp (king prawns)

a few mint leaves, chopped

salt and pepper

Plunge the clams into a bowl of cold water and let them degorge for 1 hour to get rid of any sand. Preheat the oven to 500°F/260°C/Gas mark 10.

Put the bell peppers in a roasting pan and roast in the oven for 25 minutes until bubbles form on the skin. Carefully put the roasted bell peppers in a plastic bag and let cool. Once cooled, peel off the skins, cut the peppers in half, and remove and discard the seeds and inner membrane.

Meanwhile, heat a drizzle of oil in a skillet (frying pan), add the onions and a pinch each of salt and pepper, and fry over medium heat for 5 minutes, or until soft and transparent.

Put the roasted bell peppers and fried onions into a food processor and process until the mixture is smooth.

Carefully clean the mussels with a small metal brush, then use tweezers to pull off the beards (the brown fibrous threads hanging from the shells) and rinse thoroughly.

Put the mussels and clams in a large pan, add a drizzle of oil and the tomatoes, cover, and cook over high heat for 5 minutes, or until all the shells have opened. Discard any that do not open. Set aside in their cooking liquor.

Cook the pasta in a large pan of boiling salted water according to the package directions until al dente, then drain well.

Transfer the drained pasta to the skillet with the mussels and clams and cook over low heat for 3 minutes, then add most of the bell pepper purée and shrimp (prawns) and sauté for a few minutes until heated through. Stir in the mint and serve immediately with additional sauce on the side.

⊙   Preparation time: 15 minutes

       Cooking time: 10 minutes

Ⴘ   Wine suggestion: Cerasuolo d'Abruzzo

Bucatini Pasta Amatriciana

Serves 4

5 oz/150 g pancetta or bacon,
   cut into strips
extra virgin olive oil
1/3 cup plus 1 tablespoon
   (3 1/2 fl oz/100 ml) white wine
1 1/2 cups (11 oz/300 g)
   chopped canned tomato
12 1/2 oz/360 g bucatini pasta
   (or other long pasta)
1 1/4 cups (3 1/2 oz/100 g) grated
   pecorino cheese (ideally
   Pecorino Romano cheese)
salt and pepper
basil leaves, to garnish
   (optional)

Heat a nonstick skillet (frying pan), add 3 1/2 oz/100 g of the pancetta or bacon, and cook over medium heat for 2–3 minutes until crisp. Drain the fried pancetta on paper towels.

Pour a drizzle of oil into the skillet, add the remaining pancetta, and cook over medium heat for 3 minutes, then pour over the wine and cook for 4–5 minutes until the wine has evaporated. Add the tomato pulp, then taste to check the seasoning and add salt and pepper if necessary. Cook over medium heat for 10 minutes, or until you have a homogenous thick sauce.

Cook the pasta in a large pan of boiling salted water according to the package directions until al dente. Drain well.

Transfer the drained pasta to the skillet with the sauce and cook over medium heat for 2–3 minutes until heated through. Remove from the heat and whisk in the pecorino.

Serve sprinkled with the crisp pancetta and garnished with a few basil leaves, if liked.

NOTE   The right kind of pancetta is fundamental to the success of a good pasta amatriciana: choose one that is from a single piece, dry and seasoned, pinkish-white in color, and cut into thick slices (rashers). This particular type of sauce is particularly suited to long pastas such as bucatini or spaghetti.

⊙ Preparation time: 10 minutes, plus marinating and cooling
Cooking time: 20 minutes

♀ Wine suggestion: Vernaccia di San Gimignano

Cold Fusilli Pasta with Tuna, Eggplant, and Cheese

Serves 4

²/₃ cup (5 fl oz/150 ml) extra virgin olive oil
1 large eggplant (aubergine), chopped
1 clove garlic, unpeeled
1 hot chile, chopped
4–5 mint leaves, chopped
2–3 basil leaves, chopped
1 (7-oz/200-g) tuna fillet, diced
1 tablespoon soy sauce
grated zest of 1 unwaxed lemon
12 oz/350 g fusilli pasta
5 oz/150 g sheep milk, semi-soft cheese (ideally primo sale cheese), diced
salt and white pepper

To serve
cherry tomatoes, quartered
a few herbs of your choice

Heat ½ cup (4 fl oz/125 ml) of the oil in a large skillet (frying pan), add the eggplant (aubergine), garlic, and chile, and cook over medium heat for 10 minutes, or until softened and golden. Let cool, then stir in the mint and basil. Taste to check the seasoning and add salt and pepper if necessary.

Put the tuna in a bowl with the remaining oil, and the soy sauce and lemon zest, cover with plastic wrap (clingfilm), and marinate in the refrigerator for 20 minutes.

Cook the pasta in a large pan of boiling salted water according to the package directions until al dente, then drain well. Let cool.

Toss the cooled pasta with the eggplant and tuna mixture and the primo sale. Let stand for at least 5 minutes, and remove the garlic clove, before serving.

Serve the salad with cherry tomatoes and a few herbs of your choice, if liked.

TIP If you do not care for raw tuna, you can sear it on one side and, once cool, add it to the pasta.

Preparation time: 20 minutes, plus marinating

Cooking time: 20 minutes

Wine suggestion: Oltrepò Pavese Metodo Classico Cruasè

Rigatoni Pasta with Tuna Carbonara

Serves 4

1 (11-oz/300-g) tuna fillet,
   cut into chunks
extra virgin olive oil
12 chives, finely chopped,
   plus extra, to serve
12½ oz/360 g rigatoni pasta
   (or other short, tubular
   pasta)
4 eggs
4 egg yolks
grated zest of ½
   unwaxed lemon
1 red onion (ideally a red
   Tropea onion), finely sliced
   and cooked in a skillet
   (frying pan) with a little olive
   oil until wilted (optional)
salt and pepper

Put the tuna in a bowl with a drizzle of oil and two-thirds of the chives, cover with plastic wrap (clingfilm), and marinate in refrigerator for 1 hour.

Heat a dry nonstick skillet (frying pan), add the tuna and cook over medium heat for 5–6 minutes until the chunks are just browned on the outside. Set aside.

Cook the pasta in a large pan of boiling salted water according to the package directions until al dente, then drain well.

Meanwhile, whisk the whole eggs and the egg yolks in a bowl with the lemon zest and plenty of pepper. As soon as the pasta has been drained, pour the egg mixture into a skillet, add the pasta and tuna, and cook over very low heat until the sauce is creamy.

Serve the pasta very hot, garnished with the remaining chives, the wilted red onion, if liked, and a very light dusting of pepper.

NOTE The machines used to make fresh pasta and give it its chosen shape can be made out of Teflon or bronze. In the latter case, the top of the pasta is rougher, which means it is better able to absorb any sauce, and it also absorbs more water during cooking, thus making it quicker to cook.

Preparation time: 10 minutes

Cooking time: 20 minutes

Wine suggestion: Collio Bianco

Bavette Pasta with Smoked Pancetta and Caramelized Red Onions

Serves 4

2 tablespoons (1¼ oz/
30 g) butter

5 oz/150 g thin slices smoked
pancetta or bacon,
cut into strips

3 red onions (ideally red
Tropea onions), cut
lengthwise into thin slices

1 tablespoon granulated
sugar

1 sprig flat-leaf parsley,
chopped

11¼ oz/320 g bavette pasta
(or other long pasta)

4 tablespoons grated
Parmesan cheese

4 tablespoons extra virgin
olive oil

salt and pepper

Heat the butter in a large skillet (frying pan), add the pancetta or bacon, and cook over medium–high heat for 2–3 minutes minutes until crisp. Remove the pancetta from the skillet and drain on paper towels.

In the same skillet, add the onions and cook over low heat for 5–6 minutes until wilted. Sprinkle over the sugar and cook for a few minutes more until caramelized, then add the parsley.

Meanwhile, cook the pasta in a large pan of boiling salted water according to the package directions until al dente, then drain well, reserving a little of the cooking water.

Transfer the drained pasta to the skillet with the onions. Add the crispy pancetta, Parmesan, oil, and 2–3 tablespoons of the reserved pasta cooking water and gently mix together. Serve with a sprinkling of pepper.

NOTE   The best type of onion to use for this sauce is the red Tropea onion (*Rossa di Tropea*). This variety, which is grown in the Calabria region of Italy, is characterized by a sweet taste, a tender consistency, and a white-pink, almost lilac color.

⊙ Preparation time: 20 minutes
Cooking time: 25 minutes

♀ Wine suggestion: Riviera Ligure di Ponente Pigato

Farfalle Pasta with Pesto and Zucchini

Serves 4

6 zucchini (courgette) flowers
6 tablespoons extra virgin
  olive oil
1 white onion, thinly sliced
2 large zucchini (courgettes),
  cut into rounds
1 small bunch basil
1 tablespoon pine nuts
2 tablespoons grated
  Parmesan cheese
11¼ oz/320 g farfalle pasta
salt

Gently open out the zucchini flowers, taking care not to break them, remove and discard the inner pistils, and cut the flowers into strips.

Heat 1 tablespoon of the oil in a large skillet (frying pan), add the onion and 2 tablespoons of water, and cook over medium heat for 5 minutes, or until the onion has softened. Add the zucchini (courgettes), season lightly with salt, and cook over low heat for 10–15 minutes until soft. Stir in the zucchini flowers.

Meanwhile, put the basil leaves, pine nuts, Parmesan, and the remaining oil into a food processor and process until the mixture is smooth.

Cook the pasta in a large pan of boiling salted water according to the package directions until al dente, then drain well, reserving some of the cooking water.

Transfer the drained pasta to the skillet with the zucchini, along with a few tablespoons of the reserved pasta cooking water, and sauté over medium heat for 2–3 minutes until heated through. Add the pesto, stir well, and serve.

NOTE This pesto has to be made fairly speedily, because basil blackens quickly and can become bitter. In the traditional recipe it is made using a marble mortar and a wooden pestle, which enables the cook to keep the bright green color of the basil leaves.

⊙   Preparation time: 15 minutes

        Cooking time: 15 minutes

♀   Wine suggestion: Fiano di Avellino

Ziti Pasta with Cheese, Crisp Pancetta, and Asparagus

Serves 4

1 (14-oz/400-g) bunch asparagus spears

1/3 cup plus 1 tablespoon (3½ fl oz/100 ml) whipping cream

7 oz/200 g semi-soft, washed rind cheese (ideally Taleggio cheese)

4 oz/120 g thin slices pancetta or bacon

11¼ oz/320 g ziti pasta (or other long, tubular pasta)

salt and pepper

Break off the tough part at the base of the asparagus spears and discard. Using a mandoline, cut the spears lengthwise into thin slices.

Heat the cream in a small pan, being careful not to let it boil. Remove from the heat, add the cheese, and stir until the cheese has melted and you have a thick and homogenous cream sauce. Keep warm.

Heat a dry nonstick skillet (frying pan), add the pancetta or bacon, and fry over medium heat for 2–3 minutes until crisp. Drain the fried pancetta on paper towels and then break up into smaller pieces.

Cook the pasta in a large pan of boiling salted water according to the package directions until al dente, adding the asparagus 2 minutes before the end of the cooking time. Drain well.

Gently toss the drained pasta and asparagus with the cheese sauce and serve sprinkled with the crisp pancetta and dusted with pepper.

TIP   Ziti probably originated in Sicily, where in the past it would be served at engagement or wedding parties; this is, however, typical of southern Italy as a whole. It is a durum wheat pasta, elongated in shape, tubular, hollow, and smooth, and it is traditionally served cut up by hand directly onto the plate with a ground (minced) meat and eggplant (aubergine) sauce.

THE RIGHT
SAUCE

The relationship between pasta and sauce is a true love affair, where passion and affinity are essential. It is a delicate balance and must take into account the type of pasta used, whether it has a smooth or lined surface, its length, and its shape.

The simplest match is straightforward and so easy—pasta al dente, with a drizzle of extra virgin olive oil and a basil leaf—but good-quality pasta, dressed in the right sauce, can open the doors to heaven. Combining shape and sauce is simple; all you have to do is follow a few simple rules, starting with the combination of thickness and size. The larger and thicker the pasta shape, the more adventurous you can be with complex, tasty sauces that are flavorsome and aromatic.

SMOOTH OR LINED SURFACE

Another rule to keep in mind for tasty matches is the pasta "skin". Smooth pasta shapes such as penne, mezze penne, and sigarette, are enhanced by creamy, binding sauces that envelop them without sliding off when the pasta is picked up with a fork. These shapes are therefore well matched with sauces based on cream, ricotta, béchamel sauce, and melted cheeses that will adhere to the pasta and not be left behind on the plate. They also go well with sauces made with eggs.

DOC (Denominazione di Origine Controllata)-classified carbornara sauce, for example, is made with smooth penne, both in its classic version and for lighter preparations with vegetables or fish.

Lined pasta shapes, with a rougher surface, such as tortiglioni, rigatoni, sedani, conchiglie, pipe rigate, ruote, and penne rigate, are perfect for retaining more "slippery" sauces. This means they go well with grainy sauces such as amatriciana, Bolognese sauce, and all sauces with small chunks of vegetables. In this case the sauce fills the grooves, adheres to the surface, and creates a perfect combination of pasta shape and flavor.

SHAPE

Long pasta, such as linguine, bavette, bucatini, ziti, tagliatelle, and spaghetti alla chitarra, combines well with smooth sauces and uniform pesto preparations, which coat them perfectly. You can therefore experiment with sauces made with cheese, purées, béchamel, or walnut sauce but also with chopped fish and vegetables cut into julienne strips. Creamy sauces that can be rolled with the pasta on a fork are perfect.

All twisted pasta shapes, such as fusilli, caserecce, cellentani, and castellane can be combined with sauces made with tomatoes, legumes (pulses) ragouts, and chopped fish or meat, which collect in the pasta folds.

Farfalle, reginette napoletane, pappardelle ricce, and generally speaking all flat pasta shapes, go well with creamy sauces made with cheese, such as ricotta, cream, or Gorgonzola, or with vegetable purées, aromatic herbs, and spices. Sardinian gnocchetti are best matched with particularly robust and flavorsome sauces such as those made with beef, lamb, or game, and spicy sauces.

So there are only a few rules to keep in mind, to find the perfect combination of pasta and sauce, and to create unforgettable dishes. From the simplicity of oil and basil, to the creativity of more complex sauces that enhance the quality of the shape they are matched with. And let's not forget, after all, that as the Italians say, serving macaroni without sauce is like having a party without friends.

Preparation time: 15 minutes

Cooking time: 15 minutes

Wine suggestion: Vermentino di Sardegna

Trofie Pasta with Tuna Bottarga and Pistachios

Serves 4

1¾ cups (9 oz/250 g) cherry
  tomatoes
5 tablespoons extra virgin
  olive oil
2 cloves garlic, crushed
⅓ cup (3¼ oz/90 g) pesto
  (ideally made with
  pistachios)
1½ oz/40 g tuna bottarga,
  half chopped into small
  pieces and half grated
12 oz/350 g trofie pasta
  (or other short, thin pasta)
salt
unsalted pistachios, to garnish

Bring a large pan of water to a boil. Meanwhile, lightly score a cross into the skin of each tomato. Drop the tomatoes into the boiling water and leave them for 30 seconds. Drain the tomatoes, then carefully peel off the skins and discard.

Heat the oil in a large skillet (frying pan), add the garlic and the cherry tomatoes, and cook over low heat for 7–8 minutes until the tomatoes have softened. Turn off the heat and then stir in the pesto and chopped tuna bottarga.

Cook the pasta in a large pan of boiling lightly salted water according to the package directions until al dente, then drain well.

Transfer the drained pasta to the skillet with the sauce and sauté over medium heat for 3–4 minutes until heated through. Stir in the remaining grated tuna bottarga.

Divide the pasta among serving plates, garnish with a few pistachios, and serve.

NOTE Bottarga is salted, cured roe. It should be cooked over medium heat to avoid it hardening and losing flavor. Prepare the sauce at least 20 minutes before you drain the pasta so that the saltiness of the "bottarga" comes out and its taste is less aggressive. Remember also to salt the cooking water for the pasta sparingly.

Preparation time: 35 minutes

Cooking time: 40 minutes

Paccheri Pasta with Ricotta Cheese, Radicchio, and Pecorino Cheese

Serves 6–8

1 lb 5 oz/600 g paccheri pasta (ideally Gragnano pasta, or other short, tubular pasta)
generous 2 cups (17 fl oz/ 500 ml) milk
2 tablespoons (1¼ oz/ 35 g) butter, plus extra for greasing
¼ cup (1¼ oz/35 g) all-purpose (plain) flour
extra virgin olive oil
1 shallot, chopped
1⅔ heads radicchio (about 14 oz/400 g), cut into ¾-inch/2-cm pieces (about 10 cups prepared)
2½ cups (1 lb 5 oz/600 g) cow milk ricotta cheese
1¼ cups (3½ oz/100 g) grated Parmesan cheese
2 eggs, beaten
1¼ cups (3½ oz/100 g) grated pecorino cheese (ideally Pecorino Romano cheese)
salt and pepper

Cook the pasta in a large pan of boiling salted water according to the package directions until al dente, then drain well. Transfer to an ovenproof dish, drizzle with a little oil, and mix well to prevent the pasta sticking together. Let cool.

Make the béchamel sauce. Heat the milk in a pan until just about to boil. In a separate pan, melt the butter, then add the flour and cook over low heat for a few minutes, stirring to make sure there are no lumps. Gradually add the hot milk, stirring briskly, then cook the sauce for 3 minutes, or until smooth and silky.

Heat a little oil in a nonstick skillet (frying pan), add the shallot, and cook over low heat for 3–4 minutes until soft and translucent. Add the radicchio and cook over high heat for a few minutes until wilted. Let cool.

In a large bowl, mix together the radicchio, ricotta, Parmesan, and eggs. Season to taste with salt and pepper. Spoon the mixture into a pastry (piping) bag fitted with a ½-inch/1-cm tip (nozzle).

Preheat the oven to 350°F/180°C/Gas mark 4. Grease an ovenproof dish with butter—you need a dish that is large enough to contain all the pasta arranged hole-side up in a single layer.

Pour the béchamel sauce into the prepared ovenproof dish. Arrange the pasta on top of the sauce—the pasta tubes should be vertical (hole-side up) and close together. Pipe the filling into the pasta tubes. Sprinkle the pecorino over the top, drizzle with a little oil, and bake in the oven for 25–30 minutes until golden.

WINE SUGGESTION Vespa Rosso is a red wine that balances power and sophistication. This is achieved by the careful combination of native and international grape varieties: merlot, Refosco, Cabernet Sauvignon, and Cabernet Franc. With spicy, fruity, and earthy notes, this wine's roundness and structure is an ideal accompaniment for this dish.

Preparation time: 15 minutes
Cooking time: 15 minutes
Wine suggestion: Capalbio Rosé

Spaghetti Pasta with Fennel Salami

Serves 4

10 oz/280 g spaghetti pasta
  (ideally spaghetti alla
  chitarra pasta)
2 tablespoons extra virgin
  olive oil
1/2 red onion (ideally a
  Certaldo onion), thinly sliced
3 1/2 oz/100 g fennel salami
  (ideally finocchiona
  salami), diced
8–10 sun-dried tomatoes, cut
  into thin strips
3 teaspoons dried
  tomato pâté
1 tablespoon fennel seeds,
  coarsely crushed
pinch of chili powder
salt
grated Parmesan cheese,
  to serve

Cook the pasta in a large pan of boiling salted water according to the package directions until al dente, then drain well, reserving some of the cooking water.

Meanwhile, heat the oil in a skillet (frying pan), add the onion, and cook over medium heat for 5 minutes, or until golden brown. Add the salami, sun-dried tomatoes, tomato pâté, fennel seeds, chili powder, and a couple of tablespoons of the reserved pasta cooking water, and cook for a few minutes over high heat.

Transfer the drained pasta to the skillet with the sauce, add another couple of tablespoons of the reserved pasta cocking water, and gently stir to combine. Serve with the remaining crushed fennel seeds and a sprinkling of Parmesan.

NOTE   Spaghetti alla chitarra get its name from the pasta-cutting machine that is traditionally used to make it. A chitarra is a wooden contraption with highly strung wire threads: sheets of pasta are laid on the wire threads and then rolled over with a rolling pin to cut the pasta into ribbons. Spaghetti alla chitarra is typical of the Abruzzo region of Italy, but is also found in Latium.

Preperation time: 15 minutes

Cooking time: 25 minutes

Wine suggestion: Bianco d'Alcamo

Macaroni Pasta in Onion Sauce

Serves 4

extra virgin olive oil

1 white onion, finely chopped

1 red onion, finely chopped

3 oz/80 g sardines preserved
  in salt

11¼ oz/320 g macaroni
  (ideally maccheroni
  al ferretto pasta)

salt

2 thyme sprigs, leaves only,
  to garnish

Heat a drizzle of oil in a large skillet (frying pan), add the onions, and cook over medium heat for 10 minutes, or until caramelized, adding a little water now and again if necessary to ensure the onions do not burn.

Meanwhile, carefully desalt the sardines under cold running water and remove the bones. Add the sardines to the onions and cook over very low heat for 5–6 minutes until completely dissolved.

Cook the maccheroni al ferretto in a large pan of boiling salted water according to the package directions until al dente, then drain well, reserving a little of the cooking water.

Transfer the drained pasta to the skillet with the sauce, add 2 tablespoons of the pasta cooking water, and cook for 2 minutes until well mixed and heated through. Serve garnished with thyme.

N O T E   Typical of the Lucania and Calabria regions of Italy, maccheroni al ferretto is a fresh eggless pasta made with durum wheat flour, water, and salt. It is created by rolling pieces of pasta dough around a thin metal skewer until a kind of large bucatini pasta is made, about 6 inches/15 cm long and about ¼ inch/7 mm thick. Maccheroni al ferretto goes very well with rich, flavorful sauces.

CHEF

Enrico Panero

Preparation time: 25 minutes, plus degorging

Cooking time: 15 minutes

Pasta with Cavolo Nero Pesto and Clams

Serves 4

1 lb 2 oz/500 g small
   ridged clams (ideally
   carpetshell clams)
extra virgin olive oil
1½ oz/40 g grissini
   breadsticks, coarsely broken
   into pieces
½ small hot chile, chopped
1 flat-leaf parsley sprig,
   chopped
11¼ oz/320 g linguine
   pasta (ideally Linguine di
   Gragnano pasta)

For the cavolo nero pesto
11 oz/300 g cavolo nero
   (Tuscan black cabbage),
   central ribs removed
⅓ cup (1½ oz/40 g) unsalted
   pistachios, toasted
1 cup (3 oz/80 g) grated
   pecorino cheese
1 teaspoon salt
⅓ cup (2¾ fl oz/80 ml) extra
   virgin olive oil

Plunge the clams into a bowl of cold water and let them degorge for 1 hour.

Make the pesto. Bring a large pan of water to a boil. Meanwhile fill a large bowl with iced water and set it beside the stove. Drop the cavolo nero (Tuscan black cabbage) into the boiling water and leave for 2 minutes. Drain, plunge into the iced water, then drain again thoroughly. Put the cavolo nero into a food processor with the pistachios, pecorino, salt, and oil, and process until the mixture reaches the desired consistency.

Heat a drizzle of oil in a skillet (frying pan), add the grissini, and cook over medium heat for 2–3 minutes until golden and crisp. Set aside.

Heat a drizzle of oil in a separate large skillet with a lid, add the chile, parsley, clams, and 1 tablespoon of water, cover with the lid, and cook over medium heat for 5 minutes, or until all the clams have opened. Discard any that do not open. Shell the clams, reserving a few whole ones for garnish.

Cook the pasta in a large pan of boiling salted water according to the package directions until al dente. Drain well, reserving ¾ cups plus 1 tablespoon (7 fl oz/200 ml) of the cooking water.

Transfer the drained pasta to the skillet with the clams. Add the reserved pasta cooking water and cook over medium heat for 3–4 minutes until all the water has been absorbed. Remove from the heat and stir in the pesto.

Serve the pasta in a nest shape, garnished with the reserved whole clams and sprinkled with crisp grissini crumbs.

WINE SUGGESTION Barbera Superiore Borgogno 2013. This wine comes from the most cultivated vineyard in the Piedmont region of Italy. Aged in casks, it has aromas of black fruits, violets, and spices, and is rounded on the palate and full of flavor. It goes very well with clams and is dedicated to those who are never satisfied.

CHEF
Enrico Panero

Preparation time: 20 minutes
Cooking time: 1¼ hours

Mixed Pasta with Octopus, Ricotta Cheese, and Citrus Fruits

Serves 4

1 lb 2 oz/500 g octopus, cleaned
1 celery stalk
1 carrot
1 white onion
extra virgin olive oil
½ chile, cut into strips
1 teaspoon sweet paprika
1½ tablespoons chopped flat-leaf parsley
11 oz/300 g mixed pasta shapes (ideally from Gragano)
grated zest of 1 unwaxed lemon
⅓ cup (3½ oz/100 g) cow milk ricotta cheese
1 dill sprig, chopped
grated zest of 1 unwaxed orange
grated zest of 1 unwaxed lime
salt and pepper

Bring a large pan of salted water to a boil. Add the octopus, celery, carrot, and onion, and cook for 1 hour. Drain, reserving the cooking liquid and discarding the vegetables, and cut the octopus tentacles into rounds.

Heat a drizzle of oil in a large skillet (frying pan), add the chile, paprika, and 1 tablespoon of the parsley, and cook over low heat for 2 minutes. Pour over ¾ cup plus 1 tablespoon (7 fl oz/200 ml) of the octopus cooking liquid and 1⅔ cups (14 fl oz/400 ml) water, add the pasta, and cook for about 10 minutes until al dente, adding the octopus 2 minutes before the end of the cooking time. Drizzle with a little oil and then stir in the remaining parsley and half the grated lemon zest.

Divide among soup plates and top with a few quenelles of ricotta. Serve drizzled with a little oil, dusted with pepper, and sprinkled with the dill and the remaining citrus fruit zest.

WINE SUGGESTION Dolcetto Borgogno 2013. This wine was already talked of at the end of 1500 and it is known to have been one of Napoleon's favorite wines during his stay in Italy. Dolcetto was born in Barolo and it is a concentrated and contemporary wine, with its aromas of rose, black currant, and hints of undergrowth. It is fresh on the palate with moderate tannins. It is perfect to counterbalance a dish of character such as this one.

Preparation time: 10 minutes

Cooking time: 25 minutes

Wine suggestion: Garda Classico Chiaretto

Whole Wheat Tagliatelle Pasta with Four Types of Tomato

Serves 4

3 tablespoons extra virgin
    olive oil
1 onion, cut into thin rounds
1 dried chile, crumbled
12 cherry tomatoes,
    quartered
12 small yellow tomatoes,
    quartered
1 cup (7 oz/200 g) tomato
    pulp
8 sun-dried tomatoes,
    chopped
11¼ oz/320 g whole wheat
    (wholemeal) tagliatelle pasta
5–6 basil leaves, chopped
salt

Heat the oil in a large skillet (frying pan), add the onion and chile, and cook over low heat for 3 minutes. Add the cherry and yellow tomatoes and let soften slightly, then add the tomato pulp, sun-dried tomatoes, and ⅓ cup plus 1 tablespoon (3½ fl oz/100 ml) water. Check the seasoning, adding salt if necessary, and cook over low heat for 15 minutes, or until the sauce is thickened.

Meanwhile, cook the pasta in a large pan of boiling salted water according to the package directions until al dente, then drain well, reserving some of the cooking water.

Transfer the drained pasta to the skillet with the reserved water and the tomato sauce, and cook over high heat for 2 minutes. Stir in the basil and serve.

NOTE   The yellow variety of the Piennolo tomato, the only true "pomo d'oro", has been known since 1544, thanks to the Camaldoli monks from Nola, near Naples, who grew it. It is very popular because of its sunny yellow color, and for the reduced size of its fruit. It has a thick skin and a sweet, intense flavor. It is also the only winter tomato, and its long keeping power enables it to be commercially available until the April following the harvest.

RICE

Preparation time: 20 minutes
Cooking time: 15 minutes
Wine suggestion: Colli di Luni Vermentino

Rice Salad

Serves 4

2 cups (14 oz/400 g) fino rice
 (ideally Sant'Andrea rice)
extra virgin olive oil
2 zucchini (courgettes), diced
2 carrots, diced
2 red bell peppers, cored,
 seeded, and diced
4 eggs
1¼ cups (7 oz/200 g) drained
 canned corn
salt
a few basil leaves, to garnish

For the pesto (optional)
2 bunches basil
⅓ cup plus 1 tablespoon
 (3½ fl oz/100 ml) extra
 virgin olive oil
10 peeled almonds
pinch of salt

Cook the rice in a large pan of boiling salted water for about 15 minutes until tender. Drain well.

Meanwhile, heat a little oil in a skillet (frying pan), add the zucchini (courgettes), carrots, and bell peppers, and cook over high heat for 4–5 minutes until golden and crisp.

Bring a large pan of water to a boil, then add the eggs and boil for 6 minutes until hard-cooked (hard-boiled). Drain and cool under cold running water. Remove the shells and chop up the eggs.

Put the drained rice, fried zucchini, carrots, and bell peppers, chopped eggs, corn, and olives into a large bowl and mix well.

If you are making the optional pesto, put the basil, oil, almonds, and salt into a food processor and blend until smooth.

To serve, place the rice salad in bowls. Drizzle over the pesto and garnish with a few basil leaves.

NOTE Sant'Andrea is an Italian variety of rice that is grown in Baraggia (the area between the Italian provinces of Biella, Vercelli, and Novara). The rice has a long grain and is excellent to use for making risottos as it retains its shape during cooking and easily absorbs flavors. Sant'Andrea rice is also ideal for use in soups, desserts, timbales, and salads.

Preparation time: 35 minutes, plus degorging
Cooking time: 30 minutes
Wine suggestion: Vermentino di Gallura

Mussel and Saffron Risotto

Serves 4

1 lb 2 oz/500 g mussels
4¼ cups (34 fl oz/1 liter) fish
  broth (stock)
2 g saffron threads
extra virgin olive oil
1 shallot, finely chopped
1¼ cups (9 oz/250 g)
  Carnaroli or Arborio rice
⅓ cup plus 1 tablespoon
  (3½ fl oz/100 ml) white wine
1 flat-leaf parsley sprig,
  chopped
2 tablespoons grated
  Parmesan cheese
salt and pepper

Plunge the mussels into a bowl of cold water and leave to degorge for 1 hour.

Pour the broth (stock) into a pan, bring to a boil, then reduce to a simmer. Keep over a low heat while you make the risotto. Pour a little of the broth into a small heatproof bowl, add the saffron, and let infuse for 10 minutes.

Heat a little oil in a large pan, add the shallot, and cook over low heat for 2 minutes, or until it starts to sweat. Add the rice and cook for a few minutes, stirring with a wooden spoon, until the rice is translucent. Pour over 3½ tablespoons of the wine and cook over high heat until it has evaporated. Add a ladleful of broth and cook over medium–high heat, stirring frequently, for about 9 minutes, gradually adding in more broth a ladleful at a time, making sure each addition is absorbed by the rice before adding the next ladleful.

Meanwhile, clean the mussels with a small metal brush, then use tweezers to pull off the beards (the brown fibrous threads hanging from the shells). Rinse thoroughly. Heat a little oil in a skillet (frying pan), add the mussels and the remaining wine, cover, and cook over medium heat for 5 minutes, or until all the shells have opened. Discard any that do not open.

Add the saffron water and mussels to the risotto and cook for 9 minutes more, continuing to stir and adding the broth a ladleful at a time. The risotto is ready when the rice is cooked through but still al dente. Remove from the heat, season with salt and pepper, and stir in the parsley, Parmesan, and a drizzle of oil. Let rest for a few minutes before serving.

TIP   You can make your own fish broth (stock). First clean and bone a 1 lb 10 oz/750 g sea bass: remove and discard the gills, the inside of the mouth, the eyes, and skin; set aside the fillets to cook at another time. Put the bones and fish head into a stock pot (stew pan) and pour over 8½ cups (68 fl oz/2 liters) cold water. Add ½ carrot, 1 small celery stalk, ½ onion, 2 sage leaves, 1 bay leaf, 1 rosemary sprig, 5 parsley sprigs, 1 teaspoon ground pepper, and a pinch of salt. Bring to a boil and then cook over low heat for 30 minutes, skimming the surface occasionally. Strain the broth through a fine-mesh strainer (sieve). The broth can be stored in the refrigerator for 2 days or in the freezer for up to 1 month.

Stuffed Rice Balls

Serves 6

2½ cups (1 lb 2 oz/500 g) Carnaroli or Arborio rice

⅛ teaspoon saffron powder (or you could use 1½ saffron threads)

2 tablespoons (1¼ oz/ 30 g) butter

3 tablespoons grated mature pecorino cheese

1 (3½ -oz/100-g) slice ham, diced

2 oz/50 g stretched-curd cheese (ideally caciocavallo cheese), diced

3½ oz/100 g mozzarella cheese, diced

1¾ cups (7 oz/200 g) type 00 flour

6⅔ cups (11 oz/300 g) fresh breadcrumbs

sunflower oil, for deep-frying

salt and pepper

For the stuffing

3 tablespoons extra virgin olive oil

½ onion, chopped

5 oz/150 g ground (minced) pork

⅓ cup plus 1 tablespoon (3½ fl oz/100 ml) red wine

¾ cup (7 oz/200 g) tomato purée (passata)

⅔ cup (3½ oz/100 g) shelled fresh peas

Cook the rice in a pan with 5½ cups (44 fl oz/1.3 liters) boiling salted water for 15 minutes, or until all the water has been absorbed by the rice and the rice is dry and compact.

In a small bowl, mix the saffron powder with a little cold water. Pour the saffron water over the cooked rice and stir in the butter and pecorino. Spread out the rice on a large plate or baking sheet, cover with plastic wrap (clingfilm), and let cool.

Meanwhile, make the stuffing. Heat the olive oil in a skillet (frying pan), add the onion, and cook over low heat for 3–4 minutes until soft and translucent. Add the ground (minced) pork and cook over high heat until golden brown. Pour over the red wine and cook for a few minutes until it has evaporated, then add the tomato purée (passata) and cook over medium heat for at least 15 minutes until sauce has thickened. Stir in the peas, season with salt and pepper, and cook for 5 minutes more.

Using your hands, shape two tablespoonfuls of the cooled rice mixture into a ball. Make a hole into the center with your finger and fill it with 1 tablespoon of the stuffing and a few pieces of the ham, caciocavallo, and mozzarella. Close up the hole with a little more of the rice mixture and reshape into a ball. Repeat until you have used up all the rice mixture, stuffing, ham, and cheese. Chill in the refrigerator for 20 minutes.

Make a batter by mixing the flour, 1¼ cups (10 fl oz/300 ml) cold water, and a pinch of salt together in bowl. Spread out the breadcrumbs in a shallow dish. Dip each rice ball into the batter and then roll it in the breadcrumbs to coat.

Pour enough sunflower oil for deep-frying into a deep-fat fryer or large deep pan and heat the oil to 350°F/180°C. Carefully add the rice balls to the hot oil, a few at a time, and cook for 3–4 minutes until golden brown. Remove with a slotted spoon and drain on paper towels. Repeat until all the rice balls are cooked.

⊙ Preparation time: 15 minutes
Cooking time: 20 minutes
♀ Wine suggestion: Alto Adige Valle Isarco Sylvaner

Asparagus and Cheese Risotto

Serves 4

15 asparagus spears
4¼ cups (34 fl oz/1 liter)
  vegetable broth (stock)
1½ tablespoons (¾ oz/
  20 g) butter
1 shallot, finely chopped
1¼ cups (9 oz/250 g)
  Carnaroli or arborio rice
3½ oz/100 g soft, stretched-
  curd cheese (ideally
  stracciatella cheese)
²/₃ cup (2 oz/50 g) grated
  Parmesan cheese
salt

Break off the tough part at the base of the asparagus spears and discard. Cut the asparagus spears into diagonal slices, leaving the tips whole.

Pour the broth (stock) into a pan and bring to a simmer. Keep over a low heat while you make the risotto. Put the asparagus tips in the stock to cook for 2 minutes then remove and reserve for serving.

Melt the butter in a large pan, add the shallot, and cook over medium heat for a couple of minutes until soft and translucent. Add the rice and toast over a high heat for a few minutes. Add a ladleful of the broth and cook over medium–high heat, stirring frequently, for about 8 minutes, gradually adding in more broth a ladleful at a time and making sure each addition is absorbed by the rice before adding the next ladleful. Add the asparagus and cook for 6–7 minutes more, continuing to stir and adding the broth a ladleful at a time. The risotto is ready when the rice is cooked through but still al dente. Remove from the heat and stir in the Parmesan and soft cheese, laying some of the soft cheese in strips on the very top with the reserved tips. Let rest for a few minutes before serving.

NOTE Stracciatella is a fresh cheese made from buffalo or cows' milk. It is made from shreds of mozzarella cheese soaked in fresh cream, and it is also the oozy middle part of a burrata cheese. Stracciatella is made in particular in the province of Foggia in the Apulia region of Italy. The cheese is delicious eaten on its own or added to first courses, bruschetta, or pizza.

Preparation time: 25 minutes
Cooking time: 30 minutes
Wine suggestion: Etna Bianco Superiore

Caper, Anchovy, and Oven-baked Tomato Risotto

Serves 4

2 cups (3¹/₂ oz/100 g) fresh
  breadcrumbs
1 flat-leaf parsley sprig,
  chopped
¹/₂ chile, seeded and chopped
10 anchovies preserved in
  salt, well rinsed, boned, and
  chopped
6 vine-ripened tomatoes,
  halved
4¹/₄ cups (34 fl oz/1 liter)
  vegetable broth (stock)
  without any added salt
extra virgin olive oil
¹/₂ onion, chopped
1¹/₄ cups (9 oz/250 g)
  Carnaroli or Arborio rice
20 capers preserved in salt,
  well rinsed, plus extra to
  garnish
2–3 basil leaves, torn
salt and pepper

To garnish
4 anchovy fillets preserved in
  oil, drained
a few marjoram leaves

Preheat the oven to 350°F/180°C/Gas mark 4. Grease an ovenproof dish with oil.

Mix together the breadcrumbs, parsley, chile, and one-tenth of the anchovies in a small bowl and season with salt and pepper. Place the tomatoes, cut-side up, in the prepared ovenproof dish, sprinkle over the breadcrumb mixture, and bake in the oven for 10 minutes. Transfer to a food processor and blend to a purée.

Meanwhile, pour the broth (stock) into a pan and bring to a simmer. Keep over a low heat while you make the risotto.

Heat a little oil in a large pan, add the onion, and cook over low heat for 2 minutes, or until the onion starts to sweat. Add the rice and toast over high heat for a few minutes. Add a ladleful of the broth and cook over medium–high heat, stirring frequently, for about 8 minutes, gradually adding in more broth a ladleful at a time and making sure each addition is absorbed by the rice before adding the next ladleful. Add the capers and the remaining anchovies, season with salt and pepper, and cook for 8 minutes more, continuing to stir and adding the broth a ladleful at a time. The risotto is ready when the rice is cooked through but still al dente. Stir in the puréed oven-baked tomatoes and cook for a few minutes more until heated through. Remove from the heat and stir in a little oil and the basil. Let rest for a few minutes before serving.

To serve, divide the risotto among serving plates and garnish each dish with 1 anchovy fillet, a few capers, and a few marjoram leaves.

Preparation time: 10 minutes

Cooking time: 30 minutes

Wine suggestion: Collio Chardonnay

Artichoke, Pecorino Cheese, and Lemon Risotto

Serves 4

extra virgin olive oil

1/2 onion, chopped

1 1/4 cups (9 oz/250 g)
  semifino rice (ideally
  Vialone Nano rice)

1/3 cup plus 1 tablespoon
  (3 1/2 fl oz/100 ml) white wine

4 artichokes

3 1/3 cups (27 fl oz/800 ml)
  vegetable broth (stock)

1 1/4 cups (3 1/2 oz/100 g)
  grated pecorino cheese
  (ideally Pecorino Romano
  cheese)

grated zest of 1
  unwaxed lemon

a few thyme sprigs, to garnish

salt and pepper

Heat a little oil in a large pan, add the onion, and cook over low heat for 3–4 minutes until golden brown. Add the rice and toast over high heat for a few minutes. Pour over the wine and cook until it has evaporated.

Meanwhile, trim the artichokes, discarding the inner chokes, the tougher outermost leaves, and their spiny tips. Peel and chop the artichoke stalks. Cut the artichokes into segments.

Pour the broth (stock) into a pan, add the chopped artichoke stalks, and bring to a simmer. Keep over a low heat while you make the risotto.

Once the wine has evaporated, add the artichoke segments to the pan with the rice, then add a ladleful of the broth and cook over medium–high heat, stirring frequently, for about 17 minutes, gradually adding in more broth a ladleful at a time and making sure each addition is absorbed by the rice before adding the next ladleful. The risotto is ready when the rice is cooked through but still al dente. Remove from the heat, stir in the pecorino, most of the lemon zest, and a little oil (oil is better than butter for this recipe, but only use a little). Season with salt and pepper and let rest for a few minutes before serving. Serve garnished with the remaining lemon zest and a few thyme sprigs.

NOTE You can use Vialone Nano Veronese rice for this recipe. Its consistency and starch content mean it does not lose its shape when cooked and perfectly absorbs flavors and seasoning. Grown in various areas in the province of Verona, which has an ideal climate and abundant supplies of pure water, Vialone Nano Veronese rice is one of the oldest cross-bred rice varieties (a cross between Vialone Nero and Nano). It was the first rice to obtain PGI (Protected Geographical Indication) status in 1996.

METHODS OF COOKING RICE

It is estimated that rice is consumed daily by more than half the world's population, with the highest consumption in Asia. In Italy, it is used mainly as a first course, in soups, or risotto, while in the rest of the world it is often used as a side dish.

The simplest recipe is boiled rice, where the rice is cooked in abundant salted boiling water. It is then dressed with olive oil or butter and Parmesan cheese. Rice can also be served in a salad. In this case choose parboiled or superfine rice, cook until al dente, drain the rice, and rinse quickly in cold water before adding the dressing.

A VERY ITALIAN DISH: RISOTTO

Of the preparations suggested, risotto is by far the most typically Italian. Two essential steps give it its specific characteristics: toasting the rice and cooking in broth, which is added gradually.

For good results it is necessary to choose rice that, when cooked, releases some of its starch but not too much, to avoid glutinosity: the best varieties are Carnaroli, Arborio, Vialone Nano, which remains solid and in separate grains, and Roma, ideal for very soft risottos.

First of all, heat the oil or butter in a wide, shallow Dutch oven (casserole dish) and soften some finely chopped aromatic ingredients (often only onion is used) along with any ingredients that require a longer cooking time. Then turn the heat up and toast the rice until the grains become almost transparent. At this point add a little wine, normally white, and once this has evaporated, start adding boiling broth (stock). Add a sufficient quantity to cover the rice to start with. When this has evaporated, add a ladleful at a time.

It is necessary to stir often during cooking, using a wooden spoon, and taste the rice, adding salt to taste when the rice is almost done. Some ingredients (such as vegetables, fish, and shellfish) are added pre-cooked a few minutes before the end. When the rice is al dente, turn the heat off, add a few shavings of butter and grated cheese if desired, and let the risotto rest for a few minutes. The consistency of the risotto should be soft but not liquid ("flowing in waves"), or a little bit more compact.

RICE AS A SIDE DISH

There are various methods for cooking rice as a side dish. Steaming is typical of the Orient, and for this a long-grain variety, such as basmati, is advised. Grains needs to be soaked in cold water for a few hours, then drained and steamed in a steamer until al dente. Rice cooked in this way is ideal as a side dish or for salads.

Cooking techniques that use absorption, such as pilaf, Creole, and Eastern-style, are often used to cook rice for side dishes.

For pilaf rice, melt a little butter in a pan and soften a finely chopped onion in the butter before adding cloves, then the rice. Let the rice absorb the flavors and at this point add boiling water or broth, twice as much volume as the volume of the rice. Let the liquid come to a boil again, then cover and bake in an oven, preheated to 400°F/200°C/Gas mark 6 without stirring, until the liquid has been completely absorbed. This is a Middle-eastern preparation that is normally used to accompany fish, shellfish, vegetables, meat, and legumes (pulses).

For Creole cooking, bring salted water to a boil (double the volume of the rice), add a little butter and then the rice. Let it cook over a moderate heat until the water has been completely absorbed.

Finally, a perfect cooking method for varieties such as basmati or Thai rice is the so-called Eastern-style, in which the rice is immersed in twice its weight in cold water, together with cardamom, cloves, and saffron. The rice is then cooked until all the water has been absorbed. This is excellent with sautéed shrimp (prawns).

⊙ Preparation time: 10 minutes
   Cooking time: 35 minutes
♀ Wine suggestion: Alto Adige Terlano Bianco

Nettle Risotto

Serves 4

3 tablespoons extra virgin
   olive oil
1 small white onion, finely
   chopped
2 oz/50 g lardo, finely
   chopped
1 flat-leaf parsley sprig, finely
   chopped
2 handfuls nettle tops (see
   tip), chopped
generous 2 cups (17 fl oz/
   500 ml) vegetable broth
   (stock)
1½ cups (11 oz/300 g)
   semifino rice (ideally
   Vialone Nano rice)
3 tablespoons grated
   Parmesan cheese
salt and pepper

Heat the olive oil in a large pan, add the onion, lardo, and parsley, and cook over medium heat for 2–3 minutes until the onion is sweated and the lardo has melted. Add the nettle tops, pour over two ladlefuls hot salted water and cook for 15 minutes until the nettles start to disintegrate and the water has evaporated.

Meanwhile, pour the broth (stock) into a pan and bring to a simmer. Keep over a low heat while you make the risotto.

Add the rice to the pan with the nettle tops and toast over high heat for 1 minute. Add a ladleful of the broth and cook over medium–high heat, stirring frequently, for about 17 minutes, gradually adding in more broth a ladleful at a time and making sure each addition is absorbed by the rice before adding the next ladleful. The risotto is ready when the rice is cooked through but still al dente. Season with salt and pepper and stir in the Parmesan. Let rest for a few minutes before serving.

TIP The nettle is a very common wild plant that grows on uncultivated land, and it is considered to be a weed. You should wear gloves when picking nettles because the leaves are covered in fine hairs that release a liquid that stings. The nettle tops and young leaves have a pleasant, slightly bitter taste and can be used to make frittatas, risottos, and the filling for stuffed pasta.

Rice and Ham Croquettes

Serves 4

1 cup (7 oz/200 g) Carnaroli
or Arborio rice

1½ tablespoons (1½ oz/
40 g) butter

1 tablespoon chopped flat-
leaf parsley

8 (1¼-oz/30-g) slices ham

8 (¾-oz/20-g) slices Gruyère
cheese

1 egg

pinch of salt

5½ cups (9 oz/250 g) fresh
breadcrumbs

vegetable oil, for frying

Cook the rice in a large pan of boiling salted water for about 18 minutes until al dente. Drain well, transfer to a large bowl and stir in the butter and parsley.

Lay out the slices of ham on the countertop. Put one slice of Gruyère on top of each slice of ham, then spread a little of the rice mixture over each slice of Gruyère. Carefully roll up the ham slices with the rice and cheese inside.

Beat the egg and salt well in a shallow dish. Spread out the breadcrumbs in a separate shallow dish. Dip each ham roll into the beaten egg, then roll it in the breadcrumbs to coat.

Pour enough oil into a deep skillet (frying pan) so that it is about 1¼ inches/ 3 cm deep. Heat the oil to 340°F/170°C, then carefully add the croquettes, in batches if necessary, and fry for 2–3 minutes until golden brown. Remove with a slotted spoon, drain on paper towels, and serve hot.

NOTE   Carnaroli rice, known as "the king of rices", is a high quality, superfine rice. It has large, long grains that keep their shape during cooking, making it ideal for risottos and timbales. Carnaroli rice is grown in Pavia, Novara, and Vercelli in the Italian region of Piedmont. The rice husk is removed by stone-milling, which keeps all the rice's nutritional properties intact. Carnaroli rice can be aged for one year, which stabilizes the starch and ensures perfect cooking.

Preparation time: 15 minutes, plus cooling
Cooking time: 40 minutes
Wine suggestion: Colli Piacentini Ortrugo

Black Rice Salad
with Julienne Vegetables

Serves 4

1¹/₃ cups (10 oz/280 g) black
rice (ideally Venere rice)
2 tablespoons extra virgin
olive oil
1 fennel bulb, cut into thin
strips
2 carrots, cut into thin strips
2 zucchini (courgettes), cut
into thin strips
2 tablespoons
(1¹/₄ oz/30 g) butter
7–8 walnuts, finely chopped
5 tablespoons
whipping cream
salt and pepper

Cook the rice in a large pan of boiling salted water for 40 minutes, or until the rice is al dente. Drain well, cool under cold running water, then drain again.

Meanwhile, heat the oil in a skillet (frying pan), add the fennel, carrots, and zucchini (courgettes), season with salt and pepper, and cook over medium heat for 4–5 minutes until the vegetables are just starting to soften but still retain their bite. Alternatively, blanch the vegetables in a pan of boiling salted water for 2 minutes, then drain, plunge the vegetables into a large bowl of iced water, and drain again.

To make the walnut sauce, melt the butter in a small pan, add the walnuts and ¹/₃ cup plus 1 tablespoon (3¹/₂ fl oz/100 ml) water, and cook over low heat for 5 minutes, or until one third of the liquid has evaporated. Remove from the heat, season with salt and pepper, and stir in the cream. Let cool.

Put the drained rice and vegetables into a large bowl, season with salt and pepper, and toss to mix well. Serve with the walnut sauce.

NOTE   Venere rice should not be confused with wild red rice, which though similar in appearance is not actually rice but the seed of the plant *Zizania aquatica*. The average to long grains of Venere rice are deep red, with a full flavor that is sweet after cooking. It has a high vitamin, mineral, salt, and fiber content, and is ideal for delicious salads or to serve with fish dishes.

Preparation time: 15 minutes

Cooking time: 40–45 minutes

Wine suggestion: Alto Adige Val Venosta Riesling

Black Rice with Cheese and Broccoli

Serves 4

2 tablespoons extra virgin
  olive oil
1/4 cup (1 1/2 oz/40 g) chopped
  shallot
1 cup (7 oz/200 g) black rice
  (ideally Venere rice)
2/3 head broccoli (about
  1 lb 2 oz/500 g), broken
  into florets
3 1/3 cups (27 fl oz/800 ml) hot
  vegetable broth (stock)
7 oz/200 g semi-soft, washed
  rind cheese (ideally Taleggio
  cheese), cut into pieces
salt and pepper

Heat the oil in a large pan, add the shallot, and cook over low heat for 4–5 minutes until brown. Add the rice and 2 cups (12 oz/350 g) of the broccoli florets and cook for a few minutes, then pour over the broth (stock) to cover the rice and broccoli. Season with salt and pepper, stir well, and cook for 35–40 minutes until the rice is tender.

Meanwhile, bring a pan of water to a boil. Fill a large bowl with iced water and set it beside the stove. Drop the remaining broccoli into the boiling water and leave for 8 minutes. Drain, plunge into the iced water, then drain again thoroughly.

When the rice is cooked, stir in the Taleggio and serve, garnished with the blanched broccoli florets.

NOTE Vegetable growing is a long-standing tradition in Irpinia in the Campania region of Italy, particularly in the area of Paternopoli. The few market gardeners that continue to work here—despite an earth-quake and after farming areas further inland have been abandoned—have selected to grow a variety of spring broccoli called Aprilatico, which is very dark green, with crunchy florets and a pleasant taste, making it ideal for first courses or as an accompanying vegetable. Today, Aprilatico broccoli, the symbol of a long-standing tradition of horticulture that is deeply rooted in the local community, is protected by a Slow Food Presidia label.

Preparation time: 10 minutes

Cooking time: 25 minutes

Wine suggestion: Barbera d'Alba

Red Wine Risotto

Serves 4

5 cups (40 fl oz/1.2 liters)
vegetable broth (stock)

2 tablespoons extra virgin
olive oil

2 tablespoons chopped onion

7oz/200 g sausages, skins
removed and finely chopped

1 1/2 cups (11 oz/300 g)
Carnaroli or Arborio rice

3/4 cup plus 1 tablespoon
(7 fl oz/200 ml) full-bodied
red wine

1 1/2 tablespoons (1 1/2 oz/
40 g) butter

2 tablespoons grated
Parmesan cheese

pinch of ground nutmeg
grated zest of 1/2 unwaxed
lemon

salt

Pour the broth (stock) into a pan and bring to a simmer. Keep over a low heat while you make the risotto.

Heat the oil in a pan, add the onion, and cook over low heat for 3–4 minutes until soft and translucent, then add the sausage and stir with a wooden spoon until the meat is well browned. Add the rice and toast over high heat for 1 minute, then pour over the red wine, season with salt, and cook until the wine has evaporated. Add four ladlefuls of broth and cook over medium–high heat, stirring frequently, for about 18 minutes, gradually adding in more broth a ladleful at a time and making sure each addition is absorbed by the rice before adding the next ladleful. The risotto is ready when the rice is cooked through but still al dente. Remove from the heat and stir in the butter, Parmesan, nutmeg, and lemon zest. Let rest for a few minutes before serving.

TIP For an excellent red wine risotto, choose Barbera d'Alba. Produced in the Cuneo area of Italy, this wine's garnet red color will give the dish an attractive appearance and a dry taste. If you like strong flavors, try replacing most of the vegetable broth (stock) with wine, using 3 cups (25 fl oz/750 ml) wine to cook the risotto. Bring the wine gently to a boil, as if it were broth, then gradually add it to the rice in the same way as the broth in the recipe above.

Preparation time: 40 minutes

Cooking time: 40 minutes

Wine suggestion: Trento Metodo Classico Brut

Black Rice with Vegetables, Fried Basil, and Pea Pods

Serves 4

2 cups (14 oz/400 g) black
  rice (ideally Venere rice)
5 oz/150 g fresh peas in
  their pods, shelled and
  pods reserved
2 cups (7 oz/200 g)
  trimmed (topped and tailed)
  green beans
extra virgin olive oil
10–15 cherry tomatoes,
  halved, seeded
  and chopped
2 celery stalks, strings
  removed and chopped
14 basil leaves, 4 leaves torn,
  the rest left whole
1 flat-leaf parsley sprig,
  chopped
2/3 cup (2 1/4 oz/60 g) pitted
  (stoned) black olives
grated zest of 1
  unwaxed lemon
salt and pepper

Cook the rice in a large pan of boiling salted water for 40 minutes, or until the rice is tender, then drain well. Alternatively, use a pressure cooker and reduce the cooking time to about 20 minutes.

Meanwhile, bring a large pan of salted water to a boil. Fill a large bowl with iced water and set it beside the stove. Drop the peas and green beans into the boiling water and leave for 4–5 minutes. Drain, plunge into the iced water, then drain again thoroughly. Cut the green beans into pieces.

Heat a little oil in a skillet (frying pan), add the peas, green beans, cherry tomatoes, and celery, and cook over medium heat for 5–6 minutes until brown. Add the drained rice, torn basil leaves, parsley, black olives, and lemon zest, season with salt and pepper, and mix well.

Heat 3/4 cup plus 1 tablespoon (7 fl oz/200 ml) oil in a large skillet, add the whole basil leaves and reserved pea pods and cook over medium heat for 3–4 minutes until they become crispy.

Place a large metal ring or cookie cutter in the center of each plate, fill it with the rice mixture, then carefully remove the ring or cutter. Drizzle over a little oil and garnish with the fried basil and pea pods.

CHEF
Ugo Alciati

Preparation time: 15 minutes
Cooking time: 16 minutes

Plum Tomato Risotto with Basil Purée

Serves 4

8 ripe plum tomatoes
(about 1 lb 2 oz/500 g)
10 basil leaves
2 ice cubes
3½ tablespoons extra virgin
olive oil
3 tablespoons (1½ oz/
40 g) butter
1¼ cups (8½ oz/
240 g) risotto rice, such
as Carnaroli, Arborio,
or Vialone Nano
½ cup (2 oz/50 g) grated
Parmesan cheese
salt

Put the tomatoes into a food processor and process until smooth. Push the tomato mixture through a strainer (sieve) into a bowl and discard the pulp.

Pour 4¼ cups (34 fl oz/1 liter) water into a pan, bring to a boil, and season lightly with salt.

Put the basil, ice cubes, and oil into a food processor or blender and process until you have a homogenous and smooth mixture.

Melt half the butter in a large pan, add the rice, and toast over high heat for a couple of minutes. Add two ladlefuls of the boiling water and half the tomato mixture and cook for 14 minutes, gradually adding in more boiling water, a ladleful at a time, until all the liquid is absorbed by the rice, adding the remaining tomato mixture 2 minutes before the end of the cooking time. Turn off the heat and whisk the Parmesan and the remaining butter into the rice. Let rest for a few minutes before serving.

Divide the risotto among serving plates and drizzle with the basil purée.

WINE SUGGESTION Marin Langhe Bianco 2014 is a very big wine that is born of the union between two extraordinary vines, Riesling and Nascetta, both cultivated in the high parts of the hills round the Langhe region of Italy. The acidity of the former and the body and nose of the latter balance each other out, a bit like the acidity of the plum tomato joining the fragrant basil in this classic Italian dish.

Preparation time: 20 minutes, plus chilling
Cooking time: 40 minutes
Wine suggestion: Ischia Biancolella

Risotto with Black Salsify and Parsley Butter

Serves 4

1½ tablespoons (1½ oz/
40 g) butter, softened
2 tablespoons chopped flat-
leaf parsley
grated zest and juice of
1 unwaxed lemon
9 oz/250 g black salsify
4¼ cups (34 fl oz/1 liter)
vegetable broth (stock)
2 tablespoons extra virgin
olive oil
1 leek, chopped
1⅔ cups (11¼ oz/320 g)
semifino rice (ideally
Vialone Nano rice)
⅓ cup plus 1 tablespoon (3½
fl oz/100 ml) white wine
½ cup (1½ oz/40 g) grated
Parmesan cheese
salt and pepper

First make the parsley butter. Put the butter, parsley, and lemon zest into a small bowl and beat until creamy and well combined. Let chill in the refrigerator until hard.

Peel the salsify and put it into a bowl of cold water with the lemon juice to stop it from turning brown.

Bring a large pan of lightly salted water to a boil, add the salsify, and cook over medium heat for 15 minutes, or until soft and a cocktail stick (toothpick) inserted into the salsify comes out easily. Drain and slice into rounds.

Pour the broth (stock) into a pan and bring to a simmer. Keep over low heat while you make the risotto.

Heat the oil in a large pan, add the leek, and cook over low heat for 2–3 minutes until soft. Add the rice and toast over high heat for a few minutes. Pour over the wine and cook over high heat until it has evaporated. Pour over enough broth to cover the rice, add the sliced salsify, and continue to cook over medium–high heat, stirring frequently, for about 16 minutes, gradually adding in the remaining broth a ladleful at a time and making sure each addition is absorbed by the rice before adding the next ladleful. The risotto is ready when the rice is cooked through but still al dente. Remove from the heat, stir in the Parmesan, the parsley butter, and a pinch of pepper. Let rest for a few minutes before serving.

NOTE Black salsify is a winter root vegetable that originated in eastern Europe. It is mainly grown in Piedmont and Liguria, but also grows wild in other areas of northern Italy. Salsify peel is very dark—practically black—and the flesh is white and firm, with a bitterish taste. After peeling with a potato peeler, you can boil the salsify to make purées or warm salads or pan fry. It is delicious raw or grated and dressed with lemon juice, and is a perfect accompaniment to red meat.

Preparation time: 15 minutes, plus cooling
Cooking time: 45 minutes
Wine suggestion: Alto Adige Lagrein Rosato

Rice Gnocchi

Serves 4

1¹/₂ cups (11 oz/300 g)
  fino rice
  (ideally Sant'Andrea rice)
extra virgin olive oil,
  for greasing
3 eggs, beaten
³/₄ cup (3¹/₂ oz/100 g) type
  00 flour
1¹/₄ cups (3¹/₂ oz/100 g)
  grated Parmesan cheese
1³/₄ cups (3 oz/80 g)
  fresh breadcrumbs
1¹/₂ tablespoons (1¹/₂ oz/
  40 g) butter, melted
salt and pepper

Bring 6¹/₄ cups (50 fl oz/1.5 liters) salted water to the boil in a pan. Add the rice and cook for about 30 minutes until all the water has been absorbed. Remove from the heat and let cool.

Preheat the oven to 350°F/180°C/Gas mark 4. Grease a large ovenproof dish with oil. Spread out the flour in a shallow dish.

Transfer the cooled rice to a bowl, add the eggs, 4 tablespoons of the Parmesan, and the breadcrumbs, and mix well. Season with salt and pepper. Using your hands, shape the mixture into balls about ³/₄ inch/2 cm in diameter and place them in the prepared ovenproof dish.

Pour the butter over the rice balls, sprinkle over the remaining Parmesan, and bake in the oven for 15 minutes, or until golden. Serve hot.

Granny Smith Apple and Speck Ham Whole Grain Risotto

Serves 4

4¼ cups (34 fl oz/1 liter) vegetable broth (stock)

extra virgin olive oil

3 tablespoons finely chopped shallot

1 (5-oz/150-g) slice speck ham, diced

2 Granny Smith apples

1⅓ cups (9 oz/250 g) whole grain rice

3½ tablespoons brandy

2 tablespoons (1¼ oz/ 30 g) butter

3 tablespoons grated Parmesan cheese

2 thyme sprigs, leaves only, to garnish

Pour the broth (stock) into a pan and bring to a simmer. Keep over a low heat while you make the risotto.

Heat a little oil in a large pan, add the shallot, and cook over medium heat for a couple of minutes until soft and translucent. Add the speck ham and fry for a few minutes.

Meanwhile, core the apples and cut the flesh into cubes.

Add the apple cubes to the pan with the speck ham and cook for 3–4 minutes until brown. Add the rice and toast over high heat for a couple of minutes, then pour over the brandy and cook until it has evaporated. Add a ladleful of the broth and cook over medium–high heat, stirring frequently, for 25–30 minutes, gradually adding in more broth a ladleful at a time and making sure each addition is absorbed by the rice before adding the next ladleful. The risotto is ready when the rice is cooked through but still al dente. Remove from the heat and stir in the butter and Parmesan. Let stand for 1 minute. Serve the risotto garnished with thyme leaves.

NOTE Unlike white rice, only the outer hull, which is not edible, and the chaff are removed from whole grain rice during the husking process. Whole grain rice is more nutritious than processed rice as it contains more protein, lipids, mineral salts, and fiber, but it does take longer to cook.

⊙ Preparation time: 20 minutes, plus cooling
Cooking time: 40–45 minutes

♀ Wine suggestion: Planeta Sicilia Chardonnay

Rice and Herb Flan

Serves 4

extra virgin olive oil
cornstarch (cornflour),
   for dusting
1¼ cups (9 oz/250 g)
   semifino rice (ideally
   Vialone Nano rice)
¼ teaspoon ground turmeric
2 scallions (spring onions),
   chopped
3 cups (7 oz/200 g)
   chopped chard
4 cups (7 oz/200 g)
   chopped spinach
3 eggs
3 tablespoons grated
   pecorino cheese
sea salt

Preheat the oven to 375°F/190°C/Gas mark 5. Grease a 9½ x 5½-inch/ 24 x 14-cm ovenproof dish with oil, then dust it with cornstarch (cornflour). Alternatively, you could use individual ovenproof dishes.

Bring a pan with generous 2 cups (17 fl oz/500 ml) salted water to a boil, add the rice and turmeric and cook for 8 minutes. Remove from the heat, pour over 1 tablespoon oil, and mix well. Let cool.

Meanwhile heat a little oil in a large pan, add the scallions (spring onions), and cook over low heat for a few minutes, then add the chard, spinach, and a pinch of salt and cook for about 10 minutes until softened.

In a large bowl, beat the eggs. Stir in the pecorino, then add the cooled rice and chard and spinach mixture and mix well. Pour the mixture into the prepared ovenproof dish, or individual dishes, and level it out with the back of a spoon. Bake in the oven for 25–30 minutes until golden and crisp on the top. Serve warm.

⊙   Preparation time: 10 minutes
    Cooking time: 25 minutes
♀   Wine suggestion: Oltrepò Pavese Rosso

Risotto alla Milanese

Serves 4

4¼ cups (34 fl oz/1 liter)
   vegetable broth (stock)
extra virgin olive oil
4 tablespoons (2¼ oz/
   60 g) butter
½ yellow onion, finely
   chopped
1½ oz/ 40 g beef bone
   marrow
1½ cups (11 oz/300 g)
   risotto rice, ideally Carnaroli
   or Arborio rice
⅓ cup plus 1 tablespoon (3½
   fl oz/100 ml) white wine
large pinch of saffron threads,
   plus extra to garnish
2 tablespoons grated
   Parmesan cheese
salt and pepper

Pour the broth (stock) into a pan and bring to a simmer. Keep over a low heat while you make the risotto.

Heat a little oil and half the butter in a large pan, add the onion and bone marrow, and cook over medium heat for 3–4 minutes until brown. Add the rice and toast over a high heat for 2 minutes, stirring with a wooden spoon. Pour over the wine and cook until it has evaporated. Add the saffron and a ladleful of the broth and cook over medium–high heat, stirring frequently, for about 18 minutes, gradually adding in more broth a ladleful at a time and making sure each addition is absorbed by the rice before adding the next ladleful. The risotto is ready when the rice is cooked through but still al dente. Remove from the heat and stir in the remaining butter and the Parmesan. Season with salt and pepper. Let rest for a few minutes. Serve garnished with a few extra saffron threads.

NOTE   Saffron risotto is a classic dish from Milan. It is mentioned in books on Milanese cooking that date as far back as the nineteenth century, although legend has it that on September 8, 1574, a dish of rice colored with saffron was served during the wedding banquet of the daughter of master glassmaker Valerio di Fiandra. However, the recipe as we know it today was probably created in later centuries. In 1809, *Cuoco Moderno (The Modern Cook)* published a recipe for Fried Yellow Rice, where rice is fried in butter, with the addition of *cervellato* (spiced meat and brain sausage), bone marrow, onion, hot broth (stock), and saffron.

Preparation time: 10 minutes

Cooking time: 25 minutes

Wine suggestion: Oltrepò Pavese Bonarda

Sausage and Cranberry Bean Risotto

Serves 4

4 tablespoons extra virgin
olive oil

1/2 white onion, chopped

2 bay leaves, plus extra to
garnish

3 1/2 oz/100 g sausages,
skins removed and finely
chopped

6 1/4 cups (50 fl oz/1.5 liters)
meat broth (stock)

1 1/4 cups (9 oz/250 g)
semifino rice (ideally
Vialone Nano rice)

1/3 cup plus 1 tablespoon
(3 1/2 fl oz/100 ml) white wine

6 1/4 oz/180 g cooked
cranberry (borlotti) beans
(see page 58)

white pepper

Heat the oil in a large pan, add the onion and bay leaves, and cook over low heat for 3–4 minutes until the onion browns. Add the sausages and cook, stirring all the time, for 5 minutes.

Meanwhile, pour the broth (stock) into a pan and bring to a simmer. Keep over a low heat while you make the risotto.

Add the rice to the pan with the sausages and toast over high heat for 1 minute. Pour over the wine and cook until it has evaporated. Add a ladleful of the broth and cook over medium–high heat, stirring frequently, for about 10 minutes, gradually adding in more broth a ladleful at a time and making sure each addition is absorbed by the rice before adding the next ladleful. Add the cranberry (borlotti) beans and cook for 5 minutes more, continuing to stir and adding the broth a ladleful at a time. The risotto is ready when the rice is cooked through but still al dente. Let rest for a few minutes. To serve, sprinkle the risotto with white pepper and garnish with a few extra bay leaves.

TIP   Try making this risotto with Pantano di Pignola red beans instead of cranberry (borlotti) beans. This soft-skinned bean is ideal for making starters, vegetable accompaniments, and soups. The Pantano di Pignola bean is grown around a lake at an altitude of 3,280 feet (1,000 meters) in the Potenza area of Basilicata in Italy. These beans, which may have been introduced by the Spanish on their return from the Americas, became a fundamental crop for farming families in the Napoleonic era. Today, the Pantano di Pignola bean is protected by a Slow Food Presidia label, and after years of being overlooked it is now slowly regaining popularity.

Preparation time: 10 minutes

Cooking time: 30 minutes

Wine suggestion: Colline Lucchesi Vermentino

Langoustine Risotto

Serves 4

extra virgin olive oil

1 white onion, chopped

4 tablespoons canned tomato
purée (passata)

1 lb 5 oz/600 g raw
langoustines (Dublin Bay
prawns) in their shells

juice of 1 lemon

1½ cups (11 oz/300 g) risotto
rice, ideally Carnaroli or
Arborio rice

1½ tablespoons (¾ oz/
20 g) butter

1 flat-leaf parsley sprig,
chopped

salt and pepper

Heat 4 tablespoons oil in a large pan, add the onion, and cook over low heat for 3–4 minutes until soft and translucent. Add the puréed canned tomatoes (passata) and a ladleful warm water, season with salt and pepper, and cook for 5 minutes. Add the langoustines (Dublin Bay prawns) and lemon juice, stir well. Remove from the heat.

Meanwhile, pour 4¼ cups (34 fl oz/1 liter) water into a pan and bring to a simmer. Keep over a low heat while you make the risotto.

In a separate pan, heat a little oil, add the rice, and toast over high heat for a few minutes. Pour over 2–3 ladlefuls hot water and cook over medium–high heat, stirring occasionally, for 10 minutes, gradually adding in more hot water a ladleful at a time and making sure each addition is absorbed by the rice before adding the next ladleful. Add the tomato sauce to the rice (setting the langoustines aside on a plate), season with salt and pepper, and cook for 8 minutes more, continuing to stir and adding the hot water a ladleful at a time. The risotto is ready when the rice is cooked through but still al dente. Remove from the heat and stir in the butter and parsley, retaining some to garnish. Let rest for a few minutes. Serve the risotto, garnished with the langoustines.

TIP Which rice varieties do chefs choose to use for making risotto? The answer: Carnaroli and Vialone Nano. The secret lies in the grains, which keep their shape perfectly during cooking, even after a risotto has been thickened with butter and cheese. Risotto must always be cooked over medium–high heat at a steady temperature, and the cooking liquid—broth (stock) or water—must be kept simmering in a separate pan.

○ Preparation time: 5 minutes

Cooking time: 25 minutes

♀ Wine suggestion: Colli Berici Garganega

Pea Risotto

Serves 4

3 cups (24 fl oz/700 ml)
  vegetable broth (stock)
4 tablespoons (2¼ oz/60 g)
  butter
2 oz/50 g pancetta or
  bacon, chopped
1 onion, chopped
2⅔ cups (14 oz/400 g)
  shelled fresh peas
1¼ cups (9 oz/250 g)
  semifino rice (ideally
  Vialone Nano rice)
1 flat-leaf parsley
  sprig, chopped
3 tablespoons grated
  Parmesan cheese
salt and pepper

Pour the broth (stock) into a pan and bring to a simmer. Keep over a low heat while you make the risotto.

Melt half the butter in a large pan, add the pancetta or bacon and onion, and cook over low heat for 5 minutes, or until soft and translucent. Add the peas and 2 ladlefuls of broth and cook for 5 minutes. Stir in the rice and cook over medium–high heat, stirring frequently, for 15–18 minutes, gradually adding in more broth a ladleful at a time and making sure each addition is absorbed by the rice before adding the next ladleful. A few minutes before the end of the cooking time, stir in the parsley. The risotto is ready when the rice is cooked through but still al dente. Remove from heat. Taste to check the seasoning, adding salt and pepper if necessary, then whisk in the remaining butter and the Parmesan. Let the risotto rest for a few minutes before serving.

NOTE   The combination of rice and peas is very much appreciated throughout Italy, but it is mainly in the Veneto region, and particularly in Vicenza, that risi e bisi (literally, "rice and peas") is cooked. It is a dish that is halfway between a moist risotto and a soup. The peculiarity of risi e bisi is that the pea pods themselves are cooked and puréed into a cream that is added to the risotto rice.

Preparation time: 30 minutes
Cooking time: 1 hour 10 minutes

Wild Rice with Cranberry Beans and Mint

Serves 4

²/₃ cup (5 fl oz/150 ml) extra
  virgin olive oil, plus extra
  for drizzling
½ leek, cut into strips
⅓ cup (1¼ oz/30 g) diced
  celery root (celeriac)
⅓ cup (2 oz/50 g)
  diced carrots
²/₃ cup (¾ oz/20 g)
  rosemary, chopped
¾ cup (1¼ oz/30 g) basil
  leaves, chopped
3 tablespoons chopped
  wild fennel
2²/₃ cups (11 oz/300 g)
  shelled fresh cranberry
  (borlotti) beans
4¼ cups (17 fl oz/1 liter)
  vegetable broth (stock)
1²/₃ cups (2 oz/50 g) sliced
  mint leaves (cut into strips)
⅓ cup (1 oz/30 g) grated
  unwaxed orange zest
¾ cup plus 2 tablespoons
  (5 oz/150 g) wild rice
salt

Heat the oil in a large pan, add the leek, celery root (celeriac), carrots, rosemary, basil, and wild fennel, and cook over medium heat for 5 minutes, or until soft and translucent. Add the cranberry (borlotti) beans and cook for a minute, then pour over enough broth (stock) to cover and cook for at least 1 hour until the beans are tender and soft. Transfer three-quarters of the mixture to a food processor and blend to a purée, then return to the pan and mix well. Taste to check the seasoning and add salt if necessary. Stir in the mint and orange zest.

Meanwhile, put the rice into a wide pan and pour over enough of the remaining broth to cover it by ¾ inch/2 cm. Season with salt. Cook over low heat for 45 minutes, or until the rice has absorbed all the liquid and is tender.

Divide the cranberry beans and rice among serving plates, drizzle over a little oil, and serve.

WINE SUGGESTION Uomo is made with a blend of Nero d'Avola and Merlot grapes. They blend harmoniously together, one with vibrant acidic and tannic properties, the other rich in fruit flavors, opulence, and silkiness. The sum of the two is greater than the two individual wines. This wine is excellent paired with the wild rice and minted beans.

CHEF
Elena Verzeroli

Preparation time: 35 minutes
Cooking time: 20 minutes
Wine suggestion: Giulio Ferrari Riserva del Fondatore

Summer Rice Salad with Crawfish

Serves 4

8½ cups (68 fl oz/2 liters)
  vegetable broth (stock)
1 (2-inch/5-cm) piece fresh
  ginger (about 3½ oz/
  100 g), cut into four pieces
1⅓ cups (9 oz/250 g)
  long-grain rice
⅓ cup plus 1 tablespoon
  (3½ fl oz/100 ml) soy sauce
⅓ cup plus 1 tablespoon
  (3½ fl oz/100 ml)
  raspberry vinegar
2 tablespoons honey (ideally
  rhododendron honey)
12 raw red crawfish (crayfish),
  peeled and deveined
extra virgin olive oil
3–4 chives, finely chopped
2 zucchini (courgettes), cut in
  half lengthwise and sliced
½ lemon, quartered
  and sliced
salt and pepper

To garnish
cherry tomato confit (see tip)
  (optional)
sea salt flakes
a few fresh herbs

Pour the broth (stock) into a large pan and bring to a boil. Add the ginger, 2 teaspoons salt, and the rice and then cook the rice according to the package directions until tender.

Meanwhile, mix the soy sauce, vinegar, and honey together in a bowl. Add the crawfish (crayfish), toss to coat, and let marinate for 10 minutes.

Drain the rice, discarding the ginger. Transfer to a bowl, stir in a little oil and the chives, and season with salt and pepper.

Heat a little oil in a skillet (frying pan), add the zucchini (courgettes) and a pinch of salt, and cook over medium heat for 5 minutes until brown. Add the zucchini to the rice mixture, then add the lemon and mix well.

Drain the marinade from the crawfish and cut them into pieces. Heat a little oil in the a skillet, add the crawfish, and cook over medium heat for 1–2 minutes until the crawfish changes color and becomes red. Add the crawfish to the rice mixture and mix gently.

To serve, garnish the salad with cherry tomato confit, if liked, a few sea salt flakes and some fresh herbs.

TIP Try adding some cherry tomato confit to this dish. Cut a slit in the skins of 2 cups (11 oz/300 g) cherry tomatoes. Bring a large pan of water to a boil. Meanwhile, fill a large bowl with iced water and set it beside the stove. Drop the tomatoes into the boiling water and leave for a few seconds. Drain, plunge into the iced water, then drain again thoroughly. Carefully peel off the skins, cut the tomatoes in half and remove the seeds. Preheat the oven to 215°F/100°C/Gas mark ¼. Line a baking sheet with parchment (baking) paper. Arrange the tomatoes, cut-side up, on the baking sheet and sprinkle over ¼ teaspoon salt, 1 teaspoon confectioners' (icing) sugar, the grated zest of 1 unwaxed lemon, the grated zest of 1 unwaxed orange, 1 halved clove of garlic, a few thyme leaves, and a little oil. Bake in the oven for 1½ hours, or until the tomatoes start to sweat and dry.

SAVORY TARTS AND PIES

Preparation time: 30 minutes, plus chilling

Cooking time: 40 minutes

Wine suggestion: Collio Sauvignon

Shortcrust Pie with Vegetable Whirls

Serves 4–6

For the shortcrust pie dough (pastry)

1²/₃ cups (7 oz/200 g) type 00 flour, plus extra for dusting

7 tablespoons (3¹/₂ oz/100 g) cold butter, cut into small pieces

pinch of salt

For the filling

1 carrot, thinly sliced lengthwise

1 zucchini (courgette), thinly sliced lengthwise

extra virgin olive oil

¹/₂ eggplant (aubergine), halved and very thinly sliced lengthwise

1 egg

1 saffron thread

¹/₃ cup (1 oz/30 g) Parmesan cheese, grated

4 tablespoons light (single) cream

6 cherry tomatoes, sliced

salt and pepper

First make the shortcrust pie dough (pastry). Sift (sieve) the flour into a mound on the countertop, make a well in the center, and put the butter, salt, and 2 tablespoons iced water into this. Work the ingredients together quickly with your fingertips and then use your knuckles to make a smooth dough. Wrap the pie dough in plastic wrap (clingfilm) and chill in the refrigerator for at least 1 hour.

Bring a large pan of salted water to a boil. Meanwhile, fill a large bowl with iced water and set it beside the stove. Drop the carrot and zucchini (courgette) into the boiling water and leave for 1 minute. Drain, plunge into the iced water, then drain again thoroughly and lay out on a dish towel to dry.

Heat 1 tablespoon oil in a nonstick skillet (frying pan) and fry the eggplant (aubergine) slices on both sides until lightly browned. Drain on paper towel.

Put the egg in a bowl with the saffron, Parmesan, and a pinch each of salt and pepper and beat lightly with a whisk. Add the cream and whisk until well blended.

Preheat the oven to 350°F/180°C/Gas mark 4. Line a 6–7-inch/15–18-cm round springform pan with parchment (baking) paper, allowing the paper to overlap the sides of the dish.

Roll out the pie dough on a lightly floured countertop and use it to line the base and sides of the prepared pan. Arrange the vegetables, thin-side up, in concentric circles, alternating the different varieties, until you have filled the pastry shell (case). Pour the egg and cream mixture over the top, fold any dough that overlaps the edge inward, and bake in the oven for 30–35 minutes, or until the pastry is golden brown and the filling has set.

Preparation time: 15 minutes, plus chilling
Cooking time: 40 minutes
Wine suggestion: Bolgheri Vermentino

Pumpkin, Broccoli, Zucchini, and Asparagus Tart

Serves 4–6

**For the shortcrust pie
dough (pastry)**
1²/₃ cups (7 oz/200 g) type 00
    flour, plus extra for dusting
7 tablespoons (3¹/₂ oz/100 g)
    cold butter, cut into
    small pieces
pinch of salt

For the filling
4 asparagus spears, tough
    parts at the base broken
    off and discarded
extra virgin olive oil
²/₃ cup (3¹/₂ oz/100 g) diced
    pumpkin flesh
1 zucchini (courgette), diced
1¹/₂ cups (3¹/₂ oz/100 g)
    diced broccoli
1 cup (9 oz/250 g)
    ricotta cheese
³/₄ cup plus 1 tablespoon
    (7 fl oz/200 ml) light
    (single) cream
2 tablespoons grated
    Parmesan cheese
4 eggs, lightly beaten
salt and pepper

First make the shortcrust pie dough (pastry). Sift (sieve) the flour into a mound on the countertop, make a well in the center, and put the butter, salt, and 2 tablespoons iced water into this. Work the ingredients together quickly with your fingertips and then use your knuckles to make a smooth dough. Wrap the pie dough in plastic wrap (clingfilm) and chill in the refrigerator for at least 1 hour.

Heat a little oil in a skillet (frying pan), add the pumpkin, zucchini (courgette), and broccoli, and cook over medium heat for a few minutes, then add the asparagus, season with salt and pepper, and cook for about 5 minutes until the vegetables are browned and slightly sweated. Let cool.

Put the ricotta into a large bowl and beat with a fork until creamy. Stir in the cream, Parmesan and eggs, followed by the cold vegetables.

Preheat the oven to 350°F/180°C/Gas mark 4. Line a 9¹/₂-inch/24-cm pie dish with parchment (baking) paper, allowing the paper to overlap the sides of the dish.

Roll out the pie dough on a lightly floured countertop and use it to line the base and sides of the prepared pie dish. Pour in the filling and bake in the oven for 30 minutes, or until the pastry is golden brown and the filling has set.

⊙   Preparation time: 40 minutes, plus resting

Cooking time: 40 minutes

♀   Wine suggestion: Conegliano Valdobbiadene Prosecco Extra Dry

Zucchini and Ham Pie

Serves 4

2 zucchini (courgette) flowers
1 cup (9 oz/250 g) cow milk
   ricotta cheese
3½ oz/100 g mozzarella
   cheese, cut into cubes
3 slices cooked ham, chopped
2 zucchini (courgettes),
   thinly sliced
1 tablespoon extra virgin
   olive oil
salt and pepper

For the pie dough (pastry)
1 cup (2 oz/50 g) oat flakes
1 cup (4¼ oz/125 g) all-
   purpose (plain) flour, plus
   extra for dusting
⅔ cup (2¾ oz/75 g) whole
   wheat (wholemeal) flour
pinch of salt
3 tablespoons extra virgin
   olive oil

First make the pie dough (pastry). Put the oat flakes into a food processor and pulse until roughly ground. Put the ground oatflakes and flours into a mound on the countertop, make a well in the center, and put the salt and oil into this. Using your hands, mix the ingredients together and then knead, gradually adding ½ cup (4½ fl oz/130 ml) cold water a little at a time, until the dough is soft and smooth. Cover the pie dough with a damp dish towel and let rest for 30 minutes.

Preheat the oven to 350°F/180°C/Gas mark 4. Line a 8¾-inch/22-cm pie dish with parchment (baking) paper, allowing the paper to overlap the sides of the dish.

Divide the pie dough into two portions. Roll out half the dough on a lightly floured countertop and use it to line the prepared pie dish.

Gently open out the zucchini (courgette) flowers, taking care not to break them, and remove and discard the inner pistils. Wash the flowers very gently under a trickle of cold running water. Cut the flowers into strips.

Spread the ricotta over the bottom of the pastry shell (case), then add a layer of mozzarella, followed by the zucchini flowers, then the ham, and finally the zucchini. Season with salt and pepper and drizzle with the oil.

Roll out the remaining pie dough on a lightly floured countertop and use it to cover the pie, pressing the edges of the pie to seal the borders firmly and pricking the surface with a fork. Bake in the oven for about 40 minutes until golden brown.

SAVORY TARTS AND PIES:
BASIC PIE AND
PASTRY DOUGH

To make savory pies, which are excellent as a single course meal, for picnics, or buffets, it is possible to experiment with flavor combinations and give free rein to the imagination, both in terms of the fillings and the pie dough (pastry) used. Depending on personal taste and experience, in fact, it is possible to modify and enrich basic pie dough (shortcrust pastry) by adding aromatic herbs and spices, or by choosing flours other than the ones most commonly used, for example whole wheat (wholemeal) flours, type 1 and type 2 wheat flour, spelt, quinoa, buckwheat, or cornmeal. However, not all types of basic pie dough are suitable for adapting to personal taste: a piecrust pastry is certainly easier to modify than a phyllo (filo) pastry, for example. Let's see which types of pastry are the most commonly used.

PIECRUST PASTRY OR PIZZA DOUGH

These are the most versatile types of preparations, because they are the simplest ones to make: finely chopped aromatic herbs can enrich a piecrust pastry without compromising its success, while it is possible to use practically all types of flour suitable for leavening (so not only durum wheat flour, for example) when making dough for pizza.

Piecrust pastry is obtained by mixing 1⅔ cups (7 oz/200 g) flour with 3½ oz/100 g cold butter, cut into small pieces, 2 tablespoons of water and a pinch of salt (to make about 11 oz/300 g of pie dough). Arrange the flour in a mound on a countertop and add the water, then quickly mix in the butter and the salt. Leave to rest for about 30 minutes in the refridgerator wrapped in plastic wrap (clingfilm) before using. To make a more crumbly pie dough, replace the butter with extra virgin olive oil or vegetable oil, or replace part of the water with dry white wine. A lighter pie dough can be achieved by increasing the quantity of water and reducing the fat.

For pizza dough, use 2 cups (9 oz/250 g) flour and ¾ cup plus 1 tablespoon (7 fl oz/200 ml) warm water, half a pack of brewer's yeast (1½ teaspoons active dry yeast) or 2 oz/50 g of mother dough (starter yeast), and a pinch of salt. The exact quantity of water needed will depend on the type of flour used. Let the dough rise for 1–2 hours if brewer's yeast is used, or 5–6 hours if mother dough is used. These types of dough tend to inflate with cooking, with the consequent creation of air bubbles. To avoid this inconvenience, it is useful to prick the dough base with a fork after stretching it out on the baking sheet.

PUFF AND PHYLLO PASTRY

Puff and phyllo pastries require more time and more manual labor than the previously described options.

For puff pastry, use 1⅔ cups (7 oz/200 g) flour, 7 oz/200 g cold butter, cut into small chunks, ⅓ cup plus 1 tablespoon (3½ fl oz/100 ml) of water and a pinch of salt (to make about 1 lb 2 oz/500 g of pastry). Mix the flour with water and salt and let it rest for about 30 minutes, then roll out the pie dough with a rolling pin to a thickness of 3–4 mm and arrange the butter on top. Fold the pie dough on the butter as if it were a parcel, overlapping the edges, then roll out again with the rolling pin. Repeat the process five or six times to ensure that the pie dough incorporates some air, which will cause it to produce flaky layers during cooking.

Phyllo pastry is the lightest of the pie doughs used for savory pies, as the basic recipe does not require any fat, but it is also the most difficult to make if you are not adept at using a rolling pin. The pie dough (made with 2 ⅓ cups (11 oz/300 g) flour, ¾ cup plus 1 tablespoon (7 fl oz/200 ml) tepid water and a pinch of salt) needs to be worked for a long time and stretched into wafer-thin layers, with the subsequent risk of breaking. In any case, the presence of small holes does not necessarily compromise its use, as the pie dough is commonly used in two or more layers, one on top of the other, in savory pies, roulades, etc.

⊙   Preparation time: 40 minutes, plus chilling

Cooking time: 30 minutes

♀   Wine suggestion: Etna Rosé

Pesto and Cherry Tomato Pie

Serves 4–6

**For the shortcrust pie
dough (pastry)**

1²/₃ cups (7 oz/200 g) type 00
flour, plus extra for dusting

7 tablespoons (3¹/₂ oz/100 g)
cold butter, cut into
small pieces

pinch of salt

For the filling

2 oz/50 g basil leaves

¹/₃ cup plus 1 tablespoon
(3¹/₂ fl oz/100 ml) extra
virgin olive oil

4 tablespoons grated
Parmesan cheese

1 tablespoon hazelnuts

20 cherry tomatoes (ideally
Pachino tomatoes), halved

2–3 tablespoons
fresh breadcrumbs

salt

Sift (sieve) the flour into a mound on the countertop, make a well in the center, and put the butter, salt, and 2 tablespoons iced water into this. Work the ingredients together quickly with your fingertips and then use your knuckles to make a smooth dough. Wrap the pie dough in plastic wrap (clingfilm) and chill in the refrigerator for at least 1 hour.

Make the pesto by blending the basil, oil, Parmesan, hazelnuts, and a pinch of salt in a food processor until very smooth.

Preheat the oven to 350°F/180°C/Gas mark 4. Line a 9¹/₂-inch/24-cm baking pan (tin) with parchment (baking) paper, allowing the paper to overlap the sides of the dish.

Roll out two-thirds of the pie dough on a lightly floured countertop and use it to line the prepared baking pan. Spread the pesto evenly over the bottom of the pastry shell (case), place the tomatoes, cut-side up, on top of the pesto, and sprinkle over the breadcrumbs. Roll out the remaining pie dough, cut it into strips, and use to decorate the top of the tart with a lattice of pie dough, just like a sweet pie. Bake in the oven for 30 minutes, or until golden brown.

T I P   You can replace the basil with the same quantity of arugula (rocket): the slightly bitter taste of the arugula contrasts pleasingly with the sweetness of the Pachino cherry tomatoes. This pie is an ideal picnic treat that will delight your guests.

🕐   Preparation time: 45 minutes, plus draining and resting

Cooking time: 25 minutes

♀   Wine suggestion: Orvieto Classico

Mediterranean Stuffed Pastry Roll

Serves 6

1 eggplant (aubergine),
  thinly sliced
coarse salt, for sprinkling
sunflower oil, for deep-frying
1 egg yolk
1 teaspoon milk
9 oz/250 g puff pastry
  (see page 197)
3–4 basil leaves
9 oz/250 g mozzarella cheese,
  very thinly sliced
½ cup (2¼ oz/60 g) semi-
  dried cherry tomatoes
⅓ cup (1¼ oz/30 g) grated
  Parmesan cheese

To serve (optional)
mixed baby leaf salad
cherry tomatoes

Place the eggplant (aubergine) in a colander, sprinkle with salt, and let drain for 30 minutes. Rinse the eggplant, drain again, then squeeze tightly to expel any excess moisture.

Pour enough oil for deep-frying into a deep-fat fryer or large deep pan and heat the oil to 340°F/170°C. Add the eggplant to the hot oil and cook until golden brown. Remove with a slotted spoon and drain on paper towels.

Beat the egg yolk lightly with the milk in a small bowl and set aside.

Roll out the puff pastry on a lightly floured countertop surface into a rectangle about ⅕ inch/3 mm thick. Arrange alternating layers of eggplant, basil, mozzarella, and semi-dried cherry tomatoes on top of the pastry, sprinkling each layer with Parmesan. Continue layering until you have used up all the ingredients. Carefully roll up the pie dough and its contents, taking care not to tear the pie dough. Brush the pastry with the egg yolk and milk glaze, sprinkle with a little salt, and let rest for 25 minutes.

Preheat the oven to 350°F/180°C/Gas mark 4. Carefully transfer the stuffed pastry roll to a baking sheet lined with parchment (baking) paper and bake in the oven for about 15 minutes until golden brown.

When ready to serve, cut the stuffed pastry roll into slices and serve with a salad of mixed leaves and cherry tomatoes, if liked.

⊙ Preparation time: 25 minutes, plus cooling
Cooking time: 45 minutes
♀ Wine suggestion: Molise Falanghina

Artichoke and Mint Pie

Serves 4–6

4 young, tender artichokes
3 tablespoons extra virgin
   olive oil
1 clove garlic, chopped
1 flat-leaf parsley sprig, finely
   chopped
¾ cup (7 oz/200 g) cow milk
   ricotta cheese
4 tablespoons grated
   Parmesan cheese
2 eggs, beaten
4–5 wild or garden mint
   leaves, finely chopped
9 oz/250 g shortcrust
   pie dough (pastry) (see
   page196)
salt and pepper

First prepare the artichokes. Trim the artichokes, discarding the inner chokes, the tougher outermost leaves, and their spiny tips. Cut the artichokes into thin slices.

Heat the oil in large skillet (frying pan), add the garlic and parsley, and cook over low heat for 1–2 minutes until the garlic begins to brown. Add the artichokes and cook over medium heat for 10–15 minutes, moistening with a little water if necessary, until soft. Season with salt and pepper, then remove from the heat and let cool.

Once the mixture has cooled, transfer to a bowl and add the ricotta, Parmesan, eggs, and mint, season with salt and pepper, and stir until evenly mixed.

Preheat the oven to 400°F/200°C/Gas mark 6. Line a 9½-inch/24-cm round pie dish with parchment (baking) paper, allowing the paper to overlap the sides of the dish.

Roll out the pie dough (pastry) on a lightly floured countertop and use it to line the prepared pie dish, allowing the pie dough to overlap the edge a little. Pour in the vegetable filling, smoothing the surface level with a rubber spatula. Fold the dough that overlaps the edge inward and bake in the oven for about 25 minutes until the pastry is golden brown and the filling has set. Serve this pie lukewarm or cold.

TIP   If you want to enhance this savory dish, add 2 cups (7 oz/200 g) finely diced hard cheese (Asiago would be perfect) to the filling—this cheese sets off the taste of the artichokes to perfection. This pie can be served as a main course, accompanied with a seasonal fresh salad or with broiled (grilled) vegetables.

⊙ Preparation time: 1 hour, plus resting
Cooking time: 50 minutes
♀ Wine suggestion: Cinque Terre

Easter Pie

Serves 6–8

4 cups (1 lb 2 oz/500 g) type
    00 flour
4 tablespoons extra virgin
    olive oil, plus extra for
    greasing and brushing
1 lb 2 oz/500 g mixed
    greens (ideally a mixture of
    cultivated and wild leaves)
5 tablespoons grated
    Parmesan cheese
2 marjoram sprigs, leaves
    chopped
1 bread roll
5 medium (small) eggs
1/3 cup plus 1 tablespoon (3 1/2
    fl oz/100 ml) milk
1 1/4 cups (11 oz/ 300 g) cow
    milk ricotta cheese
4 tablespoons (2 1/4 oz/60 g)
    butter, half melted and half
    cut into small pieces
salt and pepper

Sift (sieve) the flour and a generous pinch of salt into a mound on the counter-top, make a well in the center, and pour 4 tablespoons oil into it. Using your hands, mix together to form a homogenous dough, adding just enough water to make it smooth and soft. Divide the dough into 33 small pieces, line these up on the countertop, cover with a dish towel, and let rest for 1 hour.

Wash the leafy green vegetables thoroughly, then place them in a large pan of boiling salted water and cook for 3 minutes. Drain well, squeezing tightly to remove any excess moisture. Spread out the leaves on a plate, chop well, and sprinkle with a little salt, 1 tablespoon of the Parmesan, and the marjoram.

Remove the soft crumbs from the inside of the bread roll, discarding the crust, and place them in a bowl with the milk. Let soak briefly, then remove and squeeze the breadcrumbs to get rid of any excess milk.

Lightly beat two of the eggs with 2 tablespoons of the Parmesan in a large bowl. Add the soaked breadcrumbs, the chopped leafy green vegetables, and ricotta and mix thoroughly.

Preheat the oven to 375°F/190°C/Gas mark 5. Grease a 8¾-inch/22-cm pie dish with oil.

Roll out each piece of dough into a very, very thin sheet. Place ten sheets of dough in the prepared pie dish, brushing each piece of dough with oil, then covering it with another. Pour the ricotta and vegetable mixture on top. Using the back of a tablespoon, press down to create three evenly-spaced hollows in the filling—the hollows need to be deep enough to crack an egg into. Pour ¼ oz/10 g of the melted butter into each hollow and then break an egg into each hollow. Sprinkle the eggs with the remaining Parmesan, and season with salt and pepper. Cover the filling with the remaining dough sheets, brushing each layer of dough with oil and dotting it with the small pieces of butter. Fold any overlapping pieces of dough inward and prick the surface with a fork. Bake in the oven for about 45 minutes until golden brown.

⊙ Preparation time: 25 minutes

Cooking time: 35 minutes

♈ Wine suggestion: Riviera Ligure di Ponente Pigato

Asparagus and Pecorino Cheese Puff Pastry Pie

Serves 4–6

1 (11-oz/300-g) bunch
  asparagus spears
extra virgin olive oil
1/3 cup plus 1 tablespoon (3½
  fl oz/100 ml) milk
½ cup (1½ oz/40 g) grated
  mild pecorino cheese
1 cup (9 oz/250 g)
  ricotta cheese
2 eggs
1 flat-leaf parsley sprig,
  finely chopped
7 oz/200 g puff pastry
  (see page 197)
salt and white pepper

Break off the tough part at the base of the asparagus spears and set aside. Keep 10 asparagus spears whole and slice the rest into thin rounds.

Bring a large pan of salted water to a boil. Meanwhile, fill a large bowl with iced water and set it beside the stove. Drop the whole asparagus spears into the boiling water and leave for 3 minutes. Drain, plunge into the iced water, then drain again thoroughly.

Heat a little oil in a skillet (frying pan), add the sliced asparagus spears and 2 tablespoons water, and cook over medium heat for 7–8 minutes until tender. Transfer to a food processor, add the milk, pecorino, ricotta, and eggs, and blend to a purée. Season with salt and pepper then stir in the parsley.

Preheat the oven to 350°F/180°C/Gas mark 4. Grease an 11-inch/28-cm pie dish with oil.

Roll out the puff pastry on a lightly floured surface to a thickness of 1/5 inch/ 3 mm and use it to line the base and sides of the prepared pie dish. Pour the asparagus purée into the pastry shell (case) and arrange the whole asparagus spears on top like the spokes of a wheel. Bake in the oven for 20–25 minutes, or until the pastry is golden brown and the filling has set.

TIP   For a more refined version of this tart, use white asparagus, such as White Asparagus of Bassano DOP (Protected Designation of Origin). White asparagus grows underground, out of reach of the sunshine, and remains very pale. It has a sweet-sour taste that is perfect with the eggs and cheeses in this recipe, producing a mouthwatering combination of tastes.

⊙ Preparation time: 25 minutes

Cooking time: 50 minutes

♀ Wine suggestion: Sannio Piedirosso

Radicchio, Walnut, and Smoked Cheese Strudel

Serves 4

9 oz/250 g puff pastry (see page 197)

2 heads radicchio, sliced

1 clove garlic, unpeeled

1 teaspoon acacia honey

type 00 flour, for dusting

2³⁄₄ oz/70 g smoked, soft-spun cheese (ideally smoked scamorza cheese), cut into small cubes

¹⁄₃ cup (2 oz/50 g) chopped walnuts

extra virgin olive oil

salt and pepper

Heat a little oil and the whole clove of garlic in a skillet (frying pan), add the radicchio, and cook over medium heat for 10 minutes, or until soft, adding the honey at the last minute to offset the slightly bitter taste. Season with salt and pepper and let cool.

Preheat the oven to 350°F/180°C/Gas mark 4. Line a baking sheet with parchment (baking) paper.

On a lightly floured countertop, roll out the pastry into a rectangle about ¹⁄₈ inch/4 mm thick. Arrange the cooked radicchio along the center of the pastry and sprinkle over the scamorza and walnuts. Fold the long edges of the pastry over to form a sausage shape and gently press to seal the edges.

Carefully transfer the strudel to the prepared baking sheet, seal-side down. Using a sharp knife, cut a few transverse slits in the top of the strudel. Lightly brush the pastry with oil and bake in the oven for 40 minutes, or until golden. Serve hot or warm.

TIP You could use Belgian chicory (endive) instead of the radicchio for the strudel filling. Slice the chicory lengthwise and sauté in a skillet (frying pan) with the oil and the garlic, then cook over medium heat for 7–8 minutes until soft. Add the honey and season with salt and white pepper. Proceed as in the recipe above, using 2 oz/50 g chopped hazelnuts or pine nuts instead of the walnuts.

FILLINGS: COMBINATIONS
FOR ALL TASTES

Savory pies are the best type of dish to experiment with new combinations. Every recipe can be enriched or modified according to personal taste. The possible combinations for fillings are in fact countless, from the simplest ones to the most elaborate. Generally speaking a savory pie requires, in addition to the pie dough (pastry), a "solid" component—made up of vegetables and/or meat or fish—and a fluid component—generally made up of eggs, milk, and dairy products—with or without added flour, which coagulates when cooked, supporting the other ingredients.

Even with regard to shape, pies are not restricted to the classic round shape. For example, depending on one's own abilities, it is possible to make little parcels, and use pie dough for strips to make a bow, or leaves, flowers, and other elements to decorate the surface of the pie. If you wish, you can also cover the pie with a crust, which can be brushed with egg yolk and milk, and sprinkled with sesame, linseed (flax seed), sunflower seeds, or cloves.

It is normally preferable to cook the ingredients for the filling before baking the pie, to compensate for different cooking times, but there is nothing preventing the use of uncooked fillings, for example those based on fresh cheese. In this case the pie dough will need to be cooked in a mold first, lined with parchment (baking) paper covered with pie weights (baking beans) to ensure the desired shape is preserved.

COMBINATIONS

Generally speaking, to ensure a harmonious and balanced result, it is preferable to avoid the use of strong flavors in pie fillings. If dairy products with an intense flavor are used, it is best to use vegetables with a delicate or neutral flavor, such as potatoes, peas, beets (beetroot), or zucchini (courgette). Dried meats, sausages, or fish and seafood, for example shrimp (prawns), go well with cream, béchamel sauce, or simply milk and eggs, but pancetta or bacon can be combined to good effect with cheeses with a strong flavor, such as provolone.

The most common fillings are those made with fresh vegetables and cheeses, as in the classic combination of stracchino and spinach. For an alternative to spinach you could use bitter or wild herbs, which are excellent with cheeses such as mascarpone or ricotta. For a Mediterranean flavor, onions, leeks, tomatoes, eggplants (aubergine), rosemary, sage, or chile peppers can be used, ensuring in this case that the fluid part of the filling has a more neutral flavor.

Ingredients that are less common but which can result in a pleasant surprise are dried fruit or nuts. Walnuts and pine nuts are the perfect way to enrich classic fillings, and those who like contrasts might want to try combining the sweetness of sultana raisins, dried prunes, or dates with speck ham, cabbage, or radicchio.

ALTERNATIVES

If you wish to avoid the use of ingredients sourced from animals, because of food intolerances or for personal taste, fillings can be made with vegetable purées, such as pumpkin, legumes, or potatoes, which are used to bind the other ingredients. Soya milk can be used to replace dairy milk, and also to make béchamel sauce, and similarly tofu is a good alternative for cheese. Vegetarians and vegans can also use vegetable cream and margarine, but make sure to choose varieties free from hydrogenated fats.

In vegetarian or vegan recipes, mushrooms, olives, or vegetables with a distinctive taste, such as asparagus, Savoy cabbage, or peppers can be used if strong flavors are preferred.

☉   Preparation time: 20 minutes
    Cooking time: 50 minutes
♀   Wine suggestion: Cerasuolo d'Abruzzo

Egg and Pancetta Tartlets

Serves 4

1 (3-oz/80-g) slice smoked
   pancetta or bacon, cut into
   small cubes
4 eggs
1/3 cup (1 1/4 oz/30 g) grated
   Parmesan cheese
3/4 cup (6 1/2 fl oz/180 ml)
   whipping cream
2 small thyme sprigs,
   leaves only
butter, for greasing
type 00 flour, for dusting
7 oz/200 g shortcrust pie
   dough (pastry) (see p.196)
salt and pepper

Heat a dry skillet (frying pan), add the pancetta or bacon, and cook over medium heat for 3–4 minutes until crisp. Season with pepper and let cool.

Lightly beat the eggs with the Parmesan and a pinch each of salt and pepper in a bowl. Add the cream, thyme (reserving some leaves to garnish), and crisp pancetta and stir thoroughly.

Preheat the oven to 350°F/180°C/Gas mark 4. Grease four 4-inch/10-cm tartlet pans with butter, then dust them with flour.

Divide the pie dough into four pieces. Roll out each piece on a lightly floured countertop into a circle slightly larger than the diameter of the tartlet pans and use it to line one of the prepared tartlet pans. Prick the surface of the pie dough with a fork.

Fill the tartlet shells (cases) with the filling and bake in the oven for 45 minutes, or until golden brown. (If using a fan oven, switch off the fan 10 minutes before the end of the cooking time.) Serve warm, garnished with the remaining thyme.

TIP   If you'd prefer your tartlets to be less rich but just as tasty, substitute the pancetta or bacon with cooked smoked ham, finely dicing a thick slice of smoked ham and adding it to the filling mixture without frying it. You could also use low-fat fresh ricotta cheese instead of the cream. For a finishing touch, add a little dried oregano to the filling.

⊙ Preparation time: 15 minutes

Cooking time: 50 minutes

♈ Wine suggestion: Alto Adige Müller Thurgau

Zucchini and Gorgonzola Cheese Tart

Serves 4–6

extra virgin olive oil

4 zucchini (courgettes), sliced

2 cloves garlic, crushed

2 eggs

¾ cup plus 1 tablespoon
   (7 fl oz/200 ml) light (single)
   cream

pinch of ground nutmeg

9 oz/250 g puff pastry
   (see page 197)

9 oz/250 g Gorgonzola
   cheese, sliced

salt

arugula (rocket) salad,
   to serve (optional)

Heat a little oil in a skillet (frying pan), add the zucchini (courgettes) and garlic, and cook over low heat for 20 minutes, or until the zucchini are soft.

In a small bowl, lightly beat the eggs with the cream and a pinch each of nutmeg and salt.

Preheat the oven to 350°F/180°C/Gas mark 4. Grease a 10¼–11-inch/26–28-cm round pie dish with oil.

Roll out the pastry on a countertop and use it to line the prepared pie dish. Prick the surface of the pastry with a fork. Arrange the Gorgonzola in a layer to cover the bottom of the pastry shell (base), cover with the cooked zucchini, and pour the cream and egg mixture over the top. Bake in the oven for 30 minutes, or until golden brown.

Serve the tart warm—not hot—with an arugula (rocket) salad, if liked.

TIP   For a less rich, more delicately flavored version of this recipe, use mozzarella and Parmesan cheeses instead of the Gorgonzola cheese and cream. If making this dish in summer, use baby zucchini (courgettes) but be careful not to overcook them: they should be tender but not mushy.

🕐   Preparation time: 30 minutes, plus cooling

        Cooking time: 1 hour

🍷   Wine suggestion: Fiano di Avellino

Sweet Bell Pepper, Smoked Cheese, and Herb Flan

Serves 4–6

1 red bell pepper

1 yellow bell pepper

2 eggs

1 cup (8 fl oz/250 ml) milk

1 tablespoon finely chopped
    mixed herbs, such as
    marjoram, thyme, and basil

pinch of ground nutmeg

9 oz/250 g shortcrust
    pie dough (pastry)
    (see page196)

5 oz/150 g smoked, soft-spun
    cheese (ideally smoked
    scamorza cheese), cut into
    small cubes

salt and pepper

Preheat the oven to 350°F/180°C/Gas mark 4. Line a 10¼-inch/26-cm round pie dish with parchment (baking) paper, allowing the paper to overlap the sides of the dish.

Put the bell peppers into a roasting pan and roast in the oven for 30 minutes or until bubbles form on the skin. Carefully wrap the roasted bell peppers in aluminum foil or put them into a plastic bag and let cool for 10 minutes—the moisture they release will make them easy to peel. Peel off the skins and cut the peppers into ¾-inch/2-cm slices, discarding the seeds and white inner membrane.

Beat the eggs in a large bowl with a fork, then beat in the milk, herbs, and a pinch each of nutmeg, salt, and pepper.

Roll out the pie dough (pastry) on a lightly floured countertop to a thickness of ⅛ inch/4 mm and use it to line the prepared pie dish. Arrange the bell pepper slices in the pastry shell (case) like the spokes of a wheel, alternating the red ones with the yellow ones. Sprinkle with the scamorza then pour over the egg mixture. Bake in the oven for 30 minutes, or until golden brown. Let cool a little and serve lukewarm.

TIP   Here's an alternative filling for this tasty and colorful savory flan. Heat a little extra virgin olive oil in a skillet (frying pan), add 2 diced bell peppers, 1 finely chopped onion, 1 finely chopped carrot, 1 finely chopped celery stalk, 1 finely sliced leek, and a pinch of salt, and cook over low heat for 10 minutes. Transfer this mixture to the pastry shell (case), having used shortcrust pie dough (pastry) or puff pastry if you prefer, and top with grated mature hard goat cheese. Bake in the oven for 25–30 minutes until golden brown. Let cool a little and serve warm.

⊙ Preparation time: 30 minutes

Cooking time: 30 minutes

♀ Wine suggestion: Custoza Superiore

Savoy Cabbage Strudels with Cheese Cream

Serves 4–6

extra virgin olive oil

1 (2-oz/50-g) slice pancetta or
  bacon, cut into small cubes

1/2 head Savoy cabbage, cut
  into thin strips

1 teaspoon dried dill

9 oz/250 g puff pastry
  (see page 197)

type 00 flour, for dusting

1 egg, beaten

2/3 cup (5 fl oz/150 ml)
  whipping cream

5 oz/150 g semi-soft, washed
  rind cheese (ideally Taleggio
  cheese), cut into cubes

salt and pepper

1 small flat-leaf parsley sprig,
  chopped, to garnish

First make the filling. Heat a little oil in a pan, add the pancetta or bacon and cook over medium heat for 2–3 minutes until crisp, then add the cabbage. Cook for 10 minutes, or until wilted. Stir in the dill and then season with salt and pepper.

Preheat the oven to 400°F/200°C/Gas mark 6. Line a baking sheet with parchment (baking) paper.

Divide the puff pastry into four pieces and roll out each piece on a lightly floured countertop into 4¾ x 3¼-inch/12 x 8-cm rectangles. Spoon a quarter of the filling along the center of a pastry rectangle, then fold the long edges of the pastry over to form a sausage shape and tuck the ends under, gently pressing to seal the parcel. Repeat with the remaining pastry and filling.

Carefully transfer the strudels to the prepared baking sheet. Using a sharp knife, cut three transverse slits in the top of each strudel. Brush the pastry with beaten egg and then bake in the oven for 12 minutes, or until golden brown.

Meanwhile, heat the cream in a small pan, being careful not to let it boil. Remove from the heat, add the cheese, and stir until it has melted. Use an immersion blender to blend the sauce until creamy. Keep warm.

Serve the strudels with the cheese cream and garnish with parsley.

NOTE   Savoy cabbage, also known as Milan cabbage, is formed by large rippled and deeply ribbed leaves wrapped around a light green stem. The leaves, especially the tender inside leaves, are excellent raw but are usually boiled. Savoy cabbage is used in many traditional Italian recipes, especially those of northern Italy.

Preparation time: 40 minutes, plus chilling
Cooking time: 20–25 minutes
Wine suggestion: Valle d'Aosta Pinot Nero

Zucchini, Speck Ham, and Cheese Pastry Wheels

Makes 6–8

For the shortcrust pie dough (pastry)
1²/₃ cups (7 oz/200 g) type 00 flour
7 tablespoons (3¹/₂ oz/100g) cold butter, cut into small pieces
pinch of salt

For the filling
2 zucchini (courgettes), thinly sliced lengthwise
2 tablespoons extra virgin olive oil
5 oz/150 g speck ham, thinly sliced
5 oz/150 g mild semi-firm cheese (ideally fontina cheese), thinly sliced

First make the shortcrust pie dough (pastry). Sift (sieve) the flour into a mound on the countertop, make a well in the center, and put the butter, salt, and 2 tablespoons iced water into this. Work the ingredients together quickly with your fingertips and then use your knuckles to make a smooth dough. Wrap the pie dough in plastic wrap (clingfilm) and chill in the refrigerator for at least 1 hour.

Preheat the oven to 350°F/180°C/Gas mark 4. Line a baking sheet with parchment (baking) paper.

Heat a griddle pan or skillet (frying pan) over high heat. Brush the zucchini (courgettes) with the oil, then add them to the hot griddle pan or skillet and cook for 1–2 minutes on each side until just starting to color.

Roll out the pie dough on a lightly floured countertop into a rectangle about ¹/₈ inch/3 mm thick. Arrange the zucchini in a layer on top of the pie dough, followed by a layer of speck ham, and then a layer of fontina. Carefully roll up the pie dough and its contents, taking care not to tear the pie dough, then cut the roll into 6–8 1-inch/2.5-cm thick slices. Lay the slices, spiral-side up, on the prepared baking sheet and bake in the oven for about 20 minutes until golden brown. Set aside to cool on a wire rack.

TIP These stuffed pastry wheels will be all the more delicious if you use Taleggio cheese instead of fontina cheese. Taleggio DOP (Protected Designation of Origin) has been made in the province of Bergamo in Italy since ancient times. It has a thin mold-covered rind, it melts very easily, and its sweet aromatic taste goes perfectly with the other ingredients in this recipe.

Romanesco Broccoli, Onion, and Cheese Tart

Serves 6–8

For the pie dough (pastry)
2 cups (9 oz/250 g) type 00 flour, plus extra for dusting
pinch of salt
1 egg yolk
1 stick (4¼ oz/125 g) butter, softened

For the filling
2 lb 5 oz/1.1 kg romanesco broccoli, broken into small florets
extra virgin olive oil
5 oz/150 g yellow onion, finely chopped
pinch of chili powder
1 egg
⅓ cup plus 1 tablespoon (3½ fl oz/100 ml) heavy (double) cream
4 tablespoons grated pecorino cheese
salt and pepper

First make the pie dough (pastry). Sift (sieve) the flour into a mound on the countertop, make a well in the center, and put the salt, egg yolk, and butter into this. Using your fingertips, mix these ingredients into the flour, gradually adding 1¾ fl oz/50 ml cold water a very little at a time, until you have a smooth and homogenous dough. Shape the pie dough into a ball, wrap it in plastic wrap (clingfilm), and chill in the refrigerator for at least 1 hour.

Bring a large pan of salted water to a boil. Meanwhile, fill a large bowl with iced water and set it beside the stove. Drop the broccoli into the boiling water and leave for 5 minutes. Drain, plunge into the iced water, then drain again thoroughly.

Heat a little oil in a pan, add the onion, and cook over medium heat for 5 minutes, or until soft. Add the broccoli and cook for 5 minutes, or until tender, adding a little water if necessary. Stir in the chili and let cool.

Meanwhile, prepare the cheese sauce. Whisk together the egg and cream in a bowl, stir in 3 tablespoons of the pecorino, and season with salt and pepper.

Preheat the oven to 350°F/180°C/Gas mark 4. Grease a 9½-inch/24-cm pie dish with oil.

Roll out half the pie dough on a lightly floured countertop to a thickness of ⅝ inch/1.5 cm and line the prepared pie dish. Spread the broccoli mixture out over the bottom of the pastry shell (case), sprinkle over the remaining pecorino, then pour over the cheese sauce mixture. Bake in the oven for about 40 minutes until golden brown.

WINE SUGGESTION Verdicchio dei Castelli di Jesi Classico Superiore would be an imaginative choice to accompany this dish, with its fugitive scents of white flower and aromatic herbs. It is a wine of great class and prestige that goes perfectly with the pecorino cheese and vegetables. Serve well chilled (47–50°F/8–10°C).

CHEF
Fabio Nitti

Preparation time: 55 minutes, plus chilling
Cooking time: 1 hour 10 minutes
Wine suggestion: Dororosso Rosso Conero

Pumpkin, Leek, and Sausage Tart

Serves 6–8

For the pie dough (pastry)
2 cups (9 oz/250 g) type 00
  flour, plus extra for dusting
1 teaspoon salt
1 egg yolk
1 stick (4¼ oz/125 g) butter,
  softened, plus extra
  for greasing

For the savory custard
1 egg
⅓ cup plus 1 tablespoon (3½
  fl oz/100 ml) heavy
  (double) cream
4 tablespoons grated
  Parmesan cheese, plus extra
  for sprinkling
salt and pepper

For the filling
1 lb 5 oz/600 g pumpkin,
  peeled, seeded, and cut
  into chunks
extra virgin olive oil
3½ tablespoons thyme leaves
⅓ cup (¼ oz/10 g) marjoram
  leaves
12 oz/250 g leeks, sliced
11 oz/300 g sausagemeat,
  crumbled
salt and pepper

First make the pie dough (pastry). Sift (sieve) the flour into a mound on the countertop, make a well in the center, and put the salt, egg yolk, and butter into this. Using your fingertips, mix these ingredients into the flour, gradually adding 3½ tablespoons cold water a very little at a time, until you have a smooth and homogenous dough. Shape the pie dough into a ball, wrap it in plastic wrap (clingfilm), and chill in the refrigerator for at least 1 hour.

Preheat the oven to 325°F/165°C/Gas mark 3. Line a baking sheet with parchment (baking) paper.

Spread the pumpkin in a single layer on the prepared baking sheet. Season with salt and pepper, drizzle with a little oil, and sprinkle with marjoram and thyme, retaining some of the leaves to garnish the cooked tart. Bake in the oven for 35 minutes, or until soft. Transfer the pumpkin to a colander, place a plate and weight on top, and let drain for 30 minutes to get rid of any excess moisture.

Heat a little oil in a pan, add the leeks, and cook over medium heat for 6–7 minutes until soft and transparent but not browned. Add the sausagemeat and cook, stirring and turning, for a few minutes until it is cooked through (the sausagemeat will change color, becoming lighter, as it is cooked). Let cool.

Make the savory custard. Put all the ingredients into a small bowl and use an immersion blender to beat them together.

Preheat the oven to 350°F/180°C/Gas mark 4. Grease a 9½-inch/24-cm pie dish with butter.

Roll out half the pie dough on a lightly floured surface to a thickness of ¼ inch/5 mm and use it to line the prepared pie dish. Arrange the pumpkin and sausagemeat in alternating layers in the pastry shell (case). Pour over the savory custard, sprinkle with a little extra Parmesan, and bake in the oven for 30–35 minutes until golden brown.

FISH AND SEAFOOD

Preparation time: 25 minutes

Cooking time: 40 minutes

Wine suggestion: Trentino Nosiola

Baked Sea Bass with Vegetables and Parsley Mayonnaise

Serves 4

3 large potatoes, unpeeled

4 (7-oz/200-g) sea bass fillets

4 zucchini (courgette) flowers

3 tablespoons extra virgin
olive oil, plus extra to drizzle

2 thyme sprigs, leaves
finely chopped

3–4 basil leaves, finely
chopped, plus a few extra
leaves to garnish (optional)

sliced cherry tomatoes,
to garnish (optional)

For the parsley mayonnaise

2 egg yolks

1/2 teaspoon white
wine vinegar

1 cup (8 fl oz/250 ml) extra
virgin olive oil

juice of 1 lemon

1¼ cups (2¼ oz/60 g) finely
chopped flat-leaf parsley

salt and pepper

Put the potatoes into a large pan of cold water, bring to a boil, and cook over medium heat for 40 minutes (including the time it took for the water to come to a boil), or until a knife inserted into the potatoes comes out easily. Drain and then carefully peel and slice the potatoes while still hot. Put the sliced potatoes into a large bowl and set aside.

Meanwhile, make the mayonnaise. Put the egg yolks, vinegar, 1 teaspoon salt, and 1/4 teaspoon pepper into a bowl. Using an electric whisk, whisk the eggs until they have increased in volume, then, continuing to whisk, start pouring in the oil in a very slow and steady stream until the mayonnaise is thick and smooth. Whisk in the lemon juice and then stir the parsley into the mayonnaise. Cover and set aside in the refrigerator.

Cook the sea bass in a steamer for 10 minutes, or until just cooked through.

Meanwhile, gently open out the zucchini (courgette) flowers, taking care not to break them, and remove and discard the inner pistils. Wash the flowers very gently under a trickle of cold running water. Cut the flowers into strips and store in the refrigerator.

In a small bowl, whisk together the oil, thyme, basil, and a pinch each of salt and pepper. Pour the dressing over the sliced potatoes.

Spoon some of the parsley mayonnaise onto the center of each serving plate and spread out with the back of a spoon. Arrange the sea bass fillets and potatoes on top of the mayonnaise, drizzle with a little extra oil, and sprinkle with a pinch of salt. Garnish with the zucchini flowers and extra basil leaves and sliced cherry tomatoes, if liked.

⊙　　Preparation time: 45 minutes, plus degorging
　　　Cooking time: 1 hour 20 minutes
♀　　Wine suggestion: Cerasuolo d'Abruzzo

Fish Soup with Fregola Pasta

Serves 4

3½ oz/100 g octopus,
　cleaned
3½ oz/100 g mussels,
　cleaned and debearded
　(see page 74)
3½ oz/100 g clams
8 raw jumbo shrimp (king
　prawns) in their shells
1 lb 2 oz/500 g rockfish
extra virgin olive oil
4 tablespoons (2 oz/
　50 g) butter
1 onion, cut into small cubes
1 celery stalk, cut into
　small cubes
1¼ cups (10 fl oz/300 ml)
　white wine
2¼ lb/1 kg ice cubes
3 tablespoons tomato
　paste (purée)
14 oz/400 g fregola pasta
　(or pearl couscous)
1 clove garlic, chopped
2 tablespoons chopped
　flat-leaf parsley, plus extra
　to garnish
½ cup (3 oz/80 g) cherry
　tomatoes (ideally Pachino
　tomatoes), halved
salt

Cook the octopus in a large pan of boiling lightly salted water for 20 minutes, then let cool in the water. Once cooled, cut the octopus into pieces and refrigerate.

Meanwhile, wash the mussels and clams under cold running water, then place in a large bowl of cold salted water and let soak for around 30 minutes to degorge.

Rinse the shrimp (prawns) under running water. Remove the heads and shells and reserve, keeping the tails intact. Using a sharp knife, cut through the back of each shrimp and remove and discard the intestine, being careful not to break it. Set aside the shelled prawns in the refrigerator. Gut, clean, scale, and fillet the rockfish, reserving all the fish trimmings. Cut each fillet into two or three pieces and refrigerate.

Make the fish broth. Heat a drizzle of oil and the butter in a skillet (frying pan), add the onion and celery, and cook over medium heat for 3–4 minutes until the onion has become translucent. Add the shrimp heads and shells and fish trimmings, and cook over high heat for 2–3 minutes to let the flavors blend. Pour over ¾ cup plus 1 tablespoon (7 fl oz/200 ml) wine and cook for 5 minutes, or until the wine has evaporated. Reduce the heat, add enough ice cubes to cover the fish, and let simmer over low heat for 50 minutes, skimming off any scum from the surface from time to time, and adding the tomato purée (paste) halfway through the cooking time. Strain the fish broth through a fine strainer or a colander lined with a fine-mesh cloth.

Cook the pasta in a large pan of boiling salted water for 4 minutes, then drain well, cool under cold running water, and drain again. Heat a little oil in a large pan, add the drained pasta and shelled shrimp, and cook over medium heat, gradually adding the fish broth a ladleful at the time, for 10 minutes, or until the pasta is al dente and the shrimp are cooked.

Meanwhile, heat a little oil in a large pan, add the garlic and parsley, and cook over medium heat for 2–3 minutes. Add the mussels and clams and when they are very hot add the tomatoes and the remaining wine. Cover and cook over medium heat until the shells have opened. Discard any that do not open. Add the mussels and clams to the pan with the shrimp and pasta, then add the fish and octopus, and continue to cook for another 10–15 minutes until heated through. Taste to check the seasoning and serve drizzled with a little oil and garnished with extra parsley.

Preparation time: 20 minutes, plus cooling and standing
Cooking time: 45 minutes
Wine suggestion: Vermentino di Gallura Superiore

Octopus and Cranberry Bean Salad

Serves 6

1 lb 2 oz/500g fresh cranberry
(borlotti) beans in their
pods, shelled (2$\frac{1}{2}$
cups prepared)
2$\frac{1}{2}$ lb/1.2 kg octopus,
cleaned
2 tablespoons extra virgin
olive oil
2 tablespoons white wine
vinegar
1 clove garlic, finely chopped
1 small bunch flat-leaf
parsley, chopped
5–6 tomatoes, cubed or sliced
salt

Cook the beans in a very large pan of boiling lightly salted water for 45 minutes, or until tender and soft. Drain well.

Meanwhile, cook the octopus in a large pan of boiling water for 40 minutes, or until the octopus is soft and a cocktail stick (toothpick) inserted into the flesh comes out easily. Drain well and let cool. Once cool, cut the octopus into small pieces.

Transfer the octopus to a bowl. Add the oil, vinegar, garlic, and parsley and mix well, then stir in the drained beans and tomatoes. Let the salad stand for 1 hour at room temperature to let the flavors infuse before serving.

TIP To give the octopus a deeper flavor, add 1 halved unwaxed lemon, 1 chopped carrot, 1 chopped onion, 1 chopped celery stalk, 2 bay leaves, and a few peppercorns to the water it will be cooked in. To ensure the octopus is tender, turn off the heat after it has cooked for 30 minutes and let it cool in the cooking liquid.

Preparation time: 20 minutes

Cooking time: 15 minutes

Wine suggestion: Trebbiano d'Abruzzo

Monkfish with Rosemary

Serves 4

1³/₄ lb/800 g monkfish

6 tablespoons extra virgin
olive oil

2 cloves garlic, peeled

1 red chile, halved, seeded,
and finely chopped

3 rosemary sprigs, leaves
finely chopped

¹/₄ teaspoon salt

To garnish
a few rosemary sprigs
4 red chiles (optional)

Gut, clean, skin, and fillet the monkfish (see tip). Cut the fillets into medium-sized cubes.

Heat a little oil in a skillet (frying pan), add the whole garlic cloves, chile, and rosemary, and cook over medium heat for 2 minutes. Add the fish cubes and cook for 5 minutes until golden brown, then add the salt, cover, and cook for 10 minutes. Serve garnished with rosemary and whole chiles, if liked.

TIP   To clean a monkfish, using a sharp knife, cut off and discard the head, then rinse the fish under cold running water. Grip one edge of the skin and pull it in the direction of the tail until the skin comes off. Cut off the internal membrane and discard it, then cut an incision along either side of the backbone to obtain two large fillets.

⊙ Preparation time: 35 minutes, plus soaking and cooling
Cooking time: 25 minutes

♀ Wine suggestion: Valdobbiadene Superiore di Cartizze Brut

Fried Salt Cod Fish Balls

Serves 4

4 potatoes, peeled and cut
  into small cubes
1 lb 5 oz/500 g salt cod,
  desalted (see tip), cleaned,
  and cut into small cubes
generous 2 cups (17 fl oz/
  500 ml) milk
1 small bunch flat-leaf parsley,
  finely chopped
9 slices (9 oz/250 g) bread
  without crusts
3¾ cups (6 oz/175 g) fresh
  breadcrumbs
sunflower oil, for deep-frying
ketchup, mayonnaise,
  or dill mayonnaise, to serve
  (optional)

Put the potatoes and cod into a pan, pour over the milk, and cook over low heat for 15 minutes, or until the potatoes are soft. Drain well, transfer the potatoes and cod to a bowl, stir in the parsley, and let cool.

Transfer the potato and cod mixture to the bowl of a stand mixer, add the bread and 1 tablespoon of the breadcrumbs, and mix until you obtain a compact and dry mixture. Using your hands, shape the mixture into balls, each about 1½ inches/4 cm in diameter.

Spread out the remaining breadcrumbs in a shallow dish and roll each fish ball in the breadcrumbs to coat.

Pour enough sunflower oil for deep-frying into a deep-fat fryer or large deep pan and heat the oil to 340°F/170°C. Carefully add the fish balls to the hot oil and cook for 3–4 minutes until golden brown. Remove with a slotted spoon and drain on paper towels.

Serve immediately, with ketchup, mayonnaise, or dill mayonnaise, if liked.

TIP Salt cod is simply northern cod—from the Baltic and the Atlantic—that has been filleted and preserved in salt. Before cooking the salt cod needs to be soaked for 2 days in cold water, changing the water several times during this period. The best salt cod are not too small (at least 16 inches/40 cm in length) and have a light but not yellowish color. Fillets that are too white should be avoided as they may have been artificially bleached.

Preparation time: 30 minutes, plus marinating

Cooking time: 15 minutes

Wine suggestion: Vermentino di Gallura

Grilled Salmon with Milk Mayonnaise

Serves 4

juice of 1 lemon

extra virgin olive oil

1 clove garlic, crushed

4 (5–7-oz/150–200-g)
  salmon steaks

¾ cup plus 1 tablespoon
  (7 fl oz/200 ml) milk

1⅔ cups (14 fl oz/400 ml)
  sunflower oil

1 small bunch wild fennel,
  chopped

salt

First make a dressing. Put half the lemon juice, a similar quantity of extra virgin olive oil, a pinch of salt, and the garlic into a small bowl and whisk together.

Put the salmon steaks onto a plate and sprinkle over the dressing. Cover with plastic wrap (clingfilm) and let marinate in the refrigerator for 15 minutes.

Prepare the milk mayonnaise. Put the milk in a small bowl or container and use an immersion blender to whisk the milk, adding the sunflower oil in a very slow and steady stream until the mixture is the consistency of mayonnaise. Whisk in the remaining lemon juice and season to taste with a little salt.

Heat a cast-iron griddle pan until very hot. Drain the salmon, add it to the hot griddle pan, and cook over medium heat for 6 minutes on each side until golden brown.

Spread out the fennel on a shallow plate. Dip one side of each steak into the fennel to coat and then transfer to serving plates. Serve the salmon with the milk mayonnaise.

TIP To make a perfect mayonnaise, use a smallish container, just large enough to accommodate the immersion blender. The secret is to emulsify the milk quickly, keeping the immersion blender at the bottom of the container and then lifting it slowly.

⊙ Preparation time: 15 minutes, plus degorging
Cooking time: 10 minutes

♀ Wine suggestion: Verdicchio di Matelica

Parsley-scented Mussels and Clams

Serves 4

1 lb 5 oz/600 g mussels
1 lb 5 oz/600 g clams
2 tablespoons extra virgin
 olive oil
2 cloves garlic, coarsely
 chopped
1 small bunch flat-leaf parsley,
 coarsely chopped, plus
 extra to garnish
salt

Wash the mussels and clams under cold running water, then place in a large bowl of cold salted water and let them degorge for around 30 minutes to get rid of any sand.

Carefully clean the mussels with a small metal brush, then use tweezers to pull off the beards (the brown fibrous threads hanging from the shells) and rinse thoroughly.

Put the mussels and clams in a large pan and cook over high heat for 4–5 minutes until all the shells have open. Discard any that do not open. Strain the shellfish, reserving the cooking liquor, and set aside.

Meanwhile, heat the oil in a pan, add the garlic and parsley, and cook over medium heat for 2 minutes, then add the clams and mussels and a little of the reserved cooking liquid and cook for 6 minutes to allow the shellfish to absorb the flavors. Discard any that do not open. Taste to check the seasoning and add salt if necessary. Serve the mussels and clams hot, garnished with extra parsley.

NOTE The Italian Portonovo wild mussel (*mosciolo* in Italian) is protected by the Slow Food Presidia label. These mollusks live and reproduce naturally on the Conero coast in the Italian province of Ancona, where they are gathered only from April to October. Portonovo wild mussels are traditionally consumed as soon as they are harvested, cooked on a metal plate resting over a fire or in a marinara sauce.

Preparation time: 15 minutes

Cooking time: 10 minutes

Wine suggestion: Collio Chardonnay

Hake Steaks with Aromatic Herbs

Serves 4

1¾ cups (3 oz/80 g) fresh
   breadcrumbs
1 small bunch aromatic herbs,
   such as flat-leaf parsley,
   marjoram, chives, and sage
3½ slices (3½ oz/100 g) stale
   bread, crumbled
1 egg
3 tablespoons milk
4 (4-oz/120-g) hake fillets
6 tablespoons extra virgin
   olive oil
salt

Put the breadcrumbs and herbs into a food processor and process until the mixture is the texture of fine breadcrumbs. Transfer to a shallow dish and mix in the stale bread.

Whisk the egg with the milk and a pinch of salt in a separate shallow dish.

Dip the fish fillets into the egg mixture, then coat them in the breadcrumbs, pressing lightly to ensure they are well coated.

Heat the oil in a skillet (frying pan), add the fish fillets, and cook over medium heat for 3–4 minutes on each side until golden. Drain on paper towels and serve immediately.

NOTE Hake belongs to the cod and haddock family and is a common white fish. Its size varies from between 8 inches/20 cm and 3 feet/1 meter. The hake's flesh is very delicate and easily digestible. It can be cooked simply, either boiled or steamed, or its flavors can be enriched by frying, stewing, or making into fish cakes.

COOKING METHODS
FOR FISH

When cooking fish, first of all it is essential to take into account the tenderness and the delicate flavor of this type of food. It is also necessary to remember that different varieties lend themselves to different cooking methods and that it is important to select the best method, on the basis of the size of the piece to be cooked: whether whole fish are to be cooked, and are thus protected by their skin, or whether slices or fillets will be used instead. It is also advisable to avoid prolonged cooking times at high temperatures, as this risks drying the fish and damaging its texture.

SIMPLICITY IS RESPECTFUL

Steaming is one of the simplest methods of cooking, and one of the healthiest, and it is also extremely respectful of the delicacy of the fish. It is suitable for small or medium-sized fish, both whole and filleted, and requires the use of a special pan with a steamer inside. Cooking takes an average of 15 minutes per 2¼ lb/1 kg.

One of the most typical preparations for cooking fish is court bouillon. The name is taken from the aromatic liquid in which the fish is cooked, either whole or in slices. A blend of water and wine is poured into the pan, with sliced carrots, onions cut into rings, stalks of celery, parsley, and peppercorns. The liquid is then gradually brought to a temperature of around 175–185°F/80–85°C. As with steaming, it takes around 15 minutes to cook 2¼ lb/1 kg of fish.

Baking, at a maximum temperature of 400°F/200°C, is suitable mainly for oily fish of medium or large size, cooked whole. It is advisable to marinate the fish first.

A variant of this is cooking en papillot, which allows the fish to retain its juices while cooking it in contact with herbs and spices. The fish is wrapped in aluminum foil or parchment (baking) paper, with aromatic herbs, vegetables, and seasoning to taste, and baked at 350–400°F/180–200°C for 20–25 minutes. This method can be used for whole fish but also for slices and fillets. The fish can be served still wrapped up, if preferred.

A second variation of this method is to bake, en croute or in a salt crust, which is particularly suitable for bass, snapper, or bream. Cooking in a crust allows the flesh to remain moist, and the fish to retain its flavor, while protecting it from direct heat. To cook the fish in this way, cover it completely with coarse salt and bake at 400°F/200°C (1 hour per 2¼ lb/1 kg of fish). Alternatively, breadcrumbs, piecrust dough, or even clay can be used.

OUT OF THE FRYING PAN ...

Frying is considered to be the cooking method with the most calories, but it certainly is also one of the tastiest, as long as it is done in the best way. The fish should be immersed in oil at a temperature of at least 350°F/180°C but lower than the smoke point. At these temperatures the sugar content in the skin, combined with flour or other starches, allows the immediate formation of a crispy crust over the entire surface. This protects the flesh from the cooking fat, making it very light and tasty, with a pleasant contrast between the outer crispiness and the softness inside. Small fish and small-sized seafood are suitable for frying. To ensure the fried fish does not become soggy, it is essential for the salt to be added just before the food is served.

The most suitable cooking method for fish with firm meat, for larger fish slices, and for oily fish, such as eel, sardine, mackerel, and salmon, is broiling (grilling) on a hot plate. The fish can be marinated before cooking (without scaling the fish, as the scales protect it from the heat), and cooked on a hot broiler (grill), making sure the fish is not too close to the heat. It is best to use a lower heat to cook larger fish, brushing it with oil during cooking. Add salt to the fish before turning it over and then again when it is nearly ready. A variant of this is cooking in embers, in a wood-fired oven, or on a barbecue, which is suitable for very firm fish, like tuna, bream, brill, or turbot.

◷ Preparation time: 20 minutes

Cooking time: 25 minutes

♀ Wine suggestion: Vernaccia di San Gimignano

Baked Red Mullet with Thyme and Olives

Serves 4

4 (4-oz/120-g) red mullet
or red snapper, gutted,
cleaned, and scaled
(see tip on page 248)
1 unwaxed lemon, sliced
2 tablespoons pitted (stoned)
black olives (ideally
Taggiasca olives)
2 tablespoons capers
preserved in salt, well rinsed
4 thyme sprigs
extra virgin olive oil,
for drizzling
salt

Preheat the oven to 350°F/180°C/Gas mark 4. Cut four large squares out of parchment (baking) paper.

Arrange each fish in the middle of a square of parchment paper, divide the lemon slices, olives, capers, and thyme among the fish, and sprinkle with a pinch of salt. Fold up the paper, crimping it over the top to seal.

Place the parcels on a baking sheet and bake in the oven for 25 minutes, or until the fish flesh comes easily away from the bone. Transfer each parcel to a serving plate, open the parcels, and drizzle with a little oil before serving.

NOTE   Red mullet are well known and valued by chefs but often overlooked by consumers. This pink-colored sea fish is characterized by its very fragile flesh, which means that it needs to be cleaned very gently. Red mullet can be prepared in many ways but it is not suitable for stewing as the flesh would be likely to fall apart.

🕐 Preparation time: 20 minutes, plus resting

Cooking time: 30 minutes

🍷 Wine suggestion: Alto Adige Müller Thurgau

Trout with Thyme

Serves 4

4 cups (7 oz/200 g) fresh
  breadcrumbs
2 cloves garlic, finely chopped
2 rosemary sprigs, leaves
  finely chopped
1 flat-leaf parsley sprig,
  finely chopped
2–3 thyme sprigs
extra virgin olive oil
4 (6¼–7-oz/180–200-g)
  rainbow trout, gutted,
  cleaned, and scaled
  (see tip on page 248)
2 unwaxed lemons, 1 juiced
  and 1 sliced
salt and pepper

Preheat the oven to 400°F/200°C/Gas mark 6. Line a baking sheet with parchment (baking) paper.

Put the breadcrumbs, garlic, herbs, ¼ teaspoon salt, and 2 tablespoons oil into a small bowl and mix well.

Wash the fish thoroughly and pat dry with paper towels. Sprinkle some lemon juice inside the cavity of each fish, then fill the cavities with most of the herb and breadcrumb mixture, reserving a couple of tablespoons, and the lemon slices.

Arrange the stuffed fish on the prepared baking sheet. Drizzle a little oil over the fish and then sprinkle over a pinch each of salt and pepper and the reserved herb and breadcrumb mixture. Bake in the oven for 30 minutes, or until the fish are crisp and golden. Let rest for 10 minutes before serving.

TIP You can use the same herb and breadcrumb mixture to stuff bream, small sea bass, or other delicately-flavored white-fleshed fish. To bake bream or small sea bass, reduce the cooking time to 15–18 minutes.

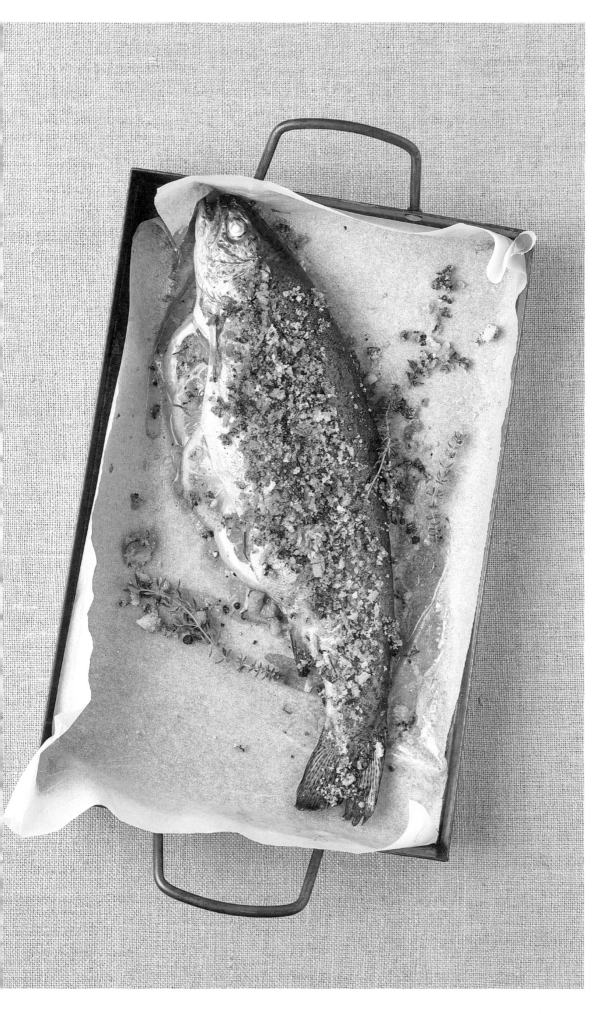

Preparation time: 20 minutes, plus marinating

Cooking time: 8 minutes

Wine suggestion: Bianco d'Alcamo

Striped Mullet with Fresh Herbs

Serves 4

2 (1 lb 5-oz/550-g) striped (grey) mullet
½ cup (4 fl oz/125 ml) extra virgin olive oil
1 teaspoon chopped oregano
1 flat-leaf parsley sprig, chopped
juice of 1 lemon
salt and pepper

Gut, clean, scale, and bone the fish, then cut the fillets in half. Rinse the fillets under cold running water and pat dry with paper towels. Put the fillets onto a plate and drizzle with half the oil. Sprinkle over the oregano and a pinch each of salt and pepper and let marinate in the refrigerator for 1 hour.

Heat a cast-iron griddle pan until very hot, add the fish fillets, and cook over medium heat for 3–4 minutes on each side until golden brown.

Meanwhile, make a dressing. Pour the remaining oil into a small bowl, add the parsley, lemon juice, and a pinch each of salt and pepper, and whisk with a fork to obtain a smooth emulsion.

Arrange the fish on a serving dish, pour over the dressing sauce, and serve straight away.

NOTE Bottarga is made from mullet eggs that have been cured with salt and dried. It is excellent served in thin slices or used as an ingredient for pasta dishes. Bottarga from Orbetello in Tuscany is protected by the Slow Food Presidia label and, unlike Sardinian bottarga, it is ready in just 15 days. It has a compact consistency, an amber color, and a pungent odor.

Preparation time: 20 minutes
Cooking time: 40 minutes
Wine suggestion: Colli Tortonesi Cortese

Spicy Mackerel with Baked Potatoes

Serves 4

7 potatoes (about 1³/₄ lb/
   800 g), peeled and cut into
   wedges ·
5–6 tablespoons extra virgin
   olive oil
3 cloves garlic, 1 clove
   crushed, 2 cloves chopped
4 (9-oz/250-g) mackerel
6 wild fennel sprigs, chopped
2 red chiles, seeded
   and chopped
salt
sprigs of thyme, to garnish

Preheat the oven to 400°F/200°C/Gas mark 6. Line a baking sheet with parchment (baking) paper.

Cook the potatoes in a large pan of boiling salted water for 5 minutes, then drain well. Arrange the potatoes on the prepared baking sheet, drizzle over the oil, sprinkle with the crushed garlic, and toss to ensure the potatoes are evenly coated with the oil and garlic. Bake in the oven for 10 minutes, or until golden brown.

Meanwhile, gut and clean the mackerel (see tip on page 248), wash them under cold running water, then pat dry with paper towels. Using a sharp knife, cut a few slanting incisions in the sides of the fish.

In a small bowl, mix together most of the fennel with the chopped garlic and half the chile. Use a quarter of this mixture to fill the cavity of each fish.

Arrange the fish at the center of the baking sheet with the potatoes, sprinkle over the remaining fennel and chile, and season with salt. Return to the oven and bake for an additional 25 minutes, or until the fish flesh comes easily away from the bone. Serve garnished with sprigs of thyme.

NOTE For a long time mackerel was considered a second-class product at Italian fish markets. It is, however, rich in nutrients, versatile in the kitchen, and can be used to make some very tasty dishes. Mackerel, like other varieties of blue fish, has an oily flesh that deteriorates quickly so it needs to be consumed very fresh. It can be cooked simply and quickly, and can also be preserved in oil.

⊙ Preparation time: 45 minutes
♀ Wine suggestion: Gavi

Fish Tartare

Serves 4

1 lb 2 oz/500 g very fresh
  umbrine or sea bass
5 tablespoons extra virgin
  olive oil
2 celery stalks, strings
  removed and cut into
  small cubes
1 cucumber, peeled and cut
  into small cubes
1 Granny Smith apple,
  peeled, cored, and cut into
  small cubes
1 orange, peeled, divided
  into segments, and
  membrane removed
1 kiwi fruit, peeled and cut
  into small cubes
1 x ¾-inch/2-cm piece
  fresh ginger, peeled
  and finely grated
juice of 1 grapefruit
salt

To garnish
pink salt crystals
a few small salad
  leaves (greens)

Gut, clean, scale, and bone the fish (see tip), then cut the fillets into small cubes. Transfer to a bowl, sprinkle with a pinch of salt, and drizzle with 2 tablespoons of the oil. Cover with plastic wrap (clingfilm) and chill in the refrigerator for 10 minutes.

Put the celery, cucumber, apple, orange, and kiwi fruit in a bowl. Drizzle over 2 tablespoons of the oil, sprinkle with a pinch of salt, and mix together gently.

To make a dressing, whisk together the ginger, a pinch of salt, the remaining oil, and the grapefruit juice in a small bowl. Pour half the dressing over the fish and toss thoroughly.

Place a large metal ring or cookie cutter in the center of each serving plate, arrange a layer of the fruit and vegetable salad on the bottom, top with a layer of the fish tartare, and drizzle with the remaining dressing. Carefully remove the rings or cutters and garnish with pink salt crystals and a few small salad leaves (greens).

TIP   To clean white fish, cut the fins off the fish with scissors, then use a sharp knife to slit open the belly and discard the innards. Scale the fish using the appropriate tool or a smooth-bladed knife. Using a sharp knife, make an incision under the head and along the back, then open the fish like a book and pull the flesh away from the backbone. Remove any remaining fish bones with tweezers.

⊙ Preparation time: 30 minutes

♀ Wine suggestion: Gavi

Salmon Tartare with Peas and Cucumber

Serves 4

1 (14-oz/400-g) very fresh
  salmon fillet, finely diced
1 large cucumber, finely diced
2 large scallions (spring
  onions), thinly sliced
²/₃ cup (3¹/₂ oz/100 g)
  shelled fresh peas
1 flat-leaf parsley sprig,
  chopped
5 tablespoons extra virgin
  olive oil
2 tablespoons lime juice
salt and pepper
mixed baby leaf salad,
  to garnish

Put the salmon, cucumber, scallions (spring onions), peas, and parsley into a bowl, season with salt and pepper, drizzle over 1 tablespoon of the oil, and mix well. Spoon the mixture into four ramekins or molds, pressing down lightly. Let chill in the refrigerator for 15 minutes.

Meanwhile, make a dressing. Whisk together the remaining oil with the lime juice and a pinch each of salt and pepper in a small bowl.

To serve, unmold the tartares by inverting them onto serving plates, then garnish with mixed baby leaf salad and drizzle over the dressing.

TIP   For a more refined version of this recipe, replace the salmon with the same quantity of very fresh raw tuna. Cut the tuna into small pieces and place in a bowl. Make a dressing with 2 tablespoons capers (rinsed thoroughly to get rid of any excess salt or vinegar), a drizzle of extra virgin olive oil, a chopped mint sprig, a chopped chervil sprig, the juice of 1 lemon, and a pinch each of salt, and pepper. Pour the dressing over the tuna, add 3¹/₂ oz/100 g shelled fresh peas, toss gently, and serve.

CHEF
Viviana Varese

⊙ Preparation time: 15 minutes, plus soaking
Cooking time: 2–2½ hours

Chickpea Soup with Red Mullet and Rosemary Oil

Serves 4

4 (3½-oz/100-g) red mullet
  or red snapper, gutted,
  cleaned and filleted
scant ½ cup (3½ oz/
  100 g) cherry tomato confit
  (see p.188)
1 shallot, sliced
rosemary oil, for drizzling

For the chickpea soup
1 cup (7 oz/200 g)
dried chickpeas
2 teaspoons extra virgin
  olive oil
1 bay leaf
1 rosemary sprig, plus extra
  to garnish
1 teaspoon salt

Soak the chickpeas in a large bowl of cold water overnight.

The next day, rinse the chickpeas under cold running water. Put the chickpeas and the remaining soup ingredients into a pressure cooker, pour over enough water to cover the ingredients by at least 1½ inches/4 cm, and cook for 2 hours until the chickpeas are soft and slightly melted. Alternatively, put the ingredients into a pan, bring to a boil, then reduce the heat, cover and cook for 2½ hours.

Cook the red mullet in a steamer for 4 minutes, or until just cooked through.

Ladle the chickpea soup into serving bowls, arrange the red mullet on top, then add the cherry tomato confit and shallots. Drizzle over a little rosemary oil and garnish with a few extra rosemary leaves.

♀ **WINE SUGGESTION** Cabochon Brut 2009 is complex and very pleasantly drinkable, making it the ideal accompaniment for this soup. This Franciacorta wine is able to enhance a "poor" but surprisingly adaptable fish.

Preparation time: 35 minutes, plus soaking

Cooking time: 1 hour 10 minutes

Wine suggestion: Colli Martani Grechetto

Cuttlefish Stuffed with Pigna Bean Purée

Serves 4

1 cup (7 oz/200 g) dried white Pigna beans (or substitue with lima/butter beans)

4 (5-oz/150-g) cuttlefish

1 French baguette, soft inside part of the bread removed and crusts discarded

1/3 cup plus 1 tablespoon (3 1/2 fl oz/100 ml) milk

1 small bunch flat-leaf parsley, finely chopped

3/4 cup (7 oz/200 g) ricotta cheese

1 egg

extra virgin olive oil

salt and pepper

chopped flat-leaf parsley, to garnish

toasted slices of rustic bread, to serve (optional)

Soak the beans in a large bowl of cold water overnight.

The next day, drain the beans and then cook them in a large pan of boiling salted water for at least 1 hour until soft.

Meanwhile, clean the cuttlefish and remove the ink sacs. Remove the heads and tentacles, chop finely and set aside. Open out the cuttlefish in half and cook them in a large pan of boiling salted water for 20 minutes, or until soft. Drain well.

Make the filling. Put the soft inside part of the French bread into a bowl with the milk and let soak for 10 minutes, then remove the bread and squeeze out any excess milk. Put the soaked bread into a large bowl, add the chopped cuttlefish heads and tentacles, parsley, ricotta, and egg, season with salt and pepper, and mix well. Stuff the cuttlefish with this filling.

Heat a cast-iron griddle pan until very hot, brush with a little oil, then add the stuffed cuttlefish and cook over medium heat for 5 minutes on each side, or until colored.

Once the beans are cooked, drain, reserving a little of the cooking liquid. Transfer the beans to a food processor and blend to a purée, adding a little of the cooking liquid if necessary, to obtain a smooth, very thick, velvety sauce.

Cut the stuffed cuttlefish into slices, divide among serving plates, and spoon over the bean sauce. Garnish with parsley and a drizzle of oil and serve with toasted slices of rustic bread, if liked.

NOTE Pigna beans are protected by a Slow Food Presidia label and are grown on the hinterland terraces in the Italian province of Imperia. They are harvested from mid-September to mid-October, but are available dried all year round. In the town of Pigna itself, these beans are cooked with goat as a local specialty.

Preparation time: 35 minutes, plus chilling

Cooking time: 45 minutes

Wine suggestion: Alezio Rosé

Sea Bream, Artichoke, and Sun-dried Cherry Tomato Strudel

Serves 4–6

For the pie dough (pastry)
1²/₃ cups (7 oz/200 g) type 00
  flour, plus extra for dusting
pinch of salt
3 tablespoons extra virgin
  olive oil

For the filling
2 artichokes
extra virgin olive oil
2 (5-oz/150-g) sea
  bream fillets
1²/₃ (3¹/₂ oz/100 g)
  sun-dried cherry tomatoes
  preserved in oil, drained
  and cut in half
2 small thyme sprigs, leaves
  finely chopped
1 rosemary sprig, leaves
  finely chopped
salt and pepper

First make the pie dough (pastry). Sift (sieve) the flour into a mound on the work surface, make a well in the center, and put the salt and oil into this. Using your hands, mix the ingredients together, gradually adding about ¹/₃ cup plus 1 tablespoon (3¹/₂ fl oz/100 ml) water a little at a time, until the dough is very firm and smooth. Continue kneading the dough for about 15 minutes. Shape the pie dough into a ball, wrap it in plastic wrap (clingfilm), and chill in the refrigerator for at least 20 minutes.

Trim the artichokes, discarding the inner chokes, the tougher outermost leaves, and their spiny tips. Cut the artichokes into thin slices.

Heat a little oil in a skillet (frying pan), add the artichokes, and cook over medium heat for 15 minutes, or until soft. Season with salt and pepper.

Meanwhile, heat a little oil in a separate skillet, add the fish fillets, skin-side down, and cook over medium heat for 2–3 minutes until the edges of the fillets start to turn white, then turn over and cook for an additional 3–4 minutes. Cut the fillets in half.

Preheat the oven to 350°F/180°C/Gas mark 4. Line a baking sheet with parchment (baking) paper.

Roll out the pie dough on a lightly floured work surface into a rectangle about ¹/₄ inch/4 mm thick. Arrange the fish, sun-dried cherry tomatoes, and the artichokes on top of the pie dough and sprinkle over the thyme and rosemary. Carefully roll up the pie dough and its contents, taking care not to tear the pie dough. Carefully transfer the strudel to the prepared baking sheet and bake in the oven for 30 minutes, or until golden brown.

MEAT

⊙ Preparation time: 25 minutes

Cooking time: 55 minutes

♀ Wine suggestion: Nebbiolo d'Alba

Succulent Hamburgers

Serves 4

1 lb 5 oz/600 g lean ground
   (minced) beef
extra virgin olive oil
salt and pepper

For the potato purée
4 potatoes, unpeeled
generous 2 cups (17 fl oz/
   500 ml) milk
3¹/₂ tablespoons whipping
   cream
4 tablespoons (2 oz/50 g)
   butter, cut into small pieces

Put the beef into a bowl, add 2 tablespoons oil, season with salt and pepper, and mix together thoroughly. Chill in the refrigerator for 20 minutes.

Meanwhile, make the potato purée. Cook the potatoes in a large pan of boiling salted water for 40 minutes. Just before the end of the cooking time, pour the milk into a small pan, bring to a boil, then remove from the heat. Drain the potatoes and carefully peel them while still hot. Pass the potatoes through a ricer or vegetable mill into a clean pan. Add the cream and the butter and stir gently over a low heat until the butter has melted, then gradually add the hot milk, a little at a time, until the potato purée is smooth and homogenous. Remove from the heat and keep warm.

Using your hands, shape the meat into 4 hamburger patties without flattening them too much. Heat a cast-iron griddle until very hot, add the hamburgers and cook over medium–high heat for 4 minutes on each side, or until golden brown. Serve with the potato purée and salad, if liked.

NOTE   These hamburgers are succulent, and irresistible! The best beef used in Italy for an outstandingly delicious hamburger is Chianina beef, which comes from a breed of Italian beef cattle that are reared in the Chiana Valley in Tuscany. Renowned for its excellent taste and very compact texture, Chianina beef is best served very pink and tender, but if rare meat is not to your taste then cook it for a few minutes longer. The beef's marbled fat will ensure that it is tender and juicy inside, with a delectable crust on the outside. If you prefer, you can serve these hamburgers with a salad of wild salad leaves and tomatoes and roasted potatoes instead of the potato purée.

⊙ Preparation time: 30 minutes, plus chilling
Cooking time: 25 minutes
♀ Wine suggestion: Cerasuolo d'Abruzzo

Asparagus, Ham, Chicken, and Cheese Roll

Serves 4

18–20 asparagus spears
(about 11 oz/300 g)
4 large thin slices chicken
breast
5 oz/150 g sliced cooked ham
3½ oz/100 g soft-spun cheese
(ideally scamorza cheese),
cut into small cubes
extra virgin olive oil
3–4 sage leaves
2 rosemary sprigs
1 clove garlic, chopped
½ cup (4 fl oz/125 ml) dry
white wine
2 carrots, diced
salt and pepper

Line up the tips of the asparagus and cut off the tough lower section at the base of the spears so they are all an even length. Peel the spears, exposing the paler layer of the stalk and discarding the green, stringy layer.

Bring a large pan of water to a boil. Meanwhile, fill a large bowl with iced water and set it beside the stove. Drop the asparagus into the boiling water and leave for 4 minutes. Drain, plunge into the iced water, then drain again thoroughly.

Place the slices of chicken flat on the countertop, slightly overlapping the slices with each other. Cover the chicken with the ham, arrange the asparagus spears in groups along the length of the chicken, reserving 4–5 asparagus spears to garnish, then sprinkle the cheese over the asparagus. Carefully roll up the chicken, enclosing the other ingredients, and secure the roll with kitchen string. Brush all over with oil and then season. Cover and chill in the refrigerator for 2 hours.

Preheat the oven to 350°F/180°C/Gas mark 4.

Heat a little oil in a nonstick skillet (frying pan), add the sage, rosemary, and garlic, then add the roll and cook over medium heat for about 5 minutes, turning from time to time, until brown all over. Pour over the wine and cook for 5 minutes more. Transfer to an ovenproof dish and bake in the oven for 15 minutes, or until the chicken is cooked through and well done.

Meanwhile, cut the reserved asparagus spears into lozenge-shaped slices. Heat a little oil in a skillet, add the sliced asparagus and the carrots and cook over medium heat for 3 minutes. Cut the roll into slices and serve with the asparagus and carrots.

NOTE   Chicken is so digestible, versatile, and affordable that it is one of the most popular meats in Italy. This huge demand has led to a degradation in its quality. It is therefore advisable to buy a whole chicken, locally reared by producers who follow genuine free-range methods and feed their birds with organic foodstuffs. The parts of the chicken needed for a particular recipe can be carved from the bird.

CHEF

Antonio Bufi

Preparation time: 15 minutes
Cooking time: 40 minutes

Suckling Pig Shoulder with Fava Beans and Saffron

Serves 4

pinch of saffron threads
extra virgin olive oil
¼ red onion, cut into thin strips
1½-inch/4-cm piece fresh ginger, peeled and cut into thin strips
1 lemongrass stalk, cut into thin rounds
⅓ cup (½ oz/15 g) mint leaves
2 cups (11 oz/300 g) shelled fresh fava (broad) beans
4¼ cups (34 fl oz/1 liter) hot vegetable broth (stock)
1 lb/450 g suckling pig shoulder, chopped
1 clove garlic, crushed
1 rosemary sprig
salt

Soak the saffron in ¾ cup plus 1 tablespoon (7 fl oz/200 ml) warm water in a small bowl for 10 minutes.

Heat ⅓ cup plus 1 tablespoon (3½ fl oz/100 ml) oil in a skillet (frying pan), add the onion, ginger, lemongrass, and mint, and cook over low heat for 5 minutes. Add the fava (broad) beans and cook for a few minutes, then pour over the vegetable broth (stock) and infused saffron water and cook for 25–30 minutes until the fava beans are very soft and disintegrating. At the end of the cooking time, beat the mixture until the beans break down to a thick purée. Taste to check the seasoning and add salt if necessary. Keep warm.

Put the pork, 2 tablespoons oil, and a pinch of salt into a bowl and mix well. Heat a separate dry nonstick skillet, add the pork, garlic, and rosemary, and cook over high heat for 4–5 minutes until slightly browned and cooked through.

Serve the fava bean purée with the meat.

WINE SUGGESTION Nero d'Avola is the king of Sicilian wines. It comes from coastal vineyards that overlook the Strait of Sicily, and it develops cherry, red berry, and licorice aromas. This wine has a vibrant tannin content that underlies its softness, and it should be drunk with meats.

⊙   Preparation time: 25 minutes

        Cooking time: 20 minutes

♀   Wine suggestion: Fiano di Avellino

Sirloin Steak with Herbs

Serves 4

7 oz/200 g pearl (baby)
   onions (ideally Borettane
   onions), unpeeled

3½ tablespoons balsamic
   vinegar

2 teaspoons superfine (caster)
   sugar

¼ oz/10 g butter

2 cups (11 oz/300 g) peeled
   and diced potatoes

1 mint sprig, leaves chopped

2–3 basil leaves, chopped

1 marjoram sprig, leaves
   chopped, plus extra to
   garnish

4 sprigs thyme, to garnish

4 tablespoons extra virgin
   olive oil

4 (5-oz/150-g) beef sirloin
   steaks

salt

Cook the onions in a large pan of boiling salted water for 6–7 minutes until soft. Let cool.

Peel the onions, leaving them whole. Put the onions, vinegar, sugar, butter, and a pinch of salt into a pan and cook over low heat for 7–8 minutes until caramelized.

Meanwhile, cook the potatoes in a large pan of boiling salted water for 12–15 minutes until they just start to disintegrate. Drain well. Transfer to a bowl and mash the potatoes with a fork, then add the herbs, oil, and a pinch of salt and mix well.

Heat a cast-iron griddle pan until very hot, add the steaks, and cook over high heat for 1 minute on each side.

To serve, divide the potatoes among serving plates, put the steaks on top, garnish with a few extra marjoram and thyme sprigs, and accompany with the glazed onions.

🕐 Preparation time: 20 minutes

Cooking time: 25 minutes

🍷 Wine suggestion: Oltrepò Pavese Barbera

Osso Buco

Serves 4

4 (7–9-oz/200–250-g) beef
  shanks (shin)
extra virgin olive oil
1 onion, finely chopped
type 00 flour, for dusting
⅓ cup plus 1 tablespoon (3½
  fl oz/100 ml) white wine
¾ cup plus 1 tablespoon
  (7 fl oz/200 ml) hot
  vegetable broth (stock)
1 celery stalk,
  coarsely chopped
1 carrot, coarsely chopped
grated zest of 1 unwaxed
  lemon
1 flat-leaf parsley sprig,
  chopped
salt and pepper
Potato Purée (see page 256),
  to serve

Wash the beef shanks (shin), dry with paper towels, and use a knife to make two little cuts in the side of each shank—this will help them to keep their shape while cooking.

Heat a little oil in a pan, add the onion, and cook over low heat for 3–4 minutes until soft.

Dust the shanks with flour and then add them to the pan with the onion and cook for 3 minutes on each side, or until brown. Pour over the wine and cook until the wine has evaporated, then pour over the broth (stock) and cook for 5 minutes more. Add the celery, carrot, lemon zest, and most of the parsley and season with salt and pepper. Cook, stirring, for a few minutes, then cover and cook for an additional 5 minutes.

Divide the beef shanks and sauce among serving plates, garnish with the remaining parsley, and serve with quenelles of potato purée.

⊙ Preparation time: 15 minutes
   Cooking time: 15 minutes
♀ Wine suggestion: Trento Rosé Metodo Classico

Pork with Sauerkraut and Prunes

Serves 4

8 (2¹/₄-oz/60-g) slices pork loin
type 00 flour, for dusting
4 tablespoons sunflower oil
¹/₂ cup (4 fl oz/125 ml) dry
   white wine
¹/₄ cup (2 oz/50 g) sauerkraut
12 prunes, pitted (stoned)
salt and pepper
1 flat-leaf parsley sprig, finely
   chopped, to garnish

Place the slices of pork loin on the countertop and lightly beat them with a meat tenderizer to flatten and enlarge them. Dust both side of the pork loin with flour and season with salt and pepper.

Heat the oil in a skillet (frying pan), add the meat, and cook over medium heat for 2–3 minutes on each side until the meat changes color. Pour over the wine and cook until the wine has evaporated, then add the sauerkraut and prunes, cover, and cook over low heat for 5 minutes more.

To serve, divide among serving plates and garnish with the parsley.

NOTE Sauerkraut is a specialty of the Trentino and Alto Adige regions of Italy. Made by fermenting cabbage and turnips, sauerkraut has an acid taste and is pale yellow in color. Starting with a layer of cabbage leaves, the sauerkraut is made by packing alternating layers of thinly sliced cabbages and turnips into a barrel and sprinkling each layer with salt and flavorings. Once the barrel is full, a final layer of cabbage leaves is added and then a weight is placed on top to press down firmly on the contents. After a fermentation period of 1 week at room temperature, followed by 3–4 weeks in a cool place, the sauerkraut is ready to be used.

HOW TO RECOGNIZE GOOD-QUALITY MEAT

Which is the best cut of meat? Depending on how the meat is cooked, it is possible to make the most of any cut. However, it is essential to choose a product of "traceable" quality.

REARING

There are various ways to rear animals but it is generally preferable to choose meat from animals that live and are fed in a natural way, free-range (or mostly free-range), rather than animals that are reared indoors. Free-range living contributes to the quality of life of the animal and therefore to the flavor and healthiness of the meat.

Conventional intensive rearing takes little account of the animal's welfare or its impact on the environment. It has also contributed to the extensive use of very productive breeds that are suitable for indoor rearing, and thus to the disappearance of ancient breeds. For this reason, the FAO (Food and Agriculture Organization) considers the livestock sector to be one of the industries with the greatest responsibility for the loss of our planet's biodiversity.

In Europe, ovines and poultry dominate the market and have facilitated the development of industrial breeding methods. For this reason, if possible, it is best to try alternatives such as turkey, pigeon, guinea fowl, duck, and pheasant. We also advise choosing meat from animals bred and slaughtered locally, from species linked to the traditions of the land and from groups, associations, or farms abiding by rigorous protocols.

CUTS

No cut is absolutely the best: for every cut it is possible to create dishes that enhance their specific characteristics. For example, the best cut for vitello tonnato (veal with tuna sauce) is a lean cut such as the round or rump roast (silverside), while cheek is excellent for stews. Tenderloin or filet mignon (fillet steak) is not the only choice of beef cut; choosing lesser-known and cheaper cuts also means reducing waste. Generally speaking, a cut rich in connective tissue (such as chuck or shoulder, also known as "the priest's hat") needs longer cooking times at lower temperatures while a lean cut (such as tenderloin) should be cooked quickly at a high temperature, broiled (grilled), or spit-roasted.

Let's not forget offal: pickled tongue, stewed tripe, and thinly sliced kidneys cooked in garlic and parsley are classic dishes made with the "fifth quarter" of the animal (left over when the two front quarters and the two hindquarters are removed). Chicken or pigeon giblets can be a tasty ingredient for many preparations, such as sauces and risotto.

QUALITY AND TRACEABILITY

There are few but essential elements to determine the quality of meat, starting with marbling: the presence of intramuscular fat, characteristic of pasture-raised cattle. The fat makes cooked meat more tender and more flavorsome. If the fat is yellowish it is not necessarily a bad sign, because some animals reared on pasture graze on grasses rich in carotene, which will make their fat yellow; in this case the color is a sign of the animal's good health.

Hanging, or aging the meat at low temperature after slaughter, is just as important. This process lasts a few days for chickens, 4–10 days for pigs, sheep, and goats, and 8–20 days for beef. In particular, in the case of beef and game, hanging tenderizes the meat and makes it tastier.

Finally, it is essential to be able to trace the meat, as this helps to retrace the animal's history. Ask your trusted butcher or read the labels, which say much but not everything. Look for: country of origin (breeding, rearing, and slaughter); the name and address of the company that has selected the animal and packaged the cut for retail; weight and commercial definition (species, category, and cut); sell-by date; and recommendations for storage.

To sum up, be wary of prices that are too low, which often indicates the very poor quality of the feed used. Good-quality meat costs more to produce, and this justifies its higher price.

Preparation time: 15 minutes

Cooking time: 40 minutes

Wine suggestion: Alto Adige Pinot Bianco

Chicken with Grapes

Serves 4

4 tablespoons vegetable oil

1 (1³/₄–2¹/₄ lb/800 g–1-kg) chicken, cut into pieces (see tip on pag 278)

¹/₃ cup plus 1 tablespoon (3¹/₂ fl oz/100 ml) white wine

2 cloves garlic

1 rosemary sprig

2 sage leaves

5 juniper berries

1²/₃ cups (9 oz/250 g) mixed seedless green and red grapes

salt and pepper

Heat the oil in a large skillet (frying pan), add the chicken, and cook over medium heat until golden all over. Carefully spoon off the fat from the skillet, then pour over the wine and cook until the wine has evaporated. Add the whole garlic cloves, herbs, and juniper berries and season with salt and pepper. Cover and cook over medium heat for 30 minutes, turning the chicken frequently. Add the grapes and cook for 5 minutes more. Serve hot or warm.

TIP You can serve this chicken with polenta bruschetta. Pour 4¹/₄ cups (34 fl oz/1 liter) salted water into a pan and bring to a boil, then gradually sprinkle in 2 cups (9 oz/250 g) coarse cornmeal, stirring all the time with a wooden spoon to prevents lumps forming. Cover and cook over low heat for 40 minutes, stirring from time to time. Pour the polenta onto a wooden board and let cool. Cut the polenta into ¹/₂-inch/1-cm slices. Heat a cast-iron griddle pan until very hot, then add the polenta and cook over medium heat for 5–6 minutes until it forms a crust. Serve the polenta bruschetta plain or top it with a little stracchino cheese or lardo.

Preparation time: 30 minutes

Cooking time: 50 minutes

Wine suggestion: Verdicchio dei Castelli di Jesi

Beef and Potato Gratin

Serves 4

2½ tablespoons extra
   virgin olive oil, plus extra
   for greasing
1 small onion, chopped
1 carrot, chopped
1 celery stalk, chopped
1 clove garlic, crushed
14 oz/400 g coarsely ground
   (minced) beef
1¼ cups (11 oz/300 g)
   canned crushed tomatoes
4 cups (1 lb 5 oz/600 g)
   peeled and diced potatoes
⅓ cup plus 1 tablespoon
   (3½ fl oz/100 ml) milk
2 tablespoons (1¼ oz/
   30 g) butter
pinch of ground nutmeg
scant 1 cup (3½ oz/100 g)
   grated Emmental cheese
salt

Heat the oil in a large skillet (frying pan), add the onion, carrot, celery, and garlic, and cook over medium heat for 3–4 minutes until brown. Add the meat and cook for 10 minutes, stirring frequently, until brown. Add the tomatoes, season with salt, and cook over medium heat for about 20 minutes until the sauce has thickened.

Meanwhile, cook the potatoes in a pan of boiling salted water for 20 minutes, or until a knife inserted into them comes out easily. Drain well. Return the potatoes to the pan, mash with a potato masher, then stir in the milk, butter, nutmeg, and ½ teaspoon salt.

Preheat the oven to 400°F/200°C/Gas mark 6. Grease an 8 x 6-inch/20 x 15-cm ovenproof dish with oil.

Pour the meat sauce into the prepared ovenproof dish and level it out with the back of a spoon. Cover with the mashed potatoes and then sprinkle the Emmental over the top. Bake in the oven for 25 minutes, or until golden.

TIP If you prefer a dish with bolder flavors, replace the mild Emmental cheese with the same quantity of fontina cheese. Fontina cheese is made in the Aosta Valley region of Italy, where cows graze at high altitude on aromatic flowers and herbs to produce a tasty POD (Protected Designation of Origin) cheese that is ideal for hot dishes, and melts to a smooth and creamy consistency.

⊙ Preparation time: 15 minutes

Cooking time: 20 minutes

♀ Wine suggestion: Chianti Colli Fiorentini

Veal Medallions with Endive and Pumpkin Purée

Serves 4

2²/₃ cups (14 oz/400 g) diced pumpkin flesh

2 tablespoons (1¼ oz/30 g) butter

2 heads Belgian endive (chicory), cut into quarters lengthwise

extra virgin olive oil

1 clove garlic, crushed

1 rosemary sprig, plus extra to garnish

14 oz/400 g fillet of veal, cut into slices about ⅝ inch/ 1½ cm thick

salt and pepper

Put the pumpkin into a pan with ¾ cup plus 1 tablespoon (7 fl oz/200 ml) water and cook over medium heat for 15 minutes until soft and dry, adding a little more water to the pan if it starts to dry out before the pumpkin is cooked. Transfer to a food processor, add the butter and a pinch each of salt and pepper, and blend until creamy. If the consistency is too thick, add a little milk to loosen the mixture.

Meanwhile, preheat the oven to 400°F/200°C/Gas mark 6. Line a baking sheet with parchment (baking) paper.

Arrange the endive (chicory) on the prepared baking sheet, drizzle over a little oil, sprinkle with a pinch of salt, and bake in the oven for 8 minutes.

Heat a little oil in a large skillet (frying pan), add the garlic and rosemary, and cook over medium heat for 1 minute, then add the veal medallions and cook for 2–3 minutes on each side until brown but still rare inside. Season with salt.

Garnish the medallions with a few extra rosemary sprigs and serve with the endive and pumpkin purée.

NOTE Veal from suckling calves (exclusively fed on their mothers' milk) has a milky taste and a very light pink color, with fat that is white without any darker shades. If the fat has a reddish color or the meat is darker, the animal has been reared with flour, grass, or cereals. The taste of veal is not as strong as beef and this is why it is ideal for so many different recipes, from vitello tonnato (veal with tuna sauce) to roasts or medallions, like this recipe, which are cooked for a short time so the meat stays tender.

Guinea Fowl with White Grapes and Pancetta

Serves 4

4²/₃ cups (1 lb 8¹/₂ oz/700 g) white grapes, cut in half and seeded
extra virgin olive oil
7 oz/200 g smoked pancetta or bacon, cut into strips
¹/₂ white onion, chopped
8 guinea fowl thighs
salt
a few sage leaves, to garnish

Preheat the oven to 350°F/180°C/Gas mark 4.

Put half the grapes into a food processor and blend until smooth. Strain the mixture through a cheesecloth (muslin) into a bowl, squeezing the grape pulp well to extract all the juice.

Heat a little oil in a large pan, add the pancetta or bacon and onion, and cook over low heat for 5 minutes, or until brown. Add the guinea fowl thighs and cook for about 5 minutes until brown all over. Add the grape juice and the remaining grapes and cook over medium heat for about 15 minutes until reduced by one third. Season with salt. Transfer to an ovenproof dish and bake in the oven for 10 minutes.

To serve, divide among serving plates and garnish with sage.

NOTE   A guinea fowl is halfway between a chicken and a pheasant, and it is classed as poultry. If a guinea fowl is more than 8 months old then it needs to be hung. The meat is dark with a full, strong flavor. It is very lean, but contains plenty of essential protein and iron. Guinea fowl is often used in dishes served for special occasions, usually stuffed with chestnuts or prunes, or flavored with spices and herbs, such as juniper. If you like strong, bold flavors, try a stuffing made from sausage, walnuts, and Gorgonzola cheese, which is perfect for the winter months.

CHEF
Lorenza Alcantara

Preparation time: 20 minutes, plus marinating
Cooking time: 20 minutes

Five-spice Beef with Onion and Orange and Fennel Sauce

Serves 4

14 oz/400 g beef tenderloin,
   cut into even-sized pieces
1¼ teaspoons Chinese
   five-spice powder
3 tablespoons soy sauce
extra virgin olive oil
11 oz/300 g fennel, chopped
1 scallion (spring
   onion), chopped
grated zest of 1
   unwaxed orange
⅓ cup (2¼ oz/60 g) superfine
   (caster) sugar
2 red onions (ideally red
   Tropea onions),
   cut into wedges
scant ½ cup (3½ fl oz/100 ml)
   white wine vinegar
salt

To garnish
orange slices
mixed baby leaf
   salad (optional)

Put the beef, Chinese five-spice powder, soy sauce, and 3 tablespoons oil into a bowl and stir well. Cover and let marinate in the refrigerator for 2 hours.

Make the sauce. Heat a little oil in a pan, add the fennel, scallion (spring onion), and orange zest, and cook over low heat for 15 minutes, or until the fennel is soft. Stir in a pinch of salt, then transfer to a food processor or blender and blend until smooth. Keep warm.

Make a dressing by bringing the vinegar and sugar to a boil in pan, then remove from the heat, and let cool.

Meanwhile, bring a large pan of water to a boil. Fill a large bowl with iced water and set it beside the stove. Drop the onions into the boiling water and leave for 2 minutes. Drain, plunge into the iced water, then drain again thoroughly. Transfer to a bowl, pour over the dressing, and toss thoroughly.

Heat a little oil in a skillet (frying pan), add the marinated beef and a pinch of salt, and cook over high heat for 5 minutes, or until the outside of the beef changes color.

To serve, spoon the sauce onto serving plates, then top with the beef and the onions, garnish with orange slices and some mixed baby leaf salad (if using), and drizzle over a little oil.

WINE SUGGESTION Arnus Langhe Arneis 2013 is a wine made from Arneis grapes that are left to macerate at low temperatures to bring out vibrant notes. Arnus has a decisive taste and is easy to drink. A tricky food combination is proposed here. We will let the wine tasters decide …

COOKING MEAT

Cooking meat is one of the most common operations in the kitchen and yet, at the same time, it is an art that requires experience, especially when aiming for excellence.

This topic can be dealt with from different points of views: from considering the physical-chemical variables that act on the molecular structure of the meat, to the meat's sensory characteristics, to the practices of the gastronomic traditions in different countries.

EXPERIENCE AND BALANCE

Italy boasts a wide range of cooking techniques, depending on the type of meat and the desired result: roasting, braising, broiling (grilling), cooking with gravies and sauces, en croute, boiling, and frying. At the heart of every recipe is the delicate balance of the different chemical reactions involved, which have both positive and negative effects. First of all, cooking causes the deterioration of proteins: in other words, it irreversibly alters the meat's molecular structure. This increases its digestibility, as it frees amino acids, but at the same time has an impact on its consistency, causing hardening of the muscular fibers. On the other hand, cooking also has an impact on fat and collagen, causing them to melt and thus softening the meat. It is therefore always necessary to adapt the type and time of cooking to the cut and type of meat (white, red, or game). Keep in mind that other factors will also have an impact on the final result, such as hanging time (the time between slaughter and consumption), the meat's fat content, and its marbling pattern.

A MATTER OF TIME AND TEMPERATURE

Italy's countless traditional recipes can be grouped into two main methods: whether the meat is in contact with accompanying liquids or exposed directly to the heat. Under the first heading there are braising and boiling, cooking in gravy, and roasting, while under the second we find broiling, spit-roasting, and frying.

The high temperature used in boiling guarantees a greater degree of tenderness, because it causes the tightening of pores in the outer layer of the meat. This prevents the meat's juices from dispersing. On the other hand, to make broth (stock) and gravy it is preferable to add the meat to liquid that is still cold, to ensure a greater exchange of flavors and aromas.

Another variable to take into consideration is the intensity of the heat: in the case of boiled and braised meats, the cooking must be slow and even, over a low heat. High heat, however, is well suited to quickly sautéing smaller cuts in a skillet (frying pan).

For successful broiling or spit-roasting, and for frying, it is essential to have good control of times and temperatures. A high heat ensures the formation of a sealed outer surface, which retains the meat's juices: in this way the meat will be crisp on the outside while still tender on the inside. It is necessary to achieve a good balance between cooking time and distance from the heat source, especially in the case of the broiler (grill) or spit-roast, to avoid burning the outside of the meat while leaving the inside uncooked.

Finally, the same recipe can be adapted to individual taste by choosing three levels of cooking: "rare", "medium", or "well done". In this case it is very useful to have a meat thermometer to measure the internal temperature, which cannot be easily determined otherwise.

Preparation time: 25 minutes, plus soaking
Cooking time: 30 minutes
Wine suggestion: Colli di Luni Rosso

Stuffed Veal Rolls

Serves 4

1 bread roll
³/₄ cup plus 1 tablespoon
   (7 fl oz/200 ml) white wine
1¹/₄ oz/30 g dried mushrooms
7 oz/200 g ground
   (minced) veal
1 clove garlic, crushed
1 flat-leaf parsley sprig,
   chopped
2 marjoram sprigs,
   leaves chopped
1 tablespoon pine nuts
2 eggs, beaten
¹/₃ cup (1¹/₄ oz/30 g) grated
   Parmesan cheese
8 (2–2¹/₄-oz/50–60-g)
   slices veal
piece of butter
1¹/₄ cups (11 oz/300 g) tomato
   purée (passata)
¹/₃ cup plus 1 tablespoon (3¹/₂
   fl oz/100 ml) hot vegetable
   broth (stock)
salt and pepper

To serve
vegetable crudites
mixed baby leaf salad
extra virgin olive oil

Remove the soft crumbs from the inside of the bread roll, discarding the crust, and place them in a bowl with ¹/₃ cup plus 1 tablespoon (3¹/₂ fl oz/100 ml) of the wine. Let soak briefly, then remove and tear the bread into small pieces.

Put the dried mushrooms in a bowl, cover with warm water, and let soak for 10 minutes. Remove the mushrooms, squeeze out any excess water, and chop into small pieces.

Heat a dry skillet (frying pan), then add the ground (minced) veal, garlic, parsley, marjoram, pine nuts, mushrooms, and soaked bread and cook over medium heat for 10–15 minutes until the meat is brown. Transfer to a bowl and let cool. Add the eggs, Parmesan, and a pinch each of salt and pepper and mix well—the mixture should have a thick consistency.

Lay out the slices of veal on the countertop and spread the ground veal mixture on top. Roll up the veal slices and secure them with kitchen string.

Melt the butter in a large pan, add the veal rolls, and cook over medium heat for 5 minutes, or until brown on all sides. Pour over the remaining wine and cook over high heat until the wine has evaporated, then add the puréed canned tomatoes (passata) and broth (stock) and cook for 15–20 minutes until the veal is soft and a cocktail stick (toothpick) inserted into the meat comes out easily.

Cut the veal rolls into slices. Divide among serving plates and serve with the sauce, accompanied with some vegetable crudites, a mixed baby leaf salad, and a small dipping bowl of olive oil seasoned with salt and pepper.

Preparation time: 20 minutes
Cooking time: 40 minutes
Lager suggestion: Pale lager

Chicken with Lager

Serves 4

4 onions (about 1 lb 2 oz/ 500 g), thickly sliced
3½ oz/100 g pancetta or bacon, diced
generous 2 cups (17 fl oz/ 500 ml) pale lager
1 (2¼-lb/1-kg) chicken, cut into pieces (see tip)
3 rosemary sprigs, plus extra to garnish
salt and pepper

Heat a dry nonstick skillet (frying pan), add the onions, pancetta or bacon, and 4 tablespoons of the lager, and cook over medium heat for 4–5 minutes until the fat from the pancetta has melted. Add the chicken pieces to the skillet, piling the onions and pancetta on top. Season with salt and pepper, pour over the remaining lager, add the rosemary and sage, and cook over medium heat for 30 minutes. Transfer to the serving platter and garnish with extra rosemary leaves.

TIP To prepare a whole chicken, burn off any remaining feathers with a lighted taper, then wash the bird thoroughly, rinse, and wipe dry. Using a pair of poultry shears, cut the chicken in half, starting by cutting along the breastbone and then along the backbone. Cut each half in two and then slice the resulting pieces in half, so you have eight pieces. Detach the wings from the breast and the drumsticks from the thighs.

🕐　Preparation time: 20 minutes

　　Cooking time: 25 minutes

♀　Wine suggestion: Verdicchio del Castelli di Jesi Classico Superiore

Baked Chicken Rolls

Serves 4

4 skinless chicken breasts
1 rosemary sprig, leaves
　finely chopped
2–3 sage leaves,
　finely chopped
2 bay leaves, finely chopped
1 thyme sprig, finely chopped
extra virgin olive oil
20 slices pancetta or bacon
2 onions, chopped
1/3 cup plus 1 tablespoon
　(31/2 fl oz/100 ml) white wine
salt and pepper

To serve
salad leaves (greens)
pickled onions

Preheat the oven to 350°F/180°C/Gas mark 4.

Butterfly the chicken breasts. Using a sharp knife, cut each breast along its length, stopping just before you reach the other side. Open out each breast, cover it with plastic wrap (clingfilm), and pummel gently with a rolling pin until it is an even thickness.

In a small bowl, mix together the herbs and with 1/2 teaspoon salt. Sprinkle the herb and salt mixture all over the butterflied chicken breasts and then drizzle 2 tablespoons oil over the chicken.

Lay two slices of pancetta or bacon on top of a chicken breast, then roll it up into a cylinder, wrap another three slices of pancetta around the roll, and secure with kitchen string. Repeat with the remaining chicken breasts and pancetta.

Heat a little oil in a Dutch oven (casserole dish), add the onions, and cook over low heat for 4–5 minutes until golden. Add the chicken rolls and cook for 5–6 minutes, turning occasionally, until lightly brown on all sides. Pour over the wine and cook until it has evaporated. Season with pepper. Bake in the oven for 15 minutes until golden and cooked through.

Transfer the chicken rolls to a carving board, reserving the cooking juices, and cut into slices.

Pour the reserved cooking juices into a bowl and use an immersion blender to blend to a smooth sauce.

Serve the slices of chicken roll with the sauce, accompanied with some salad leaves (greens) and pickled onions.

Preparation time: 25 minutes
Cooking time: 50 minutes
Wine suggestion: Etna Rosso

Rabbit with Grapes and Porcini Mushrooms

Serves 4

1 (2¼-lb/1-kg) rabbit,
    cut into pieces
4 tablespoons extra virgin
    olive oil
³⁄₄ cup plus 1 tablespoon
    (7 fl oz/200 ml) white wine
1 (4-oz/120-g) slice pancetta
    or bacon, diced
2–3 sage leaves
2 bay leaves
³⁄₄ cup plus 1 tablespoon
    (7 fl oz/200 ml) hot
    vegetable stock
14 oz/400 g small porcini
    (ceps), sliced
1 clove garlic, crushed
1 tablespoon chopped
    flat-leaf parsley
2 cups (11 oz/300 g)
    mixed seedless green
    and red grapes
salt and pepper

Season the rabbit with salt and pepper. Heat 2 tablespoons of the oil in a pan, add the rabbit, and cook over medium heat for 7–8 minutes until golden all over. Pour over the wine and cook until the wine has evaporated. Lower the heat, add the pancetta or bacon, sage, and bay leaves, cover, and cook for 30 minutes, checking from time to time and adding a little vegetable stock if the cooking juices dry up.

Meanwhile, heat the remaining oil in a skillet (frying pan), add the mushrooms and garlic, cover, and cook over medium heat for a few minutes until brown. Stir in the parsley and season with salt.

Add the mushrooms and grapes to the pan with the rabbit and cook for an additional 10 minutes. Serve hot.

NOTE An ancient method for breeding rabbits is used on the island of Ischia, near Naples, and this technique has been recognized by a Slow Food Presidium. Caves that are 10–13 feet/3–4 meters deep are dug into the ground and used to breed rabbits. These caves are similar to burrows where the rabbits can move and dig, as if they were living in the wild. The small Liparina and a' Paregn rabbit breeds were once common here, but have now disappeared. A few of the caves on Ischia are still in use, but thanks to the Slow Food Presidium, efforts are being made to reinstate this technique—restoring some of the thousand or so caves that still exist—to promote this traditional method of breeding.

⊙   Preparation time: 25 minutes

       Cooking time: 30 minutes

♀   Wine suggestion: Sannio Piedirosso

Meatballs with Tomato Sauce

Serves 4

1 cup (3½ oz/100 g) fine,
  slightly stale breadcrumbs

1 cup (8 fl oz/250 ml) milk

12 oz/350 g mixed ground
  (minced) meats

2 eggs, beaten

2 tablespoons finely chopped
  flat-leaf parsley

1 clove garlic, crushed

3 tablespoons grated
  pecorino cheese (ideally
  Percorino Toscana cheese)

⅓ cup (1¼ oz/30 g) grated
  Parmesan cheese

3 tablespoons extra virgin
  olive oil

1 small onion, finely chopped

½ cup (4 fl oz/125 ml)
  dry white wine

1¼ cups (10½ oz/300 g)
  canned chopped tomatoes

salt and pepper

Put the breadcrumbs and milk into a bowl and let soak for 10 minutes, then remove the bread and squeeze out any excess milk.

Mix together the ground (minced) meats, eggs, 1 tablespoon of the parsley, garlic, pecorino and Parmesan in a large bowl. Season with salt and pepper, add the soaked bread, and mix thoroughly. Using your hands, shape the mixture into round meatballs, each about ¾ inch/2 cm in diameter.

Heat the oil in a large skillet (frying pan), add the onion, and cook over low heat for 2–3 minutes until the onion starts to sweat. Add the meatballs and cook for 5–6 minutes, turning frequently, until lightly brown all over. Pour over the wine and cook until the wine has evaporated, then add the tomatoes and simmer for 20–25 minutes until the meatballs are cooked through and the sauce has thickened. Sprinkle over the remaining parsley and serve.

TIP   This recipe can be made into a more substantial one-course dish with the addition of peas and serving it with bread or a rice pilaf. Follow the recipe above, adding 1½ cups (7 oz/200 g) petits pois with the chopped tomatoes. If there is some tomato and pea sauce left over, reheat it the next day to accompany short pasta, and sprinkle with grated Parmesan just before serving.

⏱ Preparation time: 20 minutes
Cooking time: 10–15 minutes
Ⴘ Wine suggestion: Cerasuolo di Vittoria

Fillet of Beef with Pistachios

Serves 4

1¼ cups (10 fl oz/300 ml)
   red wine
¼ cup (2 oz/50 g)
   chestnut honey
extra virgin olive oil
8 slices smoked pancetta
   or lean (streaky) bacon
4 (3½-oz/100-g) fillets
   of beef
salt

To garnish
¾ cup (3½ oz/100 g) shelled
   unsalted pistachios,
   coarsely chopped
rosemary sprigs (optional)

Prepare the wine glaze. Pour the wine into a small pan, add the honey, and boil until the mixture has thickened. (If you have a kitchen thermometer, check the temperature: when it reaches 210°F/100°C the glaze is ready.) Keep warm.

Wrap the pancetta or bacon around the circumference of the beef fillets and secure with kitchen string. If you prefer your steak well done, preheat the oven to 400°F/200°C/Gas mark 6.

Heat a little oil in a skillet (frying pan). When the oil is very hot, add the beef fillets and cook over medium heat for 2–3 minutes until brown, then turn over, sprinkle with a little salt, and cook for an additional 2–3 minutes until the other side is well colored. For well-done steak, transfer the beef fillets to a roasting pan and bake in the oven for 5 minutes more.

When the beef is cooked to your liking, remove the string and transfer to serving plates. Drizzle over the wine glaze and garnish with the pistachios and a few tender tips of rosemary, if liked.

NOTE From the nineteenth century onwards the Piedmontese white cattle became the ideal breed of cattle in the region of Alba and Cuneo in Piedmont. Although the rearing of this breed has drastically declined, the Slow Food Presidium has recently encouraged it and now small producers have to adhere to a very strict code of practice, feeding the animals only on natural fodder. This meat is exceptional: its cholesterol content is very low and it contains the ideal amount of intra-muscular fat that keeps the meat lean but makes it incredibly tasty.

CHEF
Gianluca Esposito

Preparation time: 45 minutes, plus resting
Cooking time: 2 hours
Wine suggestion: Barolo Brandini 2008

Pork Shank with Cavolo Nero and Potatoes

Serves 4

1 clove garlic, chopped
1 rosemary sprig, chopped
2–3 sage leaves, chopped
1 bay leaf, chopped
3¼-lb/1.5-kg pork shanks
   (shins)
¾ cup plus 1 tablespoon
   (7 fl oz/200 ml) dry white
   wine (ideally Pignoletto)
extra virgin olive oil
7½ cups (1 lb 2 oz/
   500 g) chopped cavolo nero
   (Tuscan black cabbage)
2 cups (11 oz/300 g) peeled
   and chopped potatoes
1 small yellow onion, chopped
salt and pepper

Mix together the garlic, herbs, and ½ teaspoon salt in a small bowl. Rub the herb and salt mixture all over the meat. Cover and let rest in the refrigerator overnight.

Preheat the oven to 350°F/180°C/Gas mark 4.

Put the shanks (shins) into a large roasting pan and pour over the wine and 4 tablespoons oil. Bake in the oven for 30 minutes. Pour over just enough hot water (or you could use broth/stock) so that three-quarters of the meat is covered. Cover with aluminum foil, return to the oven and bake for 1 hour, checking every so often that there is still cooking liquid in the pan and topping up with a little more hot water if necessary. The meat is ready when it is soft and comes easily away from the bone. Put the meat onto a warmed platter, cover, and let rest for 15 minutes while you make the sauce and the potatoes and cavolo nero (Tuscan black cabbage).

To make the sauce, strain the meat cooking juices into a small pan and cook over medium heat for 7–8 minutes until reduced by one third.

Cook the potatoes and cavolo nero in a large pan of boiling salted water for 10 minutes until soft. Drain well.

Meanwhile, just before the end of the cooking time for the potatoes and cavolo nero, heat a little oil in a large skillet (frying pan), add the onion, and cook over low heat for 5–6 minutes until soft and translucent.

Add the drained potatoes and cavolo nero to the skillet with the onion and cook until the potatoes break up and are mixed with the cavolo nero. Season with salt and pepper and stir in 2 tablespoons oil.

Glaze the meat with the sauce and serve with the cavolo nero and potatoes.

CHEF
Gianluca Esposito

⊙ Preparation time: 40 minutes
Cooking time: 3 hours 35 minutes
♀ Wine suggestion: Brandini & Brandini Langhe Rosso 2012

Chicken Breasts with Red Bell Pepper Sauce and Poached Eggs

Serves 4

extra virgin olive oil
3 red bell peppers, cored,
   seeded, and cut into strips
1 clove garlic, unpeeled
1 marjoram sprig
¼ cup (1¼ oz/30 g)
   well-rinsed capers
1 tablespoon white
   wine vinegar
4 eggs
4 (3½-oz/100-g) skinless
   chicken breasts
2 cups (3½ oz/100 g)
   fresh breadcrumbs
chili flakes, for sprinkling
salt

For the chicken broth (stock)
1 lb 5 oz/600 g raw chicken
   carcasses
1 celery stalk, chopped
1 carrot, chopped
1 onion, chopped
1 thyme sprig
¾ cup plus 1 tablespoon
   (7 fl oz/200 ml) white wine

Preheat the oven to 400°F/200°C/Gas mark 6.

Make the chicken broth (stock). Wash the chicken carcasses and dry them with paper towels. Place them in a roasting pan and roast in the oven for 10–15 minutes until browned all over. Add the celery, carrot, onion, and thyme and roast for 10 minutes more. Transfer to a stock pot (stew pan), pour over the wine, and add just enough cold water to cover the carcasses and vegetables. Bring to a boil, then reduce the heat and simmer for 2 hours, skimming the surface occasionally. Strain the broth through a fine-mesh strainer (sieve) into a clean pan and boil until the broth has reduced by three quarters.

Heat a little oil in a separate pan, add the bell peppers, garlic, marjoram, capers, and a pinch of salt, cover, and cook over low heat until the liquid released by the peppers has evaporated, then pour over the chicken stock and cook for 10 minutes. Transfer to a food processor, blend until smooth, then strain through a fine-mesh strainer (sieve) into a clean pan. Keep warm.

Fill a small pan with water, add a pinch of salt and the vinegar, and bring to a boil. Break an egg into the pan and cook for a few minutes until the white is solid and the yolk is still soft. Remove with a slotted spoon and drain on paper towels. Repeat with the remaining eggs.

Under a hot broiler (grill) toast the bread for 5–6 minutes until golden and crispy. Crumble into fine crumbs.

Heat 2 tablespoons oil in a skillet (frying pan), add the chicken breasts, and cook over high heat for 10–12 minutes, turning the chicken halfway through the cooking time, until well browned but tender. Season with salt. Remove from the pan and cut each chicken breast into four pieces.

To serve, pour the bell pepper sauce over the plate and place a sliced chicken breast on top, sprinkle the chicken with the toasted breadcrumbs, arrange a poached egg on top, and sprinkle with chili flakes.

VEGETABLES AND LEGUMES

Preparation time: 15 minutes

Cooking time: 5 minutes

Wine suggestion: Vernaccia di San Gimignano

Panzanella Salad

Serves 4

8 slices stale rustic bread,
cut into chunks

1 cucumber, trimmed
and cubed

4 ripe tomatoes, thinly sliced,
plus extra to serve (optional)

1 red onion, thinly sliced

a few basil leaves, torn into
small pieces, plus extra to
serve (optional)

1/3 cup plus 1 tablespoon
(3 1/2 fl oz/100 ml) extra
virgin olive oil

3 tablespoons red
wine vinegar

vegetable oil, for deep-frying
type 00 flour, for coating

salt and pepper

Soften the bread with a little bit of water, then squeeze the excess water out, crumble the bread by hand, and transfer to a large salad bowl. Add the cucumber, tomatoes, a quarter of the onion, and the basil.

To make a dressing, whisk together the olive oil and vinegar in a small bowl and season with salt and pepper.

Pour the dressing over the salad and stir thoroughly, then place the salad in the refrigerator until you are ready to serve.

Meanwhile, pour enough vegetable oil for deep-frying into a deep-fat fryer or large deep pan and heat the oil to 340°F/170°C. Dip the remaining onion slices in flour, then carefully add the onions to the hot oil and cook until crispy. Remove with a slotted spoon and drain on paper towels. Season with salt.

Transfer the salad onto individual serving plates, sprinkle over the deep-fried onions, and garnish with some extra tomato slices and basil leaves, if liked.

NOTE Panzanella is a typical summer dish of central Italy, and there are many variations from region to region. In Tuscany, for instance, the bread is crumbled and then mixed with the other ingredients, whereas in Marche the bread slices are left whole, with the dressing put on top. Feel free to make your own variations: try a white onion instead of the red one, for example, or add some diced celery or a few olives.

⊙ Preparation time: 15 minutes
Cooking time: 15 minutes
♀ Wine suggestion: Collio Sauvignon

Omelet with Asparagus, Saffron, and Pecorino Cheese Cream Sauce

Serves 4

12 asparagus spears
5 eggs
2 teaspoons milk
1 saffron thread
1 tablespoon grated
  Parmesan cheese
4 tablespoons light
  (single) cream
5 oz/150 g grated pecorino
  cheese
extra virgin olive oil,
  for greasing
salt and pepper
mixed salad leaves (greens),
  to serve

Break off the tough part at the base of the asparagus spears and discard. Bring a large pan of salted water to a boil. Meanwhile, fill a large bowl with water and ice and place it beside the stove.

Add the asparagus to the boiling water and cook for a few minutes until al dente. Drain, plunge the asparagus immediately into the bowl of iced water, then drain again. Cut the asparagus spears into slices about 1/4 inch/5 mm thick, reserving the asparagus tips.

Beat the eggs in a large bowl. Add the milk, saffron, Parmesan, and a pinch of salt and pepper and beat again, then add the asparagus slices.

Heat the cream in a small pan, being careful not to let it boil. Remove from the heat, add the pecorino, and stir until the cheese has melted and you have a thick and homogenous cream sauce. Keep warm.

Grease a large nonstick skillet (frying pan) or baking pan with a little oil and heat the pan over high heat until hot. Pour the egg and asparagus mixture into the skillet, lower the heat, and cook the omelet for 3 minutes on each side, turning it with the help of a small plate or rubber spatula.

Divide the omelet into quarters and place on serving plates. Top the omelets with the reserved asparagus tips halved lengthwise and pour over the pecorino cream sauce. Serve immediately with a few mixed salad leaves (greens).

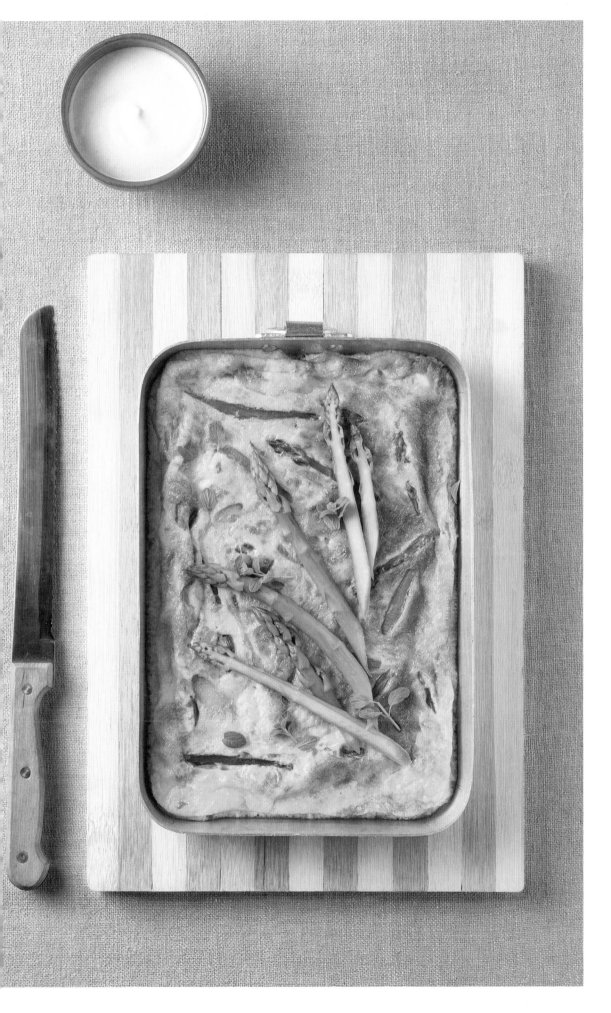

⊙ Preparation time: 20 minutes

Cooking time: 35 minutes

♀ Wine suggestion: Etna Rosé

Vegetable Couscous with Roasted Bell Pepper Sauce

Serves 4

1 cup (6¼ oz/180 g) couscous
extra virgin olive oil
2 red bell peppers
1 scallion (spring onion),
sliced
4 tablespoons vegetable
broth (stock)
1 carrot, diced
1 zucchini (courgette), diced
1 eggplant (aubergine), diced
½ red chile, finely chopped
1¼ cups (7 oz/200 g) rinsed
and drained canned
chickpeas
a few basil leaves, finely
chopped, plus extra to
garnish (optional)
a few mint leaves, finely
chopped, plus extra to
garnish (optional)
salt and pepper

Preheat the oven to 350°F/180°C/Gas mark 4.

Pour 1⅔ cups (14 fl oz/400 ml) water into a large pan, bring to a boil, and season lightly with salt. Remove from the heat, pour in the couscous, cover with a lid, and let stand for 10–15 minutes, or according to the package directions. Drizzle with a little oil and then use a fork to separate the couscous grains.

Meanwhile, put the bell peppers in a roasting pan and roast in the oven for 25 minutes or until bubbles form on the skin. Carefully put the roasted bell peppers into a plastic bag and let cool.

Meanwhile, heat a drizzle of oil in a skillet (frying pan), add the scallion (spring onion) and braise over low heat for 5 minutes until wilted.

Once the roasted bell peppers have cooled, peel off the skins, remove and discard the seeds and inner membrane, and coarsely chop the flesh. Transfer to a small bowl and use an immersion blender to purée the roasted bell peppers, adding a little of the vegetable broth (stock), if necessary, to dilute the sauce to a smooth and thick consistency. Stir in the braised scallion, taste to check the seasoning, and add salt and pepper if necessary.

Heat 3 tablespoons oil in a large skillet, add the remaining vegetables, chile, and chickpeas, and sauté over medium heat for 10 minutes until the vegetables are cooked. Season with salt and add the herbs. Stir the vegetable and chickpea mixture into the couscous.

Serve the vegetable couscous garnished with a few extra basil and mint leaves, if liked, with the bell pepper sauce on the side.

THE HEALTH BENEFITS
OF VEGETABLES

Every type of vegetable offers specific benefits for both health and sensory experience and a wide range of preparation and cooking methods are available to make the best of them.

RAW AND COOKED

Vegetables are good for us: it is a well known statement, but the manner in which vegetables are prepared and consumed is fundamental in ensuring an optimal absorption of the potentially beneficial substances they contain.

Vegetables must be grown using sustainable methods, they must be used in season and they must be, as far as possible, locally sourced. Otherwise there is the risk of dealing with products that are tasteless and lacking in nutrients, that are vegetables in name only, and are not only without any benefits but also have a negative impact on sustainability and the environment.

The benefits offered by vegetables start when we shop for them. Look for local varieties, have an inquiring approach, and a new world of flavors will open up to you.

Most vegetables can be used uncooked or cooked. The essential thing is that the product is fresh to start with. In many cases, from a nutritional point of view, it is better to consume uncooked vegetables, perhaps dressed to taste with extra virgin olive oil, which in the case of tomatoes and bell peppers facilitates the absorption of carotenoids, which are powerful antioxidants. However, some vegetables do need cooking.

Cooking, in any form, transforms the vegetable's molecular structure and breaks up nutrients, but also softens tissues that would otherwise be too tough. It also neutralizes poisonous or indigestible substances (as in the case of potatoes) and eliminates potentially harmful bacteria. Vegetables can be fried, sautéed, broiled (grilled), baked au gratin, boiled, parboiled, roasted, stewed, and poached (cooked in a liquid at a temperature of around 175°F/80°C, a delicate cooking method that, for example, makes spinach tender without altering its taste).

Alternatively, vegetables can be steamed to ensure that fewer minerals and vitamins are lost. Bell peppers, for example, retain a good proportion of their vitamin C.

WHY VEGETABLES ARE GOOD FOR US

Generally speaking vegetables are rich in fiber and low in calories (with the exception of potatoes) and therefore they help prevent obesity and diabetes. The main characteristics of the better-known and most frequently used vegetables are listed below.

Asparagus are diuretic and cleansing, and their benefits for the kidneys have been known since ancient times.

Carrots come in various forms and colors but the most commonly available carrots are yellow-orange and cylindrical ones, which are rich in carotene (a precursor of vitamin A) and antioxidants. They stimulate the production of melanin, boost eyesight and the immune system, and contain calcium to reinforce bones and teeth.

Onions are diuretic, rich in vitamins and minerals and also have antibiotic properties and help boost the immune system, all of which has a significant impact on the control of blood pressure and cholesterol. Cooking means that many of these qualities are lost but it makes them easier to digest.

Potatoes contain carbohydrates in the form of starch, as well as vitamins and minerals, such as potassium.

Bell peppers stimulate gland secretions and aid digestion. They are rich in carotenoids, minerals, and vitamins, containing more vitamin C than oranges.

Tomatoes are made mainly of water (90 percent) but contain vitamins, citric acid, and carotenoids (lycopene in particular), especially when ripe.

Finally, zucchini (courgettes) are rich in vitamins, calcium, iron, and phosphorous, and have diuretic, detoxing, and anti-inflammatory properties.

Preparation time: 10 minutes, plus desalting
Cooking time: 5 minutes
Wine suggestion: Bardolino Chiaretto

Tomato Salad with Salt Cod

Serves 4

14 oz/400 g salt cod, desalted
  (see tip on page 28), skin
  and bones removed, and
  cut into small pieces
1½ cups (10¾ fl oz /320 ml)
  extra virgin olive oil
grated zest of ½
  unwaxed lemon
a few black peppercorns
1 bay leaf
1 anchovy
2 tablespoons red
  wine vinegar
14 oz/400 g mixed varieties
  of tomatoes, thickly sliced
a few basil leaves
salt and pepper

To serve
salad leaves (greens)
toasted bread rubbed with
  garlic (optional)

Put the cod in a large pan with 1¼ cups (10 fl oz/300 ml) of the oil, the lemon zest, peppercorns, bay leaf, and anchovy. Cook over very low heat for 5 minutes, then remove from the heat, cover the pan with plastic wrap (clingfilm), and let stand for 10 minutes. Drain the cod thoroughly on paper towels.

To make the salad, whisk together the remaining oil and vinegar in a small bowl and season with salt and pepper. Put the tomatoes and basil in a salad bowl, pour over the dressing and toss well.

Serve the tomato salad and the cod with some salad leaves (greens) and large pieces of toasted bread rubbed with garlic, if liked.

Preparation time: 30 minutes
Cooking time: 45 minutes
Wine suggestion: Campi Flegrei Falanghina

Artichoke Parcels

Serves 4

3 artichokes
3 tablespoons extra virgin
   olive oil
2–3 slices hot chile
2¼ oz/60 g mozzarella
   cheese, diced
2 oz/50 g creamy, rindless
   cheese (ideally crescenza
   or other stracchino
   cheese), diced
¾ cup (2¼ oz /60 g) grated
   Parmesan cheese
2 eggs
⅓ cup (2¾ fl oz/80 ml) light
   (single) cream
butter, for greasing
type 00 flour, for dusting
11 oz/300 g puff pastry
1 egg yolk, beaten
salt and pepper

First prepare the artichokes. Trim the artichokes, discarding the inner chokes, the tougher outermost leaves, and their spiny tips. Cut them into wedges.

Heat the oil in a skillet (frying pan), add the chile, and cook over low heat for 1 minute, then add the artichoke wedges and cook for about 15 minutes until soft. Transfer the artichokes to a large bowl, add the mozzarella, crescenza, Parmesan, eggs, and cream, season with salt and pepper, and mix thoroughly.

Preheat the oven to 350°F/180°C/Gas mark 4. Grease a baking sheet with butter and dust with flour.

Roll out the puff pastry on a lightly floured countertop and cut out four large squares, about 4¾ x 4¾ inches/12 x 12 cm. Place a spoonful of the filling in the center of each square and then fold the corners of the pastry square toward the center to close up the parcels.

Place the parcels on the prepared baking sheet and brush the outsides of the parcels with the beaten egg yolk. Bake in the oven for 25–30 minutes until golden brown.

NOTE Cultivated artichokes can be split into two basic categories: with or without thorns. For this recipe we recommend using the Brindisi artichoke, which doesn't have thorns. This variety of artichoke is distinguished by its particularly tender flower head: the basal part of its leaves are compact, fleshy, and tender and the head is meaty and flavorful. Its sweet taste means that it is also perfect for eating raw.

Preparation time: 20 minutes, plus draining
Cooking time: 1 hour 15 minutes
Wine suggestion: Alcamo Rosé

Eggplant Caponata

Serves 4

4 eggplants (aubergines), cut
into small chunks
3 tablespoons extra virgin
olive oil
1 cup (3½ oz/100 g) pitted
(stoned) green olives
1 tablespoon capers
preserved in salt, rinsed
1 celery stalk, finely diced
3¼ lb/1.5 kg vine tomatoes,
chopped (about 8 ⅓ cups)
¼ cup (2 oz/50 g)
granulated sugar
3 tablespoons white
wine vinegar
salt and pepper

Place the eggplants (aubergines) in a colander, sprinkle with salt, and let drain for 30 minutes. Rinse the eggplants, drain again, then squeeze tightly to expel any excess moisture.

Heat the oil in a very large pan and cook the eggplant over medium heat for 8 minutes, then add the olives, capers, and celery and cook for 10 minutes more. Add the tomatoes and cook for 1 hour, stirring in the sugar and vinegar at the end of the cooking time. Taste to check the seasoning and add salt and pepper if necessary. Stir again.

The caponata can be served hot, warm, or cold, depending on your preference. It will keep for 2–3 months, stored in sterilized glass jars (see tip below) and kept in the refrigerator.

TIP To sterilize glass jars and lids, wash them in water and detergent, then heat them in a large pan of boiling water for 20 minutes, making sure they are covered by the water at all times. Lift the jars and lids out of the water with tongs and drain upside down on a clean dish towel. Dry thoroughly before filling the jars.

Preparation time: 20 minutes

Cooking time: 10 minutes

Wine suggestion: Colli Bolognesi Pignoletto Frizzante

Zucchini and Ham Salad

Serves 4

1 head or bunch of lettuce

1 zucchini (courgette),
   sliced lengthwise

4 tablespoons extra virgin
   olive oil

2 slices whole wheat
   (wholemeal) bread, cut into
   small cubes

4 slices cooked ham, cut into
   thin strips

2 tablespoons apple
   cider vinegar

1 tablespoon plain yogurt

1 teaspoon mild mustard

salt and pepper

Wash the lettuce and gently dry it. Cut it into fairly thin slices and put it in a large salad bowl.

Heat a griddle pan or skillet (frying pan) over high heat and cook the zucchini (courgette) for 1–2 minutes on each side until just starting to color.

Heat 2 tablespoons of the oil in a skillet, add the bread, and pan-fry over low heat for 5–6 minutes until golden brown and crisp.

Add the zucchini, ham, and bread cubes to the salad bowl and carefully toss to mix with the lettuce.

Make a dressing by stirring together the remaining oil, and the cider vinegar, yogurt, and mustard. Taste to check the seasoning and add salt and pepper if necessary. Pour the dressing over the salad, and serve immediately.

NOTE Among the many varieties of long zucchini (courgette), the dark green Genoese zucchini is particularly suitable for eating raw, broiled (grilled), or thinly sliced and cooked with oil, garlic, and parsley. Try marinating the zucchini for this salad instead of broiling them: slice the zucchini, then place them in a bowl with a dressing made of oil, salt, plenty of lemon juice, and parsley and marinate for 1 hour. Drain and then add to the salad with the ham.

Preparation time: 15 minutes, plus draining and cooling
Cooking time: 15 minutes
Wine suggestion: Riviera del Garda Bresciano Chiaretto

Puff Pastry Cake with Tomatoes, Cheese, and Olives

Serves 4

2 ripe tomatoes, diced
9 oz/250 g puff pastry
  (see p. 197)
type 00 flour, for dusting
3½ oz/100 g pecorino
  cheese, cut into thin strips
10 black olives, pitted
  (stoned) and coarsely
  chopped
2 tablespoons extra virgin
  olive oil
1 thyme sprig,
  leaves chopped
3–4 basil leaves, chopped
salt

Place the tomatoes in a colander, season with salt, and let drain for 30 minutes.

Preheat the oven to 400°F/200°C/Gas mark 6.

Roll out the puff pastry on a lightly floured countertop into a rectangle about ¼ inch/1.5 cm thick. Place the pastry on a baking sheet and bake in the oven for 15 minutes, or until golden and risen. Let cool and then cut the pastry in half horizontally to form two layers.

Mix the tomatoes, pecorino, and olives together in a bowl. Pour over the oil, add the aromatic herbs, and mix well.

Spread the tomato mixture over one of the bottom layers of pastry and then place the other layer of pastry on top. Divide into quarters and serve.

NOTE To give an original touch to your recipe, why not try using Taggiasca olives instead of the usual black ones? Taggiasca olives are grown in Imperia, Italy, and were brought to the region by the monks of San Colombano. Taggiasca olives are distinguished by a color that goes from green to black, through various shades of brown. These olives may be small in size but they have an intense, sweet, and refined flavor that makes them suitable for either eating on their own or being used in many recipes.

COOKING TIMES
FOR LEGUMES

Legumes (pulses) are edible seeds belonging to the Leguminosae family. There are many different plants that produce edible legumes, and in many cases the same species may include several varieties that lend themselves to different preservation methods as well as different uses in recipes.

DRYING AND SOAKING

Fresh legumes have a short storage life: a crisp shell and bright color indicates their freshness. If possible, seeds should be removed from the shell shortly before cooking, to prevent them from becoming dark and hard.

Dry legumes are sold both loose and already packaged. The former need to be stored in hermetically sealed containers and used as soon as possible, while the latter can be stored for several months if the packaging has not been opened.

Before boiling, dry legumes need to be thoroughly washed under cold running water to remove impurities and dust. Then they are generally soaked for a time, depending on the degree of dryness, the type of seed, and its size.

Soak them in a bowl with lots of cold water, ensuring the water is changed a couple of times and is not used for cooking.

COOKING

After soaking, discard the water, disposing of any floating seeds, and rinse well. Cook over low heat, covered, in a pan with cold water, preferably an earthenware container, as cooking will be more uniform. After 10–20 minutes it may be necessary to skim the surface of the water to remove impurities.

It is advisable to add salt only toward the end of the cooking time to prevent the skin of the seeds from hardening. When cooked, turn the heat off and leave the legumes to rest in the pan for about half an hour. Cooked legumes are easily mashed with a fork.

Some legumes are also commercially available with their skins removed, for example peas and fava (broad) beans. The skin is the least easily digestible part of the seed, and legumes without skins need shorter soaking and cooking times.

Generally speaking, legumes cooked in a pressure cooker require less cooking time. It is also necessary to keep in mind that older legumes require longer cooking times.

⊙ Preparation time: 30 minutes

Cooking time: 20 minutes

♀ Wine suggestion: Colli Albani Spumante

Deep-fried Zucchini Flowers Filled with Mozzarella and Anchovies

Serves 4

8 zucchini (courgette) flowers

¾ cup (3½ oz/100 g) type
   00 flour

pinch of salt

2 teaspoons crumbled
   brewer's yeast or ¾
   teaspoon instant yeast

4¼ oz /125 g extremely
   fresh cow milk mozzarella
   cheese, diced

2 oz/50 g anchovy fillets
   preserved in oil, drained
   and sliced

vegetable oil, for deep-frying

Gently open out the zucchini (courgette) flowers, taking care not to break them, and remove and discard the inner pistils. Wash the flowers very gently under a trickle of cold running water.

Put the flour, salt, and yeast into a bowl and stir together. Gradually pour in ¾ cup plus 1 tablespoon (7 fl oz/200 ml) warm water, stirring all the time, until you have a very soft, smooth, and homogenous batter.

Fill each flower with a few pieces of the mozzarella and the anchovies and then twist the tapering ends of the petals to seal.

Pour enough vegetable oil for deep-frying into a deep-fat fryer or large deep pan and heat the oil to 340°F/170°C. Preheat the oven to 225°F/110°C/Gas mark 1/4.

Quickly dip the stuffed flowers into the batter, then carefully add them to the hot oil in batches and cook until crisp. Remove with a slotted spoon, drain on paper towels, and keep warm in the oven for a few minutes while you cook the remaining batches. Serve immediately.

NOTE Zucchini (courgettes) have two kinds of flower: male and female. The former are the classic flowers with a stem, available in markets in bunches, and are excellent, as this recipe suggests, served fried or filled. The latter, on the other hand, are not gathered at all because they give rise to the fruits. It is possible, however, to pick young zucchini with the flowers still attached.

⊙ Preparation time: 40 minutes

Cooking time: 15 minutes

♀ Wine suggestion: Conegliano Valdobbiadene Prosecco Superiore Extra Dry

Winter Vegetable Salad

Serves 4

4 potatoes, peeled, cut into
  small cubes, and rinsed
10 cups (11 oz/300 g) spinach
1/2 head broccoli, broken
  into florets
vegetable broth (stock)
1/3 cup (1 1/4 oz/30 g) grated
  Parmesan cheese
4 artichokes
2 carrots, finely sliced
2 tablespoons extra virgin
  olive oil
1 tablespoon white
  wine vinegar
1 cooked beetroot, cut into
  small cubes
juice of 1 lemon
salt and pepper

To garnish
seeds from 1 pomegranate
a few aromatic
  herbs (optional)

Cook the potatoes in a large pan of well-salted boiling water for 15 minutes. Drain and set aside.

Meanwhile, bring a large pan of water to a boil. Fill a large bowl with iced water and set it beside the stove. Drop the spinach into the boiling water and leave for a few minutes. Drain, plunge into the iced water, then drain again thoroughly.

Cook the broccoli in a separate large pan of boiling salted water for 5 minutes. Drain and set aside.

Put the potatoes and spinach into a food processor and blend until smooth, gradually adding just enough broth (stock) to obtain a creamy mixture, then stir in the Parmesan and a pinch each of salt and pepper.

Trim the artichokes, discarding the inner chokes, the tougher outermost leaves, and their spiny tips. Cut the artichokes into thin slices.

Put the broccoli, artichokes, and carrots into a large bowl, add the oil and vinegar, season with salt, and mix together.

Put the beetroot into a small bowl, sprinkle over the lemon juice and a pinch of salt.

Divide the potato and spinach cream among plates, add the other vegetables and garnish with pomegranate seeds and a few aromatic herbs, if liked.

NOTE Carrots are among the most commonly used vegetables in cooking. They can be included as flavoring, as a main ingredient, or as a garnish as the carrot's brilliant color does not fade when it comes into contact with the air. It is best to use extra virgin olive oil in condiments as it allows for the optimal assimilation of the vitamins and beta-carotene in carrots.

⊙ Preparation time: 30 minutes

♀ Wine suggestion: Garda Classico Groppello

Beef Carpaccio with Artichokes

Serves 4

11 oz/300 g thinly sliced
   beef carpaccio
2 tablespoons soy sauce
6 tablespoons extra virgin
   olive oil
4 artichokes
juice of ½ lemon
1 carrot, cut into very
   small cubes
1 orange, peeled, segmented,
   membranes removed,
   and segments cut into
   very small cubes
juice of 1 lime
1 tablespoon white
   wine vinegar
salt and pepper
mixed baby leaf salad,
   to serve

Put the beef into a bowl with the soy sauce, 3 tablespoons of the oil, and a pinch of salt, toss to coat, and let marinate for 10 minutes.

Meanwhile, trim the artichokes, discarding the inner chokes, the tougher outer-most leaves, and their spiny tips. To prevent discoloring, place the artichokes in a bowl of cold water into which you have added the lemon juice.

Put the carrot and orange in a bowl, pour over 1 tablespoon of the oil, sprinkle with a pinch each of salt and pepper, and toss to mix well.

Drain the artichokes and dry them with paper towels. Cut the artichokes into very thin wedges and transfer to a bowl. Pour over the lime juice, the remaining oil, and the vinegar, and toss to mix well.

Arrange the beef carpaccio on a serving platter with the artichokes and the carrot and orange and serve with a mixed baby leaf salad.

Preparation time: 35 minutes

Cooking time: 5 minutes

Wine suggestion: Colli Tortonesi Timorasso Derthona

Mixed Mushroom Salad with Vegetables

Serves 4

9 oz/250 g white
  button mushrooms

6 tablespoons extra virgin
  olive oil

1 small bunch flat-leaf parsley,
  finely chopped

9 oz/250 g pioppini
  mushrooms

1 tablespoon white
  wine vinegar

2 carrots, cut into thin strips

2 celery stalks, cut into small
  cubes

4¼ oz/120 g mixed baby
  leaf salad

salt and pepper

3½ oz/100 g mature pecorino
  cheese shavings, to garnish

Cut off the earthy ends of the button mushroom stems and discard. Wash the button mushrooms under cold running water, dry them, and slice thinly. Drizzle with olive oil, and half the chopped parsley. Set aside.

Wash the pioppini mushrooms under cold running water and then cut off and discard the bottom part of their stems. Boil for 5 minutes in lightly salted water. Drain the pioppini mushrooms. Place them in a bowl with the remaining parsley, vinegar, a pinch each of salt and pepper, and 2 tablespoons of the oil and gently toss to coat the mushrooms.

Put the carrots and celery into a bowl, drizzle over the remaining oil, season with salt and toss to mix well.

Put the two types of mushrooms, carrots and celery, and mixed baby leaf salad into a salad bowl and mix gently. Serve garnished with pecorino shavings and a drizzle of oil.

TIP   To make this salad extra special, replace the button mushrooms with very fresh Caesar's mushrooms (known as ovoli mushrooms in Italy). These rare mushrooms, picked while they are still immature and closed, have a delicate scent, and are particularly suitable for use raw.

⊙ Preparation time: 25 minutes, plus cooling
Cooking time: 1¼ hours

♀ Wine suggestion: Ormeasco di Pornassio Sciac-trà

Polenta with Brussels Sprouts

Serves 4

1 tablepoon extra virgin
  olive oil
1¾ cups (9 oz/250 g)
  coarse cornmeal
5⅔ cups (1 lb 2 oz/500 g)
  Brussels sprouts
1¼ cups (3½ oz/100 g)
  grated pecorino cheese
3 tablespoons (1½ oz/
  40 g) butter, plus extra
  for greasing
1 clove garlic
2 anchovy fillets preserved
  in salt, rinsed
salt

First make the polenta. Bring 4¼ cups (34 fl oz/1 liter) of water to boil in a pan, add the oil and 1 tablespoon salt and then gradually sprinkle in the cornmeal, whisking all the time to prevents lumps forming. Cook over low heat for 1 hour, stirring continuously.

Grease a 9½-inch/24-cm cake pan with butter.

Cook the Brussels sprouts in a pan of boiling salted water for 8 minutes, then drain well. Coarsely chop two-thirds of the Brussels sprouts and cut the remaining sprouts in half.

Stir the chopped Brussels sprouts and pecorino into the polenta. Pour the mixture into the prepared cake pan and let stand at room temperature until cool. Unmold the polenta and cut it into ⅝-inch/1.5-cm slices.

Heat the broiler (grill) to high. Place the polenta slices on a baking sheet and broil (grill) for 5 minutes, or until golden brown.

Meanwhile, melt the butter in a small pan, add the whole clove of garlic and anchovies, and cook over low heat for 2–3 minutes until the anchovies have dissolved. Discard the garlic and then stir in the halved Brussels sprouts.

Serve the polenta with the anchovy-flavored sprouts.

NOTE   Small, round, and a vivid green, Brussels sprouts are the buds of the plant and sprout from a tall, thick stem, crowned by fully developed leaves. Unlike cauliflower and broccoli plants, which produce just one large central bud, Brussels sprouts produce around 40 sprouts on each stem. The sprouts contain high quantities of vitamin C and beta-carotene, as well as other antioxidants, and their availability in the winter season makes them a precious addition to a healthy and balanced diet.

⊙ Preparation time: 30 minutes

Cooking time: 55 minutes

Y Wine suggestion: Lambrusco Mantovano

Pumpkin, Sausage, and Radicchio Pie

Serves 4

4¹⁄₃ cups (1 lb 2 oz/500 g)
small pumpkin flesh cubes
3 eggs
¹⁄₃ cup plus 1 tablespoon
(3¹⁄₂ fl oz/100 ml)
whipping cream
3 tablespoons grated
Parmesan cheese
pinch of ground nutmeg
9 oz/250 g sausages
1 head radicchio, cut
into strips
2 tablespoons extra virgin
olive oil
3¹⁄₂ tablespoons red wine
2 tablespoons (1¹⁄₄ oz/30 g)
butter, for greasing
1 tablespoon
fresh breadcrumbs
salt

Put the pumpkin in a Dutch oven (casserole dish), pour over ¹⁄₃ cup plus 1 tablespoon (3¹⁄₂ oz/100 ml) water, cover, and cook over low heat for 15 minutes, or until the pumpkin is soft and dry, adding a little more water if all the water evaporates before the pumpkin is cooked.

Transfer the pumpkin to a food processor and blend until creamy. Add the eggs, cream, Parmesan, nutmeg, and a pinch of salt and process for a few seconds more to ensure the ingredients are well blended and creamy.

Skin the sausages and crumble the sausagemeat into a bowl.

Heat the oil in a skillet (frying pan), add the radicchio and a pinch of salt, and cook over medium heat for 3–4 minutes until the radicchio begins to sweat. Add the sausagemeat and red wine and cook for 5 minutes more.

Preheat the oven to 350°F/180°C/Gas mark 4. Grease a 12 x 7-inch/30 x 18-cm ovenproof dish with butter.

Stir the radicchio and sausagement mixture into the pumpkin cream and mix well. Pour into the prepared ovenproof dish and sprinkle over the breadcrumbs. Bake in the oven for 30 minutes, or until golden.

TIP If you want a striking presentation for this dish, you can use a hollow pumpkin shell instead of an ovenproof dish. Before filling the pumpkin shell with the mixture, bake the shell in an oven preheated to 350°F/180°C/Gas mark 4 for 15 minutes to soften it and ensure it does not taste raw.

CONDIMENTS AND DRESSINGS

It is fashionable these days to call them dressings because they are used to "dress" salads, to enrich and enhance their flavors. More traditionally, they are called condiments.

LET'S START WITH THE INGREDIENTS

The ingredients for condiments can be divided into five subsections: oils, acids, sauces, spices, and aromatic herbs.

Oils In addition to extra virgin olive oil, which can be more or less delicate depending on personal taste, these include corn oil or sunflower oil and, for a more distinctive taste, walnut oil.

Acids The list includes vinegars (wine, red or white, rice, balsamic) and lemon juice.

Sauces These range from classic mustard, to honey, Worcestershire sauce, and Tabasco, right up to the more exotic yogurt and sour cream.

Spices The only restriction here is a matter of taste, so pepper, chili powder, curry, mustard seeds, and so on.

Aromatic herbs In the case of aromatic herbs it is also a matter of personal taste: garlic, onion, oregano, chervil, chives, and so on.

THE CLASSIC COMBINATION: OIL AND VINEGAR

Strictly linked to Italian gastronomic culture, olive oil, extra virgin or not, enhances every dish. Every type has its own unique personality, defined by the type of olive used, agronomic practice, timing, harvesting system, and pressing techniques. It is possible to think of distinctions along the lines of fruity or delicate oils and peppery oils. In dressings, the former is suitable for salads, boiled vegetables, steamed fish, and sauces, while more pungent oils work better in dressings for legumes (pulses) and soups.

There are no specific rules on the use of vinegar. They are suitable for enhancing the flavor of aromatic, bitter, and textural herbs, in addition to being one of the basic ingredients of a perfect dressing. They also play an important role in taste and presentation. Balsamic reductions are ideal for enhancing dishes based on shellfish or strips of meat.

OTHER TYPES OF DRESSING

Starting with the classic vinaigrette and citronnette. Vinaigrette is an emulsion of oil, vinegar, and salt, vigorously stirred to blend the ingredients. For citronnette, replace the vinegar with lemon juice. There are numerous variations of both preparations, depending on the additional ingredients used, such as mustard, honey, or maple syrup. In addition, lemon juice can be replaced with orange or grapefruit juice in citronnette.

Creamy dressings are particularly suitable for ingredients with a more compact texture such as potatoes, carrots, and radishes. They are prepared using a creamy base—yogurt or sour cream—blended with oil, salt and, if preferred, mustard and various spices, depending on one's own taste.

When using ingredients with more compact textures, coarsely chopped walnuts or olives can also be added.

The exotic Indian sauce, suitable for more substantial mixes of salad leaves and mixed vegetables, is prepared by blending in a food processor half an apple with half an onion and 1 tablespoon of lemon juice, then adding sour cream and curry powder.

For the classic cocktail sauce, add mustard, Worcestershire sauce, mayonnaise, ketchup, and 1 tablespoon of Cognac to a fresh cream base.

Tapenade is a Provençal dressing made with black olives, preserved anchovy fillets, and capers. It can be more or less spicy, depending on preference. Once the base ingredients have been finely minced, they can be blended with extra virgin olive oil to make a soft cream, finished off with lemon juice and pepper.

Marinades, as well as being used for infusing fish and meat fillets, are also perfect for flavoring uncooked salads to which fish and meat fillets have been added. They can be sweet and sour, or spicy, depending on the spices used.

⊙ Preparation time: 20 minutes

Cooking time: 20 minutes

♀ Wine suggestion: Bianco di Alessano

Egg-free Spinach and Carrot Frittata

Serves 4

¹/₃ cup (2 oz/50 g) fine
cornmeal, sifted

¹/₃ cup (2 oz/50 g) all-purpose
(plain) flour, sifted

³/₄ cup plus 1 tablespoon
(7 fl oz/200 ml) soy milk

1 teaspoon baking soda
(bicarbonate of soda)

2 carrots, grated

1 cup (2 oz/50 g) finely
chopped baby leaf spinach

extra virgin olive oil

salt and pepper

First make the batter. In a large bowl, mix together the cornmeal, flour, soy milk, baking soda (bicarbonate of soda), and a pinch each of salt and pepper. Add the carrots and spinach and gently mix until well blended.

Heat 1 tablespoon oil in a nonstick skillet (frying pan). When hot, pour a small quantity of the batter into the pan with a ladle and cook over medium heat for a few minutes on each side until golden brown. Remove the fritter from the skillet and keep warm. Repeat until all the batter has been used, adding a little more oil to the skillet between fritters if necessary.

TIP For a tastier and more substantial version of this recipe, serve the frittata topped with pieces of very fresh, rindless soft cheese (ideally stracchino cheese).

⊙ Preparation time: 35 minutes
Cooking time: 45 minutes

𝑌 Wine suggestion: Cinque Terre

Salsify and Fennel Crumble

Serves 4

2²/₃ cups (12 oz/350 g) peeled
  and sliced salsify
2 fennel bulbs, cut into cubes
2 tablespoons extra virgin
  olive oil, plus extra
  for greasing
1 small onion, sliced
5 oz/150 g rindless
  soft cheese (ideally
  crescenza cheese),
  cut into small pieces
1 tablespoon pumpkin seeds
salt and pepper

For the crumble
1¹/₄ cups (5 oz/150 g)
  all-purpose (plain) flour
1¹/₄ cups (3¹/₂ oz/100 g)
  grated Parmesan cheese
1¹/₄ sticks (5 oz/150 g) cold
  butter, cut into cubes
1 small thyme sprig,
  leaves only

Cook the salsify in a large pan of lightly salted water for 10 minutes, adding the fennel halfway through the cooking time. Drain well.

Heat the oil in a skillet (frying pan), add the onion and a pinch of salt, and cook over medium–low heat for 3–4 minutes until soft and transparent. Add the fennel and the salsify and cook for 5 minutes more to allow the flavors to blend.

Meanwhile, make the crumble mixture. Put the flour, Parmesan, butter, thyme, and a pinch each of salt and pepper into a bowl. Using your fingertips, rub the ingredients together until the mixture resembles breadcrumbs.

Preheat the oven to 350°F/180°C/Gas mark 4. Grease a 8 x 6-inch/20 x 15-cm ovenproof dish with oil.

Transfer the fennel and salsify mixture to the prepared ovenproof dish. Sprinkle the crescenza over the vegetables and then cover the cheese and vegetables with the crumble mix. Sprinkle the pumpkin seeds over the top and bake in the oven for about 25 minutes until golden brown and crisp.

TIP   This recipe is also excellent if you replace the salsify with celery root (celeriac), a vegetable with a very aromatic flavor that is similar but more delicate than that of celery. Peel ²/₃ head celery root (about 12 oz/350 g), cut it into cubes, then cook it in the same way as the salsify in the recipe above.

⊙   Preparation time: 10 minutes

Cooking time: 20 minutes

♀   Wine suggestion: Alto Adige Riesling

Brussels Sprouts with Sesame Seeds

Serves 4

5 cups (1 lb 2 oz/500 g)
    Brussels sprouts, trimmed
    and harder outer leaves
    removed
2–3 tablespoons extra virgin
    olive oil
zest and juice of 1 unwaxed
    orange—the zest needs to
    be cut into very thin strips
juice of 1/2 lemon
2 tablespoons sesame seeds
salt and pepper

Cook the Brussels sprouts in a large pan of boiling salted water for 10 minutes, or until tender. Drain well.

Heat the oil in a skillet (frying pan), add the drained Brussels sprouts, and cook over medium heat for 10 minutes, or until they are soft and a knife inserted into them comes out easily. Add the orange and lemon juices, orange zest, and sesame seeds and shake the pan to coat the Brussels sprouts. Continue to cook for a few minutes to let the flavors blend, then season with salt and pepper and serve hot.

NOTE   Originally from India but now also grown in Sicily, sesame seeds can be used to enrich cereal and vegetable dishes, flavor breads and bread sticks, make delicious honey brittle, or they can be added to vegetable sauces. Sesame seeds are often lightly toasted to release their flavor. They are rich in fiber and mineral salts, such as magnesium, calcium, phosphorus, silicon, and iron, as well as B vitamins.

◷   Preparation time: 30 minutes

Cooking time: 55 minutes

♀   Wine suggestion: Curtefranca Bianco

Polenta with Cheese, Baked Radicchio, and Leek

Serves 4

1²/₃ cup (9 oz/250 g)
coarse cornmeal

3¹/₂ tablespoons
whipping cream

3¹/₂ oz/100 g semi-soft,
washed rind cheese (ideally
Taleggio cheese), cut into
small cubes

3 tablespoons (1¹/₂ oz/40 g)
butter, cut into small cubes

1 head radicchio, sliced

1 small leek, sliced

2 tablespoons extra virgin
olive oil

salt

Bring 4¹/₄ cups (34 fl oz/1 liter) water to a boil in a heavy pan, add a pinch of salt, then gradually sprinkle in the cornmeal, stirring all the time with a wooden spoon to prevents lumps forming. Cover and cook over low heat for 40 minutes, stirring from time to time. Remove from the heat and stir in the cream and cheese. Pour the polenta into individual gratin dishes and then dot the surfaces with butter.

Preheat the oven to 350°F/180°C/Gas mark 4.

Put the radicchio and leek into a nonstick ovenproof dish. Pour over the oil and a few tablespoons of water, sprinkle with a pinch of salt, and stir well to combine.

Bake the polenta and the radicchio and leek in the oven for 15 minutes, or until golden. Serve the polenta with the baked radicchio and leek spooned over the top.

TIP   As an alternative to the baked radicchio and leek, cut 1 head radicchio into wedges and cook in a dry nonstick skillet (frying pan) over medium heat for 2–3 minutes on each side until golden and crunchy, then season with salt and pepper, drizzle over a little oil, and serve with the polenta. The most suitable radicchio variety is Radicchio di Verona PGI (Protected Geographical Indication).

⊙ Preparation time: 25 minutes

Cooking time: 2 minutes

♀ Wine suggestion: Colli Orientali del Friuli Verduzzo

Apple and Celery Root Salad

Serves 4

¹⁄₃ celery root (celeriac;
   about 7 oz/200 g),
   cut into very thin strips
   (1¹⁄₃ cups prepared)
1 Fuji apple
2 tablespoons lemon juice
4 teaspoons soy cream
   (or you could use soy
   yogurt instead)
½ cup (3¹⁄₂ oz/100 g) egg-free
   rice mayonnaise
   (see tip)
salt and pepper

To garnish
¼ cup (1 oz/25 g)
   chopped walnuts
¼ cup (1 oz/25 g)
   chopped almonds

Bring a large pan of water to a boil. Meanwhile, fill a large bowl with iced water and set it beside the stove. Drop the celery root (celeriac) into the boiling water and leave alone for 2 minutes. Drain, plunge into the iced water, then drain again thoroughly.

Peel and core the apple, cut the flesh into very thin strips, and sprinkle with the lemon juice to prevent discoloration.

Gently blend the rice mayonnaise with the soy cream in a small bowl and season with pepper.

Put the apple and celery root into a large bowl, add the mayonnaise mixture, and mix well. Taste to check the seasoning and add salt and pepper if necessary. Garnish the salad with almonds and walnuts and serve.

TIP   Rice mayonnaise is made without eggs. To make homemade rice mayonnaise: put 2 tablespoons lecithin in a bowl with a little rice milk and let soak for 10 minutes. Add a little bit more rice milk (you will need 4 tablespoons rice milk in total for the recipe), and use an immersion blender to blend until the mixture is fluffy, gradually adding ½ cup (3³⁄₄ fl oz/110 ml) corn oil, followed by 1 teaspoon lemon juice. Finally, stir in 1 tablespoon mustard (choose whichever mustard you prefer) and a pinch of salt.

⊙ Preparation time: 20 minutes

Cooking time: 10 minutes

♀ Wine suggestion: San Severo Bianco

Fried Cauliflower with Mixed Salad

Serves 4

¾ cup (3¹/₂ oz/100 g)
   all-purpose (plain) flour
2 eggs
4 cups (7 oz/200 g)
   fresh breadcrumbs
1 large cauliflower, broken
   into florets
vegetable oil, for deep-frying
6 cups (6¹/₄ oz/180 g) mixed
   baby leaf salad
1¹/₃ cups (7 oz/200 g)
   boiled shredded cabbage,
   to garnish

For the dressing
3¹/₂ tablespoons extra virgin
   olive oil
1 small bunch flat-leaf parsley,
   finely chopped
2–3 chives, finely chopped
1 tablespoon white wine
   vinegar
salt and pepper

Spread out the flour in a shallow dish. Beat the eggs well in a separate shallow dish. Put the breadcrumbs into another shallow dish.

Dip each cauliflower floret in turn first into the beaten egg, then roll it in the flour, then dip again in the beaten egg, and finally roll it in the breadcrumbs.

Pour enough vegetable oil for deep-frying into a deep-fat fryer or large deep pan and heat the oil to 340°F/170°C. Carefully add the florets to the hot oil and cook for 3–4 minutes until soft. Remove with a slotted spoon and drain on paper towels.

Meanwhile, make the dressing. Whisk together the olive oil, parsley, chives, and vinegar in a small bowl. Season to taste with salt and pepper.

Put the mixed salad into a bowl, pour over the dressing, and gently toss together.

Garnish the fried cauliflower with a little boiled shredded cabbage and serve with the salad.

N O T E Cauliflower is part of the brassica family, a group of plants that grew across the Mediterranean basin in ancient times and were used and valued by the Greeks and Romans. The cauliflower is a round, fleshy inflorescence, normally white, that can be harvested, depending on its variety, in the autumn, winter, or at the start of spring.

Preparation time: 15 minutes

Cooking time: 10 minutes

Wine suggestion: Vernaccia di San Gimignano

Fennel au Gratin

Serves 4

2 fennel bulbs
½ clove of garlic, chopped
3 tablespoons
 sunflower seeds
3 tablespoons whole
 wheat (wholemeal)
 fresh breadcrumbs
2 tablespoons extra virgin
 olive oil, plus extra
 for greasing
salt

Preheat the oven to 350°F/180°C/Gas mark 4. Grease an ovenproof dish with oil.

Chop the fennel stalks and fronds and thinly slice the bulbs. Keep separate.

To make the topping, put the chopped fennel stalks and fronds, garlic, sunflower seeds, breadcrumbs, 1 tablespoon of the oil, and a pinch of salt into a bowl and mix well.

Arrange the sliced fennel bulbs in a single layer in the prepared ovenproof dish. Sprinkle over the topping and bake in the oven for 10 minutes, or until golden.

NOTE In Chinese medicine fennel is believed to aid digestion and to generate warm energy, which makes this dish an ideal meal for those cold days toward the end of winter. Fennel bulbs can have a round or oblong shape: the former is more suitable for eating raw as it is sweeter and more tender, while the latter is best for cooking.

CHEF
Giorgio Chiesa

Preparation time: 30 minutes
Cooking time: 1 hour 20 minutes

Cabbage Millefeuille with Potatoes, Pesto, and Cheese

Serves 4

1 head cabbage,
  leaves separated
3 yellow potatoes (about
  12 oz/350 g), unpeeled
4¼ cups (34 fl oz/1 liter)
  whole (full-fat) milk
1 stick (3¾ oz/110 g) butter,
  plus extra for greasing
½ cup (2¾ oz/70 g)
  all-purpose (plain) flour
11 oz/300 g soft stretched-
  curd cheese (ideally
  stracciatella cheese)
¾ cup (7 oz/200 g) pesto
1¼ cups (3½ oz/100 g)
  grated Parmesan cheese
salt

Bring a large pan of salted water to a boil. Meanwhile, fill a large bowl with iced water and set it beside the stove. Drop the cabbage leaves into the boiling water and leave for 2 minutes. Drain, plunge into the iced water, then drain again thoroughly.

Cook the potatoes in a large pan of boiling salted water for 40 minutes, or until a knife inserted into them comes out easily. Drain well. Carefully peel the potatoes. Let cool and then mash.

Make the béchamel sauce. Heat the milk in a pan until just about to boil. In a separate pan, heat 2¾ oz/70 g of the butter, then add the flour and cook over low heat for a few minutes, stirring to make sure there are no lumps. Gradually add the hot milk, stirring briskly, then season with salt, and cook the sauce for 3 minutes, or until smooth and silky.

Preheat the oven to 350°F/180°C/Gas mark 4. Grease a 8 x 6-inch/20 x 15-cm ovenproof dish with butter.

Melt the remaining butter in a separate pan. Pour a thin layer of béchamel sauce onto the bottom of the prepared ovenproof dish. Arrange a layer of cabbage leaves on top, cover with another thin layer of béchamel sauce, then add a layer of mashed potatoes, followed by a little of the curd cheese, a little of the pesto, and some of the Parmesan. Repeat these layers until the dish is full and then pour over the remaining melted butter. Bake in the oven for 40 minutes, or until golden brown. Let rest for a few minutes before serving.

WINE SUGGESTION   Ribolla Gialla Vini Orsone is made with a grape variety native to the area between Friuli and Slovenia. The wine has intense notes, a great fresh bouquet, and excellent acidity. It is a perfect match to the pesto and the fior di latte stracciatella cheese.

Preparation time: 25 minutes

Wine suggestion: Greco di Tufo

Chickpea Salad

Serves 4

2 cups (11 oz/300 g) rinsed
and drained, canned
chickpeas

10 cups (7 oz/200 g) arugula
(rocket)

2 cucumbers, thinly sliced
using a mandoline
or potato peeler

2 large scallions (spring
onions), cut into rounds

5 tablespoons extra virgin
olive oil

1 clove garlic, minced (grated)

1/2 cup (4 fl oz/125 ml) low-fat
plain (natural) yogurt

1 mint sprig, leaves chopped

1 oregano sprig, leaves only

1/2 cup (2 oz/50 g) drained
sun-dried tomatoes
preserved in oil, cut into
thin strips

salt and pepper

Put the chickpeas, arugula (rocket), cucumbers, and scallions (spring onions) into a large bowl, drizzle over 2 tablespoons of the oil, and stir together gently. Season with salt and pepper.

In a small bowl, stir the garlic into the yogurt. Season with salt and pepper and then add the remaining oil and the mint and mix well.

Garnish the chickpea and vegetable salad with the sun-dried tomatoes and oregano. Serve the salad with the yogurt dressing on the side.

TIP   If you like pronounced flavors you can enrich the yogurt dressing with spices instead of the mint leaves. For example, add 1/2 teaspoon curry powder, a pinch of ground ginger, and a few drops of lemon juice for a slightly spicy taste.

Preparation time: 25 minutes

Cooking time: 45 minutes

Wine suggestion: Colli di Luni Vermentino

Potato, Green Bean, and Pesto Bake

Serves 4

4 potatoes (about 1 lb
  2 oz/500 g), unpeeled
3 cups (11 oz/300 g) trimmed
  green beans
1/2 cup (21/4 oz/60 g)
  cornstarch (cornflour)
extra virgin olive oil
coarse or flaked sea salt

For the pesto
1 small bunch basil
sliver of garlic
1/4 cup (11/4 oz/30 g) walnuts
21/2 tablespoons pine nuts
1/4 cup (11/4 oz/30 g)
  cashew nuts

Put the potatoes into a large pan of cold water, bring to the boil, and cook the potatoes for 20–25 minutes until a knife inserted into them comes out easily. Drain well. Peel the potatoes and then lightly crush them using the back of a fork.

Meanwhile, cook the green beans in a pan of boiling water for 15 minutes, or until tender. Drain well and cut the green beans into 11/4–11/2-inch/3–4-cm lengths.

Preheat the oven to 350°F/180°C/Gas mark 4. Grease a 7 x 43/4-inch/18 x 12-cm baking pan with oil.

Make the pesto. Put the basil, garlic, walnuts, pine nuts, and cashew nuts into a food processor, season with salt, then blend to a purée.

Mix the crushed potatoes and green beans together in a large bowl. Spoon over the pesto and stir together gently. Taste to check the seasoning and add more salt if necessary.

Sprinkle most of the cornstarch (cornflour) over the bottom of the prepared baking pan. Spread out the potato and green bean mixture in an even layer in the baking pan (it should be about 5/8–3/4 inch/1.5–2 cm thick), dust the top with the remaining cornstarch, and sprinkle with a little oil. Bake in the oven for 15 minutes, or until a golden crust forms on top. Serve lukewarm or cold.

TIP If you want to make this potato dish more filling so it can be served as a main course, spread half the potato and green bean mixture in an ovenproof dish, sprinkle over 11 oz/300 g diced hard cheese (ideally Asiago cheese), cover with the remaining potato and green bean mixture, dust the surface with plenty of grated Parmesan cheese instead of the cornstarch (cornflour), and bake in the oven as above. Serve very hot.

Preparation time: 20 minutes, plus soaking
Cooking time: 1 hour
Wine suggestion: Frascati

Cannellini Bean and Pecorino Cheese Salad with Balsamic Vinegar

Serves 4

1¹/₃ cups (9 oz/250 g) dried cannellini beans

¹/₂ cup (1¹/₂ oz/40 g) grated aged pecorino cheese (ideally Pecorino Toscano cheese)

3 tablespoons extra virgin olive oil

2 tablespoons balsamic vinegar

3¹/₂ cups (3¹/₂ oz/100 g) mixed baby leaf salad

3¹/₂ cups (3¹/₂ oz/100 g) ricotta cheese or primo sale cheese, cut into pieces

salt and pepper

Soak the cannellini beans in a large bowl of cold water overnight.

The next day, rinse the beans under cold running water, then cook them in a pressure cooker for 30 minutes, or until soft, using unsalted water to prevent the beans' skins from hardening. Alternatively, cook the beans in a large pan of boiling water, covered, for 1 hour, or until tender. Drain.

Put the cooked beans, pecorino, oil, balsamic vinegar, and a pinch of salt into a bowl and stir well so the flavors combine.

Divide the mixed baby leaf salad among four plates. Spoon the cannellini bean mixture over the top and top with the ricotta or primo sale. Season with pepper and serve.

TIP To vary the taste of this recipe, substitute wild arugula (rocket), which has a pleasantly bitter, slightly peppery aftertaste, for the mixed baby leaf salad. You can also enrich the salad by adding coarsely chopped walnuts; their intense flavor makes an interesting contrast with the other ingredients.

Preparation time: 15 minutes
Cooking time: 5 minutes
Wine suggestion: Fiano di Avellino

Fava Bean Salad with Anchovies and Semi-dried Cherry Tomatoes

Serves 4

2²/₃ cups (14 oz/400 g) shelled
  fresh fava (broad) beans
1 cup (3¹/₂ oz/100 g) drained
  semi-dried cherry tomatoes
  preserved in oil, halved
8 anchovy fillets preserved in
  oil, drained and chopped
3–4 basil leaves, chopped
2–3 tablespoons extra virgin
  olive oil
salt
a few fresh herbs (basil,
  tarragon, and chives),
  to garnish

Cook the fava (broad) beans in a large pan of boiling salted water for 4 minutes. Drain well and let cool.

Put the drained beans, semi-dried cherry tomatoes, anchovies, and basil into a large bowl. Season with a pinch of salt, drizzle over the oil, and toss to mix well. Serve garnished with a few fresh herbs.

⊙   Preparation time: 25 minutes, plus soaking

Cooking time: 3 hours 10 minutes

⟟   Wine suggestion: Frascati Superiore

Barley with Chickpeas and Crispy Pancetta

Serves 4

¹/₂ cup (3¹/₂ oz/100 g)
   dried chickpeas

2 cups (14 oz/400 g)
   pearled barley

8¹/₂ cups (68 fl oz/2 liters)
   vegetable broth (stock)

extra virgin olive oil

1 tablespoon butter

¹/₃ cup (1¹/₄ oz/30 g) grated
   Parmesan cheese

8 slices pancetta or bacon
   (ideally guanciale)

1 flat-leaf parsley sprig,
   chopped, to garnish

Soak the chickpeas in a large bowl of cold water overnight.

The next day, rinse the chickpeas under cold running water and then cook them in a large pan of boiling water for 2 hours. Drain well. Put half the chickpeas into a food processor and blend to a purée. Set aside the chickpea purée and the whole chickpeas.

Meanwhile, soak the barley in a large bowl of cold water for 2 hours. Drain and rinse well under cold running water.

Pour the broth (stock) into a pan, bring to a simmer, and keep over a low heat.

Heat a little oil in a large pan, stir in the pearled barley, then add a ladleful of the broth and cook over medium heat for about 1 hour, gradually adding in more broth, a ladleful at a time, until all the liquid is absorbed by the pearled barley, and adding the chickpea purée halfway through the cooking time. Add the whole chickpeas and cook for 5 minutes more. Remove from the heat and stir in the butter and Parmesan. Cover and let rest while you cook the pancetta or bacon.

Heat a dry skillet (frying pan), add the pancetta, and cook over medium heat for a few minutes until crisp. Remove the pancetta from the skillet and drain on paper towels.

Divide the barley and chickpeas among serving plates, garnish with the crisp pancetta and parsley, and drizzle over a little oil.

TIP This recipe will look truly original if you use Murgia Carsica black chickpeas. The cultivation of these chickpeas in the southwest of the Italian region of Bari was in danger of dying out but it is now protected by a Slow Food Presidia label. Shaped like sweetcorn, these chickpeas are small, wrinkled, and irregular in shape, and their black color differentiates them from other varieties. They are high in fiber and iron, which makes them an extremely healthy option.

GRAINS

Preparation time: 25 minutes, plus soaking

Cooking time: 40 minutes

Wine suggestion: Alto Adige Gewürztraminer

Beet and Gorgonzola Cheese Pearled Barley with Cream Sauce

Serves 4

1¼ cups (9 oz/250 g)
  pearled barley
2 cooked beets (beetroot),
  cut into cubes
4 tablespoons extra virgin
  olive oil
generous 2 cups (17 fl oz/
  500 ml) vegetable
  broth (stock)
¾ cup plus 1 tablespoon
  (7 fl oz/200 ml) white wine
5 oz/150 g strong Gorgonzola
  cheese, cut into cubes
3 tablespoons plus
  1 teaspoon (1¾ fl oz/
  50 ml) whipping cream
4 tablespoons (2 oz/50 g)
  butter, cut into cubes
⅓ cup (1 oz/50 g) grated
  Parmesan cheese
salt
a few thyme sprigs,
  to garnish (optional)

Soak the barley in a large bowl of cold water for 2 hours. Rinse and drain well.

Put the beets (beetroot), 2 tablespoons of the oil, a pinch of salt, and ⅓ cup plus 1 tablespoon (3½ fl oz/100 ml) of the broth (stock) into a food processor and blend to a purée.

Pour the remaining broth into a pan and bring to a simmer. Keep over a low heat while you make the risotto.

Put the drained barley into a pan, add the remaining oil and a pinch of salt, and toast the barley over medium heat for 6 minutes, stirring continuously. Add the wine and cook for a few minutes until the wine has evaporated, then add a ladleful of the broth. Cook the barley over medium heat for about 30 minutes, gradually adding in more broth, a ladleful at a time, until all the liquid is absorbed by the barley, adding the beetroot purée 10 minutes before the end of the cooking time.

Meanwhile, put half the Gorgonzola and the cream into a food processor and blend to make a light, creamy sauce.

Once the barley is cooked, remove from the heat and stir in the Parmesan, the remaining Gorgonzola, and the butter. Divide among individual serving dishes, flattening the surface with the back of a spoon. Drizzle a spiral of Gorgonzola cream sauce over the top of each dish and garnish with a drizzle of oil and some thyme leaves, if liked.

Preparation time: 25 minutes

Cooking time: 30 minutes

Wine suggestion: Albana di Romagna

Millet Gnocchi with Arugula Pesto

Serves 4

1¼ cups (9 oz/250 g) millet
¾ cup (3½ oz/100 g)
   all-purpose (plain) flour
salt and pepper

For the pesto
2½ tablespoons chopped
   hazelnuts, plus extra to
   garnish (optional)
10 cups (7 oz/200 g) arugula
   (rocket), plus extra to
   garnish (optional)
⅓ cup (1¼ oz/30 g) grated
   Parmesan cheese
⅓ cup (2¾ fl oz/80 ml) extra
   virgin olive oil

Rinse the millet thoroughly under cold running water, drain well. Cook the millet in generous 2 cups (17 fl oz/500 ml) boiling salted water for 25 minutes, or until the water is completely absorbed and the millet is tender, adding a little more hot water during cooking if necessary. Drain well.

Meanwhile, prepare the pesto. Put the hazelnuts, arugula (rocket), and Parmesan into a food processor and blend, slowly adding the oil in a thin stream, until smooth and creamy. Taste to check the seasoning and add salt and pepper if necessary.

Transfer the drained millet to the bowl of a stand mixer and slowly beat in the flour, until a smooth and rather dry mixture is obtained. Alternatively, you can beat together the millet and barley in a large bowl. Shape teaspoonfuls of the mixture into gnocchi.

Cook the gnocchi in a large pan of boiling salted water for 3–4 minutes until they rise to the surface, then drain well.

Heat a drizzle of oil in a skillet (frying pan), add the pesto and gnocchi, and cook over low heat for a few minutes until heated through and the gnocchi are well coated with the pesto. Serve immediately, garnished with a few extra hazelnuts and arugula leaves, if liked.

Preparation time: 30 minutes
Cooking time: 40 minutes
Wine suggestion: Greco di Tufo

Quinoa with Red Beets

Serves 4

2 beets (beetroot), peeled
   (you can use precooked
   beets if you prefer)
5 tablespoons extra virgin
   olive oil
1 tablespoon red wine
   vinegar (optional)
1¼ cups (7 oz/200 g) quinoa
3–4 chives, finely chopped
7 oz/200 g fresh goat cheese
   (ideally caprino cheese)
grated zest of 1
   unwaxed lemon
salt

To garnish (optional)
sprouts
aromatic herbs

Cook the beets (beetroot) in a large pan of abundantly salted water for 40 minutes. Drain and then cut them into cubes or thin slices. Put the beets into a bowl, pour over 2 tablespoons of the oil and the vinegar, if using, sprinkle with a pinch of salt, and toss to combine.

Meanwhile, cook the quinoa in a large pan of abundantly salted water for 15–20 minutes until tender. Drain and let cool, then drizzle over the remaining oil, add the chives, and mix well.

Put the caprino, lemon zest, and a pinch of salt into a small bowl and mix with a fork until smooth and well combined.

Serve the quinoa with the beetroot slices, topped with quenelles of the caprino mixture. Garnish with sprouts and aromatic herbs, if liked.

Preparation time: 25 minutes

Cooking time: 55 minutes

Wine suggestion: Langhe Bianco

Einkorn Wheat Salad with Radicchio, Chard, and Caramelized Hazelnuts

Serves 4

1¾ cups (12 oz/350 g) einkorn
   wheat (or other wheat berry)
4 tablespoons extra virgin
   olive oil
1 tablespoon
   raspberry vinegar
1⅓ cups (5 oz/150 g) coarsely
   chopped hazelnuts
1 tablespoon superfine
   (caster) sugar
5⅓ cups (12 oz/350 g) sliced
   Swiss chard
1 head radicchio, sliced
4 celery stalks, finely sliced
salt and pepper

Cook the einkorn in a large pan of abundantly salted boiling water for about 50 minutes until tender. Drain well.

Make a dressing by whisking together the oil, vinegar, and a pinch each of salt and pepper in a small bowl.

Heat a dry skillet (frying pan), add the hazelnuts and sugar, and toast over medium heat for 3–4 minutes until they start to caramelize.

Put the chard, radicchio, and celery into a salad bowl. Pour over the dressing and toss well. Add the drained einkorn, mix well, and sprinkle over the caramelized hazelnuts.

NOTE   Einkorn, enkir, and small spelt are all terms for a cereal that, according to historical research, was probably the first crop cultivated by humans in the Middle East in around 7500 BC. In recent years enkir has been cultivated in Italy, where this rather rustic plant has adapted well and bears fruit. Its nutritional properties are very interesting because its grains have a high content of fat, phosphorous, potassium, and beta-carotene, as well as a higher percentage of proteins than other cereals.

⊙ Preparation time: 40 minutes, plus soaking
Cooking time: 40 minutes

♀ Wine suggestion: Trebbiano d'Abruzzo

Asparagus, Shrimp, and Pearled Barley Salad

Serves 4

1¼ cups (9 oz/250 g)
pearled barley
half bunch (14 oz/400 g)
  asparagus spears
11 oz/300 g raw jumbo
  shrimp (king prawns)
  in their shells
extra virgin olive oil
1 zucchini (courgette),
  cut into cubes
⅔ cup (5 oz/150 g)
  mayonnaise
juice of 1 lemon
1 small flat-leaf parsley sprig,
  finely chopped
salt and pepper
a few basil leaves, to garnish

Soak the pearled barley in a large bowl of cold water for 2–3 hours. Rinse the barley under cold running water, then cook in a large pan of abundantly salted boiling water (you need about three times the barley's volume in water) for 40 minutes, or until tender. Drain well and let cool.

Prepare the shrimp (prawns). Rinse the shrimp under running water. Remove the heads and shells, keeping the tails intact. Using a sharp knife, cut through the back of each shrimp and remove and discard the intestine, being careful not to break it. Reserve a few whole shrimp for garnish, and cut the rest into cubes.

Cook the asparagus in a large pan of boiling water for 7–8 minutes, or until soft, adding the prawns 5 minutes before the end of the cooking time. Drain well. Cut the asparagus into ¼-inch/5-mm slices, discarding the tough, woody parts at the base of the spears. Place the asparagus and cubed shrimp into a salad bowl.

Heat a drizzle of oil in a skillet (frying pan), add the zucchini (courgette) and a pinch each of salt and pepper, and cook over medium heat for 5–6 minutes until light golden. Transfer to the salad bowl with the asparagus and the shrimp, then add the drained barley and toss everything together.

Put the mayonnaise, lemon juice, and parsley in a small bowl and mix well to blend everything together.

Garnish the salad with the reserved whole shrimp and a few basil leaves and serve with the flavored mayonnaise on the side.

NOTE For a more sophisticated dish, replace the jumbo shrimp (king prawns) with Mazzancolle shrimp. These Mediterranean crustaceans belong to the same family as shrimp but they have a gray or yellow-pinkish color with larger purplish stains, are bigger, and have a more delicate flavor than jumbo shrimp.

Preparation time: 15 minutes, plus cooling
Cooking time: 15 minutes
Wine suggestion: Martina Franca

Fregola Pasta Salad with Chickpeas, Red Onion, and Cherry Tomatoes

Serves 4

7 oz/200 g fregola pasta
  (or pearl couscous)
7–8 cherry tomatoes, sliced
1 red onion (ideally a red
  Tropea onion), cut into
  small wedges
2/3 cup (3 1/2 oz/100 g)
  rinsed and drained,
  canned chickpeas
1/3 cup (1 1/2 oz/40 g) pitted
  (stoned) black olives
4 tablespoons extra virgin
  olive oil
zest and juice of 1 unwaxed
  lemon—the zest needs to
  be cut into very thin strips
2 small flat-leaf parsley sprigs,
  chopped 1 tablespoon
  chopped basil
salt and pepper

Cook the pasta in a large pan of boiling salted water according to the package directions until al dente, then drain well. Spread the pasta evenly on a baking sheet and let cool.

Put the cherry tomatoes, onion, chickpeas, olives, and cooled pasta into a salad bowl. Pour over the oil and lemon juice, then add the parsley and basil, season with salt, pepper, and toss to mix well. Serve the salad garnished with some strips of lemon zest.

NOTE Fregola—or fregula—is a traditional type of pasta made with durum wheat semolina in Sardinia. It is produced by "rolling" the semolina in a large ceramic bowl and then toasting it in the oven. Fregola comes in the shape of irregular little balls about 1/8–5/8 inch/ 2–15 mm in diameter. It is ideally suited for rich fish or seafood sauces, and goes particularly well with clams.

GLU⊄EN-FREE

CEREALS

The crossed-out ear of wheat is now universally recognized as the gluten-free mark. The symbol is shown on all products that are free from gluten, either naturally or through processing and packaging, and that are suitable for consumption by people affected by celiac disease, as well as by various types of intolerance to this protein, which is present mainly in wheat and other cereals.

Nowadays it is possible to enjoy bread, cookies (biscuits), and even pizza without fear of allergic reactions.

RICE

There are many cereal alternatives that are naturally free of gluten, starting with simple rice, which is the most widely consumed gluten-free cereal in the world. There are several varieties, from brown rice, which retains all its nutritive properties as it has not been processed and bleached in any way, to refined rice, made primarily of starch, which is a sugar complex. In Italy, the land of risotto, there are at least 50 varieties of rice, differing in shape, size, and use.

AMARANTH

Amaranth is not part of the Gramineae but the Amaranthaceae family. Rich in starch and easily digestible proteins, it has a high lysine content and essential amino acids such as calcium, phosphorous, magnesium, and iron. Thanks to its sweet and slightly nutty flavor, it is perfect for soup but also as a base for cookies. Its puffed variety can be combined with yogurt.

QUINOA

Rich in lysine, phosphorous, potassium, and manganese, quinoa belongs to the Chenopodiaceae family, which also includes spinach and red turnip. It has the appearance of small seeds, similar to those of millet but flatter. It can be used as a base for soups or salads, and its flour is excellent for bread, cookies, and also for baby food.

MILLET

Similar to wheat but gluten-free, millet is one of the most widely used cereals in the world. Easily digestible and rich in starch, minerals, and vitamins A and B, millet is the most highly recommended food for pregnant women and convalescent people. In recipes it is versatile and tasty. Once cooked, thanks to its high concentration of starch, it works well as a basis for pies, croquettes, gnocchi, or meatballs. It is very good in warm salads, combined with seasonal vegetables. Millet flour can be used to make excellent dry crackers.

BUCKWHEAT

Originally from Asia, buckwheat is part of the Poligonaceae family. Rich in iron, magnesium, and vitamins B and E, it contains essential amino acids such as lysine and tryptophan, which have a good effect on the central nervous system and are beneficial in cases of physical debilitation. The biological value of its proteins is similar to that of meat and soya. It can be used as flour for pizza, pasta, or polenta, and it is the essential ingredient in Pizzoccheri Valtellinesi (see page 364).

CORN

One of the first cereals to come to Europe following Christopher Columbus, maize is particularly rich from a nutritional point of view because of its content of iron, phosphorous, potassium, and vitamin A. It is a versatile food that can be consumed after cooking or transformed into oil, popcorn, or flour. Its flour is used in many preparations, with polenta probably the better known, but it is also good for bread, desserts, and fresh pasta. When it is refined, cornstarch (cornflour) is obtained, which can be used in cooking as a thickener. Maize is rich in vitamins, fiber, and antioxidants, and is beneficial for the skin.

Preparation time: 10 minutes

Cooking time: 25 minutes

Wine suggestion: Etna Rosato

Bulgur Wheat with Green Soybean and Eggplant Sauce

Serves 4

2¹/₂ cups (20 fl oz/600 ml)
  vegetable broth (stock)
¹/₄ teaspoon ground turmeric
2 cups (11 oz/300 g)
  bulgur wheat
2 tablespoons extra virgin
  olive oil, plus extra
  for drizzling
1 clove garlic
¹/₄ teaspoon dried oregano
1 eggplant (aubergine),
  cut into small cubes
5 canned peeled
  tomatoes, chopped
2¹/₄ cups (14 oz/400 g) cooked
  fresh green soybeans
salt

Pour the broth (stock) into a pan, add the turmeric, and bring to a boil. Add the bulgur wheat to the boiling broth and cook for 10 minutes, then remove from the heat and let stand, uncovered, until all the broth has been absorbed. Use a fork to loosen the grains of bulgur wheat. Taste to check the seasoning and add salt if necessary.

Heat the oil in a skillet (frying pan), add the garlic and oregano, and cook over medium heat for 1 minute, then add the eggplant (aubergine), season with salt, and cook over a high heat for 6–7 minutes, stirring, until golden. Add the tomatoes and continue to cook for an additional 5 minutes, then add the soybeans and cook for 5 minutes more.

Serve the bulgur wheat with the soybean and eggplant sauce and drizzle over a little extra oil.

NOTE Bulgur wheat is a hard sprouted grain that has been parboiled and cracked. It is a food with a very high nutritional value. Bulgur wheat is a staple of Lebanese cuisine, and is cooked in a variety of different ways, for example molded and served with various legumes, vegetables, or meat fillings, or used to make tabbouleh, a summer salad with onions, tomatoes, flat-leaf parsley, and lemon.

Preparation time: 15 minutes, plus soaking

Cooking time: 40 minutes

Wine suggestion: Monreale Bianco

Pearled Barley with Trapanese Pesto

Serves 4

1¼ cups (9 oz/250 g)
  pearled barley
salt and pepper
coarsely ground almonds,
  to garnish

For the pesto
2 tomatoes (about 9 oz/250 g)
1 clove garlic
3½ tablespoons extra virgin
  olive oil
2 cups (2 oz/50 g) basil leaves,
  plus extra to garnish
⅓ cup (2 oz/50 g)
  peeled almonds
1 tablespoon grated
  pecorino cheese

Soak the pearled barley in a large bowl of cold water for 2–3 hours.

Meanwhile, skin the tomatoes. Bring a large pan of water to a boil. Lightly score a cross into the skin of each tomato. Drop the tomatoes into the boiling water and leave them for 30 seconds. Drain the tomatoes, then carefully peel off the skins and discard. Coarsely chop the tomatoes.

To make the pesto, put the tomatoes, garlic, oil, basil, and almonds into a food processor and process until the sauce is smooth and homogenous. Season with salt and pepper, add the pecorino and a drizzle more oil, and blend well. Transfer to a bowl and chill in the refrigerator.

Rinse the barley under cold running water, then cook in a large pan of abundantly salted boiling water for 40 minutes, or until tender. Drain well and let cool a little.

Toss the drained barley with the pesto and garnish with ground almonds and basil leaves.

TIP Classic Genoese pesto, which does not include tomatoes, can be used to replace the Trapanese pesto shown in this recipe. Put 2 cups (2 oz/50 g) basil leaves and ⅓ cup (1½ oz/40 g) pine nuts into a food processor and blend well, gradually adding extra virgin olive oil until you have a fluid cream, then stir in 1 tablespoon grated Parmesan or pecorino cheese. Cook the pearled barley as above, toss with the pesto, and garnish with coarsely chopped sun-dried cherry tomatoes that have been preserved in oil.

Preparation time: 35 minutes, plus resting
Cooking time: 20 minutes
Wine suggestion: Vermentino di Gallura

Rich Bulgur Wheat Salad

Serves 4

1 1/4 cups (7 3/4 oz/220 g)
  bulgur wheat
extra virgin olive oil
2 cloves garlic, sliced
1 small red bell pepper,
  cored, seeded,
  and chopped
1/2 eggplant
  (aubergine), diced
pinch of dried oregano
pinch of chili powder
1 cup (5 oz/150 g) rinsed and
  drained, canned chickpeas
1/2 teaspoon paprika
2 small zucchini
  (courgettes), sliced
1 mint sprig, leaves torn
2 tablespoons white
  wine vinegar
salt

Put the bulgur wheat in a pan and cover with twice its volume of water. Bring to a boil and cook over medium heat for about 20 minutes or until the water has been completely absorbed. Remove from the heat, drizzle with a little oil and then use a fork to loosen the bulgur wheat grains.

Meanwhile, heat a little oil in a pan, add half the garlic, and cook over low heat for 1 minute, then add the bell pepper, eggplant (aubergine), oregano, and chili, season with salt, and cook for 6–7 minutes, stirring continuously, until the vegetables are soft and well browned. Transfer to a large bowl and set aside.

Heat 1 tablespoon oil in a skillet (frying pan), add the chickpeas and the paprika, and cook over medium heat for 5 minutes, stirring continuously, until they are completely coated. Transfer to the bowl with the cooked vegetables.

Using the same skillet, heat a drizzle of oil, add the zucchini (courgettes), and cook over medium heat for 2–3 minutes until golden brown. Remove from the heat, add the remaining garlic, mint, and vinegar, and season with salt. Transfer to the bowl with the cooked vegetables and chickpeas.

Mix the bulgur wheat with the vegetable and chickpea mixture and let rest for at least 30 minutes before serving.

NOTE Chickpeas are one of the most common legumes (pulses) in the history of food. They are rich in elements that are effective in the control of cholesterol. There is a variety of black chickpea that is very rich in iron, which is commonly grown in the provinces of Bari and Matera in Italy (see tip on page 341).

Preparation time: 20 minutes, plus soaking

Cooking time: 55 minutes

Wine suggestion: Conegliano Valdobbiadene Prosecco Superiore Brut

Pearled Barley and Spinach Croquettes

Serves 4

1 cup (7 oz/200 g)
  pearled barley
1 onion, chopped
4 cups (7 oz/200 g) chopped
  baby leaf spinach
2 carrots, chopped
2 tablespoons
  fresh breadcrumbs
salt and pepper

Soak the pearled barley in a large bowl of cold water for 2–3 hours. Rinse the barley under cold running water, then cook in a large pan of abundantly salted boiling water (you need about three times the barley's volume in water) for 40 minutes, or until tender. Drain well and let cool.

Preheat the oven to 350°F/180°C/Gas mark 4. Line a baking sheet with parchment (baking) paper.

In a large bowl, mix together the drained barley, onion, spinach, carrots, breadcrumbs, and a pinch each of salt and pepper. Using your hands, divide the barley mixture into 12 balls and then press down each ball with the palm of your hand to shape the croquettes. Alternatively, put spoonfuls of the mixture into a large metal ring or cookie cutter, then remove the ring or cutter and press down with the palm of your hand.

Place the croquettes on the prepared baking sheet and bake in the oven for 15 minutes, or until golden brown.

TIP   These delicious, and entirely vegetarian, croquettes are perfect on their own but can also be used to fill buns, just like a burger. Choose a soft bun with a delicate taste and fill it with a few slices of tomato, some salad greens (leaves), a croquette, and a little mayonnaise.

Preparation time: 30 minutes

Cooking time: 1 hour

Green Pea Einkorn Risotto with Vegetables and Bagna Cauda

Serves 4

2/3 cup (3¼ oz/90 g)
   frozen peas
2 tablespoons extra virgin
   olive oil
½ small white onion,
   finely chopped
1 sage leaf
1¼ cups (9 oz/250 g) einkorn,
   rinsed
2 teaspoons salt
2 tablespoons (1¼ oz/
   30 g) butter
⅓ cup (1 oz/25 g) grated
   Grana Padano cheese
5¼ oz/150 g mixed
   vegetables, such as
   cauliflower, beet (beetroot),
   bell pepper

For the bagna cauda
1 clove garlic, crushed
2 anchovy fillets preserved in
   salt, well rinsed and boned
3 tablespoons extra virgin
   olive oil

Cook the peas in a pan of boiling water for 5 minutes, then drain. Transfer the peas to a food processor and blend to a purée. Pass the purée through a strainer (sieve) into a bowl and set aside.

Make the einkorn risotto. Heat a little oil in a skillet (frying pan), add the onion and sage, and cook over medium heat for 5 minutes, or until just starting to brown. Add the einkorn and cook over a low heat for 1 minute, then add 3 cups (24 fl oz/700 ml) cold water and a little salt and bring to a boil. Cook over low–medium heat for 50 minutes, or until the einkorn is al dente. Remove from the heat and stir in the butter, Grana Padano, and the pea purée.

Meanwhile, cook the mixed vegetables in a large pan of boiling water until tender. Drain and purée each vegetable separately in a food processor with a little oil. Set aside.

Make the bagna cauda. Put the garlic into a small pan, pour over just enough water to cover the garlic, and bring to a boil. Add the anchovies and oil and cook over medium heat for 3–4 minutes until the anchovies have dissolved.

To serve, divide the risotto among individual serving dishes, flattening the surface with the back of a spoon. Garnish with a few drops of the puréed vegetables and a few drops of bagna cauda.

♀ **WINE SUGGESTION**   Chianti is made with 100 percent Sangiovese grapes. It is a wine with a great personality, a good bouquet with tones of violet, red fruits, prunes, and sour cherries, and light spicy notes. Its marked acidity makes this wine a very suitable choice to match a dish with strong flavors.

⊙ Preparation time: 30 minutes, plus soaking
Cooking time: 1 hour

♀ Wine suggestion: Erbaluce di Caluso

Whole Wheat Cereal Salad

Serves 4

⅓ cup (2¼ oz/60 g)
  wheat berries
¼ cup (2¼ oz/60 g)
  hulled barley
⅓ cup (2¼ oz/60 g)
  oat groats
⅓ cup (2¼ oz/60 g)
  buckwheat, rinsed
4 teaspoons extra virgin
  olive oil
1 small tomato, cut into
  thin wedges
1 small red bell pepper,
  cored, seeded, and cut into
  small cubes
1 small yellow bell pepper,
  cored, seeded, and cut into
  small cubes
½ cup (2¼ oz/60 g)
  peeled, seeded,
  and diced cucumber
2 small flat-leaf parsley
  sprigs, chopped
salt

To serve
thinly sliced cucumber
thinly sliced tomatoes

Soak the wheat and barley in a large bowl of cold water for 8 hours. Rinse well.

Meanwhile, in a separate bowl, soak the oats in cold water for 6 hours. Rinse well.

Cook the wheat and barley in a large pan of abundantly salted boiling water for 10 minutes. Add the oats and continue to cook for 30 minutes, then add the buckwheat and cook for 20 minutes more. Drain well and transfer to a bowl. Drizzle over 3 teaspoons oil, mix well, and let cool.

Put the tomatoes, bell peppers, cucumber and drained mixed cereals into a salad bowl, drizzle over the remaining oil, sprinkle over a pinch of salt and the parsley, and toss to mix well.

Serve the salad at room temperature on a bed of sliced tomatoes and cucumber.

Buckwheat with Spinach

Serves 4

2 cups (11¼ oz/
320 g) buckwheat
4 tablespoons extra virgin
olive oil
2 cloves garlic, chopped
1 onion, chopped
pinch of chili powder
2 cups (4 oz/120 g)
sliced spinach
4 teaspoons soy sauce
thinly sliced tomatoes, to
garnish (optional)

Cook the buckwheat in a large pan of abundantly salted boiling water for 20 minutes until tender. Drain well.

Meanwhile, heat the oil in a skillet (frying pan), add the garlic, onion, and 4 tablespoons water, and cook over low heat for 5 minutes, or until soft and transparent but not browned. Add the chili powder, spinach, and soy sauce, stir well, and cook over medium heat for a few minutes until the spinach is cooked.

Transfer the drained buckwheat to the skillet with the spinach, mix well, and cook over medium heat for a few minutes until heated through. Serve hot, garnished with some thinly sliced tomatoes, if liked.

NOTE Included among the list of traditional agro-foods are Tuscan buckwheat (also called *fagopiro* or black wheat), buckwheat from the Valle Monregalese del Casotto in Piedmont, and Lombardy buckwheat flour produced in Teglio, in the province of Sondrio. There is also a Slow Food group for Valtellina buckwheat that aims to restore the typical stone-built agricultural terraces in the area.

Preparation time: 20 minutes
Cooking time: 20 minutes
Wine suggestion: Valtellina Superiore Grumello

Pizzoccheri Pasta with Cheese

Serves 4

1 potato (about 5¼ oz/
    160 g), peeled and cut into
    large pieces
2 cups (4¼ oz/125 g)
    chopped Savoy cabbage,
    Swiss chard, or spinach
12 oz/350 g pizzoccheri pasta
1 stick (4¼ oz/125 g) butter
1 clove garlic, crushed
1¼ cups (3½ oz/100 g)
    grated Parmesan cheese
5¼ oz/160 g Valtellina Casera
    cheese, thinly sliced
salt and pepper

Preheat the oven to 350°F/180°C/Gas mark 4. Place an 8 x 6-inch/20 x 15-cm ovenproof dish in the oven to warm.

Bring a large pan of abundantly salted water to a boil. Add the potatoes and the cabbage, chard, or spinach, bring back to a boil, and cook over medium heat for 5 minutes, then add the pasta and cook for an additional 12–15 minutes until the pasta and potatoes are cooked.

Meanwhile, just before the end of the cooking time, put the butter and garlic in a small pan and heat gently until the butter has melted.

Using a slotted spoon, transfer some of pasta and the vegetables to the hot ovenproof dish and spread out to form a layer in the bottom of the dish. Sprinkle over some Parmesan and then cover with some slices of Valtellina Casera. Repeat these layers until you have used up all the ingredients. Pour the melted butter and garlic mixture over the top, season with pepper, and serve immediately on hot plates.

TIP   To make homemade pizzoccheri, sift (sieve) 2 cups (12 oz/ 350 g) buckwheat flour and ¾ cup (3½ oz/100 g) all-purpose (plain) flour together into a mound on a countertop and add a pinch of salt. Using your hands, mix the ingredients together and then gradually add water, a little at a time, and knead the mixture until you have a smooth dough. Shape the dough into a ball, cover with a dish towel, and let rest for 20 minutes. Roll out the dough to a thickness of about ⅛-inch/2 mm using a rolling pin, or put it through a pasta machine. Cut the pasta into 1½-inch/4-cm strips and then cut those strips into ribbons about 2¾ inches/7 cm long. Leave the pasta to dry on a cutting (chopping) board, moving them from time to time to help them dry.

CHEF
Claudio Vicina

Preparation time: 30 minutes
Cooking time: 50 minutes

Spelt with Meatballs and Carpione Sauce

Serves 4

10 rosemary leaves
3 tablespoons extra virgin
  olive oil
1/2 small white onion,
  finely chopped
1 1/2 cups (9 oz/250 g)
  spelt, rinsed
1 3/4 teaspoons salt

For the meatballs
4 oz/120 g wet, stale bread
11 oz/300 g ground
  (minced) veal
2 tablespoons grated
  Parmesan cheese
1 teaspoon salt
1 egg
4–5 tablespoons extra virgin
  olive oil
1 1/2 tablespoons (3/4 oz/
  20 g) butter
1 rosemary sprig, leaves only

For the carpione sauce
2 tablespoons extra virgin
  olive oil
1 red onion, sliced
3 1/2 tablespoons red
  wine vinegar
1 thyme sprig, leaves only
1 rosemary sprig, leaves only
1 leaf each sage and bay
3 1/2 tablespoons red wine

Tie the rosemary leaves together with kitchen string, then put them in a large pan with 3 cups (25 fl oz/750 ml) water and bring to a boil.

Meanwhile, heat the oil in a skillet (frying pan), add the onion, and cook over low heat for 4–5 minutes until soft. Add the spelt and cook for a few minutes until starting to brown, then add the salt and a ladleful of the rosemary-flavored boiling water and cook for about 40 minutes, gradually adding in more of the boiling water, a ladleful at a time, until all the liquid is absorbed by the spelt.

Meanwhile, make the meatballs. Squeeze the bread to expel any excess moisture. Put the bread, ground (minced) veal, Parmesan, salt, and egg into a large bowl and mix together. Using your hands, shape the mixture into meatballs, each about 1 1/4 inches/3 cm in diameter.

Heat the oil and butter in a skillet with the rosemary, then add the meatballs and cook over medium heat for 7–8 minutes until cooked through.

To make the carpione sauce, heat the oil in a skillet, add the onion, and cook over low heat for 5 minutes, or until soft and transparent. Add the vinegar and cook for a few minutes until it has evaporated, then add the herbs and wine, season with salt, if necessary, and cook for 5–6 minutes until the sauce has thickened. Transfer the sauce to a food processor and blend until smooth.

Divide the spelt among serving plates, put the meatballs in the middle and garnish with a few drops of carpione sauce. Serve immediately.

WINE SUGGESTION   Vino Libero PGI (Protected Geographical Indication) is a 100-percent Sangiovese wine obtained without the use of chemical fertilizers or weed killers, and it has a very low sulfur content. It is a fresh flower-scented wine, with tones of violet and red fruits, and has a rounded taste and persistent and harmonic tannins. It is a very good accompaniment to meat.

BREADS, PIZZAS, FOCACCIAS, AND FRITTERS

Preparation time: 35 minutes, plus rising
Cooking time: 10–15 minutes
Wine suggestion: Alto Adige Gewürztraminer

Pizza with Mozzarella Cheese, Gorgonzola Cheese, Walnuts, and Pears

Makes 8 pizzas

4 cups (1 lb 2 oz/500 g)
all-purpose (plain) flour,
plus extra for dusting

3²/₃ cups (1 lb 2 oz/500 g)
whole wheat (wholemeal)
or white bread (strong) flour

2 teaspoons crumbled
brewer's yeast or
1 teaspoon active dry yeast

4 teaspoons fine salt

extra virgin olive oil,
for greasing

1 pear

1 lb 2 oz/500 g fior di latte
mozzarella cheese, cut into
small cubes

9 oz/250 g Gorgonzola
cheese, cut into small cubes

10 walnuts, halved

2 sprigs thyme, leaves only,
to garnish (optional)

Sift (sieve) the two types of flour together into a mound on a countertop and make a well in the center. Pour 2 cups (17 fl oz/500 ml) warm water into the middle and add the yeast. Using your hands, mix everything together and knead for a few minutes, then add the salt and ⅓ cup plus 1 tablespoon (3½ fl oz/ 100 ml) warm water and knead until the dough is well blended. Continue to knead, slowing adding 3½ tablespoons warm water, then shape the dough into a small loaf. Place the dough in a large oiled bowl, cover it with a damp dish towel, and let rise at room temperature for 3 hours, or until doubled in size.

Preheat the oven to 425°F/220°C/Gas mark 7. Grease several baking sheet with oil.

Divide the dough into eight pieces. Roll out the dough on a lightly floured surface into circles about 10¼ inches/26 cm in diameter and ½ inch/1 cm thick. Place the pizzas on the prepared baking sheets. Thinly slice the pear. Arrange the pear slices on top of the pizzas, then sprinkle over the mozzarella and Gorgonzola. Bake in the oven for 10–15 minutes until golden brown—you may need to bake the pizzas in batches. Garnish the pizzas with the walnuts and serve.

TIP For this recipe we suggest using walnuts from the Campania region of Italy, where the ancient Sorrento and Malizia varieties are still produced: they are grown in the fertile areas of the Nolano-Palmese-Sarnese countryside and harvested by hand in September and October. In addition to their high quality, these walnuts are characterized by the ease with which the nuts are extracted from the shells, almost always remaining whole.

Neapolitan Pizza
Versus Roman Pizza

Some people like their pizza base thin, some prefer deep-dish, some want a soft pizza while others prefer crispy, but often we forget the main thing: it should be tasty and expertly prepared. When it comes to pizza, stereotypes are plentiful and it is not uncommon for discussions to run aground on the eternal conflict between those who claim that Neapolitan pizza is stodgy and hard to digest and those who instead believe that for a pizza to be pizza, it needs to be deep and have a thick crust, forgetting that what matters is to follow precise processing stages, a correctly risen dough, and the use of quality ingredients. Preferring one type of pizza to another is a matter of taste, but it is an essential requirement for the pizza to be digestible.

AVOIDING MISUNDERSTANDINGS

Many people, when they claim their unconditional love for thin and crispy pizzas, don't know that they are in fact praising the Roman style of pizza making, called "*scrocchiarella*" in Rome, whose characteristics are the opposite of the traditional Neapolitan pizza. They neglect the fact that a heavy, rubbery, sometimes undercooked pizza that is difficult to finish and to digest means that they have consumed a product that was prepared with little care, was badly leavened, and that could be described, yes, as "deep" and "small", but is certainly not a properly Neapolitan pizza.

Let's be clear about this then. The main difference between Neapolitan and Roman pizza is not the size, the softness, or the thickness, but first of all the recipe, which requires the use of different types of flour, leavening methods, and cooking times.

NEAPOLITAN PIZZA, GUARANTEED TRADITIONAL SPECIALTY

In February 2010, Neapolitan pizza obtained recognition as a "Guaranteed traditional specialty" from the European Union, which means this is a product whose ingredients, dimensions, preparation modes, and cooking times are strictly determined.

No fats are used for the dough of Neapolitan pizza, only water, flour, brewer's yeast or mother yeast, and salt, and ambient temperature processing for 12–24 hours. In terms of liquid, the amount of water used is around 60 percent of the weight of flour used. The weight of a dough ball used for an average pizza is around 8¼ oz/230 g.

Pizza is stretched by hand to a diameter no greater than 14 inches/35 cm, respecting the honeycomb structure of the dough and without touching the edges of the baking sheet (the "cornice"), which must be ½–¾ inch/1–2 cm deep.

In terms of toppings, the only acceptable ones are peeled tomatoes, mozzarella ("Mozzarella di Bufala Campana AOP" or "Mozzarella STG"), garlic, a drizzle of olive oil, salt, and fresh basil leaves.

Cooking, which takes barely 60–90 seconds, takes place in wood-fired, low-vaulted ovens where temperatures of up to 923°F/500°C can be reached. This results in a product that is soft on the inside and crisp on the outside. An essential requirement for Neapolitan pizza is, in fact, its softness.

ROMAN SCROCCHIARELLA

Roman pizza is prepared with soft type 00 or type 0 flour, brewer's yeast or mother yeast, olive or vegetable oil, and salt, in such proportions as to obtain a compact, consistent dough with a hydration level of around 50 percent. Leavening takes place at ambient temperature for a shorter time than Neapolitan pizza—normally the dough is prepared in the morning to be used the same evening—or it is done using a cold process, where the dough is refrigerated to 39°F/4°C.

A rolling pin is normally used to stretch the dough, both because the dough is harder and because it is necessary to achieve a uniform thickness much less than for Neapolitan pizza.

The weight of dough ball used for an average pizza is around 5 oz/150 g. Cooking, which lasts more-or-less 2 minutes, takes place at a lower temperature than that used for Neapolitan pizza: in this way the dough is cooked on the inside too, and becomes crisp.

Even though it has a shorter leavening time, Roman pizza is still easy to digest because it has been cooked for longer. As the base is quite light, it is possible to use ingredients of various types as toppings, without the risk of making the pizza too rich.

⊙ Preparation time: 30 minutes, plus rising
Cooking time: 25 minutes

♀ Wine suggestion: Alghero Vermentino Frizzante

Muffins with Green Olive Pâté and Ham

Makes 8–10 muffins

1 tablespoon brewer's yeast
or ½ tablespoon active
dry yeast
4 tablespoons tepid milk
2⅓ cups (11 oz/300 g) all-
purpose (plain) flour
2½ tablespoons lard
½ teaspoon fine salt
½ cup (6¼ oz/180 g) green
olive pâté
5 oz/150 g cooked ham,
sliced (about 1 cup)

In a small bowl, dissolve the yeast with 3½ tablespoons of the milk.

Mix the flour with the lard, ⅓ cup plus 1 tablespoon (3½ fl oz/100 ml) warm water, and the yeast mixture, then add the salt, mix everything together, and knead thoroughly until smooth. Place the dough in a large bowl, cover with a dish towel, and let rise at room temperature for 40 minutes, or until doubled in size.

Divide the dough into 1½-oz/40-g portions (8–10 pieces) and flatten them to make the muffins. Place the muffins on baking sheets lined with parchment (baking) paper, cover with a dish towel, and let rise at room temperature for 20 minutes.

Preheat the oven to 350°F/180°C/Gas mark 4.

With your fingertips, make indentations onto the surface of the muffins. Brush the dough with the remaining milk and bake in the oven for 25 minutes until golden brown and crisp. Let cool.

Cut the muffins in half through the middle. Spread each bottom layer with the green olive pâté, top with sliced ham, then close with the top half of each roll.

NOTE   Nowadays lard is rarely used in our kitchens as it has been replaced by extra virgin olive oil and butter, but lard is still often used for making bread. As with oil and butter, this animal fat makes the dough more manageable, improves its taste, and makes for a softer and more aromatic bread.

⊙   Preparation time: 40 minutes, plus rising

Cooking time: 30–35 minutes

Seasoned Soft Dough Knots

Makes 7 knots

2 teaspoons crumbled
  brewer's yeast or
   1 teaspoon active dry yeast
2 teaspoons honey
2 teaspoons fine salt
4 cups (1 lb 2 oz/500 g) white
  bread (strong) flour (ideally
  W280), plus extra
  for dusting
2¹/₂ tablespoons lard
1¹/₂ tablespoons extra virgin
  olive oil

For the biga
1¹/₄ cups (5 oz/150 g)
  Manitoba flour or white
  bread (strong) flour
¹/₂ teaspoon brewer's yeast
  or ¹/₄ teaspoon instant yeast
extra virgin olive oil, for oiling

First prepare the biga. Put the Manitoba flour, yeast, and ¹/₃ cup plus 1 tablespoon (3¹/₂ fl oz/100 ml) warm water in a bowl, quickly mix with a wooden spoon, and then shape the dough into a ball. Oil the dough ball, cover it with a damp dish towel, and let rise at room temperature for 15–24 hours until doubled in size.

In a small bowl, dissolve the yeast with ¹/₃ cup plus 1 tablespoon (3¹/₂ fl oz/100 ml) warm water. In a separate small bowl, dissolve the salt and honey with ²/₃ cup (5 fl oz/150 ml) warm water.

Put the white bread (strong) flour into a mound on the countertop, make a well in the center, and put the yeast mixture, lard, and oil into this. Using your hands, mix everything together and then knead the dough, slowly adding the salt and honey mixture to the dough. Knead for a short time to mix the ingredients together, then add the biga and continue to knead until the two types of dough have been thoroughly blended and the dough is smooth and elastic. Place the dough in a large bowl, cover it with a damp dish towel, and let rise at room temperature for 10–15 minutes.

Divide the dough into seven pieces. On a lightly floured countertop, roll out each piece of dough into a cylinder about 9³/₄ inches/25 cm long, then tie into a knot and join the two free ends until a continuous knot is obtained. Place the knots on a floured baking sheet and let rise in a warm place for about 1 hour or until doubled in size.

Preheat the oven to 400°F/200°C/Gas mark 6. Bake the knots in the oven for 30–35 minutes until golden brown and crisp. Let cool.

NOTE   Biga is a rather dry preparation, obtained by mixing water, flour, and yeast, that allows you to create a lighter bread. It requires the use of strong flours. The resting time will vary depending on the temperature (the ideal temperature is between 60°F/16°C and 64°F/18°C).

⊙   Preparation time: 20 minutes, plus chilling

Cooking time: 35 minutes

♀   Wine suggestion: Valle d'Aosta Petit Rouge

Rice and Cheese Fritters

Serves 4

1½ cups (11 oz/300 g)
   Arborio or Carnaroli rice
3 eggs, beaten
⅓ cup plus 1 tablespoon
   (3½ fl oz/100 ml) milk
3½ oz/100 g mild semi-firm
   cheese (ideally fontina
   cheese), cut into cubes
⅔ cup (2 oz/50 g) grated
   Parmesan cheese
piece of butter, softened
2 marjoram sprigs, leaves
   chopped, plus extra
   to garnish
3–4 sage leaves, chopped
vegetable oil, for frying
salt and pepper

Cook the rice in a large pan of boiling salted water for 18 minutes, or until al dente. Drain and let cool.

Transfer the cooled rice to a bowl, add the eggs, milk, fontina, Parmesan, and butter, and mix well. Let chill in the refrigerator for 1 hour, then stir in the herbs and season with salt and pepper.

Pour enough oil into a deep skillet (frying pan) so that it is about ½ inch/1 cm deep. Heat the oil to 340°F/170°C, then carefully drop tablespoonfuls of the rice mixture into the skillet and cook the fritters, a few at a time, over medium heat for 2–3 minutes, turning several times, until golden brown. Remove with a slotted spoon, drain on paper towels, and keep warm while you cook the remaining fritters. Sprinkle with a little salt and serve hot.

TIP This recipe can be adapted with endless variations and is perfect for using up leftover cooked rice. Try adding different ingredients to the mixture, such as cubes of cheese, cooked vegetables, or small pieces of cooked ham. You could also change the shape and the way the fritters are cooked. Instead of making lots of small fritters, make one large fritter by heating a little oil in a nonstick skillet (frying pan), then adding all the rice mixture and cooking over medium heat for 5–6 minutes on each side until golden. Or, for a lighter version, spoon the rice mixture into a greased high-sided ovenproof dish and bake in an oven preheated to 375°F/190°C/Gas mark 5 for 12 minutes, or until golden.

⊙   Preparation time: 30 minutes, plus rising
Cooking time: 20–30 minutes

Walnut Bread

Makes 4 loaves

4 cups (1 lb 2 oz/500 g)
  all-purpose (plain) flour
4 cups (lb 2 oz/500 g) buratto
  flour or white bread
  (strong) flour
1¾ tablespoons crumbled
  brewer's yeast or
  2¼ teaspoons active
  dry yeast
4¼ cups (1 lb 2 oz/500 g)
  walnuts, chopped
1¾ tablespoons fine salt

Sift (sieve) the two types of flour together into a mound on a countertop and make a well in the center. Pour generous 2 cups (17 fl oz/500 ml) warm water into the middle and add the yeast. Using your hands, mix everything together and knead for a few minutes, then add the walnuts and knead again. Add the salt and continue to knead, slowing adding ¾ cup plus 1 tablespoon (7 fl oz/200 ml) warm water, until the dough is smooth and elastic.

Divide the dough into four pieces and shape each piece into a loaf shape—you should have four 1-lb/450-g loaves. Place the loaves on a baking sheet lined with parchment (baking) paper, cover with a dish towel, and let rise at room temperature for 3 hours, or until doubled in size.

Preheat the oven to 450°F/230°C/Gas mark 8. Bake the loaves in the oven for 20–30 minutes until golden brown. Let cool.

NOTE   One of the fundamental steps in bread making is the biological leavening that occurs due to microorganisms, which break down complex sugars and turn them into carbon dioxide. In Italy, the most commonly known yeast is fresh yeast. It can often be bought in 1-oz/2-g blocks, and should normally be stored in the refrigerator.

Olive Bread

Makes 4 loaves

4 cups (1 lb 2 oz/500 g) all-purpose (plain) flour

4 cups (1 lb 2 oz/500 g) buratto flour or white bread (strong) flour

4 teaspoons crumbled brewer's yeast or 2 teaspoons active dry yeast

3½ cups (1 lb 2 oz/500 g) coarsely chopped, pitted (stoned) olives (ideally Taggiasca olives)

1¾ tablespoons fine salt

Sift (sieve) the two types of flour together into a mound on a countertop and make a well in the center. Pour generous 2 cups (17 fl oz/500 ml) warm water into the middle and add the yeast. Using your hands, mix everything together and knead for a few minutes, then add the olives and knead again. Add the salt and continue to knead, slowing adding ¾ cup plus 1 tablespoon (7 fl oz/200 ml) warm water, until the dough is smooth and elastic.

Divide the dough into four pieces and shape each piece into a loaf shape—you should have four 1-lb/450-g loaves. Place the loaves on a baking sheet lined with parchment (baking) paper, cover with a dish towel, and let rise at room temperature for 3 hours, or until doubled in size.

Preheat the oven to 450°F/230°C/Gas mark 8. Bake the loaves in the oven for 20–30 minutes until golden brown. Let cool.

NOTE Characteristic of western Liguria in Italy, and particularly of the province of Imperia, Taggiasca olives derive their name from the Taggia area, where they were imported by the St Colombanus monks. These small olives are among the tastiest table olives. Traditionally the olive harvesting in Imperia was done by women, who hand-picked any olives that had fallen to the ground and then beat the remaining olives off the branches onto dish towels stretched underneath.

FLOURS FOR PIZZAS, BREADS, AND FOCACCIAS

Over the last few years, thanks in part to the increased popularity of homemade bread, there has been a significant increase in the types of flour available on supermarket shelves. However, with this significant increase in consumer choice, there has been no parallel increase in the detailed information available to consumers who are increasingly better informed and more demanding. Average consumers, in fact, no longer limit themselves to distinguishing between flours for cakes, sweet (type 00) flour, or flour for savory preparations (type 0), which is furthermore a simplistic and often incorrect distinction.

SOFT GRAIN FLOUR: A FEW TECHNICAL DETAILS

The flours most suitable for bread, focaccia, and pizza are those made with soft grains. The two main parameters to consider when making a choice are the flour's degree of refinement and its strength.

With flour, refining refers to the sifting rate of the grain used. For whole wheat (wholemeal) flour (100 percent rate of sifting), the whole grain is used; for type 0 flour, the rate is about 72 percent, and for type 00 flour, it is barely 50 percent (only the inner part of the grain is used).

Flour strength, on the other hand, measures its resistance to mechanical stress during processing, and depends on its protein content (gliadin and glutenin), which fuses to form gluten when liquid is added. Because of its reticular structure, gluten traps molecules of carbon dioxide, which develop during fermentation. For this reason, "strong" flours that contain a high level of gluten can be used to make dough that is resistant and elastic, which can be stretched and compressed without breaking, and which can rise without collapsing, to make products that are soft and fluffy.

Flour strength is indicated by the letter "W", but is rarely reported on flour packaging for domestic use. Packaging also often lacks nutritional information such as the level of protein, which would be a good indication of the flour's strength. For very soft bread and leavened dough (pizza and focaccia), it is necessary to use flour with a W rating of at least 160. The greater the flour strength, the greater the quantity of water absorbed and the rising time, and the fluffier the products obtained.

The quantity of gluten present in flour is also linked to the sifting rate. Type 0 flour is "weak", and for this reason it is not particularly suited to bread making. Type 00 flour (average strength, with a W rating of 180–250) can be used for some types of bread or pizza. Type 1 and type 2 flours, which are difficult to find, are excellent for bread. It is possible to strengthen weak flours by adding Manitoba flour, which is produced with special grains and has a W grade of over 350. It absorbs 90 percent of its weight in water.

Generally speaking, while it is normally preferable to use strong flours for making bread, there are different viewpoints with regard to pizza, but the choice of flour must take into account the rising time available and the desired quality of the finished product.

OTHER FLOURS

When preparing whole wheat dough for bread or pizza, it is preferable to mix flours made of other cereals with wheat flour, which is richer in gluten, while for focaccia it is possible to make greater use of flours made with other cereals to produce a leavened product.

Flours that can be added in small quantities to dough, because they contain modest quantities of gluten, are rye flour, commonly used in Western Europe, and cornstarch (cornflour), which has a sweetish taste.

Up to 50 percent spelt flour can be used in dough mixes as it has a good capacity to develop gluten. It is also delicious and rich in fiber.

Kamut® flour, obtained from a particular type of wheat, is characterized by its high nutritional value, and so is quinoa flour, which can be used for up to a third of the total of flour used.

In Tuscany and Liguria, chickpea flour, which is very high in protein content, is often used for making focaccia.

TYPES OF YEAST

In Italy, the most common type of yeast is fresh yeast, which is refrigerated and sold in compressed cakes in grocery stores. Fresh yeast is highly perishable and can be hard to find in the U.S. It can instead be substituted for fast action dry yeast or instant yeast.

MOTHER YEAST VERSUS BREWER'S YEAST

Many physical and environmental factors, as well as manual dexterity, influence the various phases of baking, in particular the leavening phase. The combination of these factors makes every bake and bread unique.

RISING

Bread making is a delicate and complex operation, requiring experience to handle every aspect. One of the key points of the process is the leavening, in which the volume of dough increases through the action of microorganisms, such as yeast and bacteria, which trigger the fermentation processes. These microorganisms transform sugars into carbon dioxide and lactic acid, or alcohol, depending on which yeast is used. A good rise depends primarily on the correct use of the yeast, avoiding temperatures that are too low, making the yeast inactive, or too high, which would kill the microorganisms. This is why it is better not to freeze fresh yeast. After removing it from the refrigerator it should be brought gradually to its ideal temperature of 68–86°F/20–30°C. Rising will be affected by the environment in which the dough is left. Overly dry or humid environments can have negative consequences on the leavening process. Moisture, for example, acts unfavourably on the crunchiness of the bread and pizza. The dough should not be left to rise in a draught either as this will also hinder the leavening process.

BREWER'S YEAST

Brewer's yeast is a type of fresh yeast. The yeast was once taken directly from beer, while today it comes from the culture of Saccharomyces cerevisiae, sold fresh in compressed cakes or in dehydrated form. It should not be confused with the dietary supplement, which is an inactive form of brewer's yeast. Brewer's yeast is able to trigger alcohol fermentation, which is responsible for, among other things, the slight hint of alcohol in freshly baked products. It has a fast metabolism, is easy to find and use, but is often associated with breads that are not of excellent quality. In actual fact, providing the flour is also good quality, correct use of brewer's yeast can produce good results for both bread and pizza, perhaps even more so for pizza, for which the process is better suited to this type of yeast. A wood-fired oven can also greatly enhance the quality of the finished product.

MOTHER YEAST

Mother yeast can also be referred to as starter yeast, mother dough, natural yeast, natural leavening, or sourdough. Before the advent of brewer's yeast, mother yeast was the primary method of baking. It can give excellent results, but requires a laboriously slow preparation. The leaven is created using a paste of flour and water (preferably in equal measures), which is naturally fermented and acidified by various microbial fauna consisting of yeasts and bacteria. This leads to three types of fermentation: alcoholic, acetic, and lactic. Its management is not easy because it requires constant reinvigorating or 'feeding' with daily additions of water and flour. The leaven is added to the dough base, acting as a leavening agent, and activating a slow rise. Rising in this way produces a final product with more fragrance, complex aromas, and a longer shelf life thanks to its high acidity, which preserves it from fungal attack and from becoming stale. Breads made with mother yeast have a more uniform crumb, because the carbon dioxide develops gradually during rising and is more easily absorbed by the dough. The consistency of the dough is also different, with a soft and elastic feel when squeezed between your fingers. Finally, the bread is more easily digestible, due to the long period of resting and maturing before cooking, which allows the bacteria to transform complex molecules into simpler ones.

⊙ Preparation time: 40 minutes, plus rising
   Cooking time: 40–45 minutes
♀ Wine suggestion: Asprinio di Aversa Spumante

Fried Pizzas with Tomatoes, Mozzarella Cheese, and Basil

Makes 18–20 fried pizzas

generous 2 cups (17 fl oz/
   500 ml) sunflower oil, for
   deep-frying
14 oz/400 g fior di latte
   mozzarella cheese, diced
a few basil leaves, to garnish

For the sauce
1³/₄ cups (14 oz/400 g) fine
   tomato pulp
extra virgin olive oil
1 teaspoon chopped oregano
pinch of salt

For the dough
4 cups (1 lb 2 oz/500 g) all-
   purpose (plain) flour
3 cups (14 oz/400 g) whole
   wheat (wholemeal) or white
   bread (strong) flour
³/₄ cup (3¹/₂ oz/100 g)
   whole wheat (wholemeal)
   Manitoba flour or white
   bread (strong) flour
1 tablespoon crumbled
   brewer's yeast or
   1¹/₂ teaspoons active
   dry yeast
1¹/₂ teaspoons malt powder
4 teaspoons (³/₄ oz/20 g)
   fine salt

First make the sauce. Place the tomato pulp in a pan with the oregano, salt, and a drizzle of olive oil and cook over low heat for 40–45 minutes until the liquid has reduced and the sauce is thick and quite dry.

Meanwhile, make the dough. Sift (sieve) the three types of flour together into a mound on a countertop and make a well in the center. Pour generous 2 cups (17 fl oz/500 ml) warm water into the middle and add the yeast and malt. Using a fork, start mixing everything together, then add the salt and knead by hand until it has dissolved into the mixture. Knead for an additional 10 minutes, slowly adding ²/₃ cup (5 fl oz/150 ml) warm water, until the dough is smooth and elastic. Shape the dough into a ball, place in an oiled bowl, cover with a damp dish towel, and let rise at room temperature for 15–20 minutes.

Make 18–20 little dough balls, weighing about 2¹/₄ oz/60 g each, and stretch them lightly into discs on a countertop.

Pour the sunflower oil into a large deep pan, or deep-fat fryer, and heat the oil to 340°F/170°C. Carefully add two or three dough discs to the oil and cook over medium heat for 3–4 minutes on each side until golden. Remove with a slotted spoon, drain on paper towels, and keep warm. Repeat until all the dough discs have been cooked.

Serve the fried pizzas topped with a little tomato sauce and mozzarella, and garnished with a few basil leaves.

Preparation time: 40 minutes, plus rising
Cooking time: 40–45 minutes
Wine suggestion: Asprinio di Aversa Spumante

Fried Pizzas with Cheese and Anchovies

Makes 18–20 fried pizzas

generous 2 cups (17 fl oz/
  500 ml) sunflower oil, for
  deep-frying
11 oz/300 g soft stretched-
  curd cheese (ideally
  stracciatella cheese)
9 anchovy fillets preserved
  in oil, drained and sliced
arugula (rocket) leaves,
  to garnish (optional)

For the dough
4 cups (1 lb 2 oz/500 g) all-
  purpose (plain) flour
3 cups (14 oz/400 g) whole
  wheat (wholemeal) or white
  bread (strong) flour
³/₄ cup (3¹/₂ oz/100 g)
  whole wheat (wholemeal)
  Manitoba flour or white
  bread (strong) flour
1 tablespoon crumbled
  brewer's yeast or
  1¹/₂ teaspoons active
  dry yeast
1¹/₂ teaspoons malt powder
4 teaspoons (³/₄ oz/20 g)
  fine salt

Make the dough. Sift (sieve) the three types of flour together into a mound on a countertop and make a well in the center. Pour generous 2 cups (17 fl oz/ 500 ml) warm water into the middle and add the yeast and malt. Using a fork, start mixing everything together, then add the salt and knead by hand until it has dissolved into the mixture. Knead for an additional 10 minutes, slowly adding ²/₃ cup (5 fl oz/150 ml) warm water, until the dough is smooth and elastic. Shape the dough into a ball, place in an oiled bowl, cover with a damp dish towel, and let rise at room temperature for 15–20 minutes.

Make 18–20 little dough balls, weighing about 2¹/₄ oz/60 g each, and stretch them lightly into discs on a countertop.

Pour the sunflower oil into a large deep pan, or deep-fat fryer, and heat the oil to 340°F/170°C. Carefully add two or three dough discs to the oil and cook over medium heat for 3–4 minutes on each side until golden brown. Remove with a slotted spoon, drain on paper towels, and keep warm. Repeat until all the dough discs have been cooked.

Serve the fried pizzas topped with the stracciatella and anchovies and garnished with a few arugula (rocket) leaves, if liked.

Bread Rolls with Sun-dried Tomatoes and Scallions

Makes about 20 rolls

2 cups (3½ oz/100 g)
   sun-dried tomatoes
2 teaspoons honey
1½ tablespoons extra virgin
   olive oil
1¾ teaspoons crumbled
   brewer's yeast or ¾
   teaspoon active dry yeast
2½ cups (12 oz/350 g) white
   bread (strong) flour
   (ideally W220)
2 teaspoons fine salt
6 scallions (spring onions),
   thinly sliced, including
   the green parts
¾ cup plus 1 tablespoon
   (5 oz/150 g) durum wheat
   farina (semolina),
   for sprinkling

For the poolish
¾ cup (3½ oz/100 g) white
   bread (strong) flour
   (ideally W280)
½ teaspoon brewer's yeast
   or ¼ teaspoon instant yeast

First prepare the poolish. Combine the flour, yeast, and 4 tablespoons warm water in a bowl and let rise at room temperature for 4 hours.

Meanwhile, soak the sun-dried tomatoes in a bowl of cold water for 1 hour, then drain, dry thoroughly, and cut into small pieces.

When the poolish is ready, pour 1 cup (8 fl oz/250 ml) warm water and the honey and oil into a small bowl and dissolve the yeast in this mixture.

Put the flour into a mound on the countertop, make a well in the center, and put the yeast mixture, salt, and poolish into this. Using your hands, mix everything together and knead until the two types of dough have been thoroughly blended. Add the tomatoes and scallions (spring onions) and continue to knead the dough for a few minutes, then cover the dough with plastic wrap (clingfilm) and let rise at room temperature for 1½ hours, or until doubled in size.

Preheat the oven to 400°F/200°C/Gas mark 6. Line 3 baking sheets with parchment (baking) paper.

Divide the dough into 2-oz/50-g portions (you should have enough dough to make about 20 rolls), shaping them as you wish. Place the rolls on the prepared baking sheets, sprinkle lightly with farina (semolina), and let rise at room temperature for about 40 minutes, or until doubled in size.

Sprinkle a little water over the rolls and bake in the oven for 10 minutes, then lower the oven temperature to 350°F/180°C/Gas mark 4 and bake for an additional 20 minutes until golden brown and dry. Let cool.

NOTE   The poolish has a semi-liquid consistency and is prepared by mixing equal quantities of water and flour. The quantity of yeast used depends on the desired leavening time: for a longer leavening time, less yeast will be necessary. A limited quantity of yeast makes for a longer-lasting bread with a better aroma.

⊙   Preparation time: 25 minutes, plus rising

        Cooking time: 45 minutes

Ⴘ   Wine suggestion: Penisola Sorrentina Gragnano Rosso Frizzante

Babà Rustico

Serves 4–6

2³⁄₄ crumbled teaspoons
  baker's yeast or
  1¹⁄₄ teaspoons active
  dry yeast
¹⁄₃ cup plus 1 tablespoon
  (3¹⁄₂ fl oz/100 ml) warm milk
  (the milk should be at
  room temperature)
¹⁄₂ teaspoon superfine
  (caster) sugar
¹⁄₃ cup plus 1 tablespoon
  (3¹⁄₂ fl oz/100 ml) extra
  virgin olive oil, plus extra
  for greasing
2 eggs
2 cups (9 oz/250 g) type
  00 flour
5 oz/150 g stretched-curd
  cheese (ideally Montalbano
  provola cheese), finely diced
3¹⁄₂ oz/100 g salami (ideally
  Felino salami), diced
3¹⁄₂ oz/100 g thickly sliced
  cooked ham
salt

Grease a 9³⁄₄-inch/25-cm rum baba mold with oil.

In a large bowl, dissolve the yeast in the milk. Whisk in the sugar, oil, and eggs. Sift (sieve) the flour into the bowl and mix to prevent any lumps forming. Add a pinch of salt and then stir in the Montalbano provola, salami, and ham. Transfer the mixture to the prepared mold and let rise at room temperature for 1 hour.

Preheat the oven to 350°F/180°C/Gas mark 4. Bake the loaf in the oven for 45 minutes, or until a skewer inserted into the middle comes out clean. Turn out of the mold and place on a wire rack to cool.

TIP This savory recipe takes its name from the rum baba, a famous Neapolitan dessert, and adopts its basic yeast dough without the sweetness. The loaf is both soft and flavorful and can be enhanced with other ingredients, such as pitted (stoned) Taggiasca olives or drained and finely chopped sun-dried tomatoes preserved in oil. Remember to be very sparing in your use of salt because the salami is already very salty.

NOT JUST BREAD

There are many alternatives to bread in traditional Italian cuisine, from carasau bread, to friselle, and grissini. Some of these are valued for their crispiness and distinctive flavor, others are softened with water before being dressed for use, but they are all linked by the ancient need to store bread for long periods.

GRISSINI

Typical of Turin cooking traditions, grissini were invented around 1675 by Antonio Brunero, baker to the Savoy court, to remedy the health problems of the future King Vittorio Amedeo II, who was so sickly he could not tolerate very soft bread. Under the guidance of the court's physician, Teobaldo Pecchio, the resourceful baker created the first ghersino, a product that was halfway between bread and a cookie (biscuit). The name derived from ghersa, a typical Piedmont bread with an elongated shape.

Grissini captivated the people's palates, at court and beyond. Napoleon fell in love with the "petites batons de Turin" to such an extent that he started a dedicated postal service so that he could have the delicious crunchy sticks sent every day directly from the capital in Piedmont.

Turin is synonymous with grissini but there is much more to grissini. There are also rubatà and stirati. Typical of the Chieri area, rubatà were immediately added to the list of traditional food products. The name derives from robat, a typical agricultural tool formed by a long wooden cylinder, which was dragged along the ground, flattening it by compression. More recent than rubatà, stirati are produced in the Lanzo, Canalese, Pinerolese, and Turin valleys. While rubatà are rolled to obtain their typical irregular shape, stirati means "stretched". The dough is first cut into 10 cm strips, then stretched the length of the baker's arms by its extremities. This process makes them crumbly and crunchy.

TARALLI

These dough rings, which country people in Apulia used to dip in a glass of wine in the fifteenth century, were devised to ensure bread was available to the poorest of families. They were less expensive than traditional bread and also had a high energy value because lard was used in making them. Taralli are available in almost infinite varieties. In Apulia, black ones are made with vincotto (a spiced cooked wine), and other varieties are flavored with capocollo (a type of cured meat), fennel seeds, sugar, or chocolate.

In Campania, woven varieties are available, made with almonds, eggs, lard, and pepper, as well as the C.O. (a municipal denomination mark) variety from Agerola, in the province of Naples. In Calabria, white taralli, soft taralli, and varieties scented with aniseed, fennel seeds, or chile peppers can be found. Aviglione taralli, made with sugar, are typical of Basilicata.

FRISELLE

Typical of cooking traditions in Apulia, friselle look like golden, crunchy, ring-shaped cookies. Their ancient origins are rooted in Phoenician times: on long sea journeys, merchants used to eat round, ring-shaped cakes, softened with seawater, and flavored with olive oil.

As well as those made according to the original recipe, nowadays it is possible to find varieties made with durum wheat, barley, and whole wheat (wholemeal) flour. The preparation is the same for all varieties: dough cylinders are shaped into a ring and, after being first partially cooked in a wood-fired oven, the cakes are cut with a string while they are still warm, to form discs with an irregular, coarse surface. The friselle are then baked again until crisp.

SCHIACCIATINE

Schiacciatine, from Mantua, have a long history. A favored food of the Gonzaga court, their origins can probably be traced to the chisoela, chisel, or mirtol of the Jewish gastronomic culture.

Today, Mantuan schiacciatina is a square or rectangular focaccia obtained by mixing soft grain flour, water, salt, and lard, and flavored with crispy ciccioli (pressed cakes of fatty pork), aromatic herbs, or onion.

CARASAU BREAD

A type of flatbread typical of the Sardinian area of Barbagia, carasau bread is also known as "sheet music". The basic ingredients are yeast, salt, water, and flour. The preparation of this bread was traditionally a ritual involving at least three women. The dough would be stretched in discs separated by linen or woolen cloth and baked in an oak-fired oven. Preparation would start at the first light of dawn and, once the bread was cooked, it would be cut in two layers with a knife and then put back in the oven to be toasted.

⊙ Preparation time: 40 minutes, plus rising
   Cooking time: 25 minutes
♀ Wine suggestion: Lambrusco di Sorbara

Focaccia with Balsamic Vinegar and Pecorino Cheese

Serves 4

1 teaspoon brewer's yeast or
   ½ teaspoon active dry yeast
1 teaspoon superfine
   (caster) sugar
1 teaspoon fine salt, plus
   extra for sprinkling
2½ cups (12 oz/350 g)
   white bread (strong) flour
   (ideally W320)
½ cup (3½ oz/100 g) starter
   yeast (also known as
   mother yeast)
½ cup (2 oz/50 g) grated
   pecorino cheese
2½ tablespoons extra virgin
   olive oil
3 tablespoons balsamic
   vinegar

In a small bowl, dissolve the yeast and sugar in ½ cup (4 fl oz/120 ml) warm water. In a separate small bowl, dissolve the salt in ½ cup (4 fl oz/120 ml) warm water.

Put the flour in a large bowl, add the yeast mixture, followed by the salted water, then the starter yeast and pecorino. Mix everything together and knead well, then add 4 teaspoons of the olive oil and knead until the dough is smooth and elastic. Place the dough in a bowl, cover with plastic wrap (clingfilm) and let rise at room temperature for 1 hour, or until doubled in size.

Grease a 12 x 16-inch/40 x 30-cm baking pan with oil.

Stretch the dough to fit the prepared baking pan and then let rise for 30 minutes. Using your fingertips, make some indentations on the surface of the dough. Lightly sprinkle over some salt and let rise for an additional 20 minutes.

Preheat the oven to 375°F/190°C/Gas mark 5.

In a small bowl, blend the remaining oil with the vinegar and 1 tablespoon water. Sprinkle the mixture over the surface of the focaccia and then bake in the oven for 25 minutes until golden brown. Turn the focaccia out of the pan and place on a wire rack to cool.

NOTE   Just like oil, balsamic vinegar can be used to enrich the flavor of a focaccia. Balsamic vinegar is a particular type of vinegar obtained from cooked grape juice. This exquisite product originated in the Duchy of Modena and Reggio Emilia and its tradition is still rooted in those two towns. Nowadays this well-known condiment is used in the kitchen for its intense, exclusive, and unique flavor. The traditional balsamic vinegar produced in Modena and Reggio Emilia was awarded the DOP (Protected Designation of Origin) mark in 2000; balsamic vinegar from Modena was awarded the PGI (Protected Geographical Indication) mark in 2009.

⊙   Preparation time: 25 minutes, plus rising

Cooking time: 35 minutes

♀   Wine suggestion: Lagrein Rosato

Potato Focaccia with Mozzarella Cheese and Porcini Mushrooms

Serves 4

300 g potatoes, unpeeled
1 tablespoon crumbled
  brewer's yeast or ¹/₂
  tablespoon active dry yeast
2¹/₃ cups (11 oz/300 g) all-
  purpose (plain) flour
2 tablespoons extra virgin
  olive oil, plus extra for
  greasing and the emulsion
7 oz/200 g buffalo mozzarella
  cheese, sliced
7 oz/200 g porcini mushrooms
  preserved in oil, drained
salt and pepper

Place the potatoes in a large pan of cold water and bring to a boil. Drain and let stand until cool enough to handle, then peel off the skins and mash the potatoes with fork.

In a small bowl, dissolve the yeast in 1¹/₄ cups (10³/₄ fl oz/320 ml) warm water.

Put the flour in mound on the countertop, add the mashed potatoes, 2 teaspoons salt, a pinch of pepper, oil, and the yeast mixture. Using your hands, mix everything together and then knead until the dough is smooth and elastic. Shape the dough into a ball, place in a bowl, cover with plastic wrap (clingfilm), and let rise at room temperature for 1 hour, or until doubled in size.

Preheat the oven to 500°F/270°C/Gas mark 10. Grease a 10¹/₄-inch/26-cm round baking pan with oil.

Divide the dough into 2 pieces. Stretch half of the dough out to fit the prepared baking pan, sprinkle the mozzarella on top, and sprinkle with salt and pepper. Stretch out the remaining dough to the same size, place it on top of the mozzarella, and gently press around the edges of the dough to seal.

Make an emulsion by mixing together a little water, oil, and salt in a small bowl. Brush the emulsion over the top of the focaccia, then let rise at room temperature for 30 minutes, or until doubled in size.

Sprinkle the mushrooms over the top of the focaccia and press them gently into the dough. Sprinkle over a little salt and then bake in the oven for 35 minutes until golden brown. Turn the focaccia out of the pan and place on a wire rack to cool a little. Serve warm.

TIP   If you want a tastier focaccia, particularly in winter, you can replace the buffalo mozzarella cheese with Morlacco del Grappa cheese. This cheese, protected by the Slow Food organization, is produced in the area of Massiccio of Mount Grappa. This alpine pasture cheese is light and soft, and it melts easily and goes well with potatoes and porcini mushrooms.

⊙ Preparation time: 20 minutes, plus rising

Cooking time: 20 minutes

♀ Wine suggestion: Penisola Sorrentina Gragnano

Baker's Pizza

Serves 4

2¹/₂ tablespoons crumbled
   brewer's yeast or
   1¹/₄ tablespoons active
   dry yeast
1 tablespoon superfine
   (caster) sugar
1¹/₄ teaspoons salt
4 cups (1 lb 2 oz/500 g)
   all-purpose (plain) flour
4 tablespoons extra virgin
   olive oil, plus extra
   for greasing
1²/₃ cups (14 oz/400 g)
   drained and chopped
   canned tomatoes
8 oz/250 g cow milk
   mozzarella cheese, diced
1 teaspoon chopped oregano

In a small bowl, dissolve the yeast and sugar in ¹/₃ cup plus 1 tablespoon (3¹/₂ fl oz/100 ml) warm water. In a separate small bowl, dissolve the salt in ³/₄ cup plus 1 tablespoon (7 fl oz/ 200 ml) warm water.

Put the flour in a mound on the countertop and make a well in the center. Pour the oil into the middle and add the sugar and yeast mixture. Using your hands, mix everything together and then knead for a few minutes, slowly adding the salted water. Continue to knead until the dough is smooth and elastic. Shape the dough into a ball, place in large bowl, cover with a damp dish towel, and let rise at room temperature for 1 hour, or until doubled in size.

Grease a 12 x 9³/₄-inch/30 x 25-cm baking pan with oil.

Stretch the dough to fit the prepared baking pan. Arrange the tomatoes on top and let rise at room temperature for another 35–40 minutes until doubled in size.

Preheat the oven to 475°F/240°C/Gas mark 9. Bake the pizza in the oven for 15 minutes, then sprinkle the mozzarella over the pizza, sprinkle over the oregano, return to the oven, and bake for 5 minutes more. To check that the pizza is cooked, carefully lift up the edge of the pizza: if the underside is golden brown, the pizza is ready.

NOTE Fior di latte mozzarella cheese is ideal for any type of pizza. In fact, it has a sweeter taste than buffalo mozzarella cheese and it also has fewer calories. Just a precaution: always choose less watery mozzarellas. Alternatively, dice the mozzarella and then leave it to drain for a few minutes on a chopping board or, even better, on a slightly sloped plate. In this way, when the mozzarella cheese is added to the pizza, it will release less liquid and the pizza will be crispier.

CHEF
Alessandro Coccia

Preparation time: 40 minutes, plus rising
Cooking time: 55 minutes

Whole Wheat Pizza with Red Onions and Cheese

Makes 6 pizzas

extra virgin olive oil
5 red onions (ideally red
   Tropea onions), sliced
1/3 cup plus 1 tablespoon
   (3 1/2 fl oz/100 ml) red wine
2 tablespoons
   balsamic vinegar
1 tablespoon superfine
   (caster) sugar
durum wheat farina
   (semolina), for dusting
1 lb 2 oz/500 g fior di latte
   mozzarella cheese, diced
7 oz/200 g mild Provalone
   cheese (ideally pancettone
   cheese), finely sliced
salt and pepper
a few basil leaves,
   to garnish (optional)

For the dough
8 1/3 cups (2 1/4 lb/1 kg) whole
   wheat (wholemeal) flour
1 tablespoon crumbled
   brewer's yeast or
   1 teaspoon instant yeast
4 teaspoons fine salt

First make the dough. Put the flour, yeast, and generous 2 cups (18 fl oz/500 ml) warm water in a large bowl and mix everything together. Knead the dough for about 5 minutes, then add the salt and continue to knead, slowly adding 1 cup (8 fl oz/250 ml) warm water, until the dough is smooth and elastic. Shape the dough into a ball, place in a large oiled bowl, cover with a damp dish towel, and let rise at room temperature for 3 hours, or until doubled in size.

Divide the dough into 6 balls, each weighing about 9 oz/250 g, cover them with a damp dish towel, and let rise at room temperature for an additional 3 hours, or until doubled in size.

Meanwhile, heat a drizzle of oil in a large skillet (frying pan), add the onions, and cook over high heat for a few minutes, then add the wine and a little water and season with salt and pepper. Cover and cook over medium heat for 30 minutes, stirring from time to time, until the onions are soft. Add the balsamic vinegar and sugar and cook for 3–4 minutes, stirring from time to time, until the onions are caramelized.

Preheat the oven to 425°F/220°C/Gas mark 7. Grease six 8–8 3/4-inch/20–22-cm baking pans with oil.

On a countertop dusted with a little farina (semolina), stretch the dough balls out to fit the prepared baking pans. Bake in the oven for 20 minutes until golden brown and dry, topping with the mozzarella and caramelized onions halfway through the cooking time.

To serve, sprinkle the pizzas with slices of pancettone and garnish with a few basil leaves, if liked.

BEER SUGGESTION Open Gold is an American pale ale with a hoppy taste. It is an excellent accompaniment for the pancettone cheese, and contrasts well with the sweet caramelized onions.

CHEF

Alessandro Coccia

🕐 Preparation time: 45 minutes, plus rising

Cooking time: 30 minutes

Whole Wheat Focaccia with Ratatouille, Mint, and Goat Cheese

Makes 6–8 focaccias

extra virgin olive oil
2 potatoes, peeled and diced
4 carrots, diced
1 celery stalk, diced
2 eggplants
   (aubergine), diced
3 zucchini (courgettes), diced
a few mint leaves, plus extra
   to garnish
durum wheat farina
   (semolina), for dusting
14 oz/400 g fresh goat cheese
   (ideally caprino cheese),
   cut into pieces
salt

For the dough
8¹⁄₃ cups (2¹⁄₄ lb/1 kg) whole
   wheat (wholemeal) flour
1 tablespoon crumbled
   brewer's yeast or
   1 teaspoon instant yeast
4 teaspoons fine salt

First make the dough. Put the flour, yeast, and generous 2 cups (18 fl oz/500 ml) warm water in a large bowl and mix everything together. Knead the dough for about 5 minutes, then add the salt and continue to knead, slowly adding 1 cup (8 fl oz/250 ml) warm water, until the dough is smooth and elastic. Shape the dough into a ball, place in a large oiled bowl, cover with a damp dish towel, and let rise at room temperature for 3 hours, or until doubled in size.

To make individual focaccias, divide the dough into balls, each weighing about 9 oz/250 g (you should have enough dough to make between six and eight balls), cover them with a damp dish towel, and let rise at room temperature for an additional 3 hours, or until doubled in size.

Meanwhile, make the ratatouille. Heat a drizzle of oil in a large skillet (frying pan), add the potatoes, and cook over high heat for 3–4 minutes, then add the carrots and cook for 3–4 minutes, followed by the celery, eggplant (aubergine), and zucchini (courgette), allowing 3–4 minutes between each addition. Stir in the mint leaves and season to taste with salt.

Preheat the oven to 425°F/220°C/Gas mark 7. Grease six to eight 8-inch/20-cm baking pans with oil.

On a countertop dusted with a little farina (semolina), stretch the dough balls out to fit the prepared baking pans. Bake in the oven for 20 minutes until golden brown and dry, spreading the ratatouille on top of the focaccia halfway through the cooking time.

To serve, sprinkle the caprino over the focaccia, garnish with a few extra mint leaves, and drizzle with oil.

🍺 **BEER SUGGESTION** Isaac Bière Blanche is a light wheat beer. The citrus notes of the coriander and orange zest complement the aroma of the focaccia's mint and caprino cheese, while the beer's freshness and delicate body make for an excellent match with the ratatouille.

FLOUR, BATTER, AND BREAD: FRIED FOOD DRESSES UP

When subjected to heat, as in the case of frying, the surface of food experiences a series of chemical reactions between its sugars and its proteins, which are responsible for the food browning and becoming crisp. To obtain this effect in foods that are low in sugars, like meat for example, it is necessary to use methods such as flouring, breading, and immersion in batter. In this way, a coating rich in carbohydrates is formed, which will react with the proteins and the lipids in the cooking fat. On the other hand, foods that are naturally rich in starch—like potatoes and batters—do not need additional coating.

For every type of preparation it is important to remove any excess flour or batter, which are likely to come loose and cloud the cooking fat. This cooking fat should not be used again because the numerous substances involved could compromise its quality.

THE CRUST

The crust, in addition to being tasty in itself, also acts to retain internal moisture and therefore ensure that the food remains soft: for example, frying meat without a crust might lead to excessive dehydration. At the same time, the crust prevents the food from becoming soaked in the cooking fat.

For an outer crust to form, the cooking fat must be quite hot. When the food is added to the pan it will lower the temperature of the cooking fat. To compensate for this, it is best to turn the heat up for a few moments before turning it down again (you could use a kitchen thermometer). The ability of the crust to retain moisture dissipates when the food is cooled: this is why fried foods are tastier and crispier if consumed immediately, before the internal moisture softens the crust.

FLOURING AND BREADING

The simplest of these methods is flouring, which consists of dipping the food in sifted flour, typically wheat or cornmeal. This type of treatment is particularly suitable for fish or meat cut into small pieces, which must be cooked very rapidly at high temperatures. Food must be floured just before cooking, to prevent the flour absorbing moisture from the food, which should in any case be as dry as possible.

Breading normally consists of dipping the food in a beaten egg and then in breadcrumbs, but there are also variations that require the food to be dipped in flour first, then the egg, and then the breadcrumbs, or in cornstarch (cornflour) instead of breadcrumbs. The egg has a double role: it acts as an adhesive between the food and the bread, and it makes for a stronger crust because it coagulates immediately on contact with the heat. Breading is therefore suitable for larger pieces of food, like the classic Milanese cutlet. Of all the methods of coating, breading is the one that is most resistant over time—though it is still tastier when consumed immediately—and food cooked in this way can also be consumed at a later time.

BATTERS

Some recipes require a coating made of batter, a semi-liquid preparation that can be used for any type of food and which is particularly suitable for shellfish, fruit, and vegetables. It is best to prepare the batter in advance and let it rest: its consistency must be quite creamy to ensure it sticks to the food and creates a uniform film.

Generally speaking the batter is made with eggs, flour, and milk, but there are many variants: with or without yeast, with butter, sugar, wine, beer, lemon, spices, water, etc. However, it's important to remember that many of these ingredients—spices in particular—speed up the process of oxidation of the cooking fat and lower the temperature of the smoke point.

⊙ Preparation time: 25 minutes, plus resting
    Cooking time: 15 minutes
Ⓠ Wine suggestion: Trento Metodo Classico Extra Brut

Vegetable and Shrimp Tempura

Serves 4

extra virgin olive oil,
    for deep-frying
20 raw shrimp (prawns),
    shelled and deveined,
    with the heads left intact
10 small squid tentacles
2 carrots, cut into strips
2 zucchini (courgettes),
    cut into strips
2 asparagus spears,
    trimmed and cut into strips
1 red bell pepper, cored,
    seeded, and cut into strips
1 eggplant (aubergine),
    cut into strips

For the tempura batter
1 cup (8 fl oz/250 ml)
    carbonated water
2 ice cubes
²/₃ cup (3¹/₂ oz/100 g) rice flour
¹/₃ cup plus 1 tablespoon
    (2 oz/50 g) all-purpose
    (plain) flour
¹/₃ cup plus 2 tablespoons
    (2 oz/50 g)
    cornstarch (cornflour)
¹/₄ teaspoon salt
1 teaspoon paprika
    or curry powder

First make the batter. Pour the carbonated water into a bowl and add the ice cubes to keep it cool. Sift (sieve) the flours, salt, and paprika or curry powder into the bowl and mix well so as to avoid the formation of lumps. Let rest in the refrigerator for 20 minutes. The batter should be liquid and creamy, but not too thick.

Pour enough oil for deep-frying into a deep-fat fryer or large deep pan and heat the oil to 325°F/160°C.

Stir the batter. Dip the vegetables, shrimp (prawns), and squid into the batter and shake off any excess (the batter should only coat the ingredients lightly enough to be a little transparent), then fry them, in batches if necessary, for 2–3 minutes until crisp. Remove with a slotted spoon and drain on paper towels. Serve immediately.

⊙ Preparation time: 45 minutes, plus rising
Cooking time: 40–45 minutes

♀ Wine suggestion: Franciacorta Brut

Small Fried Pizzas with Parmesan Cheese Cream, Asparagus, and Prosciutto

Makes 18–20 fried pizzas

10 purple asparagus spears
sunflower oil, for deep-frying
10 thin slices prosciutto
(Parma ham)
salt and pepper

For the dough
4 cups (1 lb 2 oz/500 g) all-
purpose (plain) flour
3 cups (14 oz/400 g) whole
wheat (wholemeal) or white
bread (strong) flour
3/4 cup (3 1/2 oz/100 g)
whole wheat (wholemeal)
Manitoba flour or white
bread (strong) flour
1 tablespoon crumbled
brewer's yeast or
1 1/2 teaspoons active
dry yeast
1 1/2 teaspoons malt powder
4 teaspoons (3/4 oz/20 g) fine
salt

For the Parmesan cream
3/4 cup plus 1 tablespoon
(7 fl oz/200 ml) whipping
cream
pinch of ground nutmeg
1 1/2 cups (4 1/2 oz/130 g)
grated Parmesan cheese

Make the dough. Sift (sieve) the three types of flour together into a mound on a countertop and make a well in the center. Pour generous 2 cups (17 fl oz/ 500 ml) warm water into the middle and add the yeast and malt. Using a fork, start mixing everything together, then add the salt and knead by hand until it has dissolved ino the mixture. Knead for an additional 10 minutes, slowly adding 2/3 cup (5 fl oz/150 ml) warm water, until the dough is smooth and elastic. Shape the dough into a ball, cover with a damp dish towel, and let rise at room temperature for 15–20 minutes.

Meanwhile, make the Parmesan cream. Pour the cream into a small pan, add the nutmeg, and bring to a boil. Stir in the Parmesan and cook over low heat, stirring all the time, for 10 minutes. Remove from the heat and keep warm.

Break off the tough part at the base of the asparagus spears and discard. Cut the spears into 1/5-inch/4-mm slices. Transfer to a bowl, add 2 tablespoons oil and a pinch of salt, and toss to coat.

Make 18–20 little dough balls, weighing about 2 1/4 oz/60 g each, and stretch them lightly into discs on a countertop.

Pour enough oil for deep-frying into a small deep pan, or deep-fat fryer, and heat the oil to 340°F/170°C. Carefully add two or three dough discs to the oil and cook over medium heat for 3–4 minutes on each side until golden brown. Remove with a slotted spoon, drain on paper towels, and keep warm. Repeat until all the dough discs have been cooked.

Spread a little Parmesan cream over each fried pizza, then top with some asparagus and prosciutto (Parma ham). Serve immediately.

Preparation time: 25 minutes

Cooking time: 10 minutes

Wine suggestion: Falerno del Massico Bianco

Fried Mozzarella Cheese Sandwiches

Serves 4

8 slices bread

2 (7-oz/200-g) balls buffalo
mozzarella cheese, drained
well and sliced

3½ oz/100 g pecorino cheese
shavings

4 eggs

4 tablespoons milk

4½ cups (7 oz/200 g) fresh
breadcrumbs

sunflower oil, for frying

salt and pepper

**For the mozzarella cream
sauce (optional)**

¾ cup plus 1 tablespoon
(7 fl oz/200 ml) whipping
cream

1 (7-oz/200-g) ball mozzarella
cheese, diced

Lay four slices of bread on the countertop. Divide the mozzarella and pecorino among the four slices of bread and then top each with another slice of bread to make a sandwich.

Whisk the eggs, milk, and a pinch each of salt and pepper together in a shallow dish. Spread out the breadcrumbs in a separate shallow dish. Dip each sandwich into the egg mixture, then cover it with breadcrumbs, patting it with your hands to make sure it is completely coated. Repeat the process once more.

Pour enough oil into a deep skillet (frying pan) so that it is about 2 inches/5 cm deep. Heat the oil to 340°F/170°C, then carefully add the sandwiches and cook for 3–4 minutes, turning them over occasionally, until golden brown and crisp. Remove with a slotted spoon and drain on paper towels.

Meanwhile, if liked, make a mozzarella cream sauce to accompany the sandwiches. Pour the cream into a small pan, bring to a boil, then remove from the heat and stir in the mozzarella until melted.

Cut the sandwiches into cubes and serve immediately, accompanied with the mozzarella cream sauce, if liked.

NOTE This is the main appetizer—and a very tasty one—of Neapolitan cuisine. There is also a Roman version that uses a different filling: fior di latte mozzarella, anchovies and/or cooked ham. There are differing reports as to the origin of the name *mozzarella in carrozza* (mozzarella in a carriage). According to one, the name derived from the shape of the two slices of bread that enclose the mozzarella, which looked similar to a transport carriage.

⊙ Preparation time: 30 minutes

Cooking time: 40 minutes

♀ Wine suggestion: Riviera Ligure di Ponente Vermentino

Potato Cakes with Black Olives, Zucchini, and Carrots

Serves 4

7 potatoes (about 1³/₄ lb/
    800 g), unpeeled
extra virgin olive oil
1 carrot, cut into small cubes
1 zucchini (courgette), cut into
    small cubes
2 tablespoons grated
    Parmesan cheese
1 small bunch basil, leaves
    coarsely chopped
1 small bunch chives,
    coarsely chopped
²/₃ cup (2¹/₄ oz/60 g)
    pitted (stoned) black olives
    (ideally Taggiasca olives),
    coarsely chopped
2 eggs
6²/₃ cups (11 oz/300 g) fresh
    breadcrumbs
salt

To serve (optional)
mixed salad
mayonnaise

Put the potatoes into a large pan of cold water, bring to a boil, and cook the potatoes for 30 minutes, or until a knife inserted into them comes out easily. Drain well. Carefully peel the potatoes and then mash them.

Meanwhile, heat a little oil in a skillet (frying pan), add the carrot, zucchini (courgette), and a pinch of salt, and cook over medium heat for 5 minutes until brown.

Transfer the mashed potato to a large bowl. Add the Parmesan, herbs, olives, and fried vegetables and mix gently. Using your hands, shape the potato mixture into small balls, each about 2¹/₂–2³/₄ inches/6–7 cm in diameter.

In a shallow dish, whisk the eggs with a pinch of salt. Spread out the breadcrumbs in a separate shallow dish. Dip each ball in turn first into the beaten eggs, then roll them in the breadcrumbs to coat.

Pour enough oil for deep-frying into a deep-fat fryer or large deep pan and heat the oil to 325°F/160°C. Carefully add the balls to the hot oil and cook for 2–3 minutes until golden brown. You may need to cook them in batches. Remove with a slotted spoon and drain on paper towels.

Serve immediately with a mixed salad and mayonnaise, if liked.

TIP Savory potato cakes or balls are without doubt one of the most versatile ways to recycle leftovers. Instead of zucchini (courgettes), carrots, and olives, try using different ingredients to flavor the potato cakes, for example stir-fried mushrooms or artichokes with cubes of cheese or cooked ham.

⊙ Preparation time: 30 minutes
Cooking time: 15 minutes
♀ Wine suggestion: Alto Adige Pinot Bianco

Spiced Shrimp and Swordfish Skewers with Chips

Serves 4

5 potatoes (about 1 lb
  5 oz/600 g), peeled
extra virgin olive oil,
  for deep-frying
1 cup (7 oz/200 g) durum
  wheat semolina
1 tablespoon paprika
1 tablespoon curry powder
1/2 teaspoon chili powder
2 1/4 lb/1 kg raw shrimp
  (prawns) in their shells,
  heads removed
1 lb 2 oz/500 g swordfish,
  cleaned, skinned, boned,
  and diced
salt
scallions (spring onions),
  chopped, to garnish
mixed salad greens (leaves),
  to serve

Using a mandoline, cut the potatoes into slices about 1/8 inch/2 mm thick. Transfer to a bowl filled with cold water and let soak under cold running water for 30 minutes to remove the starch.

Pour enough oil for deep-frying into a deep-fat fryer or large deep pan and heat the oil to 325°F/160°C.

Sift (sieve) the semolina and spices into a shallow dish. Coat the shrimp (prawns) and the swordfish with the spiced flour. Add the shrimp and fish to the hot oil, in batches if necessary, and cook until brown and crisp. Remove with a slotted spoon and drain on paper towels. Keep warm.

Drain the potatoes and dry them with a dish towel. Add them to the hot oil and cook for 3 minutes, or until golden brown and crisp. You may need to cook them in batches. Remove with a slotted spoon and drain on paper towels.

When ready to serve, thread the deep-fried fish and shrimp onto long skewers, alternating fish and shrimp. Divide the kebabs and chips among serving plates, sprinkle with a pinch of salt, garnish with chopped scallions (spring onions), and serve with mixed salad greens (leaves).

Preparation time: 25 minutes, plus resting

Cooking time: 25 minutes

Wine suggestion: Freisa d'Asti Frizzante

Chicken with Provençal Herbs Fritters

Serves 4

1 carrot, chopped

1/2 celery stalk, chopped

1 small onion, chopped

14 oz/400 g skinless
chicken breasts, cut into
3/4–11/4-inch/2–3-cm pieces

3 eggs

4 cups (7 oz/200 g) fresh
breadcrumbs

2 tablespoons herbs de
Provence

sunflower oil, for deep-frying

salt

Place the vegetables and chicken into a pan, cover with cold water, and add a pinch of salt. Bring to a boil and cook over medium heat for 15 minutes, or until the meat is tender. Drain well, discarding the vegetables, and dry the chicken on paper towels.

Lightly whisk the eggs in a bowl. Add the chicken, stir to coat, cover, and let rest in the refrigerator for at least 2 hours.

Pour enough oil for deep-frying into a small deep pan and heat the oil to 340°F/170°C.

Mix together the breadcrumbs and herbs in a shallow dish. Roll the chicken in the breadcrumbs to coat. Carefully add the chicken to the hot oil and cook for 10 minutes, turning occasionally, or until golden brown and crisp. You may need to cook them in batches. Remove with a slotted spoon and drain on paper towels. Serve sprinkled with a pinch of salt.

NOTE Herbs de Provence contains all the scents of the Mediterranean in their bouquet: thyme, basil, rosemary, savory, chervil, lovage, parsley, oregano, marjoram, chives, tarragon, onion, garlic, lavender, sage, and bay leaves. It is a blend particularly suitable for flavoring fish, white meats, eggs, sauces, steamed vegetable dishes, and legumes. It is also excellent for marinating meat for grilling.

⊙   Preparation time: 30 minutes, plus cooling

Cooking time: 35 minutes

♀   Wine suggestion: Etna Rosato

Tuna, Potato, and Chive Cakes

Serves 4

4 potatoes (about 1 lb
    2 oz/500 g), unpeeled
5¼ oz/160 g canned tuna
    in oil, drained
10 chives, chopped
2 tablespoons grated
    Parmesan cheese
pinch of ground nutmeg
1¼ cups (5 oz/150 g) fine
    yellow cornmeal
peanut (groundnut) oil,
    for frying
salt

Put the potatoes into a large pan of cold water, bring to a boil, and cook the potatoes for 30 minutes, or until a knife inserted into them comes out easily. Drain well and let cool. Peel the potatoes and cut them into small pieces.

Transfer the potatoes to a large bowl and add the tuna, chives, Parmesan, nutmeg, and a pinch of salt. Mash with a fork until well blended. Using your hands, shape the potato mixture into small balls, each about ¾ inch/2 cm in diameter.

Spread out the cornmeal in a shallow dish. Roll the balls in the cornmeal to coat.

Pour enough oil for deep-frying into a deep-fat fryer or large deep pan and heat the oil to 340°F/170°C. Carefully add the balls to the hot oil and cook for 2 minutes, or until golden brown. You may need to cook them in batches. Remove with a slotted spoon and drain on paper towels.

Serve hot with a sauce of your choice.

TIP   There are infinite variations of this recipe. Experiment with different and imaginative combinations of ingredients and aromatic herbs. Try, for example, replacing the tuna with the same weight of salmon fillets cooked in a dry nonstick pan over medium heat for 7–8 minutes until cooked through and then skinned and flaked, using chopped flat-leaf parsley or marjoram instead of the chives.

Preparation time: 15 minutes, plus cooling

Cooking time: 55 minutes

Wine suggestion: Valdobbiadene Superiore di Cartizze Extra Dry

Fried Polenta with Gorgonzola Cheese Fondue

Serves 4–6

1²/₃ cups (11 oz/300 g) fine
  yellow cornmeal
2 tablespoons
  (1 oz/25 g) butter
extra virgin olive oil
salt

For the fondue
11 oz/300 g mild
  Gorgonzola cheese
²/₃ cup (5 fl oz/150 ml) milk
¹/₃ cup plus 1 tablespoon
  (3¹/₂ fl oz/100 ml)
  whipping cream
1 teaspoon salt

Grease a 6 x 8-inch/ 15 x 20-cm dish with oil.

Bring 4¹/₄ cups (34 fl oz/1 liter) water to a boil in a heavy pan, add a pinch of salt, then gradually sprinkle in the cornmeal, beating briskly with a whisk to prevents lumps forming. Cook over low heat for 45 minutes, stirring continuously with a wooden spoon. Stir in the butter. Pour the polenta into the prepared dish and even it out so that it forms a layer about ¹/₂–⁵/₈ inch/1–1.5 cm thick. Let cool. Once the polenta has firmed up, cut the polenta into sticks, each about ⁵/₈ inch x 2 inches/1.5 x 5 cm.

Make the fondue. Put all the ingredients for the fondue into a pan and cook over a low heat, stirring occasionally, until a smooth cream is obtained. Pass the sauce through a strainer (sieve) into a clean pan. Taste to check the seasoning and add more salt if necessary. Keep warm.

Pour enough oil into a deep skillet (frying pan) so that it is about 1¹/₄ inches/ 3 cm deep. Heat the oil to 340°F/170°C, then carefully add the polenta sticks and cook over medium–high heat for about 5 minutes, turning halfway through the cooking time, or until they are golden brown on both sides. You may need to cook them in batches. Remove with a slotted spoon and drain on paper towels.

Serve the fried polenta with the fondue in a small bowl for dipping.

TIP   This is the perfect way to use up leftover polenta. The fried polenta can also be served with fresh cheeses, such as crescenza cheese or squacquerone cheese, or with more mature ones like Taleggio cheese.

Preparation time: 20 minutes, plus resting

Cooking time: 5 minutes

Wine suggestion: Colli di Parma Malvasia Frizzante Secco

Fried Sage

Serves 4

1 egg, separated

³/₄ cup plus 1 tablespoon
   (7 fl oz/200 ml) milk

pinch of salt

3 tablespoons all-purpose
   (plain) flour

sunflower oil, for frying

20 sage leaves

coarse salt, for sprinkling

In a bowl, whisk together the egg yolk with the milk and a pinch of salt, then gradually whisk in the flour until you have a smooth and fluid batter. Let rest in the refrigerator for 1 hour.

In a separate spotlessly clean bowl, whisk the egg white until it forms stiff peaks. Using a rubber spatula, gently fold the egg white into the batter, blending gently with a bottom-up movement to avoid deflating the egg white.

Pour enough oil for deep-frying into a small deep pan and heat the oil to 340°F/170°C.

Wash the sage leaves under cold running water and dry them on paper towels. Dip the leaves into the batter, shake off any excess, then carefully add them to the hot oil. Cook for 1–2 minutes until golden brown. Remove with a slotted spoon and drain on paper towels. Serve sprinkled with a little coarse salt.

NOTE   When it comes to deep-frying, each type of ingredient needs its own special batter. Whether you want to fry vegetables or meat, fish or sweets, the classic batter ingredients (egg, flour, and water) can be adapted to obtain tasty and appetizing results. For example, try using carbonated water or white wine instead of water; whisk the egg white to stiff peaks, or substitute rice flour for all-purpose (plain) flour. Many of these ingredients have the advantage of making the batter puff out when it comes into contact with the hot oil, making the end result fluffier, lighter, and crunchier.

CHEF

Pasquale Torrente

Preparation time: 40 minutes

Cooking time: 35 minutes

Stuffed Paccheri Pasta

Serves 6

extra virgin olive oil

1 clove garlic, unpeeled

1 cup (9 oz/250 g) crushed
   canned peeled tomatoes
   (crushed with a fork)

2¹/₂ cups (3¹/₂ oz/100 g)
   torn basil leaves

1 lb 2 oz/500 g paccheri
   pasta (or other short,
   tubular pasta)

3¹/₄ cups (1³/₄ lb/800 g)
   ricotta cheese

1¹/₄ cups (3¹/₂ oz/100 g)
   grated pecorino cheese

1¹/₃ cups (4 oz/120 g) grated
   Parmesan cheese

6 eggs

6²/₃ cups (11 oz/300 g)
   fresh breadcrumbs

sunflower oil, for deep-frying

salt and pepper

First make the sauce. Heat a little oil in a pan, add the whole clove of garlic and cook over low heat for 2 minutes to allow the garlic to release its flavor. Remove the garlic with a slotted spoon and discard, then add the tomatoes and most of the basil (reserving a few leaves for garnish), and cook for about 20 minutes until the sauce thickens.

Meanwhile, cook the pasta in a large pan of boiling lightly salted water according to the package directions until al dente. Fill a large bowl with iced water and set it beside the stove. Drain the pasta, plunge into the iced water to cool, then drain again thoroughly.

Put the ricotta, pecorino, and most of the Parmesan (reserving a small amount for sprinkling over the finished dish) into a bowl and mix well. Season with salt and pepper. Spoon the mixture into a pastry (piping) bag fitted with a ¹/₂-inch/1-cm tip (nozzle). Hold each pasta tube upright on the countertop and pipe the filling into the tube.

Beat the eggs in a shallow dish. Spread out the breadcrumbs in a separate shallow dish. Dip each filled pasta tube into the eggs, then roll it in the breadcrumbs to coat.

Pour enough sunflower oil for deep-frying into a small deep pan and heat the oil to 350°F/175°C. Carefully add the filled pasta tubes to the hot oil, in batches if necesssary, and fry for 2–3 minutes, turning them over occasionally, until golden brown. Remove with a slotted spoon and drain on paper towels.

To serve, spread a smooth layer of tomato sauce in the center of each soup plate and rest four of the stuffed paccheri vertically in the dish. Sprinkle with the reserved Parmesan and garnish with the reserved basil.

WINE SUGGESTION   Bellavista Vendemmia Brut Franciacorta Sapore Asciutto is an exceptionally elegant and satisfying wine. It has a steady robustness and excellent energy, and its harmonious acidity contributes to its great personality and character.

CHEF
Pasquale Torrente

Preparation time: 40 minutes, plus cooling
Cooking time: 1¼ hours

Supplì

Serves 6

40 fl oz/1.2 liters hot
  vegetable broth (stock)
extra virgin olive oil
3 tablespoons finely chopped
  gold-skinned onion
1 celery stalk, finely chopped
1 carrot, finely chopped
3½ oz/100 g ground
  (minced) pork
2 oz/50 g ground
  (minced) beef
2¼ oz/60 g chicken gizzards,
  cleaned and chopped
1¾ cups (14 oz/400 g) canned
  peeled tomatoes (ideally
  San Marzano tomatoes)
2 or 3 basil leaves, chopped
2½ cups (1 lb 2 oz/500 g)
  Carnaroli rice
1¼ cups (3½ oz/100 g)
  grated Parmesan cheese
7 oz/200 g mozzarella cheese,
  cut into cubes
3 eggs
3⅓ cups (5 oz/150 g)
  fresh breadcrumbs
sunflower oil, for deep-frying
salt and pepper

Pour the broth (stock) into a pan and bring to a simmer. Keep over a low heat while you make the risotto.

Heat a little olive oil in a large pan, add the onion, celery, and carrot, and cook over medium heat for 4 minutes, or until the vegetables start to sweat. Add the ground (minced) meats and chicken gizzards and cook for a few minutes until brown, then add the tomatoes and cook for 40 minutes until the sauce thickens. Season with salt and pepper and stir in the basil.

Add the rice to the pan with the sauce and cook over medium heat, stirring frequently, for about 20 minutes, gradually adding in more broth a ladleful at a time and making sure each addition is absorbed by the rice before adding the next ladleful, until the rice is cooked through and soft. Remove from the heat and stir in the Parmesan. Spread out the rice on a large baking sheet, cover with plastic wrap (clingfilm), and let cool.

Using dampened hands, shape a 4-oz/120-g portion of the cooled rice mixture into a slightly oval croquette, then make a hole into the center with your finger, fill it with a couple of cubes of mozzarella, then smooth the rice over the hole to seal in the cheese. Repeat with the remaining rice mixture and mozzarella.

Beat the eggs in a shallow dish. Spread out the breadcrumbs in a separate shallow dish. Dip each supplì into the eggs, then roll in the breadcrumbs to coat, then repeat the dipping and coating twice more.

Pour enough sunflower oil for deep-frying into a small deep pan and heat the oil to 330°F/165°C. Carefully add the supplì to the hot oil, in batches if necessary, and fry for 3–4 minutes, turning them over occasionally, until golden brown. Remove with a slotted spoon and drain on paper towels. Serve hot.

WINE SUGGESTION Bellavista Alma Terra Curtefranca is elegant and expansive with a full and inviting flavor. This wine exhibits an exquisite freshness and persistent aromatic concentration.

CHEESE

Preparation time: 20 minutes
Cooking time: 30 minutes
Wine suggestion: Lambrusco di Sorbara

Broccoli Roulade with Cheese

Serves 4

extra virgin olive oil
¼ head broccoli (about
    5 oz/150 g), broken into
    florets and finely chopped
3 eggs
½ cup (2¼ oz/60 g) all-
    purpose (plain) flour
½ cup (4 fl oz/120 ml) milk
9 oz/250 g fresh cream
    cheese (ideally
    squacquerone cheese)
8 slices cooked ham
salt

Heat a little oil in a skillet (frying pan), add the broccoli, and cook over medium heat for 5 minutes, or until soft, adding a little more oil if necessary.

Place the eggs, flour, milk, and a pinch of salt in a bowl and whisk until the mixture is smooth, adding a little extra flour if it is too liquid, or a little extra milk if it is too dry. Add the broccoli and mix well.

Heat a little oil in the skillet, then pour in one-quarter of the broccoli mixture and cook over low heat for 3 minutes, or until golden, then flip the omelet and cook for 3 minutes more. Remove the omelet from the pan and keep warm while you repeat with the remaining broccoli mixture.

Spread each omelet with a quarter of the squacquerone, top with slices of ham, then roll up the omelets. Serve hot.

NOTE   Squacquerone cheese is a fresh, soft, and rindless cheese, typical of Emilia Romagna. It has a sweet and rich flavor with pleasant, slightly sour notes. This cheese has an ancient origin: popular tradition suggests that it originated in the first century AD, but the first written reference dates from 1800—a letter from Carlo Bellisomi, the bishop of Cesena, enquiring about a batch of cheese that was ordered but never received.

Preparation time: 35 minutes, plus chilling
Cooking time: 5 minutes
Wine suggestion: Sannio Falanghina

Ricotta Cheese and Semi-dried Tomato Cheesecake

Serves 4

5 slices (5 oz/150 g) stale
  bread, cut into very small
  cubes
1/3 cup plus 1 tablespoon (3 1/2
  fl oz/100 ml) extra virgin
  olive oil
1 small thyme sprig, leaves
  chopped
2–3 mint leaves, chopped
20–30 semi-dried tomatoes,
  chopped
3–4 basil leaves, shredded
2 cups (1 lb 2 oz/500g) ricotta
  cheese (ideally buffalo milk
  ricotta cheese)
2 tablespoons confectioners'
  (icing) sugar
3 tablespoons grated
  Parmesan cheese
1 cup (8 fl oz/250 ml)
  whipping cream
1/3 cup (1 1/2 oz/40 g) pitted
  (stoned) and finely chopped
  black olives (ideally
  Taggiasca olives)
2 anchovy fillets preserved in
  salt, rinsed
salt and white pepper

To garnish (optional)
mixed baby leaf salad
slivers of cherry tomatoes

Put the bread into a bowl with a pinch each of salt and pepper, 4 tablespoons of the oil, and the thyme and mint. Heat a little oil in a skillet (frying pan), add the bread cubes, and cook over medium heat for 5–6 minutes until brown and crunchy. Transfer to a bowl, add the semi-dried tomatoes and basil, and mix well.

Put the ricotta into a bowl and soften with a rubber spatula, then mix in the confectioners' (icing) sugar, Parmesan, a pinch each of salt and pepper, and 1 tablespoon of the oil.

In a separate bowl, whip the cream until it forms stiff peaks. Using a rubber spatula, gently fold the cream into the ricotta mixture with the spatula, using a bottom-up movement to prevent the whipped cream losing its stiffness. Let chill in the refrigerator for at least 20 minutes.

Using a mortar and pestle, finely grind the olives and anchovies together with the remaining oil to make an olive cream.

Assemble the cheesecake. Place a 2 1/2-inch/6-cm metal ring in the center of each serving plate. Divide the bread mixture among the rings and press to flatten—this will be the base of the cheesecake. Spoon the ricotta mixture into the rings and smooth with a rubber spatula. Finally, carefully spread the olive cream over the top.

To serve, carefully remove the rings and garnish the cheesecake with mixed baby leaf salad and slivers of cherry tomatoes, if liked.

Preparation time: 20 minutes, plus resting
Cooking time: 10 minutes
Wine suggestion: Alto Adige Gewürztraminer

Crepes with Gorgonzola Cheese and Pancetta

Serves 6

piece of butter, for frying
12 oz/350 g rindless mild
  Gorgonzola cheese
3½ tablespoons milk
4 oz/120 g smoked pancetta
  or bacon, sliced
½ cup (4 oz/120 g) shallot or
  onion jelly (jam)

For the batter
2 cups (9 oz/250 g) all-
  purpose (plain) flour, sifted
3 eggs
generous 2 cups (17 fl oz/
  500 ml) milk
3 tablespoons (1½ oz/40 g)
  butter, melted, plus extra
  for greasing
salt

First make the batter. Mix together all the ingredients in a large bowl and whisk until the batter is smooth. Let rest in the refrigerator for at least 1 hour.

Melt a little butter a nonstick skillet (frying pan). When the skillet is very hot, pour a small ladleful of the batter into the middle of the skillet and then tilt and rotate the skillet to spread the mixture evenly over the entire surface of the skillet. Cook over medium–low heat, shaking the pan from time to time to prevent the batter from sticking, for 1 minute, or until the underside of the crepe is light brown, then flip the crepe and cook for 1 minute more, or until the other side is the same color. Turn out of the pan and keep warm while you repeat with the remaining batter, adding extra butter to the pan between crepes if necessary.

Put the Gorgonzola and milk in a small bowl and beat until soft and creamy.

Heat a dry skillet until very hot, add the pancetta or bacon, and cook over medium heat for 2–3 minutes until the fat has melted and the pancetta is crisp. Drain on kitchen paper.

Fill the crepes with the Gorgonzola, the crisp pancetta, and a little shallot or onion jelly (jam). Fold the crepes in half, and then in quarters, and serve.

THE KING,
PARMIGIANO REGGIANO

For centuries, Italian cheese makers have repeated the same process day in and day out to make the most famous Italian cheese in the world, and the one that can boast the most numerous attempts at imitation. Tasty and easily digestible, it is also a rich food from a nutritional point of view.

NINE CENTURIES OF HISTORY

Parmigiano Reggiano is a DOP (Protected Designation of Origin) hard cheese made with unpasteurized milk, without additives or preservatives. Its production area includes the provinces of Parma, Reggio Emilia, Modena, Bologna west of the river Reno, and Mantua south of the river Po. This area accounts for 360 dairies, which receive milk from 3,300 farms where the cows are fed with locally produced fodder. In 2014, these dairies produced nearly 3.3 million wheels of cheese.

Its historical origin dates back to around the twelfth century, to the Benedictine and Cistercian monasteries in the area of Parma and Reggio, and to the so-called "caselli"—small buildings with a square or polygonal base—where milk was processed. They followed a production technique similar to that of the ancient cheese from Piacento, called piacentino, and that of granone lodigiano.

Many stories and anecdotes have been collected over the centuries. It is said that Moliere asked for a sliver of Parmesan cheese before he died, and that Casanova made a gift of it to his lovers. Many others have sung its praises, from Boccaccio, who imagined mountains made of grated Parmesan cheese in his *Decameron* (1349), to Robert Louis Stevenson in his *Treasure Island* (1883), and Alberto Savinio, who in 1939 wrote that Parmigiano Reggiano performs the role the double bass plays among string instruments: it holds the harmony and supports the other instruments.

BOVINE BREEDS

At present a large proportion of production is carried out with milk from Friesian cows, introduced to the area during the last century, but the breeds traditionally used are the Rossa Reggiana, probably of Longobardic origin, and the Bianca Modenese or Valpadana (protected by a Slow Food Association), which accounted for more than 240,000 units in the 1950s, but have now reduced to only a few hundred beasts.

Unfortunately, these are breeds with quantitatively inferior milk production than that of Friesians, even though their milk is of better quality, and this explains in part why they are no longer used as much.

Thankfully, a few small dairies endure and continue to use milk from these breeds, producing a cheese of great value. Try one of the 14,000 wheels produced every year from the milk of the Rossa Reggiana and you will taste it for yourself.

HOW IT IS DONE

The secret of a good Parmesan cheese is not limited to the choice of breed that provides the prime ingredient.

The milk is collected and delivered to the dairies twice a day. The milk from the evening milking is placed in large shallow tanks to allow the fat to rise to the top. The following morning the fat is removed and the partially skimmed milk is mixed with the whole (full fat) milk from the morning milking and placed in copper tanks shaped like upturned bells. Whey inoculum (the acidified whey from the previous day's production) and natural rennet are added to the milk. The curd is broken by the cheese maker into minuscule fragments that are then slowly cooked (at 131°F/55°C), after which the extracted mass is divided into two wheels.

Each wheel is assigned a casein label with an identification number. A marking band is used to engrave the wheel with the month and year of production, the dairy identification number, and the unmistakable dotted writing all over its circumference. Some 18,600–30,300 fl oz/550–600 liters of milk are used to make a Parmesan wheel that weighs around 15 lb 7 oz/38–40 kg.

The salting and ageing phases follow. The minimum aging time is 12 months: at this point only the wheels deemed to be suitable are fire-branded and continue to age for 24–30 months or more, up to a maximum refinement of 80–90 months, which gives the cheese its unique sensory characteristics.

Preparation time: 25 minutes

Wine suggestion: Vermentino di Gallura

Flatbread Millefeuilles with Mozzarella, Tomatoes, and Pesto

Serves 4

3¹/₂ oz/100 g pane carasau
   (crisp Sardinian flatbread)
4 tomatoes, sliced
2 (9-oz/250-g) balls buffalo
   mozzarella cheese, sliced
extra virgin olive oil
salt

For the pesto
2 cups (2 oz/50 g) basil leaves,
   plus extra for garnish
¹/₃ cup (1¹/₄ oz/30 g) grated
   Parmesan cheese
1 tablespoon grated
   pecorino cheese
3¹/₂ tablespoons extra virgin
   olive oil
2¹/₂ tablespoons pine nuts
1 clove garlic
¹/₄ teaspoon salt

Put all the pesto ingredients into a food processor and blend until the mixture is a smooth sauce.

Assemble the millefeuille. Place a slice of pane carasau on a serving plate, spread with some pesto, add a slice of tomato, followed by a slice of mozzarella, drizzle with a little oil, and sprinkle with a pinch of salt. Repeat these layers until all the ingredients have been used up, finishing with a slice of pane carasau. Garnish with a few basil leaves and serve immediately.

NOTE Mozzarella di Bufala Campania, which was awarded the DOP (Protected Designation of Origin) mark in 1996, is a stretched-curd cheese produced predominantly in the provinces of Caserta and Salerno in Italy. Its origins date back to the Middle Ages, when the first references to the presence of buffalo on the plains of the Volturno and Sele rivers are found. Whether raw or cooked, this mozzarella lends itself to many uses.

🕐   Preparation time: 10 minutes

Cooking time: 20 minutes

♀   Wine suggestion: Roero Arneis

Chestnut Polenta with Cheese

Serves 4

5 cups (1 lb 2 oz/500 g)
  chestnut flour
1 (8½-oz/240-g) fresh goat
  or sheep cheese (ideally
  robiola cheese)
salt and pepper
cooked spinach, to serve

To garnish
extra virgin olive oil,
  for drizzling
chopped chives

Bring 8½ cups (70 fl oz/2 liters) of salted water to a boil in a pan. Pour the chestnut flour into the boiling water all at once, stirring briskly to avoid lumps forming. Cook over low heat for 15 minutes, stirring continuously with a wooden spoon, until the polenta is soft and creamy and easily comes away from the sides of the pan.

Put a generous spoonful of the hot polenta on the center of each plate and spread out the polenta with the back of a spoon to make a smooth base. Cover the polenta with a layer of robiola. Repeat these layers once more and then season with pepper, drizzle with a little oil, and garnish with the chives. Serve immediately with cooked spinach.

⊙ Preparation time: 10 minutes

Cooking time: 45 minutes

♀ Wine suggestion: Verdicchio dei Castelli di Jesi Classico Superiore

Baked Ricottinas with Aromatic Herbs

Serves 4

4 (3¹/₂-oz/100-g) Ricottina
cheeses (or make your own
by dividing 1²/₃ cups/
14 oz/400 g ricotta cheese
among four 1¹/₂-inch/
4-cm conical molds)
¹/₂ teaspoon dried oregano
pinch of chili powder
extra virgin olive oil
salt and pepper
4 small thyme sprigs,
leaves only, to garnish

Preheat the oven to 350°F/180°C/Gas mark 4. Grease a nonstick baking pan with oil.

Carefully remove the whole Ricottina from their baskets or molds, passing a smooth-bladed knife around the edges to loosen them if necessary and place them in the prepared baking pan. Sprinkle over the oregano, chili, a grinding of pepper, and a pinch of salt, and drizzle with oil. Bake in the oven for about 45 minutes, or until golden. Let cool.

To serve, garnish the baked Ricottinas with thyme and drizzle over a little more oil.

TIP To add a little spice to this recipe, replace the chili powder and dried oregano with curry powder and paprika. For a Mediterranean version, try adding some dried cherry tomatoes and chopped pitted (stoned) black olives. If you prefer sweet and sour flavors, we suggest a combination of honey and coarsely chopped dried fruits, or orange marmalade.

HOW TO SERVE CHEESE

In the last few years, cheese has progressed from being served as a starter, as a simple second course, or as a dessert, to being considered a course in its own right. In restaurants it is fashionable to serve samples of five or six different types of cheese, possibly with preserves or honey, accompanied by various vegetables, depending on the selection of cheeses.

In more sophisticated establishments specific wines are matched to individual cheeses to enhance their flavors. Interesting combinations in particular are those between blue cheeses and sweet, so-called meditation wines, or between very mature cheeses and very complex, aged wines such as Barolo, Taurasi, and Torgiano rosso Riserva.

SELECTION

If you decide to serve a selection of cheeses to your guests, the first issue to consider is which types of cheese to choose. The five or six types to consider should exclude very fresh cheeses and mozzarella, which are normally tasted separately. Try to include a soft cheese with a delicate flavor, a more mature soft cheese, a hard or semi-hard cheese, a spun-curd (pasta filata) cheese, a blue cheese and possibly a very mature cheese. It is best to choose one or two good quality local products and one or two goat and/or sheep milk cheeses. The ideal serving arrangement should start with the least flavorsome cheese (normally the freshest one) and end with the strongest tasting one, usually a blue cheese. Cheese must be served at room temperature; it should be taken out of the fridge one or two hours before serving. The cheese rind must not be removed.

CUTTING AND KNIVES

How a cheese is cut depends on its size and shape, but the most important thing to consider is that each guest has a chance to taste all its parts, from its rind to its heart. The way the cheese is cut is also important for correct storage of the remaining cheese.

Round or square cheeses are cut like cakes, into wedges, while cylindrical ones are sliced into regular slices around 1 centimeter thick.

Generally speaking, stretched curd cheeses are sliced, but if they are large each slice can also be cut into wedges.

Each cheese needs to be cut with an appropriate knife. Using the incorrect utensil could deform or modify the structure of the paste or rind, and therefore impact on its flavor. The general rule is that the thickness of the blade must be proportionate to the cheese's maturation period, and its length to that of the cheese's size. For very hard cheeses it is possible to use double-handled knives with a blade in the middle: push the handles down sharply with both hands after resting the blade on the cheese.

To cut into a hard-pressed cheese (canestrato pugliese or raschera) and for very soft cheeses it is more practical and more precise to use a cheese wire, a tensioned stainless steel wire stretched across a supporting frame.

To avoid spoiling their granular structure, Parmigiano Reggiano and Grana Padano are never cut but are "broken open." Using a wedge-shaped Parmesan cheese, first make a ½–¾ inch (1–2 cm) cut into the rind and then bring weight to bear on the cheese to pull off pieces, ensuring compliance with natural fracture lines.

Finally, to serve cheese portions it is best to use the forked tip of a cheese knife.

COMBINATIONS WITH HONEY AND CONSERVES

With regard to combinations, there are two schools of thought: some people insist that cheese must be served on its own to ensure that its flavor and aroma is fully appreciated; others suggest that the flavor of cheese can be enhanced by the correct combination with other foods, such as preserves and honey.

This well-established combination plays on contrasts: preserves and honeys complement the cheese, which contains very few sugars, so equilibrium between tastes is achieved. Generally speaking, honey and preserves can be matched to mature cheeses with strong flavors, enhancing their characteristics, but would overpower the flavor of fresh cheese. Honey with delicate flavors, such as acacia, is best suited to cheeses with average aromatic qualities.

🕐 Preparation time: 20 minutes

Cooking time: 1 minute

🍷 Wine suggestion: Malvasia delle Lipari

Pecorino Cheese with Grapes, Dried Figs, and Walnuts

Serves 4

2 tablespoons lime blossom
  honey
1 head radicchio (11–14 oz/
  300–400 g), leaves snapped
9 oz/250 g mature pecorino
  cheese (ideally from
  Sardinia), sliced
2 ready-to-eat dried figs,
  cut into wedges
24 walnut halves
 2¹⁄₃ cups (12 oz/350 g) white
  grapes, halved and seeded
extra virgin olive oil
salt

Gently warm the honey in a small pan until it becomes liquid.

Season the radicchio leaves with olive oil and salt.

Divide the radicchio, pecorino, figs, walnuts, and grapes among four serving plates. Drizzle over the warmed honey and serve.

TIP For an interesting alternative, trim 12 fresh figs and make a cross in the top of each one. Place the figs on a large rectangle of parchment (baking) paper. Sprinkle the figs with a pinch of cane sugar, the juice of ½ lemon, 1 tablespoon pine nuts, and 2 thyme sprigs, then bring up the sides of the parchment paper over the figs and fold a few times to seal. Place the parcel on a baking sheet and bake in an oven preheated to 300°F/150°C/Gas mark 2 for 10 minutes. Open the parcel and sprinkle over 1¹⁄₃ cups (7 oz/200 g) white grapes, halved, and 7 oz/200 g mature goat cheese, cubed. Seal the parcels again and bake for 10 minutes more. Remove and discard the thyme sprigs, drizzle with a little balsamic vinegar, and serve.

CHEF
Elena Vian

Preparation time: 30 minutes
Cooking time: 15 minutes

Polenta Gnocchi with Parmesan Cheese and Porcini Mushroom Fondue

Serves 4

For the fondue
2 oz/50 g dried porcini
extra virgin olive oil
1 cup (8 fl oz/250 ml)
    whipping cream
1 bay leaf
large pinch of ground nutmeg
2¹⁄₃ cups (7 oz/200 g) grated
    Parmesan cheese
salt and pepper

For the polenta gnocchi
1 cup (7 oz/200 g)
    cooked polenta
³⁄₄ cup (3¹⁄₂ oz/100 g)
    all-purpose (plain) flour
2 oz/50 g ricotta cheese
¹⁄₂ cup (1¹⁄₂ oz/40 g) grated
    Parmesan cheese
3 eggs
pinch of ground nutmeg
2 tablespoons (1¹⁄₄ oz/30 g)
    butter
3–4 sage leaves

Soak the mushrooms in a small bowl of tepid water for 15 minutes, then drain, squeeze to expel any excess moisture, and chop into small pieces.

Heat a little oil in a skillet (frying pan), add the mushrooms, and cook over medium heat for 5 minutes, or until brown. Transfer the mushrooms to a food processor and process until creamy.

Pour the cream into a small pan, add the bay leaf and nutmeg, and bring to a boil. As soon as the cream reaches boiling point, add the Parmesan and stir briskly to avoid the formation of lumps. Stir the creamy mushrooms into the fondue and then season to taste with salt and pepper. Keep warm.

Make the polenta gnocchi. Put the polenta, flour, ricotta, Parmesan, and eggs into the bowl of a stand mixer fitted with a flat beater and beat at a moderate speed until the mixture is soft and well blended. Season with a pinch each of nutmeg, salt, and pepper. Spoon the mixture into a pastry (piping) bag fitted with ⁵⁄₈-inch/1.5-cm tip (nozzle).

Bring a large pan of salted water to a boil. Hold the pastry bag over the pan of boiling water and gently squeeze the pastry bag to form ³⁄₄-inch/2-cm gnocchi, cutting them off with a knife and letting them drop into the water. As soon as the gnocchi rise to the surface, remove them with a slotted spoon and drain well.

Melt the butter in a skillet, add the sage leaves and the gnocchi, and cook over medium heat for 4–5 minutes until golden and heated through.

Serve the gnocchi with the fondue in a bowl on the side, with toothpicks (cocktail sticks) to skewer the gnocchi and dip them in the fondue.

WINE SUGGESTION   Nero di Troia DOC Castel del Monte is made with a native vine that produces full bunches of juicy and sweet grapes. This wine makes an interesting contrast to this dish as it has a rounded, spicy, and typically tannic flavor.

DESSERTS

Preparation time: 25 minutes, plus chilling

Cooking time: 10–15 minutes

Beer suggestion: amber beer with chestnut aromas

Chocolate Mousse with Hazelnut Brittle

Serves 6

2 gelatin sheets (leaves about
  1/8 oz/5 g)
generous 2 cups (17 fl oz/
  500 ml) whipping cream
9 oz/250 g bittersweet (dark)
  chocolate (70% cocoa
  solids), broken into pieces
1 vanilla bean (pod), split in
  half lengthwise and seeds
  scraped out

For the hazelnut brittle
1 cup (7 oz/200 g) superfine
  (caster) sugar
2/3 cups (3 1/2 oz/100 g)
  hazelnuts, coarsely chopped

To decorate (optional)
edible flowers
a few small mint leaves

Soak the gelatin in a bowl of cold water for 5–10 minutes until softened, then squeeze dry.

Meanwhile, put 8 fl oz/250 ml of the cream and the chocolate into a small pan and heat over low heat for 5–6 minutes until the chocolate has melted and the mixture is thick, full-bodied, and dense, then stir in the vanilla seeds. Remove from the heat and stir in the gelatin until dissolved. Let cool.

Pour the remaining cream into a bowl and whip until it is glossy. Gently fold the whipped cream into the chocolate cream, taking care that it does not collapse. Pour the mousse into individual serving glasses and chill in the refrigerator for at least 2 hours.

To make the hazelnut brittle, pour 4 teaspoons water into a small pan, add the sugar, and cook over low heat for 5–10 minutes until the caramel begins to darken. Remove from the heat, stir in the hazelnuts, then spread the caramel evenly over parchment (baking) paper and let cool for at least 10 minutes. Break up the hazelnut brittle with a knife.

Decorate the mousses with the hazelnut brittle and a few edible flowers and mint leaves, if liked.

MAKING ICE CREAM
WITHOUT
AN ICE CREAM MAKER

In Italy, consumption of artisanal ice cream has been increasing for many years. It is estimated that every Italian consumes on average 16 lb 7 oz/7 kg of ice cream per year. This is due, in part, to the favorable opinions of nutritionists. Ice cream, in fact, is considered to be a healthy snack, a source of "first class" proteins, lactose and sucrose (sugars that are easily broken down into energy), minerals such as calcium, phosphorous, and vitamins A, B1, and B2. This is the case, of course, providing the product is high-quality and free from hydrogenated fats, which are present in industrially made ice cream and in some bases that are also used by artisanal ice cream makers. In some cases home preparation, which allows absolute control over the quality of ingredients used, could become a valid alternative to the ice cream shop, rather than a second best or an experiment presumed to fail from the start.

ICE CREAM MAKER—YES OR NO?

There are two schools of thought among advocates of homemade ice cream: those who prefer to do it from scratch by hand, and those who insist instead that it is impossible to make a good ice cream without an ice cream maker.

In fact ice cream has existed since the sixteenth century, and the first ice cream machines, cooled by ice and salt, were patented only towards the end of the nineteenth century. The birth of the most famous Italian dessert therefore precedes by far the birth of the tool needed to cool and cream, processes that nowadays can be performed with the use of a freezer and a good supply of energy and patience. The recipe is the same, and the "no ice cream maker" school's supporters suggest that the only difference between the two types of ice cream is the preparation time and the physical effort involved.

Let's clarify first of all what differentiates a mousse ice cream and cream-based semifreddo. Unlike other preparations, mousse ice cream does not require cream or whipped egg whites or gelatin, but air, which is one of its essential ingredients, and which must be incorporated through blending. This operation is carried out by removing the stainless steel bowl of ice cream from the freezer and whisking its contents energetically for a few minutes, starting from the outer edges, where it will solidify more quickly. The process needs to be repeated five or six times in the space of two or three hours, to incorporate air and avoid the formation of ice crystals. This is because domestic freezers reach much lower temperatures than those used in artisanal ice cream workshops.

THE SECRET OF A GOOD HOMEMADE ICE CREAM

The ingredients for the preparation of ice cream are: eggs, very fresh whole (full fat) milk, sugar, cream, and a thickener.

To ensure a good ice cream, in addition to air it is essential to consider the water content in the ingredients used. For a good creamy consistency this must not represent more than 60 percent of the total weight of the ingredients (so be careful when preparing coffee ice cream!). The remaining 40 percent of the ingredients must be made up of soluble solids. It is extremely important not to use too much sugar, which inhibits freezing and prevents the ice cream from thickening. To compensate for this problem some people prefer to use invert sugar syrup, where the sucrose is decomposed into glucose and fructose by adding citric or ascorbic acids: this type of sugar tends to retain more moisture than sucrose, and therefore lowers the freezing point, avoiding crystallization (adding dextrose has the same effect).

Cream, an essential contributor of the fat element in the ice cream, must be around 10 percent of the ingredients used (if other fats are present, though, less cream is necessary), and should not be whipped because, as explained earlier, the incorporation of air into the ice cream takes place during the whisking and creaming stage.

Many people also use a small quantity of thickener to make the ice cream creamier and prevent it from freezing hard. Instead of soft grain flour, it is ideal to use carob-seed flour or carrageenan, which do not affect the flavor.

Finally, homemade ice cream must be consumed as quickly as possible because it destabilizes very quickly.

Preparation time: 30 minutes

Cooking time: 2 minutes

Wine suggestion: Conegliano Valdobbiadene Prosecco Superiore Dry

Strawberry Fruit Salad with Chantilly Cream

Serves 4–6

²/₃ cup (5 fl oz/150 ml)
  whipping cream
¾ cup (9 oz/250 g) pastry
  cream (see tip)
1²/₃ cups (9 oz/250 g)
  chopped strawberries
pinch of pepper
4 tablespoons grappa
juice of 1 lemon
²/₃ cup (3 oz/80 g) unsalted
  pistachios, chopped, plus
  extra to decorate
10 shortcrust pie dough
  (pastry) cookies (biscuits),
  crumbled

First make the Chantilly cream. Gently whisk the cream in a bowl until it forms stiff peaks. Using a rubber spatula, gently fold the pastry cream into the whipped cream.

Heat a dry skillet (frying pan), add the strawberries, pepper, grappa, and lemon juice, and cook over medium heat for 2 minutes, or until the liquid has evaporated.

To serve, spoon a layer of strawberries into individual glasses, then add a layer of pistachios, followed by a layer of biscuits, then another layer of strawberries. Top with plenty of Chantilly cream then sprinkle over extra chopped pistachios to serve.

TIP To make the pastry cream, pour generous 2 cups (17 fl oz/ 500 ml) milk into a pan, add the seeds of 1 vanilla bean (pod), and bring to a boil. Meanwhile, put 4 eggs into a bowl with ²/₃ cup (4 oz/ 120 g) superfine (caster) sugar and ¹/₃ cup plus 1 tablespoon (2 oz/50 g) all-purpose (plain) flour and whisk together. Slowly pour the hot milk over the egg mixture in a thin stream, whisking all the time, then return the mixture to the pan and cook over low heat for 1–2 minutes, stirring constantly, until it starts to thicken. Remove from the heat and let cool.

⊙ Preparation time: 20 minutes, plus cooling

Cooking time: 20 minutes

♀ Wine suggestion: Brachetto d'Acqui

Fruit Crisps with Ginger

Serves 4

1 lb 5 oz/600 g soft fruit
(raspberries, blackberries,
blueberries, Goji
berries, mulberries)
juice of ½ lemon
½ cup (3½ oz/100 g)
cane sugar
2 mint sprigs, leaves only,
chopped, plus extra mint
leaves to decorate
1½ cups (1½ oz/
40 g) cornflakes
3 tablespoons (1½ oz/
40 g) butter, softened and
cut into small pieces
½ cup (2 oz/50 g) peeled and
grated fresh ginger
⅔ cup (3 oz/80 g) 00 flour
¾ cup (7 oz/200 g)
plain yogurt

Preheat the oven to 350°F/180°C/Gas mark 4. Line a baking sheet with parchment (baking) paper.

Put the fruit into a bowl, add the lemon juice, 2 tablespoons of the sugar, and the mint, and mix gently.

Crush the cornflakes, reserving a handful of whole cornflakes for decoration, and put them into a bowl with the remaining sugar, butter, ginger, and flour. Using your fingertips, rub the ingredients together until the mixture resembles breadcrumbs. Spread out the crumb topping mixture on the prepared baking sheet and bake in the oven for 20 minutes, or until golden brown, breaking up the mixture halfway through the cooking time. Let cool.

To assemble the crisps (crumbles), drain the fruit and divide it among glasses. Spoon the yogurt over the fruit and then sprinkle with the crumb topping. Decorate with extra mint leaves and the reserved cornflakes.

NOTE Ginger is native to East Asia, but has been used in Italy since ancient times, both for its pleasant taste and health-giving properties. It is a stimulant and an astringent, and it can be used to treat arthritis, or lower cholesterol. In cooking, the fresh peeled rhizome can be grated, finely sliced, or juiced, or the dried ground powder can be used.

⊙ Preparation time: 30 minutes, plus draining
♉ Wine suggestion: Brachetto d'Acqui

Coeur de Crème with Strawberries

Serves 4

3 egg whites
1½ cups (12 fl oz/350 ml)
  whipping cream
3 tablespoons superfine
  (caster) sugar

To decorate
3¼ cups (1 lb 2 oz/500 g)
  chopped strawberries
½ cup (2¼ oz/60 g) toasted
  almonds, chopped

Line four heart-shaped molds with drainage holes in the bottom with cheese-cloth (muslin).

In a large spotlessly clean bowl, whisk the egg whites until they form stiff peaks. In a separate bowl, whisk 1 cup (8 fl oz/250 ml) of the cream to stiff peaks. Using a rubber spatula, gently fold the whipped cream into the egg whites. Pour the mixture into the prepared molds and cover with plastic wrap (clingfilm). Place on a tray and let drain in the refrigerator overnight.

The next day, whip the remaining cream with the sugar. Remove the coeur de crème from the molds and decorate with the whipped cream, strawberries, and almonds.

TIP   If you would like to serve your guests an even more sophisticated dessert, buy strawberries from Sciacca and Ribera: wild strawberries grown below lemon, orange, and peach trees in the Agrigento area of Italy. The plants probably originated from Friuli or Trentino, arriving in Sicily with soldiers returning from the Second World War. The strawberry plants adapted well, with a local ecotype developing that is now widely acclaimed for its very intense, sweet smell.

⊙ Preparation time: 25 minutes, plus chilling
Cooking time: 10 minutes
♀ Wine suggestion: Ramandolo

Citrus Fruit Panna Cotta

Serves 4

1 unwaxed orange
1 unwaxed lime
2 unwaxed lemons
generous 2 cups (17 fl oz/
   500 ml) whipping cream
²/₃ cup (5 fl oz/150 ml) milk
¹/₂ vanilla bean (pod), split in
   half lengthwise
2 gelatin sheets (leaves about
   ¹/₈ oz/5 g)
¾ cup (5 oz/150 g) superfine
   (caster) sugar

For the citrus fruit sauce
juice of 2 oranges
juice of 1 lemon
¾ cup (3¹/₂ oz/150 g) cane
   sugar

To serve
orange slices
a few mint leaves

Peel the orange, lime, and lemons and set the peel aside. Remove and discard the pith and break up the fruit into segments. Put the citrus peel and fruit segments into a bowl, add the cream, milk, and vanilla bean (pod) into a bowl and mix together. Chill in the refrigerator for 1 hour.

Soak the gelatin in a bowl of cold water for 10 minutes, then squeeze dry.

Transfer the citrus fruit mixture to a pan, add the superfine (caster) sugar, and bring to a boil, then stir in the gelatin until dissolved.

Strain the mixture into a pitcher (jug) and then pour it into four ramekins. Let cool and then cover and chill in the refrigerator for at least 3 hours until set.

Meanwhile, prepare the sauce. Pour the orange and lemon juices into a pan, add the cane sugar, and boil until the liquid reduces and has a syrupy consistency.

To unmold, dip each ramekin into warm water to loosen the panna cotta, then invert onto individual serving plates. Pour over the sauce and decorate with a few orange slices and some mint leaves.

NOTE   Whether refined or unrefined, cane sugar is ideal for making desserts because, unlike beet sugar, it has a particular aroma and taste, which is sometimes like licorice. Sugar cane is also used to produce panela (an unrefined sugar)—sugar cane juice is boiled and evaporated and the remaining syrup is then shaped into blocks, which can be crumbled. Panela has a dark amber color, characteristic aroma, and delicate taste.

Meringue Wafers

Serves 4

3½ egg whites (about
⅓ cup plus 1 tablespoon/
3½ oz/100 g)
1⅔ cups (7 oz/200 g)
confectioners' (icing)
sugar, sifted
pinch of salt
a few drops of lemon juice
2½ tablespoons unsalted
shelled pistachios
3¾ cups (1 lb 2 oz/500 g)
pistachio ice cream, to serve

Preheat the oven to 185–215°F/80–100°C. Line a baking sheet with parchment (baking) paper.

Put the egg whites into a large spotlessly clean bowl with half the confectioners' (icing) sugar and the salt and whisk until they form stiff peaks. Using a rubber spatula, carefully fold in the remaining confectioners' sugar and the lemon juice.

Spoon the meringue mixture into a pastry (piping) bag fitted with a ¼-inch/5-mm tip (nozzle). Pipe ⅜-inch/8-mm discs onto the prepared baking sheets, spacing them ¾ inch/2 cm apart. Bake in the oven for 2 hours or until dry and crisp. If the meringues start to brown, reduce the oven temperature and increase the cooking time. Let the meringues cool on the baking sheet inside the oven with the oven door open.

Put the pistachios into a food processor and process until finely chopped.

Serve a few scoops of pistachio ice cream on top of the meringue wafers and decorate with the chopped pistachios.

⊙   Preparation time: 15 minutes, plus chilling

Cooking time: 15 minutes

🍷   Wine suggestion: Oltrepò Pavese Sangue di Giuda Frizzante

Cherry and Soft Fruit Pudding

Serves 4

⅓ cup (1½ oz/40 g)
   cornstarch (cornflour)

¾ cup plus 1 tablespoon
   (7 fl oz/200 ml) red wine

¾ cup plus 1 tablespoon
   (7 fl oz/200 ml) raspberry
   or blueberry juice

¼ cup (2 oz/50 g) unrefined
   cane sugar

pinch of ground cardamom

2⅔ cups (14 oz/400 g) pitted
   (stoned) cherries, halved

2½ cups (12 oz/350 g)
   soft fruit (raspberries,
   blackberries, blueberries,
   Goji berries, mulberries)

a few mint leaves, to decorate

Put the cornstarch (cornflour) into a heavy pan with a little of the wine and cook over low heat for 3–4 minutes, stirring well to stop lumps forming, until dissolved. Pour over the remaining wine and the raspberry or blueberry juice, add the sugar and cardamom, and bring to a boil, stirring all the time. Add the cherries and cook for 7 minutes, then add the soft fruit and cook for 3 minutes more.

Spoon the fruits into four individual glasses and chill in the refrigerator for a few hours. Serve the puddings decorated with a few mint leaves.

NOTE   You can never eat just one cherry. Although similar in appearance, there are two different varieties of cherry: the sweet cherry and the sour cherry. Try replacing some of the cherries in this light and delicious recipe with Amarene Brusche di Modena PGI (Protected Geographical Indication) cherries to give the pudding a particularly intense aromatic flavor.

⊙   Preparation time: 20 minutes

Cooking time: 25–30 minutes

♀   Wine suggestion: Moscadello di Montalcino Vendemmia Tardiva

Apple Crisp with Cinnamon and Pine Nuts

Serves 4

4 apples

scant 1 cup (6¼ oz/180 g)
   superfine (caster) sugar

grated zest and juice of ½
   unwaxed lemon

1⅔ cups (7 oz/200 g)
   00 flour, sifted

1 stick (4 oz/120 g) butter,
   softened and cut into
   small pieces, plus extra
   for greasing

⅓ cup (1½ oz/40 g)
   pine nuts, chopped

pinch of ground cinnamon

Preheat the oven to 350°F/180°C/Gas mark 4. Grease four 2¾ x 2¾-inch/ 7 x 7-cm ovenproof dishes with butter.

Peel and core the apples, then cut them into ¼-inch/5-mm slices. Put the apple slices into a bowl with ¼ cup (2 oz/50 g) of the sugar and the lemon juice, toss thoroughly, and set aside.

Put the remaining sugar, flour, butter, lemon zest, pine nuts, and cinnamon into a bowl. Using your fingertips, rub the ingredients together until the mixture resembles breadcrumbs.

Arrange the apples in the prepared ovenproof dishes, sprinkle with the crumb topping, and bake in the oven for 25–30 minutes until golden brown. Serve the crisp (crumble) warm.

NOTE   There are 72 municipalities in the Italian province of Bolzano that grow Mele Alto Adige PGI (Protected Geographical Indication), which are some of the most well-known apples in Italy, and widely sold in Europe. Although all apples have a full taste and flavor, Fuji apples are the best for this recipe. Sweet and juicy, they are excellent for making desserts and strudels.

Cherries with Almond-flavored Ice

Serves 4

1²/₃ cups (9 oz/250 g) pitted
(stoned) cherries, halved,
plus extra whole cherries
to decorate
2¹/₂ tablespoons cane sugar
2 tablespoons
Maraschino liqueur
¼ cup (3 oz/80 g) marzipan
14 oz/400 g ice cubes
(about 1¾ cups crushed)

Put the cherries, sugar, and Maraschino liqueur into a bowl, mix well, and let stand for 30 minutes.

Put the marzipan into a pan with 4–5 tablespoons water and cook over medium–low heat for 4–5 minutes, stirring from time to time, until the marzipan has dissolved. Let cool.

Finely crush the ice in a food processor or blender, add the dissolved marzipan, and continue to process until you have a smooth, granita-like texture. Transfer the mixture to a plastic freezerproof container and freeze until required.

To serve, spoon a layer of the granita into four individual glasses, followed by a layer of the cherries and their juice, then repeat the layers, finishing with a layer of the granita. Decorate with a few extra cherries on top.

Preparation time: 10 minutes, plus standing
Cooking time: 5 minutes
Wine suggestion: Moscato d'Asti Frizzante

Sweet Couscous

Serves 4

²/₃ cup (5 fl oz/150 ml) apple
  juice
1 cup (5 oz/150 g) couscous
1 tablespoon rice syrup
¼ cup (2 oz/50 g) chopped
  candied fruit
2 oz/50 g bittersweet (dark)
  chocolate, coarsely chopped
grated zest of 1 unwaxed
  orange, to decorate

Bring the apple juice to a boil in a pan. Put the couscous into a separate pan, pour over the hot apple juice, cover with a lid, and let stand for 10–15 minutes, or until the couscous has soaked up all the juice.

Use a fork to separate the couscous grains, then add the rice syrup, candied fruit, and chocolate and mix well.

Divide the sweet couscous among small glasses and serve decorated with grated orange zest.

TIP   For a variation on this quick and delicious dessert, replace the apple juice with orange juice. As an alternative to serving the couscous in glasses, place a large metal ring or cookie cutter in the center of each serving plate and fill them with the couscous, then carefully remove the rings or cutters and serve with a scoop of orange or dark chocolate ice cream alongside.

Vanilla Cream with Strawberries and Port

Serves 4–6

4 eggs

1 egg yolk

1/2 cup (31/2 oz/100 g)
   superfine (caster) sugar

31/3 cups (27 fl oz/800 ml) milk

1 vanilla bean (pod), split in
   half lengthwise and seeds
   scraped out

grated zest of 1/2
   unwaxed lemon

For the decoration

1/2 cup (31/2 oz/100 g)
   cane sugar

1/3 cup plus 1 tablespoon
   (31/2 fl oz/100 ml) Port

11/4 cups (7 oz/200 g)
   chopped strawberries

Preheat the oven to 225°F/110°C/Gas mark 1/4.

Gently whisk the eggs, egg yolk, and superfine (caster) sugar in a bowl. Put the milk, vanilla seeds and lemon zest into a pan and heat the milk to 120°F/50°C. Stir the hot milk into the egg and sugar mixture, then strain into a pitcher (jug) and pour into ramekins.

Place the ramekins in a baking pan and add boiling water to the pan to come halfway up the ramekins. Bake in the oven for 40–50 minutes until the mixture is compact and jelly-like. Remove ramekins from the water and let cool.

Melt the cane sugar in a small pan over medium heat without stirring it. When it starts to turn dark, add the Port, 1/3 cup plus 1 tablespoon (31/2 fl oz/100 ml) water, and the strawberries. Remove from heat and let stand for 10 minutes.

To serve, decorate the vanilla creams with the strawberries and port.

N O T E   Made exclusively from grapes grown in the Douro region of northern Portugal, Port wine—or simply Port—is liquor-like and ideal for making desserts or accompanying them. Port is naturally sweet because of the high sugar content of the grapes, and because it is only partially fermented, which prevents all the sugar being turned into alcohol. There are seven main types of Port, from basic versions to finer Ports that have been aged for longer.

🕐 Preparation time: 20 minutes, plus chilling

Cooking time: 10 minutes

🍷 Wine suggestion: Valle d'Aosta Chambave Moscato Passito

Fruity Mascarpone Mousse with Coffee Caramel Sauce

Serves 4–6

¾ cup plus 2 tablespoons
  (7 oz/200 g)
  mascarpone cheese
⅔ cup (5 oz/150 g)
  ricotta cheese
3 egg yolks
½ cup plus 1 tablespoon
  (3¾ oz/110 g) superfine
  (caster) sugar

For the coffee caramel sauce
¼ cup (2 oz/50 g) superfine
  (caster) sugar
⅓ cup (2¾ fl oz/80 ml) coffee
3 tablespoons plus
  1 teaspoon (1¾ fl oz/
  50 ml) coffee liqueur

To decorate
3½ oz/100 g chocolate
  cookies (biscuits)
1 cup (4 oz/120 g) berries
a few coffee beans

Put the mascarpone and ricotta into a bowl and mix well with a fork.

Beat the egg yolks and sugar together in a metal bowl. Set the bowl over a pan of boiling water and whisk for 5 minutes until the mixture becomes creamy. Stir into the cheese mixture and chill in the refrigerator for 2 hours.

To make the sauce, put the sugar into a small pan and cook over low heat for 5 minutes, or until it starts to caramelize. Pour over the coffee and coffee liqueur and cook over medium heat until reduced by half.

To serve, add spoonfuls of the mascarpone mousse into glasses, crumble over the cookies, drizzle over the sauce, add some berries, and decorate with a few coffee beans.

TIP You can also serve this delicious dessert with a dark chocolate sauce instead of the coffee caramel sauce. Heat ⅓ cup plus 1 tablespoon (3½ fl oz/100 ml) whipping cream in a pan, being careful not to let it boil, then add 3½ oz/100 g chopped bittersweet (dark) chocolate, remove from the heat, and mix well until you have a smooth, dark sauce. Let cool.

⊙ Preparation time: 20 minutes, plus chilling

Summer Fruit Cups with Grand Marnier

Serves 4–6

1 peach, peeled, pitted
  (stoned), and chopped
4 plums, pitted (stoned)
  and chopped
4 apricots, pitted (stoned)
  and chopped
½ melon, peeled, seeded,
  and chopped
¼ cup (2 oz/50 g) superfine
  (caster) sugar
⅓ cup plus 1 tablespoon
  (3½ fl oz/100 ml) orange-
  flavored liqueur (ideally
  Grand Marnier liqueur)
2⅔ cups (12 oz/350 g)
  vanilla ice cream
2⅔ cups (12 oz/350 g)
  pistachio ice cream
shelled unsalted pistachios,
  to decorate

Put the fruit, sugar, and Grand Marnier into a bowl and mix well. Cover with plastic wrap (clingfilm) and chill in the refrigerator for 2 hours. Strain the liquor from the fruit.

Spoon a layer of the fruit salad into individual glasses, followed by a layer of vanilla ice cream, then another layer of fruit salad, and finish with a layer of pistachio ice cream. Decorate with pistachios and serve immediately.

TIP Plums must be bought ripe but not soft. Fresh plums are firm and the skin is shiny (though slightly opaque from the natural coating that protects the fruit from parasites). Plums should be kept in the refrigerator for no more than a week, preferably stored in glass containers rather than plastic or paper bags.

⊙ Preparation time: 25 minutes, plus cooling
Cooking time: 50 minutes
♀ Wine suggestion: Alto Adige Moscato Giallo

Crème Brûlée with Ginger

Serves 4

1²/₃ cups (14 fl oz/400 ml)
   whipping cream
3¹/₂ tablespoons peeled and
   grated fresh ginger
4 egg yolks
3¹/₂ tablespoons superfine
   (caster) sugar
¹/₂ cup (3¹/₂ oz/100 g)
   cane sugar

Preheat the oven to 325°F/160°C/Gas mark 3.

Pour the cream into a pan, add the ginger, and bring to a boil. Meanwhile, in a bowl, whisk the egg yolks with the superfine (caster) sugar until light and creamy. Strain the hot cream and then slowly pour it onto the egg mixture in a thin stream, whisking all the time. Pour the mixture into four ramekins.

Place the ramekins in a baking pan and add boiling water to the pan to come halfway up the ramekins. Bake in the oven for 45 minutes, or until set. Let cool to room temperature, then put in the refrigerator until ready to serve.

Before serving, sprinkle a layer of cane sugar over each ramekin, then caramelize it using a blowtorch. Alternatively, place the ramekins under a hot broiler (grill) for 2–3 minutes until the sugar has caramelized.

⊙ Preparation time: 25 minutes

Cooking time: 10 minutes

♀ Wine suggestion: Alto Adige Moscato Rosa

Tiramisu with Spiced Two-color Cream

Serves 6

²/₃ cup (4 oz/120 g) unrefined cane sugar

¹/₃ cup (2 oz/50 g) rice flour

4¼ cups (34 fl oz/1 liter) rice or almond milk

¼ teaspoon ground cinnamon

1 tablespoon unsweetened cocoa powder

½ vanilla bean (pod), split in half lengthwise and seeds scraped out

11¼ oz/320 g melba toasts (Danish toasts, 10–12 slices)

¾ cup plus 1 tablespoon (7 fl oz/200 ml) sweetened coffee

¼ cup (1¼ oz/30 g) toasted hazelnuts, chopped

Mix together the sugar and flour in a pan. Add a little of the rice or almond milk and stir to make a smooth cream, then slowly add the remaining rice or almond milk in a thin stream. Bring the mixture to a boil, stirring all the time, then cook over medium heat for 5 minutes, or until the cream starts to thicken.

Divide the cream mixture between two bowls. Stir the cinnamon and cocoa powder into the cream in one bowl. Stir the vanilla seeds into the other.

Put the melba toasts into a bowl and pour over the coffee. Put a layer of the soaked melba toasts in the bottom of six ramekins, then add a layer of the cinnamon and cocoa cream, followed by another layer of the soaked melba toasts, and finish with a layer of the vanilla cream. Decorate with the hazelnuts.

NOTE   The cocoa tree grows in tropical areas of Latin America, particularly in Brazil (which is one of the world's biggest cocoa producers), Central Africa, and Southeast Asia. Each tree yields 10–15 fruit (cocoa pods), each of which contain 25–40 seeds in a white, sugary, mucilaginous pulp. The dried and fermented seeds (cocoa beans) are processed to make cocoa paste and unsweetened cocoa powder. The three main types of cocoa bean are Criollo, which is considered the best, Forastero, and Trinitario.

THE IMPORTANCE
OF TEMPERING

To obtain a finished chocolate product, after they are harvested cacao beans are put through a process that lasts several days and includes fermentation, drying, mixing, conching, and tempering.

All these phases involve a certain degree of difficulty and one of the most delicate phases is tempering, which is the process before cooling.

During the phase of conching, a process invented by Rodolphe Lindt in 1880, cacao is mixed with all the other ingredients at a controlled temperature so as to achieve a dense fluid. This fluid cannot be poured into molds immediately, as chocolate tends to solidify in irregular patterns because of the fats it contains. If this happens, the final product will look dull, or the fat might come to the surface to form a white patina. The desired objective is crystallization, the solidification of the molecules in an even pattern: in this way the chocolate will have a shiny surface and a uniform and crunchy consistency. To achieve this, a pre-crystallization process is needed. This process, also called tempering, brings the chocolate to a lower melting point (between 105°F/40°C and 120°F/50°C), when the paste is still fluid enough to be molded.

When done professionally, tempering is carried out by specific machinery with thermometers, which quickly bring the temperature down from 105–120°F/40–50°C to 82°F/28°C, then return it to around 88–90°F/31–32°C (these temperatures refer to bittersweet (dark) chocolate: for milk or white chocolate the temperature is one or two degrees lower).

TEMPERING AT HOME

When working with chocolate at home, it is best to use tempering every time you need to blend chocolate to make small chocolates, pralines, and couverture chocolate.

There are machines for domestic tempering but it is also possible to try and manage this process manually. To obtain a perfect pre-crystallization, it is ideal to have a food thermometer and a marble or steel countertop.

Start by melting the chocolate in a double boiler or bain-marie, stirring until it reaches a temperature of around 113°F/45°C. At the right melting point, the chocolate should lightly coat a rubber spatula. At this point pour two-thirds of the fluid onto the marble or steel countertop, using a frosting spatula (palette knife) to spread it evenly on the surface. When the chocolate has reached a temperature of 82°F/28°C the fluid will be rather viscous and needs to be returned to the pan with the remaining hot chocolate. By stirring well, return the temperature of the chocolate to around 90°F/32°C: the chocolate is now ready to be used.

THINGS TO AVOID

When the appropriate instruments are not available, particularly a thermometer, it may be difficult to achieve a perfect crystallization, though practice and experience can help. In any case, it is essential to ensure that the chocolate does not absorb too much humidity during the process: the instruments and the countertop must be perfectly dry, and contact with the water in the bain-marie must be avoided.

If the result is not satisfactory, it is possible to repeat the tempering process, several times if necessary, but this leads to a progressive loss in the aromatic quality of the chocolate.

⊙   Preparation time: 20 minutes, plus freezing

Watermelon and Mint Granita

Serves 4

2 cups (11 oz/300 g)
  watermelon chunks, seeded
juice of ½ lemon
10 mint leaves, plus extra
  to decorate

Spread out the watermelon on a tray and then freeze for at least 2 hours.

Put the frozen watermelon, lemon juice, and mint into a food processor or blender and process until the mixture turns into granita. Serve immediately, decorated with a few extra mint leaves.

TIP   This light and fresh granita is the ideal way to round off a summer-evening barbecue. For an extra-special touch, to make a truly memorable dessert, add a dash of vodka to the granita and decorate with pieces of watermelon.

Amaretto Ice Cream with Chocolate Sauce and Peaches in Syrup

Serves 4

1½ cups (10 fl oz/300 ml) milk
¾ cup plus 1 tablespoon
  (7 fl oz/200 ml)
  whipping cream
2½ tablespoons Amaretto
  di Saronno liqueur
17 dry amaretti cookies
  (biscuits, about 3 oz/
  80 g), crumbled, plus extra
  to decorate
4 egg yolks
¾ cup (5 oz/150 g) superfine
  (caster) sugar
4 peach halves preserved
  in syrup, drained and sliced,
  to decorate

For the chocolate sauce
9 oz/250 g bittersweet
  (dark) chocolate,
  broken into pieces
1 cup (8 fl oz/250 ml) milk
⅓ cup plus 1 tablespoon
  (3½ fl oz/100 ml)
  whipping cream
⅓ cup (2¼ oz/60 g) superfine
  (caster) sugar

Pour the milk, cream, and Amaretto di Saronno liqueur into a pan, add the amaretti cookies (biscuits), and bring to a boil.

In a bowl, whisk the egg yolks with the sugar until light and creamy. Pour the hot milk mixture over the egg and sugar mixture, stirring all the time until smooth. Return the mixture to the pan, bring to a boil, and cook over low heat for a few minutes, stirring gently with a wooden spoon, until the custard begins to thicken and coats the back of a spoon. Let cool.

Pour the custard into an ice cream machine and churn for 20 minutes. Transfer the ice cream to a plastic freezerproof container and freeze until required.

Make the chocolate sauce. Put the chocolate into a microwaveable bowl and microwave in 20-second intervals, stirring after each one, until the chocolate is smooth. (Alternatively, melt the chocolate in a double boiler or in a heatproof bowl set over a pan of gently simmering water.) In a separate pan, bring the milk, cream, and sugar to the boil. As soon as the sugar has dissolved, stir in the chocolate until you have a smooth sauce. Let cool.

To serve, put some chocolate sauce on each serving plate in the shape of a tear drop, arrange some scoops of ice cream alongside, and decorate with the peaches and extra amaretto cookies.

CHEF
Marta Pavera

🕐 Preparation time: 30 minutes, plus cooling, churning, and freezing
Cooking time: 25 minutes

Ginger Ice Cream with Cocoa and Orange Crumble

Serves 4

1 cup (8 fl oz/250 ml) milk
1/3 cup plus 1 tablespoon
  (31/2 fl oz/100 ml)
  whipping cream
1 vanilla bean (pod)
1/3 cup (11/4 oz/33 g) peeled
  and grated fresh ginger
3 egg yolks
2/3 cup (4 oz/120 g) superfine
  (caster) sugar

**For the cocoa
  crumble topping**
3/4 cup (31/2 oz/100 g)
  00 flour, sifted
1/3 cup (3 oz/80 g) cane sugar
4 tablespoons (21/4 oz/60 g)
  cold butter, cut into pieces
1/2 cup (11/2 oz/40 g)
  unsweetened cocoa powder
pinch of salt

To decorate
1 orange, segmented
  and chopped
a few mint leaves

Pour the milk and cream into a pan, add the vanilla bean (pod) and ginger, and bring to a boil. Remove from the heat, cover, and let stand for 20 minutes. Remove and discard the vanilla bean.

In a bowl, whisk the egg yolks with the superfine (caster) sugar until light and creamy. Gently stir the ginger-infused cream into the egg and sugar mixture. Return the mixture to the pan, bring to a boil, and cook over low heat for a few minutes, stirring gently with a wooden spoon, until the custard begins to thicken and coats the back of a spoon. Let cool.

Pour the custard into an ice cream machine and churn for 20 minutes. Transfer the ice cream to a plastic freezerproof container and freeze until required.

Preheat the oven to 350°F/180°C/Gas mark 4. Line a baking sheet with parchment (baking) paper.

Make the cocoa crumble. Put the flour, cane sugar, butter, and cocoa powder into a bowl. Using your fingertips, rub the ingredients together until the mixture resembles breadcrumbs. Spread out the crumble mixture on the prepared baking sheet and bake in the oven for 15 minutes. Let cool.

To serve, arrange the crumble in the center of serving plates, put some scoops of ice cream on top, and decorate with orange slices and a few mint leaves.

Preparation time: 15 minutes, plus chilling

Cooking time: 15 minutes

Beer suggestion: blanche beer with chocolate aromas

Sweet Crepes

Serves 4

For the batter

1 cup (8 fl oz/250 ml) milk

1¼ cups (5 oz/150 g) 00 flour

1 medium (small) egg (about
1½ oz/40 g)

2 tablespoons superfine
(caster) sugar

1½ tablespoons (¾ oz/20 g)
butter, melted, plus extra
for greasing

1 vanilla bean (pod), split in
half lengthwise and seeds
scraped out

pinch of salt

To serve

chocolate spread

confectioners' (icing) sugar,
sifted, for dusting (optional)

mint leaves, to decorate

First make the batter. Mix together all the ingredients in a large bowl until frothy and homogenous. Chill in the refrigerator for at least 1 hour.

Grease a low-sided skillet (frying pan) with a little butter and heat it until very hot. Pour in a small ladleful of the batter—the crepes should be very thin— and let it spread out over the surface of the skillet. Cook over medium heat for 1–2 minutes until the edges of the crepe look dry, then flip the crepe and cook for 1–2 minutes more until the underside is golden brown. Turn out of the pan and repeat with the remaining batter, greasing the pan between crepes if necessary.

To serve, spread the crepes with the chocolate spread, then fold them halfway over on themselves, dust with confectioners' (icing) sugar, if liked, and decorate with mint leaves.

TIP To make homemade chocolate spread, put 1⅓ cups (9 oz/ 250 g) milk chocolate and 3½ oz/100 g bittersweet (dark) chocolate broken into pieces into a microwaveable bowl and microwave in 20-second intervals, stirring after each one, until the chocolate is smooth. (Alternatively, melt the chocolate in a heatproof bowl set over a pan of gently simmering water until a temperature of 105°F/40°C is reached.) Stir in 1⅓ cups (9 oz/250 g) hazelnut spread, followed by ⅓ cup (2¾ oz/75 g) confectioners' (icing) sugar, then stir in ⅓ cup (2¾ fl oz/75 ml) sunflower oil until the chocolate spread is homogenous and smooth. The spread can be stored in a sterilized jar (see page 306) in the refrigerator for up to 2 weeks.

Preparation time: 20 minutes, plus chilling
Cooking time: 5 minutes
Beer suggestion: Lambic Framboise

Lemon Custards in Chocolate Cups

Makes 25 cups

1 egg, plus 5 egg yolks
4 tablespoons strained lemon
 juice
1²⁄₃ cups (7 oz/200 g)
 confectioners' (icing) sugar
grated zest of ½
 unwaxed lemon
2¼ sticks (9 oz/250 g) butter
25 store-bought bittersweet
 (dark) chocolate cups
 (or you can make your own,
 see tip below)

To decorate
berries, such as strawberries
 and blackberries, sliced
kiwi, sliced

Place the egg and 5 egg yolks in a large bowl and beat lightly.

Pour the lemon juice into a pan, add the confectioners' (icing) sugar, lemon zest, and butter, and bring to a boil, stirring all the time. Pour the mixture over the beaten eggs and stir to combine. Cook in a double boiler or in a heatproof bowl set over a pan of gently simmering water until the custard reaches a temperature of 185°F/85°C. Cool the custard immediately (to avoid the eggs scrambling) by pouring the custard into a baking pan and chilling it in the refrigerator for 10–15 minutes until cool.

Transfer the custard to a bowl and use an immersion blender to blend until smooth. Fill the chocolate cups with the custard and decorate with slices of fruit.

TIP To make homemade chocolate cups, temper bittersweet (dark) chocolate (see page 460–461) and then pour it into polycarbonate molds (available from specialty stores) until they are completely full. After 2 minutes, turn the molds upside down to pour away any excess chocolate, using a pastry brush to wipe them of any dribbles. Chill the upturned molds in the refrigerator for 20–30 minutes until set (the cups need to be upturned so that the insides of the cups don't absorb any humidity). When this time is up, unmold the chocolate cups and fill them as you like.

Preparation time: 20 minutes, plus chilling
Cooking time: 10 minutes
Wine suggestion: Sagrantino di Montefalco Passito

Chocolate Puddings with Caramelized Oranges and Amaretti Cookies

Serves 6–8

4¼ cups (34 fl oz/1 liter) cold milk
¾ cup (5 oz/150 g) superfine (caster) sugar
1¼ cups (5 oz/150 g) 00 flour
1 cup (3 oz/80 g) unsweetened cocoa powder
16 amaretti cookies (biscuits), crumbled, for sprinkling

For the caramelized oranges
⅓ cup plus 1 tablespoon (3½ fl oz/100 ml) Grand Marnier
⅓ cup (2¼ oz/60 g) superfine (caster) sugar
2 oranges, peeled, divided into segments, and membrane removed

Mix together the milk and sugar in a pan, then sift over the flour and unsweetened cocoa powder and mix well. Cook over medium heat for a few minutes until thickened. Line 4-inch/10-cm nonstick individual molds (or you can use a single 6-inch/15-cm pudding mold) with plastic wrap (clingfilm) that clings very well to the edges, then pour in the mixture. Chill in the refrigerator for at least 1 hour.

Pour the Grand Marnier and sugar into a skillet (frying pan) and cook over medium heat until the sugar has disssolved and the liquid has reduced by one third. Add the oranges and cook for 1 minute, or until caramelized. Remove from the heat and let cool until lukewarm.

To unmold the puddings, pass a smooth-bladed knife around the edges of the molds and turn out onto individual serving plates. Decorate the puddings with the warm orange segments and sprinkle over the amaretti biscuits (cookies).

TIP When strawberries are in season, you can serve this pudding with whole fresh strawberries and a sauce made with 7 oz/200 g hulled strawberries: put the strawberries into a large pan with 3½ oz/100 g superfine (caster) sugar and the juice of half a lemon, cook over medium heat for 10 minutes until the strawberries are soft, then use an immersion blender to blend until smooth. To enrich this dessert further, decorate it with whipped cream.

Preparation time: 25 minutes

Cooking time: 40 minutes

Wine suggestion: Brachetto d'Acqui Passito

Stuffed Peaches

Serves 6–8

5 large peaches
1 egg
¼ cup (2 oz/50 g) superfine (caster) sugar
2½ teaspoons unsweetened cocoa powder
8 large amaretti cookies (biscuits), crumbled
2 tablespoons (1¼ oz/ 30 g) butter, plus extra for greasing

Preheat the oven to 325°F/160°C/Gas mark 3. Grease an ovenproof dish that is large enough to hold the peaches with butter.

Wash and dry the peaches, cut them in half, and discard the pits (stones). Scoop out a little flesh from the center of each peach half with a teaspoon, place the scooped-out flesh in a blender or liquidizer and blend to a puree. Add the egg, sugar, and unsweetened cocoa powder and blend again until smooth. Stir the amaretti cookies (biscuits) into the mixture.

Arrange the peaches, cut-side up, in the prepared ovenproof dish. Fill the peach hollows with the amaretti mixture and place a small piece of butter on top of each peach. Bake in the oven for about 40 minutes until the peaches are soft.

N O T E Among the very many varieties of peach cultivated in Italy, the one that most lends itself to cooking—whether in syrup or in the oven—is the Percoca peach, which is yellow-fleshed, compact, and adheres to its pit (stone), which should be detached with a small knife. Peaches are cultivated in many areas of southern Italy but the peaches produced in the Campania region are particularly noteworthy: the ruffled Percoca peach, the Percoca Puteolana peach, the reefing Percoca Terzarola peach, and the Giallona di Siano peach are all recognized as traditional food and agriculture produce.

Preparation time: 35 minutes, plus chilling
Cooking time: 10 minutes
Beer suggestion: brown ale

Butterscotch Chocolate Cups

Makes 10 cups

2¼ oz/60 g bittersweet
   (dark) chocolate, broken
   into pieces
2¼ oz/60 g milk chocolate,
   broken into pieces
¼ cup (2 oz/50 g) superfine
   (caster) sugar
¼ cup (2 fl oz/60 ml)
   whipping cream
poppy seeds, for decorating

Temper both kinds of chocolate separately (see The Importance of Tempering page 460–461).

Pour the bittersweet (dark) chocolate into five small round or heart-shaped molds until they are completely full. Fill five more molds with the milk chocolate. After 2 minutes, turn the molds upside down to pour away any excess chocolate, using a pastry brush to wipe them of any dribbles. Chill the upturned molds into the refrigerator for 20–30 minutes to set. You should now have ten small chocolate cups.

To make the butterscotch, heat the sugar in a small pan over low heat until the sugar turns dark brown. Meanwhile, heat the cream in a separate small pan, being careful not to let it boil. Drizzle the cream over the sugar, carefully stirring all the time, to obtain butterscotch. Let cool.

Just before serving, fill the chocolate cups with the butterscotch and decorate with a dusting of poppy seeds.

N O T E   Poppy seeds originated in the eastern Mediterranean and in Central Asia. Usually toasted, these small black-blue seeds seeds are extremely versatile when combined with honey or fruit desserts, and can be used as a thickening agent in sauces. Poppy seeds have a delicate flavor and aroma that derives from their prized essential oils. They are rich in Omega-6 fatty acids, B vitamins, and mineral salts such as calcium and phosphorus.

⊙ Preparation time: 15 minutes, plus chilling

⎕ Beer suggestion: Lambic Kriek

Chocolate Yogurt Mousse

Serves 4

²/₃ cup (5 fl oz/150 ml)
  coconut milk
5 dried figs
¹/₂ cup (1¹/₂ oz/40 g)
  unsweetened cocoa powder
¹/₄ cup (4¹/₄ oz/125 g)
  unsweetened soy yogurt
red currants, to decorate

Put the coconut milk and dried figs into a food processor and blend until smooth. Add the unsweetened cocoa powder and continue to blend until the mixture reaches your desired consistency. Alternatively, you could blend the ingredients together in a bowl with an immersion blender.

Divide the chocolate mixture among four glasses, then spoon over a layer of soy yogurt. Chill in the refrigerator for at least 2 hours. Serve the mousse decorated with berries.

TIP This fresh and light dessert, which is suitable for vegans thanks to its lack of animal products, lends itself well to being accompanied by the fruit of your choice, either fresh or in syrup. Try it, for instance, with homemade peaches in syrup (see page 492).

CHEF

Anna Vicina

Preparation time: 25 minutes

Cooking time: 10 minutes

Chocolate Almond Umbertini Cookies

Makes about 20 cookies

1½ cups (9 oz/250 g) almond flour

¾ cup (5 oz/150 g) superfine (caster) sugar

¼ cup (1 oz/25 g) unsweetened cocoa powder

3¼ egg whites (about ⅓ cup plus 2 tablespoons/ 3¼ oz/110 g)

1¼ cups (5 oz/150 g) confectioners' (icing) sugar, sifted

Mix together the almond flour, sugar, and unsweetened cocoa powder in a bowl.

In a separate spotlessly clean bowl, whip the egg whites until they form stiff peaks, then gradually stir in the flour mixture, a little at a time, until it forms a soft mixture.

Preheat the oven to 375°F/190°C/Gas mark 5. Line a baking sheet with parchment (baking) paper. Spread out the confectioners' (icing) sugar on a shallow plate.

Spoon the cookie (biscuit) mixture into a pastry (piping) bag fitted with a ½-inch/1-cm tip (nozzle). Pipe out small balls of the mixture, drop them into the confectioners' sugar and roll to coat in the sugar.

Lay the small balls on the prepared baking sheet and bake in the oven for 10 minutes until golden brown. Let cool on the baking sheet.

Serve these cookies singly or, if preferred, sandwich them together with a drop of melted bittersweet (dark) chocolate.

WINE SUGGESTION Barolo Chinato Montanaro is made with passion, patience, and dedication. It has bewitching ruby reflections, a rich, complex bouquet, and an authentic, pleasingly sweet/sour flavor. This wine represents a seductive meeting with the sweetness of the almond-flavored umbertini cookies.

⊙ Preparation time: 20 minutes, plus chilling
Cooking time: 10 minutes

♀ Wine suggestion: Cinque Terre Sciacchetrà

Chocolate Galettes with Mascarpone Cheese

Serves 4

6¼ oz/180 g bittersweet (dark) chocolate, broken into pieces
⅓ cup plus 1 tablespoon (3½ fl oz/100 ml) whipping cream
¾ cup (3½ oz/100 g) hazelnuts, toasted and finely chopped
4 oz/120 g white chocolate, finely chopped
¾ cup (6¼ oz 180 g) mascarpone cheese
1 tablespoon brandy

Line a baking sheet with parchment (baking) paper.

Melt the bittersweet (dark) chocolate in a double boiler or in a heatproof bowl set over a pan of gently simmering water, then add the cream and mix together. Using a tablespoon, drop one spoonful of the mixture at a time onto the prepared baking sheet and flatten it into an even disc about 2¾ inch/7 cm in diameter. When you have made 16 discs, and before the mixture sets, sprinkle four of the chocolate discs with half of the hazelnuts. Chill in the refrigerator for 2 hours or until set.

Make the filling. Melt the white chocolate in a double boiler. Put the mascarpone in a bowl, pour over the melted white chocolate and stir well until you have a smooth and homogenous mixture, then stir in the brandy and the remaining hazelnuts. Spoon the filling into a pastry (piping) bag fitted with a ½-inch/1 cm tip (nozzle).

To make the galettes: put one of the plain chocolate discs on a serving plate, pipe some of the filling onto the disc, top with another plain chocolate disc, then pipe some more of the filling onto the disc, repeat with another disc and filling, and finish with one of the hazelnut-covered chocolate discs. Repeat with the remaining discs and filling. Chill the galettes in the refrigerator for a few minutes to allow them to set before serving.

NOTE Mascarpone is a fresh cheese that is the product of mixing cream with citric or acetic acid. In Lombardy the words *mascherpa* or *mascapia* denote ricotta cheese or cream: hence the name mascarpone. Typical of the areas around Lodi and Abbiategrasso, mascarpone is a traditional regional Italian food product and is used mainly in the making of sweet creams. It is indispensable for tiramisu and for mascarpone cheese cream, a dessert that is widespread in the Emilia region.

Preparation time: 20 minutes, plus chilling
Cooking time: 10 minutes
Wine suggestion: Loazzolo

White Chocolate Puddings

Serves 8

4¼ cups (34 fl oz/1 liter) milk
7 tablespoons (3½ oz/
   100 g) butter
3½ oz/100 g white
   chocolate, chopped
¾ cup (3½ oz/100 g) 00 flour
¾ cup (4 oz/120 g)
   vanilla sugar
liqueur of your choice, for
   brushing the mold

To decorate (optional)
chocolate sauce
   (see page 454)
chocolate sprinkles
a few mint leaves

Pour the milk into a pan and bring to a boil. Remove from the heat, add the butter and chocolate, and stir until completely melted.

Sift (sieve) the flour into a bowl, add the vanilla sugar, then gradually pour in the melted chocolate, a little at a time, stirring with a whisk to prevent lumps forming. Return the mixture to the pan over medium heat and bring to a boil, stirring continuously with a wooden spoon.

Meanwhile, brush eight 2½-inch/6-cm individual molds with a liqueur of your choice—this will make it easier to unmold the puddings.

When the chocolate mixture starts to boil remove it from the heat and ladle the mixture into the prepared molds. Let the puddings come to room temperature and then chill them in the refrigerator for at least 2 hours.

To unmold the puddings, pass a smooth-bladed knife around the edges of each mold and turn them out onto serving plates. Decorate the puddings with chocolate sauce, chocolate sprinkles, and mint leaves, if liked.

TIP   You could use Maraschino liqueur for this dessert. This sweet and colorless distillation of Marasca cherries, which originated in Dalmatia, is frequently used in cooking, particularly for sweet recipes, because of its intensely aromatic scent that has no aggressive notes. Its harmonious and rounded flavor marries perfectly with white chocolate, giving it a slight flavor of Marasca cherries.

CHEF
Anna Vicina

Preparation time: 15 minutes, plus cooling
Cooking time: 25–35 minutes

Piedmontese Bonet

Serves 6

⅓ cup (2¼ oz/60 g) superfine
  (caster) sugar
1¼ cups (10 fl oz/300 ml)
  whole (full-fat) milk
2 eggs
3 tablespoons unsweetened
  cocoa powder
21 dry amaretti cookies
  (biscuits; about 3½ oz/
  100 g), plus more to serve
scant 1 teaspoon instant
  coffee powder
18 small amaretti cookies
  (biscuits), to serve
cocoa powder, sifted, to serve

Melt 6 tablespoons of the sugar in a small pan over medium heat without stirring. When the sugar has caramelized, pour it into the bottom of six 2½-inch/6-cm aluminum cups or molds. Let cool completely so that the liquid solidifies.

Preheat the oven to 275°F/140°C/Gas mark 1 or preheat a steam oven to 185°F/85°C.

Put all the other ingredients into a food processor and blend to a purée. Pour the mixture into the cups or molds and cover each with sheets of aluminum foil. Place the cups or molds in a baking tray, add enough cold water to come three-quarters of the way up the cups or molds, and bake in the oven for 30 minutes, or until set. Alternatively, cook in a steam oven for 18 minutes, or until solid.

To unmold the puddings, pass a smooth-bladed knife around the edges of each mold and turn them out onto serving plates. Decorate each pudding with three amaretti cookies (biscuit), or dust with a little bit of cocoa powder, if liked.

WINE SUGGESTION Grappa di Moscato is a generous vine that provides extraordinary gifts. Among these is Grappa di Moscato Montanaro, with its marvellous golden reflections, perfected in great oak casks for 24 months. Its all-encompassing aroma and its soft, sweet flavor are more than a match for the coffee, unsweetened cocoa powder, and almond tones of this festive dessert.

Preparation time: 10 minutes, plus churning, cooling, and freezing
Cooking time: 10 minutes

Hazelnut Ice Cream with Dark Chocolate Sauce

Serves 4–6

1¼ cups (10 fl oz/300 ml) milk
¾ cup plus 1 tablespoon
    (7 fl oz/200 ml)
    whipping cream
⅓ cup (3 oz/80 g)
    hazelnut paste
½ cup (2 oz/50 g)
    chopped hazelnuts (ideally
    Piedmont hazelnuts)
4 egg yolks
¼ cup (2 oz/50 g) superfine
    (caster) sugar

For the chocolate sauce
⅓ cup (2¾ fl oz/80 ml)
    whipping cream
5 oz/150 g bittersweet (dark)
    chocolate (70% cocoa
    solids), finely chopped

**For the caramelized
    hazelnuts**
½ cup (3½ oz/100 g)
    cane sugar
20 hazelnuts (ideally
    Piedmont hazelnuts)

Put the milk, cream, hazelnut paste, and hazelnuts into a pan, bring to a boil, then remove from the heat.

Meanwhile, whisk the egg yolks with the superfine (caster) sugar in a separate pan until light and creamy, then bring to a boil, stirring all the time. Pour the hot milk and hazelnut mixture onto the egg and sugar mixture, whisking continuously, and cook over low heat for a few minutes, stirring gently with a wooden spoon, until the custard begins to thicken and coats the back of a spoon. Let cool.

Pour the custard into an ice cream machine and churn for 20 minutes. Transfer the ice cream to a plastic freezerproof container and freeze until required.

Make the chocolate sauce. Heat the cream in a small pan, being careful not to let it boil. Remove from the heat, add the chocolate, and stir until the chocolate has melted.

Make the caramelized hazelnuts. Heat a dry skillet (frying pan), add the cane sugar and 1 tablespoon water, and cook over low heat until the sugar has dissolved. Add the hazelnuts and cook for 3–4 minutes until caramelized.

To serve, spoon some warm chocolate sauce into the center of each serving bowl, place a scoop of ice cream on top, and decorate with caramelized hazelnuts.

SWEET TARTS,
CAKES,
AND
COOKIES

⊙ Preparation time: 20 minutes
Cooking time: 20–25 minutes
♀ Wine suggestion: Brachetto d'Acqui

Raspberry Cake

Serves 8

4 eggs, separated
1 cup plus 2 tablespoons
   (7³/₄ oz/220 g) superfine
   (caster) sugar
1²/₃ cups (7 oz/200 g) type 00
   flour, sifted, plus extra
   for dusting
1³/₄ sticks (7 oz/200 g butter),
   melted and cooled, plus
   extra for greasing
grated zest of 1
   unwaxed lemon
1²/₃ cups (7 oz/
   200 g) raspberries

Preheat the oven to 325°F/160°C/Gas mark 3. Grease a 9¹/₂–10¹/₄-inch/24–26-cm round cake pan (tin) with butter, then dust it with flour.

In a large spotlessly clean bowl, whisk the egg whites with 1 cup (7 oz/200 g) of the sugar until they form very stiff peaks. Add the egg yolks and carefully stir them into the mixture using a figure-eight movement with the whisk so that the egg whites do not collapse. Continuing to stir in this way, stir in the flour, followed by the butter, and finally the lemon zest.

Pour half the cake batter into the prepared cake pan and level it out with a frosting spatula (palette knife). Arrange the raspberries on top, pour over the remaining cake batter, then sprinkle the remaining sugar over the top. Bake in the oven for 20–25 minutes, or until a skewer inserted in the middle comes out clean. Let the cake cool in the pan.

TIP You can make this cake with many types of fruit. Try replacing the raspberries with diced apples dusted with a little ground cinnamon, for example, or with thinly sliced pineapple or chopped strawberries.

⊙ Preparation time: 40 minutes

Cooking time: 45 minutes

♀ Wine suggestion: Verdicchio dei Castelli di Jesi Passito

Buckwheat Cake

Serves 4–6

2³⁄₄ sticks (11 oz/300 g) butter,
  softened and cut into cubes,
  plus extra for greasing
1¹⁄₂ cups (11 oz/300 g)
  granulated sugar
6 eggs, separated
a few drops natural
  vanilla extract
2¹⁄₂ cups (11 oz/300 g)
  buckwheat flour, sifted
3 tablespoons all-purpose
  (plain) flour, sifted, plus
  extra for dusting
1¹⁄₂ tablespoons baking
  powder
¹⁄₃ cup (4 oz/120 g) blueberry
  jelly (jam)
sifted confectioners' (icing)
  sugar, for dusting
whipped cream,
  to serve (optional)

Preheat the oven to 350°F/180°C/Gas mark 4. Grease a 10¹⁄₄-inch/26-cm round cake pan (tin) with butter, then dust it with flour.

Cream the butter and sugar in a large bowl, then add the egg yolks and vanilla extract and blend until creamy. Slowly beat in the flours and baking powder, being careful to avoid lumps forming.

In a separate spotlessly clean bowl, whisk the egg whites until they form stiff peaks. Using a rubber spatula, gently fold the egg whites into the cake batter with a bottom-up movement to avoid the egg whites losing their stiffness.

Pour the cake batter into the prepared cake pan and bake in the oven for 45 minutes, or until the top is golden brown and a skewer inserted in the middle comes out clean. Turn out of the pan and place on a wire rack to cool.

Cut the cake into two layers. Spread the blueberry jelly (jam) onto the bottom layer of cake and cover with the top layer of cake. Dust with confectioners' (icing) sugar and serve with whipped cream, if liked.

NOTE Buckwheat is a widely used cereal in Valtellina, in the Lombardy region of Italy, where buckwheat flour is used to make the traditional pizzoccheri pasta (see p.364). This hardy plant grows quickly and tolerates poor soil and damp and cold climates. Its grains have a high nutritional content because they are rich in essential amino acids, minerals, and vitamins.

Preparation time: 20 minutes, plus resting
Cooking time: 3–4 minutes
Wine suggestion: Alto Adige Moscato Rosé

Alassio's Kisses

Makes about 20 kisses

2 cups (8¼ oz/230 g)
   hazelnuts, toasted
2¼ cups (1 lb/450 g)
   superfine (caster) sugar
2 tablespoons plus
   1 teaspoon honey
¼ cup (¾ oz/20 g)
   unsweetened cocoa powder
2¾ egg whites (about
   ⅓ cup/2¾ oz/75 g)
6½ oz/185 g bittersweet
   (dark) chocolate
   (67% cocoa solids)

Put the hazelnuts and sugar into a food processor and blend to a fine powder. Transfer to a bowl, add the honey, cocoa powder, and egg whites, and mix until well combined. Spoon the mixture into a pastry (piping) bag fitted with star-shaped tip (nozzle).

Line a baking sheet with parchment (baking) paper. Pipe out about 20 ¾-inch/2-cm balls of the mixture onto the prepared baking sheet, spacing them about 1¼-inches/3-cm apart. Let rest for 8–10 hours at room temperature until a light crust forms on the dough for each cookie (biscuit).

Preheat the oven to 475°F/240°C/Gas mark 9. Bake the for 3–4 minutes until a crust forms on the top of each cookie. Let the cookies cool on the baking sheet.

Make the precrystallized chocolate couverture. Coarsely chop the chocolate on a marble cutting (chopping) board with a smooth-bladed knife. Melt the chocolate in double boiler, or in a heatproof bowl set over a pan of gently simmering water, bringing it to 115–120°F/45–50°C. Pour two-thirds of the chocolate onto the marble board (or you could use a steel plate) and set the rest of the chocolate aside. Using a rubber spatula, spread out the melted chocolate on the marble board to lower the temperature—it needs to cool to 80°F/27°C. Return the cooled chocolate to the double boiler with the remaining melted chocolate and mix well. Heat the chocolate again until the temperature reaches 86–90°F/30–32°C.

Once the cookies are cool, sandwich pairs of them together with the precrystallized chocolate couverture.

NOTE It was thanks to these cookies that the Ligurian town of Alassio joined Le Città del Cioccolato (The City of Chocolate) club in 2007. Tradition has it that the cookies were invented in 1910 by Rinaldo Balzola, pastry cook to the royal house of Savoy. He may have been inspired by the older Piedmontese baci di dama (ladies' kisses): two cookies made with the famous Piedmont hazelnuts, unsweetened cocoa powder, and honey, and sandwiched together with chocolate.

🕐 Preparation time: 30 minutes, plus chilling
Cooking time: 55 minutes

🍷 Wine suggestion: Moscadello di Montalcino

Mini Easter Cakes

Makes 12 cakes

For the pie dough (pastry)

1⅓ cups (5¾ oz/170 g)
   type 00 flour, plus extra
   for dusting

1 egg

⅓ cup (2¼ oz/60 g) superfine
   (caster) sugar

¼ cup (2¼ oz/60 g) lard,
   cut into cubes

For the filling

3½ oz/100 g grano cotto
   (cooked wheat)—available
   in jars or cans (tins) from
   Italian grocery stores

2 tablespoons milk

½ tablespoon butter

grated zest of 1
   unwaxed lemon

¾ cup (6¼ oz/180 g)
   ricotta cheese

¾ cup (5 oz/150 g) superfine
   (caster) sugar

2 eggs

1 vanilla bean (pod) split in
   half lengthwise and seeds
   scraped out

1 teaspoon orange
   flower water

pinch of ground cinnamon

¼ cup (2 oz/50 g) diced
   candied fruit, such as lemon,
   orange, and pumpkin

First make the pie dough (pastry). Put the flour in a mound on the countertop, make a well in the center, put the egg and sugar into this, and arrange the lard around edges. Using your hands, gradually gathering up all the ingredients and blend them together until you have a ball of dough. Wrap the dough in plastic wrap (clingfilm) and chill in the refrigerator for 1 hour.

Preheat the oven to 350°F/180°C/Gas mark 4. Line the cups of a 12-hole muffin pan (tin) or 12 individual ramekins with parchment (baking) paper.

Put the grano cotto (cooked wheat), milk, butter, and lemon zest into a large pan and cook over medium heat for about 10 minutes until it is the consistency of custard.

Meanwhile, in a large bowl, mix together the ricotta, sugar, eggs, vanilla seeds, orange flower water, cinnamon, and candied fruit. Pour this into the pan with the grano cotto mixture and mix well.

Divide the pie dough into 12 pieces and then roll out each piece on a lightly floured countertop to a thickness of ¼ inch/5 mm. Use the pie dough to line the cups of the prepared muffin pan or ramekins.

Spoon the filling into the pastry shells (cases) and bake in the oven for 45 minutes, or until the tops of the cakes are golden brown. Let the cakes cool in the muffin pan or ramekins.

N O T E   It is preferable to use a vanilla bean (pod) or natural vanilla instead of synthetic vanillin as the latter is inferior, though cheaper, than real vanilla. To be sure of purchasing a product containing natural vanilla, you should check that the label says "vanilla extract."

Preparation time: 30 minutes, plus chilling
Cooking time: 8–10 minutes
Wine suggestion: Recioto della Valpolicella

Rice Flour and Cocoa Powder Cookies

Makes about 20 cookies

1¼ sticks (5 oz/150 g) butter, softened and cut into cubes
½ cup (3½ oz/100 g) superfine (caster) sugar
3 tablespoons milk
2¼ teaspoons baking powder
1 cup plus 1 tablespoon (5¾ oz/170 g) rice flour, plus flour for dusting
⅔ cup (3½ oz/100 g) potato flour
⅓ cup (1¼ oz/30 g) unsweetened cocoa powder
¾ cup (3½ oz/100 g) coarsely chopped hazelnuts

Preheat the oven to 350°F/180°C/Gas mark 4. Line two baking sheets with parchment (baking) paper.

Cream the butter and sugar together in a bowl, then add the milk, baking powder, and rice and potato flours, and mix well. Add the cocoa powder and beat until you have a homogenous mixture, then stir in the hazelnuts. Using your hands, shape the cookie (biscuit) dough into a loaf shape, wrap it in parchment paper, and chill in the refrigerator for 1 hour.

Roll out the dough on a floured surface to a thickness of about ½ inch/1 cm. Cut the dough into strips about 1½ inches/4 cm wide and then cut the strips into squares. Transfer the cookies to the prepared baking sheets and bake in the oven for 8–10 minutes until golden brown. Let the cookies cool on the baking sheets.

NOTE Hazelnuts can be either round in shape or slightly elongated —the former are generally of better quality and more highly prized than the latter. It is no coincidence that the noblest hazelnuts in Italy should be round. These include the Tonda Gentile delle Langhe variety of hazelnut and others such as the Nocciola Piemonte PGI (Protected Geographical Indication), Tonda Nocciola Romana POD (Protected Designation of Origin), which has a very refined flavor, and the Nocciola di Giffoni PGI, which is dried out in the sun. Besides being ideal for sweet recipes, toasted hazelnuts can also be used to enrich breakfast cereals, flavor salads, or made into a topping for oven-baked fish fillets.

Preparation time: 15 minutes

Cooking time: 20 minutes

Wine suggestion: Recioto di Gambellara

Ugly but Tasty Cookies

Makes about 15 cookies

3½ egg whites (about ⅓ cup plus 1 tablespoon/ 3½ oz/100 g)

1 cup (7 oz/200 g) superfine (caster) sugar

1½ cups (7 oz/200 g) whole hazelnuts, three-quarters chopped and one-quarter halved

Preheat the oven to 350°F/170°C/Gas mark 4. Line two baking sheets with parchment (baking) paper.

Stir together the egg whites and sugar in a small pan, then add the hazelnuts and cook over medium heat for about 10 minutes, stirring continuously with a wooden spoon, until the mixture leaves the sides of the pan.

Using two teaspoons, place heaped spoonfuls of the cookie (biscuit) dough onto the prepared baking sheets, spacing them about 1¼–1½ inches/3–4 cm apart. Bake in the oven for 10 minutes, or until golden brown. Let the cookies cool on the baking sheet.

NOTE In Italy these cookies are known as Brutti ma Buoni, hence the name of this recipe. Many Italian regions, including Emilia Romagna, Piedmont, and Tuscany, vie for the origin of this simple but delicious recipe. These lumpy cookies (biscuits) may not look particularly tempting but they are actually wonderfully crisp morsels. You can replace the hazelnuts with sweet and bitter almonds, if liked.

Preparation time: 15 minutes

Cooking time: 40 minutes

Wine suggestion: Loazzolo

Amaretto and Peach Pastry Cake

Serves 8

2 tablespoons (1¼ oz/30 g)
   butter, for greasing
type 00 flour, for dusting
1½ quantities (14 oz/400 g)
   shortcrust pie dough (pastry,
   see Note page 494)
3 tablespoons plus
   1 teaspoon Marsala or
   dessert wine
3 tablespoons plus
   1 teaspoon strong coffee
7 oz/200 g soft amaretti
   cookies (biscuits)
3 cups (13½ oz/380 g)
   drained and sliced canned
   peaches in syrup
confectioners' (icing) sugar,
   sifted, for dusting

Preheat the oven to 350°F/180°C/Gas mark 4. Grease a 9½-inch/24-cm round cake pan (tin) with butter, then dust it with flour.

Put two-thirds of the pie dough (pastry) on a lightly floured countertop and roll out to a fairly thin disc (about ⅛ inch/3 mm thick) and use it to line the prepared cake pan—the sides of the pastry shell (case) should be about 1½ inches/4 cm deep.

Roll out the remaining pie dough to a fairly thin disc (about ¹⁄₁₆ inch/2 mm thick)—it should be large enough to cover the top of the cake pan. Set aside.

In a small bowl, stir together the Marsala or dessert wine and the coffee. Quickly dip the amaretti cookies (biscuits) into the wine and coffee mixture and then crumble them over the bottom of the pastry shell to cover it completely. Arrange the peaches on top of the crumbled cookies in a spiral pattern.

Place the rolled-out pie dough on top of the cake and crimp the edges together to seal. Bake in the oven for 40 minutes, or until golden brown. Serve the cake dusted with confectioners' (icing) sugar.

TIP   To make excellent homemade peaches in syrup, scald 13 peaches (about 4½ lb/2 kg) for 2 minutes in a large pan of boiling water with the juice of 2 lemons, then skin the peaches, cut them in half, and remove the pits (stones). Put 3¾ cups (1 lb 10 oz/750 g) superfine (caster) sugar into a large pan with 8½ cups (68 fl oz/2 liters) water, bring to a boil, and cook for a few minutes, then let the syrup cool. Transfer the peaches to sterilized jars (see page 306), cover them with the syrup, leaving a little space between the syrup and the top of the jar, and seal the jars. Place the sealed jars in a large pan of water, keeping the jars separated using a dish towel, and boil for 30 minutes. Let cool, then remove the jars and dry them. Store for 1 month before eating.

⊙ Preparation time: 10 minutes
Cooking time: 6–8 minutes

♀ Wine suggestion: Moscadello di Montalcino Vendemmia Tardiva

Ricotta Cheese, Honey, and Apple Tarts with Apple Brandy

Makes 4 tarts

1 quantity (9 oz/250 g)
   shortcrust pie dough
   (pastry, see Note)
type 00 flour, for dusting
1½ tablespoons (¾ oz/
   20 g) butter, plus extra
   for greasing
⅔ cup (5 oz/150 g)
   ricotta cheese
2 teaspoons acacia honey
2 Red Delicious apples
2 tablespoons superfine
   (caster) sugar
2 tablespoons apple brandy
   (ideally Calvados)

To decorate (optional)
apple slices
a few mint leaves, chopped

Preheat the oven to 350°F/180°C/Gas mark 4. Grease the outsides of four upturned 2½-inch/6-cm tart pans (tins) with butter, then dust them with flour and place, upside-down, on a baking sheet.

Divide the pie dough (pastry) into four pieces and then roll out each piece of pie dough on a lightly floured countertop to form a circle measuring 1½–2½ inches/4–6 cm in diameter. Lay the pie dough circles over the prepared upturned pans and bake in the oven for 6–8 minutes until golden brown. Let the pastry shells (cases) cool on top of the pans.

Meanwhile, put the ricotta and honey into a small bowl and beat together until smooth and well combined.

Peel, core, and dice the apples. Melt the butter in a skillet (frying pan), add the apples and sugar, and sauté over medium heat for 5 minutes, or until soft. Drizzle over the apple brandy, stir, then flambé by carefully igniting with a match and then letting the flames die down. Let cool.

Put 1 teaspoon of the ricotta mixture into each pastry shell and top with some of the apples. Decorate each cake with a few slices of raw apple and some chopped mint leaves, if liked.

NOTE Shortcrust pie dough (pastry) is ideal as a basis for many sweet and savory recipes. For homemade pie dough, place 1¼ cups (5 oz/150 g) type 00 flour in a mound on the countertop, put a pinch of salt in the center, and add 5½ tablespoons (2¾ oz/75 g) cold cubed butter. Mix the ingredients together by hand, adding sufficient cold water to make a firm, homogenous dough. Shape the dough into a ball, wrap it in plastic wrap (clingfilm), and let rest in the refrigerator for 1 hour before using.

⊙ Preparation time: 30 minutes, plus resting and cooling

Cooking time: 30 minutes

♀ Wine suggestion: Colli Piacentini Malvasia Passito

Honey and Nut Cake

Serves 6–8

4 cups (1 lb 2 oz/500 g) type 00 flour, sifted, plus extra for dusting

1 stick (4 oz/120 g) butter, softened, plus extra for greasing

2/3 cup (4½ oz/125 g) superfine (caster) sugar

2 egg yolks

½ cup plus 1 tablespoon (4¾ fl oz/140 ml) milk

½ cup plus 1 tablespoon (4¾ fl oz/140 ml) white wine

confectioners' (icing) sugar, sifted, to decorate (optional)

For the filling

2¼ cups (1 lb 2 oz/500 g) acacia honey

1 cup (4¼ oz/125 g) coarsely chopped walnuts

½ cup (2 oz/50 g) coarsely chopped almonds

3 cups (4¼ oz/125 g) fresh breadcrumbs

1/3 cup (2 oz/50 g) pine nuts, coarsely chopped

1/3 cup (2 oz/50 g) raisins, coarsely chopped

1–2 cloves, ground

ground cinnamon, to taste

ground nutmeg, to taste

Cream the flour, butter, superfine (caster) sugar, and egg yolks together in a bowl. Add the milk and wine and mix until you obtain a homogenous mixture. Wrap the pie dough (pastry) in plastic wrap (clingfilm) and let rest at room temperature for 20 minutes.

Make the filling. Heat the honey in a small pan and then let cool until it is lukewarm. Put all the remaining filling ingredients into a bowl, pour over the warm honey, and stir thoroughly to combine.

Preheat the oven to 355°F/170°C/Gas mark 4. Grease two 9½-inch/24-cm round cake pans (tins) with butter.

Divide the pie dough into four pieces and roll out each piece on a lightly floured countertop into a thin circle about 9½ inches/24 cm in diameter. Line the prepared cake pans with two of the pie dough circles and prick the surface of the pie dough with a fork.

Divide the filling between the two pastry shells (cases). Cover the filling with the remaining pastry circles and crimp the edges to seal. Bake in the oven for 25 minutes, or until golden brown. Let the cakes cool in the pan.

Serve the cakes dusted with plenty of confectioners' (icing) sugar, if liked.

NOTE Spongata is a traditional Italian Christmas dessert that is made, albeit with many variations, in the areas around Piacenza, Parma, Reggio Emilia, Modena, and up to La Spezia. The origins of this recipe are ancient, maybe even Hebrew, and historical sources tell us that this dessert was sent as a gift to Duke Francesco Sforza of Milan in 1454.

⊙ Preparation time: 35 minutes, plus chilling
Cooking time: 30 minutes

♍ Wine suggestion: Recioto della Valpolicella

Chocolate Layer Cake

Serves 6

For the sponge cake
butter, for greasing
³/₄ cup (3¹/₂ oz/100 g) type 00
  flour, plus extra for dusting
2¹/₂ tablespoons potato flour
³/₄ teaspoon baking powder
  (ideally vanilla-flavored)
1 tablespoon unsweetened
  cocoa powder
3 eggs
²/₃ cup (4¹/₄ oz/125 g)
  superfine (caster) sugar

For the chocolate custard
2 cups (17 fl oz/500 ml) whole
  (full-fat) milk
4 egg yolks (about ¹/₄ cup/
  2 oz/50 g), beaten
³/₄ cup (5 oz/150 g) superfine
  (caster) sugar
¹/₃ cup (2 oz/50 g) type 00
  flour
1³/₄ sticks (7 oz/200 g) butter
7 oz/200 g bittersweet (dark)
  couverture chocolate

For the frosting (icing)
1 cup (9 fl oz/250 ml)
  whipping cream
³/₄ cup (5 oz/150 g) superfine
  (caster) sugar
9 oz/250 g bittersweet (dark)
  chocolate
2 tablespoons (1 oz/25 g) butter

Preheat the oven to 350°F/180°C/Gas mark 4. Grease an 8-inch/20-cm round cake pan (tin) with butter, then dust it with flour.

Sift (sieve) together the flours, baking powder, and cocoa powder in a large bowl. In a separate bowl, beat the eggs with the sugar until light and fluffly. Use a rubber spatula to gently fold together the sifted flour and the egg, then mix until homogenous. Pour the mixture into the prepared cake pan and bake in the oven for 15 minutes, or until a skewer inserted in the middle comes out clean. Turn out of the pan and place on a wire rack to cool, covered with a dish towel.

To make the chocolate custard, break the couverture chocolate into pieces. Bring the milk to boil in a pan, add the egg yolks, sugar, and type 00 flour, and cook over medium heat for 2 minutes, stirring to avoid lumps forming, until thickened. Stir in the butter, followed by the chocolate, then pour the mixture into a steel bowl in an iced double boiler, or a bowl set over another bowl of iced water, and use an electric whisk to beat it until cold. Cover and let chill in the refrigerator.

Cut the cake into three layers. Spread half the custard onto the first layer of cake. Put another layer of cake on top and spread with the remaining custard. Top with the third layer of cake and then store in the refrigerator.

To make the frosting (icing), heat the cream and sugar in a pan over medium heat for 1 minute, then remove from the heat and let cool for 5 minutes. Meanwhile, melt the bittersweet (dark) chocolate with the butter in a double boiler, or in a heatproof bowl set over a pan of gently simmering water. Gradually whisk the melted chocolate into the cream, a little at a time, until homogenous and glossy.

Pour the frosting over the cooled cake, wait for it to set, and then serve.

⊙ Preparation time: 30 minutes, plus chilling
Cooking time: 30 minutes

♀ Wine suggestion: Moscato d'Asti

Fresh Fruit Tartlets

Makes 4 tartlets

For the pie dough (pastry)
1 stick (4 oz/120 g) butter,
   plus extra for greasing
1 vanilla bean (pod), split in
   half and seeds scraped out
2/3 cup (2³/4 oz/75 g)
   confectioners' (icing) sugar
2 eggs
1/2 teaspoon fine salt
2 cups (9 oz/250 g) type 00
   flour, sifted, plus extra
   for dusting

For the vanilla custard
2¹/4 egg yolks (about
   2 tablespoons/1¹/4 oz/30 g)
1 tablespoon (¹/2 oz/15 g)
   cornstarch (cornflour), sifted
1/3 cup (2¹/4 oz/60 g) superfine
   (caster) sugar
1 cup (8 fl oz/250 ml) whole
   (full-fat) milk
1/2 vanilla bean (pod), split in
   half lengthwise
1 tablespoon (¹/2 oz/
   15 g) butter

For the topping
2/3 cup (3¹/2 oz/100 g)
   blueberries
scant 1 cup (3¹/2 oz/100 g)
   red currants
1¹/3 cups (7 oz/200 g) strawberries
1 tablespoon apricot jelly (jam)

First make the pie dough (pastry). Cream the butter and vanilla seeds together in a bowl. Stir in the confectioners' (icing) sugar, followed by the eggs and salt, and finally the flour, working the mixture until it forms a smooth dough. Cover with plastic wrap (clingfilm) and chill in the refrigerator for at least a couple of hours.

To make the custard, whisk the egg yolks in a bowl and then gradually add the cornstarch (cornflour) and 2 tablespoons (1¹/4 oz/30 g) of the superfine (caster) sugar, stirring continuously. Pour the milk into a small pan, add the vanilla bean (pod) and the remaining sugar, stir together, then bring to a boil. As soon as the milk has come to a boil, remove and discard the vanilla bean, then bring the milk to a boil once more. Pour the milk over the egg mixture, whisking all the time. Return the mixture to the pan and cook over medium heat for 4–5 minutes, stirring continuously, until thickened. Remove from the heat, add the butter, and beat until well combined. Cover with plastic wrap and chill in the refrigerator.

Grease four 4-inch/10-cm tartlet pans with butter. Divide the pie dough into four pieces and roll out each piece on a lightly floured countertop into a circle slightly larger than one of the tartlet pans. Use the pie dough to line the prepared pans, then prick the surface of the pastry shells (cases) with a fork and chill in the refrigerator for 30 minutes.

Preheat the oven to 350°F/180°C/Gas mark 4.

Line the pastry shells with large circles of parchment (baking) paper and fill with pie weights (baking beans). Bake in the oven for 10–15 minutes until the top edges of the tarts start to brown, then remove the baking parchment and pie weights and bake for an additional 5–10 minutes until the pie dough is dry and golden brown. Carefully remove the pastry shells from their pans and place on a wire rack to cool.

Fill the pastry shells with the custard and top with fresh fruit. Melt the apricot jelly (jam) in a small pan over low heat, then brush the jelly over the fruit. Store the tartlets in the refrigerator until you are ready to serve them.

⊙ Preparation time: 10 minutes

Cooking time: 10 minutes

♀ Wine suggestion: Malvasia delle Lipari

Apricot Jelly Palmiers

Makes about 10 palmiers

14 oz/400 g puff pastry

flour, for dusting

2 tablespoons apricot jelly
(jam)

3 tablespoons superfine
(caster) sugar

Preheat the oven to 400°F/200°C/Gas mark 6. Line a baking sheet with parchment (baking) paper.

Roll out the puff pastry on a lightly floured countertop to a thickness of ⅛ inch/3 mm. Starting at both the longest edges of the rectangle, roll up the pastry toward the center, then cut the roll into about ten ⅝-inch/1.5-cm thick slices (they should resemble small hearts). Lay the slices, heart side-up, on the prepared baking sheet, leaving a little bit of space between each slice.

Melt the apricot jelly (jam) in a small pan over low heat, then brush the pastry hearts with a thin layer of hot jelly and sprinkle over a little sugar. Bake in the oven for 10 minutes, turning them over halfway through, until golden brown. Let the palmiers cool on the baking sheet.

TIP You can also use puff pastry to make glazed puff pastries. First make the glaze by lightly beating 2¼ egg whites (about ¼ cup/2¼ oz/ 60 g) with 2 cups (9 oz/250 g) confectioners' (icing) sugar and 1 teaspoon lemon juice in a bowl, then stir in ¼ cup (1¼ oz/30 g) type 00 flour. Roll out the puff pastry on a lightly floured countertop to a thickness of ⅛ inch/3 mm, then roll out the glaze directly onto the puff pastry. Spoon apricot jelly (jam) into a pastry (piping) bag, and pipe lozenge motifs onto the glaze. Cut the pastry into elongated rectangles, place them on a baking sheet lined with parchment (baking) paper, and bake in an oven preheated to 400°F/200°C/Gas mark 6 for 15 minutes, or until golden brown. Let the pastries cool on the baking sheet.

⊙ Preparation time: 35 minutes, plus chilling
Cooking time: 25 minutes

⎕ Beer suggestion: Scotch ale

Chocolate Tart

Serves 8

**For the shortcrust pie
dough (pastry)**
2¹/₃ cups (11 oz/300 g) type
00 flour, plus extra
for dusting
1³/₄ sticks (7 oz/200 g) cold
butter, cut into cubes,
plus extra for greasing
pinch of salt
¹/₄ cup (2 oz/50 g) superfine
(caster) sugar
grated zest of 1
unwaxed lemon
2 egg yolks
confectioners' (icing) sugar,
for dusting

For the filling
2³/₄ cups (1 lb 2 oz/500 g)
chocolate spread
(see Tip p.466)
1 tablespoon heavy
(whipping) cream

First make the pie dough (pastry). Put the flour, butter, and salt into a food processor and process until grainy and floury. Transfer to a large bowl or a stand mixer, then add the sugar, lemon zest, and egg yolks and mix for a few minutes, making sure the butter doesn't become too warm. Use your hands to shape the pie dough into a ball, wrap it in plastic wrap (clingfilm), and chill in the refrigerator for 1 hour.

Preheat the oven to 350°F/180°C/Gas mark 4. Grease a round 10¹/₄-inch/26-cm round tart pan (tin) with butter, then dust it with flour.

Mix the chocolate spread together with the cream in a bowl, stirring thoroughly until smooth and homogenous.

Roll out the pie dough on a lightly floured countertop to a thickness of ¹/₄ inch/5 mm and use part of it to line the prepared tart pan. Spoon the chocolate filling into the pastry shell (case) and decorate the top of the tart with a lattice of pie dough strips. Bake in the oven for 25 minutes, or until golden brown. Let cool before serving, dusted with confectioners' (icing) sugar.

⊙ Preparation time: 40 minutes
Cooking time: 30–40 minutes

♀ Wine suggestion: Colli Euganei Fior d'Arancio Passito

Apple and Yogurt Cake

Serves 6

5–6 apples (about 2¼ lb/1 kg)
grated zest and juice of
  1 unwaxed lemon
3 eggs
⅔ cup (4¼ oz/125 g)
  granulated sugar
1¼ cups (5 oz/150 g) type 00
  flour, sifted, plus extra
  for dusting
1 tablespoons baking powder
½ cup (4¼ oz/125 g)
  plain yogurt
pinch of fine salt
1 stick (4¼ oz/125 g) butter,
  melted, plus extra
  for greasing
2 tablespoons cane sugar,
  for sprinkling

Preheat the oven to 350°F/180°C/Gas mark 4. Grease a 9½-inch/24-cm round springform cake pan (tin) with butter, then dust it with flour.

Peel, core, and cut the apples into segments, then thinly slice the segments. Put the apple slices into a bowl, sprinkling the layers of apple with lemon juice to prevent them discoloring.

In a large bowl, beat together the eggs with the granulated sugar for 10 minutes, or until light and frothy.

In a separate bowl, stir together the flour with the baking powder. Fold the flour mixture into the egg mixture, then add the yogurt, lemon zest, and salt and mix thoroughly. Stir in the butter and lastly, add two-thirds of the sliced apples.

Pour the cake batter into the prepared cake pan and use a frosting spatula (palette knife) to even out the surface. Arrange the remaining apple slices over the top of the cake and sprinkle evenly with the cane sugar. Bake in the oven for 30–40 minutes until the top is golden brown and a skewer inserted in the middle comes out clean. Let the cake cool in the pan.

CHEF

Anna Vicina

Preparation time: 35 minutes, plus resting and chilling

Cooking time: 20 minutes

Brandy suggestion: 1964 vintage brandy from the Montanaro distillery

Piedmontese Chocolate Pastries

Makes about 20 pastries

For the choux pastry

7 tablespoons (3½ oz/
  100 g) butter, plus extra
  for greasing

¾ cup (3½ oz/100 g) type 00
  flour, sifted, plus extra
  for dusting

3 eggs

For the chocolate custard

3 egg yolks

½ cup (3½ oz/100 g)
  granulated sugar

2½ tablespoons type 00 flour

1¼ cups (10 fl oz/300 ml)
  whole (full-fat) milk

⅔ cup (2 oz/60 g)
  unsweetened cocoa powder

For the whipped cream

¾ cup plus 1 tablespoon
  (7 fl oz/200 ml)
  whipping cream

1 tablespoon
  granulated sugar

To decorate

confectioners' (icing)
  sugar, sifted

unsweetened cocoa
  powder, sifted

First make the pastry. Melt the butter in a pan with ¾ cup plus 1 tablespoon (3½ fl oz/100 ml) boiling water. Remove from the heat, add the flour, and mix thoroughly with a wooden spoon. Return the pan to the heat and cook over medium heat for a couple of minutes until the mixture comes away clean from the edges of the pan. Remove from the heat and mix in the eggs one by one. Wrap the pastry mixture in plastic wrap (clingfilm) and let rest for 10 minutes.

Preheat the oven to 350°F/180°C/Gas mark 4. Grease a baking sheet with butter, then dust it with flour.

Spoon the pastry mixture into a pastry (piping) bag fitted with a ⅝-inch/ 1.5-cm tip (nozzle). Pipe out 1-inch/2.5-cm balls of the mixture onto the prepared baking sheet, spacing them about 1¼ inches/3 cm apart. Bake in the oven for 10–12 minutes or until the buns are dry and golden brown. Set aside to cool.

To make the custard, mix together the egg yolks, sugar, and flour in a bowl. Bring the milk to a boil in a small pan, then add the egg mixture and cook over low heat for 5 minutes, stirring continuously, or until thickened. Remove from the heat and stir in the unsweetened cocoa powder. Transfer the custard to a clean bowl, place a sheet of plastic wrap (clingfilm) directly on top, and pierce a hole in the plastic wrap with a toothpick to make the evaporation process easier. Chill in the refrigerator.

Put the cream and sugar in a bowl and slowly whip to quite stiff peaks—it is important to whip the cream slowly as this will make tiny bubbles of air inside the cream, which will make the whipped cream lighter.

Cut off the top part of each bun and fill each bun with a layer of chocolate custard, followed by a layer of whipped cream, repeating the layers until the pastry is filled up, and ending with a layer of cream. Close the buns with their lids and dust with confectioners' (icing) sugar and unsweetened cocoa powder. Serve immediately.

⊙ Preparation time: 35 minutes, plus chilling
Cooking time: 20 minutes

♀ Wine suggestion: Vin Santo di Montepulciano

Almond and Pistachio Cookies

Makes about 35 cookies

5½ tablespoons (2¾ oz/
75 g) butter, softened
¾ cup (5 oz/150 g) superfine
(caster) sugar
1½ eggs (about
⅓ cup/2¾ oz/75 g),
at room temperature
pinch of fine salt
⅓ envelope (1 g) vanillina or
2–3 drops vanilla extract
2 cups (9 oz/250 g) type 00
flour, sifted
¾ teaspoon baking powder
⅔ cup (3½ oz/100 g)
almonds, skinned
½ cup (3 oz/80 g) unsalted
shelled pistachios

Cream the butter and sugar together in a large bowl. Stir in the eggs, salt, and vanillina or vanilla extract, then add the flour and baking powder and beat until you have a homogenous mixture. Stir in the almonds and pistachios. Shape the cookie (biscuit) dough into a ball, wrap in plastic wrap (clingfilm), and chill in the refrigerator for 1–2 hours.

Preheat the oven to 350°F/180°C/Gas mark 4. Line a baking sheet with parchment (baking) paper.

Cut the dough into three pieces and roll each piece into a log about 6 inches/ 15 cm long and 1¼ inches/3 cm wide. Place them on the prepared baking sheet and bake in the oven for 10–15 minutes until they start to turn golden brown.

Cut each of the logs diagonally into slices about ½ inch/1 cm thick. Spread them out in rows on the baking sheet, then return to the oven and bake for 8 minutes more. Let the cookies cool on the baking sheet.

Preparation time: 15 minutes, plus chilling
Cooking time: 20 minutes
Wine suggestion: Recioto della Valpolicella

Sablé Cookie Cake with Chocolate Cream

Serves 6

For the cookies (biscuits)
1¼ sticks (5 oz/150 g)
   butter, softened
2 teaspoons instant
   coffee powder
grated zest of 1
   unwaxed lemon
½ cup (3½ oz/100 g)
   superfine (caster) sugar
pinch of salt
1 egg, beaten
2 cups (9 oz/250 g)
   type 00 flour

For the chocolate cream
1 leaf gelatin
2 egg yolks
¼ cup (2 oz/50 g) superfine
   (caster) sugar
5 oz/150 g bittersweet
   (dark) chocolate, broken
   into pieces
2 tablespoons plus
   1 teaspoon coffee
1¼ cups (10 fl oz/300 ml)
   heavy (double) cream

To serve
3 tablespoons
   mandarin marmalade
cacao nibs, crushed (optional)
small mint leaves (optional)

Put the butter into a stand mixer and beat until soft. Continuing to mix, add the instant coffee powder and lemon zest, followed by the sugar and salt, then the egg. Finally, pour in the flour all at once and gently stir it into the mixture. Using your hands, shape the cookie (biscuit) dough into a cylinder. Place it on some parchment (baking) paper and chill it in the refrigerator for at least 40 minutes.

Soak the gelatin in a bowl of cold water for 10 minutes, then squeeze dry.

Meanwhile, make a custard by putting the egg yolks and sugar in a double boiler or in a heatproof bowl set over a pan of gently simmering water and whisking until the mixture becomes frothy.

Melt the chocolate with the coffee in a separate double boiler or in a heatproof bowl set over a pan of gently simmering water, then stir in the gelatin until dissolved. Remove from the heat, stir the melted chocolate into the custard, and let cool to lukewarm.

Pour the cream into a bowl and whip until it is glossy. Gently stir the whipped cream into the chocolate custard. Spoon the custard into a pastry (piping) bag fitted with a ½-inch/1-cm tip (nozzle) and chill in the refrigerator for a couple of hours.

Preheat the oven to 325°F/160°C/Gas mark 3. Line a baking sheet with parchment (baking) paper.

Roll out the cookie dough to a thickness of about 1/16 inch/2 mm and cut out 12 discs, about 3¼ inches/8 cm in diameter. Place them on the prepared baking sheet and bake in the oven for 8 minutes, or until golden brown. Transfer to a wire rack and let cool.

To serve, spread a little mandarin marmalade in the center of four serving plates, place a cookie on top of the marmalade, spread the cookie with chocolate cream, then place another cookie on top. Decorate the top cookies with a little bit more of the chocolate cream and a few cacao nibs and mint leaves, if liked.

⊙ Preparation time: 15 minutes

Cooking time: 15 minutes

♀ Wine suggestion: Moscato di Pantelleria

Wine and Raisin Cookies

Serves 4

¹⁄₃ cup (2 oz/50 g) raisins

²⁄₃ cup (5 fl oz/150 ml) Zibibbo (Muscat wine) or any sweet dessert wine

¹⁄₃ cup plus 1 tablespoon (3¹⁄₂ fl oz/100 ml) extra virgin olive oil

¹⁄₂ cup (3¹⁄₂ oz/100 g) granulated sugar

2 cups (9 oz/250 g) type 00 flour, sifted

³⁄₄ cup (3¹⁄₂ oz/100 g) cornstarch (cornflour)

2¹⁄₄ teaspoons baking powder

pinch of salt

Soak the raisins in the wine in a small bowl for 10 minutes, or until they soften.

Preheat the oven to 350°F/180°C/Gas mark 4. Line a baking sheet with parchment (baking) paper.

Pour the oil into a bowl and stir in most of the sugar, reserving a little for the tops, and the wine and raisins. In a separate bowl, mix together the flour and cornstarch (cornflour) with the baking powder and salt, then incorporate them into the raisin mixture.

With the aid of a teaspoon, drop little mounds of the cookie (biscuit) dough onto the prepared baking sheet, spacing them about 1¹⁄₄–1¹⁄₂ inches/3–4 cm apart, then sprinkle with the remaining sugar. Bake in the oven for 15 minutes, or until golden brown. Let the cookies cool on the baking sheet.

NOTE The Zibibbo grape was introduced to the island of Pantelleria, in the Strait of Sicily, in very ancient times, perhaps by the Phoenicians and certainly by the Arabs. This variety of grape gives rise to many extraordinary wines, including the famous raisin wines. Indeed, the origin of the word zibibbo derives from the Arabic zahib, which means "raisin" or "dried grape." The traditional practice of cultivating the head-trained bush vines on this arid and difficult island was recently inscribed on UNESCO's Representative Lists of Intangible Cultural Heritage of Humanity.

Preparation time: 20 minutes
Cooking time: 2 hours
Wine suggestion: Erbaluce di Caluso Passito

Chocolate Meringues with Mascarpone Cheese Filling

Makes 24 meringues

3$\frac{1}{2}$ egg whites (about
$\frac{1}{3}$ cup plus 1 tablespoon/
3$\frac{1}{2}$ oz/100 g)
1 cup (7 oz/200 g)
granulated sugar
2 drops lemon juice
2 tablespoons unsweetened
cocoa powder, sifted

**For the mascarpone
cheese filling**
1 cup (9 oz/250 g)
mascarpone cheese
$\frac{1}{2}$ cup plus 1 tablespoon
(2$\frac{3}{4}$ oz/70 g) confectioners'
(icing) sugar
grated zest of 1
unwaxed orange

Preheat the oven to 190°F/90°C. Line a baking sheet with parchment (baking) paper.

Put the egg whites into a spotlessly clean bowl and use an electric whisk to beat the egg whites until they form very stiff peaks. Gradually add the granulated sugar and the lemon juice, whisking all the time, until the mixture is firm, then gently fold in the cocoa powder.

Spoon the meringue mixture into a pastry (piping) bag fitted with a 1$\frac{1}{4}$-inch/ 3-cm smooth tip (nozzle). Pipe circles of meringue, each 1$\frac{1}{4}$–1$\frac{1}{2}$ inches/ 3–4 cm in diameter, onto the prepared baking sheet, spacing them 1$\frac{1}{2}$ inches/ 4 cm apart. Bake in the oven for 2 hours or until the surfaces starts to crackle slightly. Let the meringues cool on the baking sheet.

To make the filling, mix together the mascarpone, confectioner's (icing) sugar, and orange zest in a bowl.

Carefully peel the meringues off the parchment paper and sandwich them with the mascarpone filling.

NOTE There are different types of meringue with the most common being French meringue, made with egg whites beaten with both granulated and confectioners' (icing) sugar and piped onto a baking tray lined with parchment (baking) paper, then dried out very slowly in an oven at low temperature to achieve the crunch. In contrast, Italian meringue is made with beaten egg whites and sugar syrup and is cooked under a hot broiler (grill) until golden brown. Italian meringue is used to decorate cakes.

Preparation time: 40 minutes, plus rising and resting

Cooking time: 1 hour

Wine suggestion: Alto Adige Gewürztraminer Vendemmia Tardiva

Cinnamon Rolls

Makes 8 rolls

For the pie dough (pastry)
3²/₃ cups (1 lb 2 oz/500 g)
   type 00 flour
1³/₄ tablespoons brewer's
   yeast or 2¹/₄ teaspoons
   active dry yeast
3¹/₂ tablespoons milk,
   at room temperature
grated zest of 1
   unwaxed orange
¹/₂ cup (3¹/₂ oz/100 g)
   superfine (caster) sugar
3 eggs, beaten
1¹/₂ sticks (6¹/₄ oz/
   180 g) butter, softened,
   cut into cubes, plus extra
   for greasing

For the filling
1¹/₂ sticks (6¹/₄ oz/
   180 g) butter
¹/₃ cup (2³/₄ oz/70 g) superfine
   (caster) sugar
2 teaspoons ground cinnamon

First make the pie dough (pastry). Sift the flour into a large bowl. In a small bowl, dissolve the yeast in the milk and then slowly pour it onto the flour and mix well. Stir in the orange zest and sugar, followed by the eggs, and finally stir in 5 oz/ 150 g of the butter, a piece at a time, until it is all absorbed into the dough. Cover with plastic wrap (clingfilm) and let rise at room temperature for at least 2 hours.

Meanwhile, make the filling. Beat the butter, sugar, and cinnamon together in a small bowl until you have a frothy, soft custard.

Grease a baking sheet with butter. Roll out the pie dough on a lightly floured countertop into a rectangular shape about ¹/₂ inch/1 cm thick. Using a frosting spatula (palette knife), spread the filling onto the pie dough, leaving a ¹/₂ inch (1 cm) border around the edges. Roll the pie dough up from the longest edge of the rectangle, then cut the roll into 2¹/₂-inch/6-cm thick slices. Lay the slices, spiral-side up, on the prepared baking sheet, leaving a little bit of space between each slice. Let rest for 1 hour at room temperature.

Preheat the oven to 325°F/160°C/Gas mark 3. Brush the tops of the roll-ups with the remaining butter and bake in the oven for 1 hour, or until golden brown. Let the roll-ups cool on the baking sheet.

⊙ Preparation time: 30 minutes
Cooking time: 15 minutes

♀ Wine suggestion: Trentino Moscato Giallo Passito

Castagnole Fritters

Serves 4–6

1²/₃ cups (7 oz/200 g)
  all-purpose (plain) flour
2 eggs
¼ cup (2 oz/50 g) superfine
  (caster) sugar
3 tablespoons (1 ½ oz/40 g)
  butter, softened
1 vanilla bean (pod), split in
  half lengthwise and seeds
  scraped out
grated zest of ½
  unwaxed lemon
pinch of salt
1 tablespoon rum
2 teaspoons baking powder
sunflower oil, for frying
salt
confectioners' (icing) sugar,
  for dusting
custard, to serve (optional)

Put the flour into a bowl with the eggs, sugar, butter, vanilla seeds, salt, lemon zest, rum, and baking powder and mix until well combined. Transfer the dough to a lightly floured countertop and knead until the dough is smooth and soft. Let rest for a few minutes.

Roll the dough into a log about ¾–1¼ inches/2–3 cm thick and then cut it into ¾-inch/2-cm pieces. Using you hands, roll each piece into a ball.

Pour enough oil for deep-frying into a small deep pan and heat the oil to 340°F/170°C. Fry the dough balls, a few at the time, for 2–3 minutes, turning them over occasionally, until fluffy and golden. Remove with a slotted spoon and drain on paper towels.

Dust the fritters with confectioners' (icing) sugar and serve with custard, if liked.

NOTE   A carnival favorite, castagnole are one of the most common fried treats in Italy. The recipe is ancient and a reference to them can be found as early as the eighteenth century in the State Archives in Viterbo. Every area, and almost every family, has its own version of the recipe for this tasty sweet treat, but the main distinction is between plain castagnole and those filled with custard or cream.

GLOSSARY

ITALIAN SALUMI

The term *salumi* refers to different meat products, characterized by salting and seasoning, which allow them to be stored for a long time. It includes *salumi* made with whole pieces of meat and preparations made with minced meat. Italy is the top European country in terms of cured meat products that qualify for a DOP (Protected Designation of Origin) or IPG (Protected Geographical Information) mark.

CARPEGNA HAM DOP
Produced since the fifteenth century, it is processed and seasoned in the district of Carpegna. It is round with a delicate flavor.

MODENA HAM DOP
It is the shape of an elongated pear, has a bright red color, a strong but not salty taste, and a sweet and intense aroma.

NORCIA HAM IPG
To truly appreciate its aroma, this ham needs to be sliced by hand, with a sharp knife. Only the quantity of ham that will be consumed immediately should be cut.

PARMA HAM DOP
It weighs more than fifteen pounds (seven kilos) and has a uniform color, interspersed with the white of the fat. It is noted for its sweetness.

SAN DANIELE HAM DOP
It is seasoned by the breezes from the Adriatic and the Alps. It can be recognized by its flattened guitar shape and the classic *piedino* (small foot).

TUSCAN HAM DOP
Its fragrant and characteristic flavor comes from the brining process, which uses berries and herbs typical of the region.

VENETO BERICO-EUGANEO HAM DOP
The area between the Berici and the Euganei hills enjoys a microclimate ideal for the processing of this ham.

CULATELLO DI ZIBELLO DOP
Produced in the Parmense area, this is considered by many to be the king of cured meats. Try it on a bread *crostino*, with a little butter.

FIOCCHETTO
It is encased in a natural piece of intestine, and cured for more than six months. It has white fat and bright red, lean meat.

COOKED HAM
It is among the most widely used cured meat in Italy. The high-quality varieties are among the most valued cured meats.

SAN SECONDO COOKED SHOULDER
Typical of the Parmense area, it can be served hot or cold. It must not be sliced too thick, so that it can melt in the mouth.

CURED SHOULDER
Produced in the Bassa Parmense area, it requires great workmanship to produce and a long seasoning time. Its shape is similar to that of *culatello*.

CALABRIA CAPOCOLLO DOP
Cured for at least 100 days, it can be recognized by the traditional binding of sun-dried thin cane strips.

CAPOCOLLO DI MARTINA FRANCA
Martina Franca is a southern center of excellence for cold cuts. This capocollo is slightly smoky.

PARMA COPPA

It differs from the *coppa piacentina DOP* because it has a finer casing and a shorter seasoning time.

COPPA PIACENTINA DOP

It has a balanced content of fat and lean meat, and a sweet and tasty fragrance. It is exclusively dry salted.

ALTO ADIGE SPECK HAM IPG

It is a boned, trimmed ham, dry salted and lightly smoked. It is produced in Val Venosta.

GOLA

A cut of excellent quality, often served sliced on bread *crostini*. It is also used in making *salame* and *cotechino*.

GOTA OR GUANCIALE

Tuscan cured meat of small size, with a characteristic triangular or trapezoidal shape, made with the jowl or cheek of pigs.

LARDO D'ARNAD DOP

It has a soft and compact texture when thinly sliced, and it melts in the mouth, giving off the aromas used in its curing solution.

LARDO DI CINTA SENESE

An excellent quality lard with an intense aroma and a delicate but savory taste. Delicious served with bread.

LARDO DI COLONNATA IPG

It is at its best consumed in thin slices, with fresh bread or toast. Traditionally, marble quarry workers had this with their bread.

ALTO ADIGE PANCETTA

Its fat veins give it its subtle taste, as does the juniper wood used to smoke it.

PANCETTA PIACENTINA DOP

Dry cured (and strictly by hand) with salt, natural aromatics, and spices. It is is left to mature for at least three months.

CIAUSCOLO IPG

A spreadable cured meat, made with pork meat and fat to which garlic or *vino cotto* have been added.

FINOCCHIONA

With a soft consistency and a very fine texture, this Tuscan *salame* is flavored by the distinctive taste of wild fennel seeds.

SALAME DELLA DUJA

Covered with a layer of fat after it has been encased, it is seasoned for 3–12 months inside an earthenware pot.

SALAME DI CINTA SENESE

The *cinta senese* is a breed of pigs that is raised in a free-range environment. They feed on acorns and tubers giving their meat an intense flavor and sweet taste.

CREMONA SALAME IPG

Depite its lengthy seasoning time, it retains its softness thanks to the humid and climate of its area of origin, Cremona.

FELINO SALAME

Pure pork *salame* from the green Baganza valley, it is excellent with *torta fritta di Parma,* or as filling for sandwiches.

NEAPOLITAN SALAMI

Its curing process requires salt, pepper, chili pepper, pressed garlic cooked in wine, and, sometimes, orange zest.

VARZI SALAMI DOP

It is typical of the Pavese area. Cut into rather thick slices, it goes well with vegetables preserved in oil and cheeses from the same area of origin.

MANTUAN SALAME

There are various versions of this recipe: in the Alto Mantovano area only a little garlic is used, while in the Basso Mantovano area larger amounts of garlic are added to the mix.

SALAME PIACENTINO DOP

A slice from this *salame* has a compact appearance; red with white-pinkish chunks of lard are typical of this large-grain *salame*.

SARDINIAN HOT SALAME

Hot chili pepper, wild fennel, and other Mediterranean herbs give this cured meat its characteristic flavor.

PIEDMONTE SALAME DOP

Light, spicy aromas characterize this *salame* produced with the use of wines such as Nebbiolo, Barbera, and Dolcetto.

TUSCAN SALAME

Its surface is typically treated with fat, which preserves it and allows for a longer seasoning time.

ITALIAN SALAMINI ALLA CACCIATORA DOP

A small *salame*, traditionally prepared for woodcutters, who ate them at work or when hunting because they were easy to carry.

STROLGHINO

A *salame* with a small diameter, produced in limited quantities. It is made with *culatello* offcuts.

CALABRIAN SAUSAGE DOP

It is cylindrical in shape, woven in a distinctive chain. The color varies, depending on the use of black pepper or chili pepper.

SOPRÈSSA VICENTINA DOP

The taste is delicate yet persistent, slightly sweet and peppery with its aroma coming from the herbs and spices used in the mix.

BOLOGNA MORTADELLA IPG

The most recognized mortadella, produced only with pig meat and encased in natural intestines, not artificial ones.

COTECHINO MODENA IPG

Considered the father of *zampone*, it is made from a mix of lean pork meat, lard, rind, and herbs.

SALAMA DA SUGO

It is made with liver, tongue, meat from the pig's neck, red wine, nutmeg, cloves, and rum.

ZAMPONE MODENA IPG

It is encased in the skin from the pig's trotter. This protects it very well from breaking during cooking.

BRESAOLA DELLA VALTELLINA

It is a beef salami, salted and dried, typical of the province of Sondrio. The curing mix is enriched with pepper and wine.

BOAR CACCIATORINI
Spiced delicately to enhance the strong flavor of the boar meat; they are best eaten as fresh as possible and still soft.

GOOSE SALAME
It is produced at Mortara, in Lomellina, made from equal parts of lean cooked goose and pork meat.

SALAME MILANO
A *salame* made with minced beef and pork, with a texture like rice grains, which allows the lean and fat ingredients to be evenly distributed.

SO MANY WAYS TO SAY FRESH PASTA

Fresh pasta is available in many formats: with or without eggs, flavored or prepared with the most diverse types of flour, long or short, filled or in a gnocchi style. Italy is a veritable treasure trove in continuous evolution, even though, walking through villages, it is still possible to see women working in the kitchen, mixing flour, eggs, and water according to the ancient traditional recipe. The reputation of the most renown restaurants, and therefore of their chefs, is often based on their fresh pasta, which they serve using classic recipes or innovative and creative interpretations.

Some of the regions that have fully promoted fresh pasta are Emilia Romagna, Veneto, and practically the whole of the South of Italy, but with significant differences: the further south you travel, the more likely that soft wheat will be replaced by durum wheat. Eggs disappear from the mix and, because the number of ingredients used is very limited, other factors become more important, such as the craftsmanship and practical manual skills, as well as the temperature of the hands of the person involved, which has an impact on the drying of the dough during processing and, therefore, on the final product.

The expansion of modern production techniques has allowed the introduction of mass produced fresh pasta: in this way the product can reach every home, be it fresh or dried, nevertheless retaining the characteristics of homemade pasta.

Those who choose to make pasta in their own kitchen need a few basic tools: a wooden working surface on which to work the dough, a rolling pin, a knife with a smooth blade to cut the various shapes, and a pasta machine, which helps flatten the dough into thin sheets. Also essential are the dedicated cutters for ravioli, anolini, and lined pappardelle.

SMOOTH PASTA

Every Italian region produces different types of homemade pasta, with the recipe, as well as name in the local dialect, passed on from generation to generation. The queen of smooth fresh pasta is *tagliatelle,* but there are many other types that are worthwhile discovering.

PRESSED BIGOLI
Fat *spaghetti* of the Veneto tradition, produced with a *torchio,* a special pressing machine, called *bigolaro.*

CAVATELLI
Made only with flour and water, they are traditionally served with a meat ragu, *cardoncelli* mushrooms, or broccoli.

CHITARRA
The fresh variety of *spaghetti alla chitarra* is very popular. Their square cross-section makes a very pleasant texture in the mouth.

CORZETTI
The varieties differ: from Valpolcevera they are in an "8" shape, and there are pressed types, small disks with different motifs stamped onto the surface.

FREGOLA
Fresh pasta made with durum wheat, typical of Sardinia. It has the shape of small irregular balls, very similar to Israeli couscous.

PRESSED MACCHERONCINI
The irregular shape and the porous surface of this pasta comes from the dough being pressed in a *torchio,* a classic pressing machine.

MALTAGLIATI
A type of pasta from Emilia Romagna, made from the offcuts of dough from the production of *tagliatelle*.

MARITATI
A pasta typical of Apulia, consisting of a combination of *orecchiette* and *maccheroncini* made from durum wheat semolina.

ORECCHIETTE
Small "cups" made by hand, smooth on the side where the fingertip has pressed the dough, and rough on the other, where the dough has rubbed against the working surface.

PAPPARDELLE
The name probably derives from *pappare,* the Tuscan word meaning "eating with good appetite." They are similar to *tagliatelle* and *fettuccine.*

PICI
Widespread in the south of Tuscany, in the provinces of Siena and Grosseto. In Tuscany, *appicciare* means "working by rolling."

PISAREI
In the Piacento province, this pasta is made with flour, water, and breadcrumbs. *Pisarei e fasò* is a well known dish of this pasta served with a bean sauce.

SCIALATIELLI
The Neapolitan word *sciglà* means "ruffle," as referred to hair, because of its resemblance to messy hair when it is served.

STROZZAPRETI
The screw shape of this pasta is where the it gets its name. The pasta in fact is "twisted" (*strozzata*) to achieve the typical shape.

TROFIE
A typical pasta shape from Liguria, whose name might derive from the dialect word *strufuggià*, which means "rubbing."

GNOCCHI

The classic dough is made with potatoes but an infinite variety of ingredients can be used: from pumpkin to semolina, from stale bread to ricotta. *Chicce* and *canederli* are some of the variants of this type of fresh pasta.

POTATO GNOCCHI
They are the best known variety of gnocchi, and the simplest. Often served with just tomato sauce.

PUMPKIN GNOCCHI
Characterized by the typical, slightly sweet back taste of pumpkin, they are excellent with a little melted butter, cheese, and sage.

SARDINIAN GNOCCHI
This is Sassari's version of the better known *malloreddus*. To this day, they are made at home with durum wheat semolina, and water.

CANEDERLI
Typical of the cuisine of Alto Adige and Trentino, *canederli* can be served in broth, with a tomato sauce, or with melted butter.

CHICCHE DELLA NONNA

The name probably derives from the fact that grandmothers (*nonne*) often have little objects in their pockets for their grandchildren. They are made with *ricotta* cheese and spinach.

ROMAN GNOCCHI

Round disks made of semolina cooked in milk and enriched with cheese and egg yolks. They are served with butter and Parmesan cheese.

FILLED PASTA

Ravioli came first, then came a whole kaleidoscope of shapes and fillings that may include meat, vegetables, or fish. Almost every town has its own type of filled pasta, usually served on feast days and accompanied by the most varied of sauces: from simple melted butter with sage and cheese, to the most elaborate of ragus.

AGNOLOTTI

Filled pasta for feast days. The rich filling is made with beef, Parmesan cheese, and pancetta.

ANOLINI

A type of pasta with a filling, which must include stewed beef as well as bread and Parmesan cheese.

CAPPELLACCI

Large homemade shape with various fillings. In mountainous areas, soft cheese, mushroom, and speck ham are used.

CARAMELLE

This pasta is filled, according to taste, with meat, spinach, and ricotta cheese, or pumpkin. There are countless varieties.

CASONCELLI

Ravioli filled with meat, herbs, potatoes, and bread. There is a sweet variety that derives from a medieval recipe.

CULURGIONES

There are many Sardinian varieties, both in terms of the filling and of the sauce served with them. The dough, on the other hand, is always made with durum wheat semolina.

FAGOTTINI

They have a filling similar to that of *tortelli*, with beets and ricotta, and, like them, they can be served with melted butter and Parmesan cheese.

MARUBINI

The filling for this pasta is made with braised beef, called *pistum* (Cremona *salame* mix) in the local dialect, Parmesan cheese, and nutmeg.

MEZZELUNE

This type of *tortello*, with many different types of filling and varieties, takes different names in different Italian towns.

PANSOTTI

The name of this pasta literary means "potbellied" because of its shape. It is a traditional filled pasta shape from Liguria.

PLIN

In the Monferrato area this pasta is very small and is called *ravoli del plin*. It is filled with mixed stewed meats.

RAVIOLI

There are countless local versions so they cannot be rigidly classified, both in terms of the dough and types of filling used but all are generally of a similar shape.

TORTELLI CON LA CODA

This is the classic *ravioli* from Piacento, with a *ricotta* cheese and spinach filling. It is served with butter, sage, and Parmesan cheese.

TORTELLI

Filled with aromatic herbs, *ricotta* cheese, or other ingredients to taste, it is served with abundant melted butter and Parmesan cheese.

TORTELLINI

Ideal in chicken or beef broth, or with ragu. Bologna and Modena have made claims on the origin of this pasta since ancient times.

LONG PASTA

The main type of long dry pasta, *spaghetti*, characterizes Italian cuisine abroad. Among common types of long pasta are *perciatelli*, *ziti*, *mafalde*, and other types that offer different ways to hold the sauce and satisfy the palate.

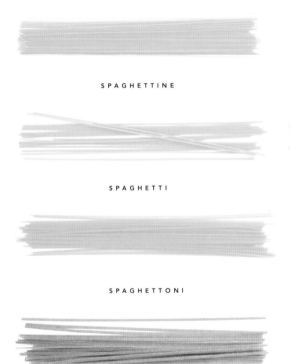

SPAGHETTINE

SPAGHETTI

SPAGHETTONI

SPAGHETTI INTEGRALI

BAVETTE

CAPELLINI

ZITIO ZITE

FUSILLI LUNCHI BUCATI

MAFALDE

PERCIATELLI

SHORT PASTA

Penne and maccheroni are the main types of short pasta. However, there are infinite varieties of short pasta that can be used in as many recipes: from the more traditional varieties such as fusilli and farfalle, to regional or local varieties, such as calamarata and anellini.

RIDGED PENNE
These are a great classic variety and their reduced length makes them ideal for any type of sauce.

HALF RIDGED PENNE
These are shorter than penne but the pasta is thicker. This shape is particularly suited to rich sauces.

RIGATONI
This pasta is originally from Rome, where tradition dictates it is used for carbonara sauce. The outside surface of the tube shape is ridged.

FARFALLE
The typical butterfly- or bow tie–shaped farfalle, among the most common varieties, is ideal for cold pasta salads, but is also used for thick and creamy sauces.

MEZZE MANICHE
A traditional short pasta type, whose name means "short sleeves," with a hollow cylindrical shape ridged on the outside. It is originally from central and northern Italy.

SHORT FUSILLI
Curlier than traditional fusilli, it is perfect for holding sauce and is particularly suited to meat-based sauces.

RIDGED PIPE
Similar to snail shells, this ridged shape is particularly suited to thick sauces, for example a meat ragu.

CONCHIGLIE
This pasta is shell-shaped and is therefore ideal for gathering sauces made with mushrooms, ham, and mozzarella.

CONCHIGLIONI
This pasta is larger than traditional shell shapes and it is so designed to hold condiments and sauces.

CASARECCE
Typical of Sicily, this pasta is said to be of Arab origins and is usually combined with a typical pesto from Trapani, made with almonds and tomatoes.

SMOOTH DITALONI
This pasta takes its name from thimbles and is normally used for rather liquid and creamy sauces.

PACCHERI
The word paccheri is reminiscent of a slapping sound, perhaps an analogy to the noise made by pasta being mixed in a bowl.

HALF PACCHERI
Smooth or ridged, it is a more practical shape, easier to mix with condiments and sauces than the larger paccheri shape.

CALAMARATA
These large rings can be used to good visual effect with sauces made with calamari, also cut into rings.

CELLENTANI
With its ridged surface and hollow corkscrew shape, *cellentani* or "corkscrews" is a shape suitable for all types of sauces.

BOMBARDINI
A smaller variety than *bombardoni*, it is typical of southern Italy, in particular Campania, Sicily, and Calabria.

SMOOTH BOMBARDONI
This pasta shape derives its name from the Italian word for the euphonium, a wind musical instrument used by traditional village bands.

GALLETTI
This pasta has a tubular, semicircular shape, and takes its name from the characteristic crest, similar to that of a rooster's comb.

CAMPANELLE
This shape takes its name from the Italian word for bell or flower, *campana*, and for this reason it is also known by the name of *gigli* (lilies).

CASTELLANE
First produced in Parma in the 1980s, this pasta is so called because its shape recalls the type of skirt worn by women in medieval courts.

SICILIAN ANELLINI
Probably of Sicilian origins, it is said that this shape was designed to look like the earrings used by African women.

RUOTE
Among the most original shapes, this wheel-shaped pasta alternates hollow spaces, which allow the pasta to retain the sauce.

FESTONATI
Originally served on feast days, the shape of this pasta is reminiscent of garland decorations.

GHIOTTOLE
This pasta is similar, but longer, than Neapolitan *fusilli* and, like them, it is well suited to thick and robust sauces.

SPECIAL PASTA

Surprising for their colors and taste: this is pasta dough flavored in the most varied of ways. The ingredients used offer diverse possibilities for interesting combinations with different ingredients, balancing the flavor of the pasta with that of the sauce, creating distinctive flavor contrasts.

ARLECCHINO
Named after harlequin, it is also called tricolor pasta, made by adding ingredients such as nettles, spinach, saffron, and carrots to the flour and water.

GREEN AND RED CONCHIGLIE
Red turnip and spinach are used as colorants for these shells, although there are varieties flavored in many other ways.

527

FOGLIE D'ULIVO
In shape and color, this pasta looks like an olive leaf, hence their name. It is originally from Apulia and goes well with vegetable-based sauces.

MUSHROOM FETTUCCINE
This pasta is typical of the Appennines region. As well as dried mushrooms, corn semolina is also added to the pasta dough.

SAGE FETTUCCINE
The intense flavor makes it possible for this pasta to be served with very simple sauces, for example butter and Parmesan cheese.

SQUID INK AND TURMERIC CONCHIGLIE
Offering a sharp visual contrast with the yellow and black colors, it is ideal for seafood or fish-based red sauces.

TRICOLORED GIGLI
Like *farfalle*, this pasta is made with a wide range of dough mixes, and is ideal for thick sauces.

COLORED FARFALLE
The butterfly shape can be mixed with the most varied ingredients. It is ideal for baked recipes.

TOMATO FARFALLE
This pasta uses the most basic foods of the Mediterranean cuisine—wheat and tomato. They are ideal for white or fish ragu.

SQUID INK TAGLIATELLE
This pasta is often used in recipes that require a more rustic and homely type than either *tagliolini* and *spaghetti*.

TRICOLORED TAGLIATELLE
It is derived from *paglia e fieno* "hay and straw" pasta, and can also be found as *fettuccine*. It is excellent with Bolognese ragu.

FLAVORED TAGLIATELLE
Tagliatelle can be flavored not only with spinach but also, for example, with saffron and nettles.

SAFFRON TAGLIATELLE
The beautiful color of this pasta is obtained by adding saffron to the dough. It is normally available in large sizes.

SQUID INK TAGLIOLINI
This pasta is differentiated from *spaghetti* by its square section and rougher surface, and it offers a different experience on the palate.

GREEN TROFIE
Trofie is the most typical pasta shape from Liguria and, even in the green variety, it goes very well with classic pesto.

RICE FUSILLI
Perfect for those on a gluten free diet, this is a tasty alternative to durum wheat pasta.

WHOLE-WHEAT FUSILLI
This pasta contains a high quantity of fiber and is very filling. It is excellent with vegetable- and cheese-based sauces.

WHOLE WHEAT SPAGHETTI
It is made with unrefined ground wheat, which allows fiber to be retained in the dough.

SQUID INK SPAGHETTI
Among the best known types of pasta, this type of *spaghetti* goes very well with fish based sauces.

SPELT SPAGHETTI
Among the most widely used spelt flours are those produced in the Langhe region and those produced in the province of Ancona.

CORN FLOUR SEDANI
This pasta can be made entirely with corn flour or mixed with potato starch and lupin flour.

PIZZOCCHERI
This pasta is made with toasted buckwheat mixed with white flour. It is an ancient pasta from the Valtellina area.

DRIED EGG PASTA

This is the traditional homemade pasta, even though these days it is possible to find some industrially produced varieties of excellent quality. In addition to wheat (and creativity), eggs have been a readily available ingredient for a long time, and this has allowed this type of pasta to become one of the main traditions of Italian cuisine.

FETTUCINE
This pasta is popular in both Rome and Tuscany. It is shaped in long ribbons and is similar to *tagliatelle*. It is often eaten with meat ragu.

PICI AI FUNGHI
Traditionally from the south of Tuscany, this *spaghetti*-like pasta is flavored with mushroom.

PAGLIA E FIENO
The name of this pasta translates as "hay and straw" and is a type of *fettuccine*. Excellent served with meat ragu.

TAGLIATELLE
This is a traditional pasta from the Emilia Romagna and Marche regions of Italy. Flat ribbon that are similar in shape to *fettuccine* and often served with meat ragu.

LASAGNA
A "regional treasure" of the Emilia region, this pasta is prepared simply as a "ribbon" to be boiled and dressed, and also in layered preparations.

FETTUCCINE
Similar to *tagliatelle*, in the Lazio region this pasta is often prepared *alla papalina* (papal style), a variant of the traditional *carbonara* sauce.

TAGLIOLINI
With a single shape and a thousand variations, this pasta type differs in thickness from region to region.

CAPELLI D'ANGELO
The name translates as "angel's hair" because of its delicate nature. It cooks in minutes and is served with both sauces and in broth.

MACCHERONCINI DI CAMPOFILONE
Very thin, elastic, and compact, this pasta is a typical shape from the Marche region. It is excellent with rich sauces.

CHITARRINE
With a square section, they take their name from *chitarra*, a guitar-shaped instrument for cutting pasta sheets in thin pasta strips.

EGG STROZZAPRETI
This pasta is the dry version of a type of fresh pasta that is produced by rotating dough strips around themselves.

TONNARELLI
This pasta is cut with "*lu carrature*," a frame made with metal wires, similar to the *chitarra* used for other pasta types.

GRATED PASTA
This pasta is made by grating fresh egg pasta dough with a special frame. Ideal for soup.

VARIETIES OF RICE

Italy is the largest European producer of unrefined rice. The numerous varieties available can be divided into two categories: *indica*, which does not easily release its starch and whose grains remain separate, and *japonica*. The cultivated varieties belong mainly to this latter group and, according to a classification based on the size of the grains, the following groups are available:
Originario or common: rice with small round grains, with limited resistance to cooking;
Semifino: rice characterized by round grains of medium length, with good resistance to cooking;
Fino: rice with tapered grains of medium length, with high resistance to cooking;
Superfino: rice with large and long grains, with very high resistance to cooking.

In addition to the characteristics deriving from the variety of rice, what determines the quality of the final product is how it has been processed. Aging is a very important phase: *risone* (the unrefined rice still in its husk) need a resting time of at least three months after being harvested, to give the flavor of the grains the time to develop fully. After being cleaned of impurities, the grains of unrefined rice have their outer layer removed through mechanical friction. Whole grain rice, which retains all other parts of the rice, is obtained when processing stops at this stage. Refined rice, on the other hand, undergoes a bleaching process: using dedicated abrasive machinery, the rice is "filed" losing its husk, middlings, and germ. The taste and appearance quality of the rice depend on the purity of its variety, a good aging process, and delicate refining.

RAW AIACE
Aiace that has not been de-husked. To be fit for consumption, it must have its husk removed.

RAW ARBORIO
Freshly harvested and dried rice before losing its outer layer.

ARBORIO
With its large and long grains, *arborio* has been considered for a long time the best symbol of quality Italian rice, particularly abroad.

ARBORIO RICE FROM SARDINIA
Sardinian paddy fields, with their natural and climatic advantages, produce *arborio* rice of excellent quality, with large and chewy grains.

RAW BALDO
Like all rice varieties, unrefined *baldo* rice is not edible in its raw state. It becomes edible after processing.

BALDO
A *superfino* rice, with a crystalline structure, used mainly for *risotto* but it is also suitable for rice salads.

CARNAROLI DI BARAGGIA
The highly valued *Carnaroli di Baraggia* has great stability, consistency, and limited stickiness.

BELGIOIOSO
A cross between *Carnaroni* and *Vialone*. Suitable for preparations that require grains to be *al dente* and do not stick together.

RAW CARNAROLI
The long grains of *Carnaroli* in their raw state. They are yet to be de-husked and bleached.

CARNAROLI
Superfino rice of excellent quality and optimum stability in cooking. It is well suited to the preparation of risotto and timbales.

SEMIREFINED ELIO
A common variety from *Balilla*. Its round grains can be used for soup or sweet recipes.

EUROPA
A cross of two different varieties, it is characterized by its long and slightly tapered grains. Suitable for risotto and side dishes.

JAPANESE
An Italian rice deriving from the *japonica* subspecies, with short grains that easily release their starch.

UNREFINED LONG INDICA
It has long grains that do not stick together even after long cooking times making it suitable for salads and pilafs.

UNREFINED
Rice is defined as unrefined when the grain is separated from its husk, through de-husking.

MARATELLI
Semifino rice with small grains that are round, light, and compact. It is very stable in cooking and it has an excellent yield.

NERONE
A new rice variety with black grains, naturally rich in nutritional and antioxidant qualities.

RAW ORIGINARIO
Originario still covered by its outer skin. It is only edible after the removal of its husk.

ORIGINARIO
Common rice with a limited resistance to cooking. Ideal for sweet recipes.

PADANO
Semifino variety with a tender paste and high content of starch. Soups, *supplí*, and *arancini* use this type of rice.

PARBOILED
After having undertaken a hydrothermal treatment, this rice becomes more resistant to cooking but it will absorb less of its sauce.

RIBE
With its compact paste and long grains, it is the most commonly used variety for parboiling. It is excellent for soups and sweet recipes.

ROMA
This *superfino* rice has a good consistency and absorbs sauces well, while keeping the grains well separated.

RED
An unrefined rice produced in limited quantities. It has a medium-long grain that goes well with foods with a strong taste.

WHOLE GRAIN SANT'ANDREA FROM BARAGGIA
This rice is typical of Baraggia, between Biella and Vercelli. It is tastier and more aromatic when only partially processed.

SANT'ANDREA
A *fino* rice, with a good balance between resistance to cooking and ability to absorb flavors from its sauce.

WHOLE GRAIN SANT'EUSEBIO
It has red grains and it is particularly rich in antioxidants, which are well preserved in this whole grain variety.

PARTIALLY REFINED
This rice has been partially processed after its initial de-husking. It cooks faster than whole grain rice.

RAW THAILBONNET
This type of rice has long, Asian-looking grains. It needs to be de-husked to be edible.

THAILBONNET
It has very long and tapered grains, with limited stickiness. Ideal for use in the preparation of salads and side dishes.

VIALONE
Rice with thick, chunky grains, with all the characteristics needed to make excellent risotto.

VIALONE NANO
This rice grows in the fertile plains in the province of Verona. Even though it is a *semifino* variety, it is one of the best types of rice for risotto.

RAW VOLANO
Before undergoing any type of processing, *Volano* is a light, yellowish brown color.

VOLANO
Superfino rice suited for the preparation of *risotto al dente*. It is one of the varieties cultivated in the Po river delta.

RICE FLOUR
This is not a typical Italian product but it is easily available. Leavening is difficult to achieve with this type of flour.

SEA FISH

There are many types of classifications used for sea fish, one of Italy's most significant food resources. One, based on the body shape, differentiates between flat, eel-like, and elongated fish. Another makes a distinction between poor and more valued fish, while nutritional characteristics divide fish into lean, moderately lean, and fatty varieties.

ANCHOVIES
They have fatty flesh but are more delicate than sardines. The ones from the Ligurian Sea preserved in salt carry the DOP mark.

SEA BASS
Its flesh is very versatile for all types of cooking, including baking, braising, and sautéeing.

RED GROUPER
It has excellent firm flesh. Thanks to its large size, it is often cooked in slices: baked, *en papillote*, or boiled.

SNAPPER
It can rearch a large size. Thanks to its fine and highly valued flesh, it is considered one of the best fish for baking or boiling.

GURNARD
There are many varieties of this fish, also known as *gallinella, luserna,* or *cuoccio*. It is found in Atlantic and Mediterranean waters.

MORMORA
Similar to *pagello*, it is highly valued for its quality. The one from Miramare (in Friuli Venezia Giulia) is a traditional variety.

HAKE
Hake, and also cod and haddock, are very delicate and easy to digest, they are well suited to boiling or steaming, but also excellent in stews.

SADDLE BREAM
Good for broiling (grilling) only if very fresh. Small, it is excellent for frying, while larger specimens are suitable for soup.

MEAGRE
Enjoyed for its white and boneless flesh, it is very delicate and versatile. When filleted it is suitable for fast sauté cooking.

GILTHEAD BREAM
Highly valued for its delicate taste and marked sea smell. It is advisable not to scale it before baking.

COMMON PANDORA
Found in the Mediterranean, it is suitable for grilling, baking, and frying. The classic recipe requires baking with potatoes and onions.

MONKFISH
Also called angler fish, its flesh is similar to that of lobster and it lends itself to the sauce accompaniments.

RAY
It is necessary to skin the fish, because the skin is thick and tough. Once boiled, it is served cold with a garlic-and-vinegar or sweet-and-sour sauce.

GREATER AMBERJACK
A species commonly found throughout the Mediterranean, it is highly regarded. In Sicily it is baked with tomatoes, capers, and herbs.

MEGRIM
Found in the northeast Atlantic and in the Mediterranean. Highly regarded taste, especially when it is small in size.

JOHN DORY
Very easy to clean into four boneless fillets. It is cooked like sole and brill or in soups.

DIPLODUS
A fish with firm and tasty flesh, excellent when baked. Other varieties can be added to soups.

SARDINES
They have fatty flesh and need to be consumed within hours of fishing. The most highly regarded ones are those fished in the spring.

ROCKFISH
A very common ingredient in Italian fish soups, from *brodetto dell'Adriatico* to *cacciucco livornese*.

MACKEREL
It is commonly found in the Mediterranean and is available fresh as well as frozen, smoked, salted, and canned.

SOLE
This fish is light colored on one side and dark on the other, able to camouflage itself against a sandy background. It is best cooked *a la meunière*.

SWORDFISH
It is highly regarded both for the quality of its flesh and for the convenience of preparation because it usually comes in thick slices.

YELLOW FIN TUNA
Fishing for this variety has dramatically increased. It is used mainly for canning.

RED MULLET
Found in the Mediterranean, North Atlantic, and the Black Sea, it has very delicate flesh, which needs careful cleaning. It is suited to all types of preparation other than boiling.

FRESHWATER FISH

There is a variety of freshwater fish in Italy, which is used in regional cookery, even though this type of fish is considered to be of lower quality. Freshwater fish are found in lakes and still waters, as well as rivers and streams. The quality of the flesh of these varieties is linked to the habitat in which they are found.

EEL
It has rather fatty flesh, with few bones. In Italy, the varieties from the Verona side of Lake Garda, from Livenza, Orbetello, and Lesina are highly regarded.

CARP
If fished in muddy waters, it needs to be soaked in vinegar for a few hours to clean the flesh.

EUROPEAN PERCH
It is normally available already filleted because of its numerous bones. It is suitable for frying and cooking in butter.

WELS CATFISH
Introduced to Italy a few decades ago, it is widespread in the basins of the Po and Adige rivers. It can be steamed, braised, or fried.

SIBERIAN STURGEON
It can reach 16 ½ feet (5 meters) in length. Its flesh, distinctly fatty, is very delicate. Farmed sturgeon is most commonly found.

RAINBOW TROUT
One of the most popular freshwater fish. It is suitable for cooking *en papillote*, baked, or boiled.

SHELLFISH

From mussels to octopus, shellfish represent a whole gastronomic universe, much loved by chefs. Both cephalopods and bivalves are included under the generic term of shellfish.

CALAMARETTO
Also called *velo calamaretto*, it is a small variety of squid. It does not need to be cleaned and it is cooked whole, often fried.

SQUID
Small ones are fried or boiled and need to be consumed right away. Larger ones are excellent broiled (grilled) or stuffed.

QUEEN SCALLOP
Similar to scallop, it can be white, yellow, pink, or purple. It is fished in winter on sandy and muddy sea floors.

RAZOR SHELL
A bivalve shaped like an elongated tube. It needs to be carefully washed to elimate sand. It can be sautéed or cooked *au gratin*.

SCALLOP
It is used mainly in the Veneto region in Italian cooking, using these two recipes: scallops *in tecia* (braised or stewed in a pan) or *au gratin*.

MUSSELS
Called *cozze* and more appropriately as *mitili*, they are the best known bivalves in Italy, and the variety most widely farmed.

COCKLES
There are several varieties, quite similar to each other. They are often added to fish soup or clam sauces.

SMOOTH CLAMS
They have a strong taste and a firm consistency. They are excellent for sauces for pasta or for making fish balls. They require a short cooking time.

SMALL SEA SNAILS
In Italy they can be picked along the coast or in the lagoon in Veneto. Once cooked, boiled, or stewed, the flesh is extracted using a pin.

MUSKY OCTOPUS
Found in the Mediterranean, there is a line of suckers on each tentacle. It can be cooked in tomato sauce or dusted in flour and fried.

OYSTERS
Sometimes called flat oysters if one of the two valves is flat, or concave oysters otherwise. Excellent raw or cooked.

LIMPETS
A shellfish with only one valve. They are traditionally consumed raw, with lemon juice.

OCTOPUS
Sometimes called rock octopus, it is best prepared in stews or cooked for seafood salads.

SEA URCHINS
Particularly tasty at the end of winter, just before the start of spring. They cook very quickly.

CUTTLEFISH

The Tuscan recipe, *in zimino* (a sauce made with beets, spinach, garlic, and parsley) is a typical use for this shellfish. The ink in its sac can also be used.

WARTY VENUS

A species of saltwater clam with an almost round, striped valve. They have a different taste to other clams, and a more elastic texture.

DONAX TRUNCULUS

Almost pyramidal in shape. It has sweet and delicate flesh. Because of its small size, it is often used with pasta.

TOTANI

Similar to squid but with a triangular fin and larger tentacles. It is often used in stews or stuffed.

VONGOLE OR LUPINI

Considered less desirable than carpetshell clams, this variety of clams is tasty and can be used in mixed fish soups and for sauces for pasta.

CARPETSHELL CLAMS

There are many varieties of clam, but carpetshell clams (the *verace* variety) is the most highly regarded.

SPINY LOBSTER

The best spiny lobsters are female, heavy but not too large. Boiled lobster salad with mayonnaise is a classic recipe.

LOBSTER

Similar to spiny lobster but with only two very large pincers. Its flesh is firmer but less delicate than the spiny lobster.

MANTIS SHRIMP

The flesh of the tail is tender and very delicate, excellent for sauces, soups, or grilled. A plump eye indicates freshness.

SHRIMP TAILS

They can be purchased fresh or frozen. They combine great taste and ease of preparation and are ideal for making sauces.

PINK SHRIMP

Pale pink, almost white in color, its flesh is good but of lesser quality than that of red or white shrimp.

RED SHRIMP

They have very tasty flesh and are easy to find, both fresh and frozen. They are usually referred to as "king prawns" or "jumbo shrimp."

CRAWFISH (CRAYFISH)

With a delicate flavor, now quite rare. The variety from eastern Venice is highly regarded.

MOLTING CRAB

Very sought-after in molting season, the molting crab is referred to as *maleca* in the Veneto region. It is normally dusted with flour and fried.

CRAB

It needs to be cleaned by being brushed under running water. The flesh can be used for pasta sauces.

SPIDER CRAB

Its flesh is particularly tasty and plentiful in females over the winter period. It is usually served boiled.

MAGNOSA
Also called *cigala*, it is rarely fished but it is still a very sought after variety. Excellent for sauces for pasta.

WHITE SHRIMP
They are grayish or pink-yellow, with almost purple patches. Not to be confused with tropical shrimp.

LANGOUSTINE
Smaller than spiny lobsters, they are cooked whole, or the shelled tails alone are used. Heads can be used for making stock or broth.

SALAD GREENS

The term "salad" normally refers to all varieties of lettuce, which owes its name to the milky liquid that seeps from its stem, leaves, and roots when they are broken. They usually have a sweet and fresh taste, and are rather tender to the bite. Varieties such as *valeriana* and arugula (rocket) are interesting options.

CURLY LETTUCE
Also called gentile lettuce, it has jugged leaves and a rather loose head. It does not keep fresh for long.

SPRING LETTUCE
Also called oak-leaf lettuce, it is a cut-and-come-again variety, among the first to be available in the spring. It has small, oval, and tender leaves.

BUTTERHEAD LETTUCE
Its large, smooth, and fleshy leaves form cup shapes and are particularly rich in minerals and vitamins.

ICEBERG LETTUCE
Like butterhead lettuce, it has a compact head, with crisp and densely packed leaves. It can be cooked.

VALERIANA OR SONCINO
Also known as corn salad or lamb's lettuce, not to be confused with *Valeriana officinalis*. It tastes best with lemon rather than vinegar.

ARUGULA (ROCKET)
It has a strong and slightly bitter taste, and can be used raw or cooked. It is excellent for making pesto.

GARLIC AND ONION

Garlic and onion are essential for adding flavor to recipes, for *soffritto* (a mixture of finely chopped onion, garlic, celery, carrot, etc. gently fried in olive oil), and in fillings. Onions can also be used raw, with an olive oil dip, or sliced in mixed salads.

WHITE GARLIC FROM VESSALICO
Cultivated in Liguria, this has a more delicate flavor than other varieties and a rather small core, which makes it easy to digest.

GARLIC FROM UFITA
It has an intense and pungent flavor, due to its high content of essential oils. It is ideal for flavoring oil.

RED GARLIC FROM CASTELLIRI

It has a pungent and spicy flavor. Its leaves are soaked in vats overnight, before being braided.

BROWN ONION

Sweeter taste notes are more prevalent early in the season, with more pungent ones becoming noticeable later. The golden onion from Parma is an excellent variety.

RED ONION FROM TROPEA PGI

Its unusual crispiness and extraordinary sweetness set it apart from any other variety of onion.

WHITE ONION FROM BORETTO

A small variety that takes its name from Boretto, in the province of Reggio Emilia. Excellent for preserves.

ASPARAGUS

A delicate vegetable, of ancient origin, used in cooking since Roman times. There are several varieties, both wild and cultivated, some of which are characterized by quite distinctive appearance and taste characteristics.

ASPARAGUS FROM BADOERE PGI

An excellent variety from Veneto. They are often served boiled or steamed, dressed with olive oil, salt, and pepper, and served with boiled eggs.

GREEN ASPARAGUS FROM ALTEDO PGI

Cultivated in the provinces of Bologna and Ferrara, its spears are characterized by a bright green color and solid and crunchy flesh.

PINK ASPARAGUS FROM MEZZAGO

Widespread in the areas of Monza and Brianza, spears are harvested when the tips turn light pink. It is quite a flavorful variety.

WHITE ASPARAGUS FROM BASSANO PDO

With a bittersweet taste, it grows underground, without sunlight. It is renowned for its texture and its generous yield.

PURPLE ASPARAGUS

A rare and highly valued variety. Its purple color depends on how it is grown and on cultivation techniques.

PURPLE ASPARAGUS FROM ALBENGA

It tastes soft and buttery, with very large spears and a light purple color due to its genetic heritage.

ARTICHOKES

The home of this vegetable is the south of Italy, where it has been cultivated since ancient times. Depending on the shape and color of the bracts, artichokes can be differentiated into spiny or spineless, and into purple or green varieties. End-of-harvest baby artichokes are suitable for preserving in oil or for freezing.

PURPLE ARTICHOKE OR ARTICHOKE FROM CATANIA

This is the most common variety in Italy. In the province of Catania, "*arrustutu*" (broiled [grilled]) artichokes are sold as street food.

ARTICHOKE FROM BRINDISI

Characterized by a compact, oval-shaped flower head, this artichoke is excellent both cooked and raw. The bracts, green with a purple hue, have no spines.

ROMAN ARTICHOKE FROM LAZIO PGI
Also called *mammola* or *cimarolo*, it is an integral part of the cuisine from the Lazio region.

SPINY PURPLE ARTICHOKE FROM ALBENGA
This artichoke is excellent raw, thanks to the tenderness of its internal leaves, which are crisp and sweet.

PROVENCAL PURPLE ARTICHOKE
This is a variety with a very generous yield, which was introduced in Sardinia in the 1980s, where it replaced the indigenous variety, the *masedu* artichoke.

TUSCAN PURPLE ARTICHOKE
Also known as *il carciofo violetto di livornese*, it is not very sweet and is excellent cooked in olive oil, garlic, and parsley.

TOMATOES

The symbol of Mediterranean cuisine and one of the most common ingredients in Italian cooking, there are in fact nearly 300 varieties of tomato available on the market, and these can be divided into three large groups: industrial tomatoes, salad tomatoes, and long lasting tomatoes, capable of being stored for a long time and intended to last through the winter.

CLUSTER TOMATOES
This type of tomato is available all year round. It is best used for preparations that require long cooking times.

SAN MARZANO TOMATO FROM AGRO SARNESE-NOCERINO PDO
Characterized by its oblong shape and firm flesh, it is best used peeled.

PERINO TOMATO
Characterized by its elongated oval shape, this tomato is crunchy and robust.

BEEFSTEAK TOMATOES
A tomato typically used for salads, it is large, pink, sweet, and solid. With a thin skin, it does not need to be skinned.

TUSCAN BEEFSTEAK TOMATO
It is a variety of beef tomato, large and of irregular shape. It has a very fleshy pulp, with few seeds.

BELMONTE TOMATO
A beefsteak tomato from Calabria, it can become very large. It has lumpy flesh and a bright, dark pink skin.

SALAD TOMATO
This is a large category of tomatoes, which can be picked before they are fully mature and used raw.

COSTOLUTO TOMATO FROM CHIVASSO
A variety grown in the province of Turin. It has a compact flesh, which is sweet and flavorful.

TOMATO FROM PACHINO PGI
This type of tomato is grown in Sicily in four different varieties, all characterized by a full flavor and compact and scented flesh.

CHERRY TOMATOES
These cluster tomatoes are round, small, and sweet, with a bright color. They are excellent eaten raw.

DATTERINO TOMATO

Very tasty and rich in sugars, it is used for *bruschetta*, salads, and tomato-based sauces.

VESUVIAN CHERRY TOMATO

Intensely red-colored, this tomato is very versatile in the kitchen and can be stored for a long time. It is ideal for sauces and preserves.

CAMONE TOMATO FROM SARDINIA

It has a spherical shape and a very firm flesh. It is ideal for salads thanks to its balanced, slightly acidic taste.

DRIED CHERRY TOMATOES

Sweeter but harder than other dried varieties, they can be rehydrated by being boiled in water for two minutes.

CARROTS AND RADISHES

These are among the most commonly available root vegetables, and both are excellent raw and dipped in olive oil. Sweet carrots are an essential ingredient in countless recipes, while radishes have an Asian origin, and are characterized by their aromatic and slightly hot flavor.

CARROT FROM ALTOPIANO DEL FUCINO PGI

It has a cylindrical shape with a rounded tip, with a bright orange smooth skin. Its flesh is very sweet and crunchy.

CARROT FROM ALBENGA

Red-colored, the root is long, with a cone shaped tip. It is an important ingredient in the cuisine of the Liguria region.

CARROT FROM ZAPPONETA

Called *pastnoc* in the local dialect, it is one of the most important vegetables in the province of Foggia, together with onions and potatoes.

WHITE TIPPED RADISH

This is the tastiest and most commonly available radish. The surface must be smooth, without any blemishes, and the leaves must be bright green.

LONG WHITE TIPPED RADISH

It has a white and crunchy flesh, with a slightly hot flavor. It is best to choose young specimens, to be used in salads.

LONG WHITE RADISH

Also known as *ice candle*, it has a compact and crunchy flesh. Larger ones tend to have a woody consistency.

EGGPLANTS

Italy is the top European country for the production of eggplants, with cultivation concentrated in the south of Italy, especially in Campania and Sicily. The elongated and round varieties are available all year round, while the purple variety is only available from spring to fall.

OVAL EGGPLANT

Specimens of this variety can be quite large, with a shiny dark purple, almost black skin. The flesh is sweet and suitable for cooking in slices.

STREAKED EGGPLANT

An ancient variety that was at risk of extinction, but has now recovered. It has a sweet taste, and a pink skin with white streaks.

ROUND EGGPLANT FROM GENOA
The end of season small fruits of this dark purple variety are in great demand for preserves in oil.

FLORENTINE PURPLE EGGPLANT
With a roundish shape and a light purple skin, this variety is valued for its tender, compact, and slightly acidic flesh.

NEAPOLITAN PURPLE EGGPLANT
This type of eggplant has a stronger flavor than round eggplants. In Naples it is often cooked *in carrozza* (two slices of eggplant with a slice of cheese in the middle, dipped in egg and breadcrumbs, then fried).

WHITE EGGPLANT
Round, smaller, and egg-shaped, this is an early variety, with a sweet taste, similar to that of mushrooms.

PEPPERS

Raw, cooked, or preserved in oil, peppers come in two main varieties: sweet and hot. The first is by far the most commonly used variety, green while they are still unripe, and in brighter yellow and red colors when they are ripe. Large and fleshy varieties are more suitable for baking, round ones can be filled, and slim ones can be fried.

PEPPER FROM CARMAGNOLA PGI
This is grown in four different varieties, all of which have a particularly sweet flavor and bright yellow and red colors.

SQUARE PEPPER FROM ASTI
Greatly valued variety from Piedmont, which is suffering from competition by less valued but more profitable varieties.

FLESHY PEPPER FROM CUNEO
Also known as square pepper from Cuneo, it is protected by a Consortium. Its fleshy crunchiness makes it unique.

PAPACCELLA PEPPER
Small, sweet, and fleshy. Preserved in vinegar, it constitutes an essential ingredient of the typical Neapolitan *rinforzo* salad (a traditional Christmas salad).

PEPPER FROM PONTECORVO PDO
Produced in the province of Frosinone, it is tasty, highly scented, and easy to digest, thanks to its thin skin.

FRIGGITELLI PEPPER
Small and dark green, its flesh is sweet and tasty. Excellent fried, stuffed, or preserved in oil.

ZUCCHINI AND CUCUMBERS

These two vegetables have a similar shape but have a completely different taste and they are used in very dissimilar ways. Zucchini color varies from dark to light green. Cucumbers, consumed raw or preserved in vinegar, are characterized by their slightly acidic and bitter taste.

ZUCCHINI FROM BORGO D'ALE
Produced in the province of Vercelli, it has a smooth skin, a vivid dark green color, very white flesh, and few seeds.

BLACK ZUCCHINI FROM MILAN
Characterized by its very dark and uniform skin, it has a compact flesh and cylindrical shape. It can grow quite large.

ROUND ZUCCHINI

Commonly used in cooking for fillings of all types. The varieties from Florence—light green, and from Piacenza—darker in color, are highly valued.

PRESERVING CUCUMBER

Only the smallest fruits, tender and young, just a couple of inches long, are suitable to be preserved in vinegar.

CAROSELLO CUCUMBER

Also known as *spuredda leccese*, it is an oval or round variety with the skin covered by a light down. It is excellent with lemon and salt.

LONG CUCUMBER

The dark green variety from Cascine, very long and of excellent quality, and also the smooth skinned variety are among the long fruit varieties available.

CRUCIFEROUS VEGETABLES

This is a family of plants that have been known in Mediterranean countries since ancient times. A first classification includes plants with large inflorescence, such as cauliflower or broccoli. Cabbages, on the other hand, are characterized by very compact heads, which can be green, red, or purple.

BROCCOLI

The edible part is the still immature flowering head, with the flowers still unopened.

SPIGARIELLI BROCCOLI

A variety of early broccoli with long leaves, similar to turnip greens but with a more delicate flavor. They are excellent with pasta.

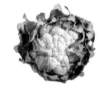

BROCCOLO DI RAPA CALABRESE

A highly valued variety that, unlike broccoli, presents many lateral shoots. It can be preserved in oil.

ROMANESCO BROCCOLI

The shape of its florets is spectacular. It has a bright light green color and it is characterized by its sweetness.

NEAPOLITAN GIANT CAULIFLOWER

The inflorescence is white if picked at just the right stage. It is an ingredient of the Neapolitan *rinforzo* salad.

CAULIFLOWER FROM FANO

A variety that lasts until mid-May, characterized by a good texture, which keeps well. It is excellent boiled.

PURPLE CAULIFLOWER

The bright color is due to the presence of vacuolar pigments in a concentration that is greater than that of white cauliflowers.

THE PURPLE OF SICILY CAULIFLOWER

The inflorescence forms a compact head with a fine texture, with brown-purple hues.

BRUSSELS SPROUTS

Characterized by a slightly bitter taste, which makes them perfect with chestnuts, chickpeas, and pork.

RED CABBAGE

Differentiated from green cabbage by its color and its sweeter taste. When cooked, it becomes a beautiful blue color.

GREEN CABBAGE
The variety used to make sauerkraut. Its leaves are covered by a waxy substance that makes them smooth. Excellent raw.

TUSCAN CURLY BLACK CABBAGE
Also known as Tuscan cabbage, it has bullous leaves that curl at their edges. Its intense flavor is irreplaceable in *ribollita toscana*.

WHITE VIENNA KOHLRABI
A cultivar of cabbage, it is widespread in Northern Europe and present in some Italian regional cuisines (Sicily, Apulia, Alto Adige).

SAVOY CABBAGE
It keeps less well than other varieties of cabbage. Its flavor is particularly delicate with a very tender core if it has had the opportunity to experience frosts.

RADICCHIO AND SPINACH

Radicchio has a stronger taste and is available in very different forms and colors. They are all characterized by an essentially bitter note. In spite of their appearance, which is similar to that of salad greens, spinach and beet leaves need to be cooked, unless baby leaves are used.

CHARD
It has a sweet taste and is consumed boiled or steamed. It is used in several traditional savory pies and filled pasta varieties.

BEET LEAVES
Very tender, with a delicate flavor similar to that of spinach. A typical filling for *tortelli parmensi*.

CATALOGNA
Many regional recipes require it to be cooked in broth and soups, which softens its slightly bitter taste.

SUGARLOAF CHICORY
It has large, fleshy, and resistant leaves with a slightly bitter taste. Its leaves are very crisp.

RED CHICORY
It is picked when its leaves are still tender. Slightly bitter, it is excellent sautéed with cubes of *pancetta*.

ENDIVE
Often incorrectly referred to as Belgian, it is also part of the chicory family. It is cultivated in the dark and is particularly bitter.

CURLY ENDIVE
With its characteristic curly leaves, it is consumed raw in salads or sautéed with olive oil, garlic, and anchovies.

FIELD RADICCHIO
In the Emilian Apennines it is cut into strips and dressed with a *soffritto* made with lard, shallots, and vinegar.

RADICCHIO DI CHIOGGIA IPG
Late in season it has a slightly bitter taste, earlier in season, it is sweeter. It is one of the varieties best suited to being cooked.

ROSSI DI VERONA RADICCHIO IPG
It is set apart by its bright red color, slightly bitter taste, and great crispiness.

RED TREVISO RADICCHIO IPG

It can be recognized by its distinctive white ribs, its bright red color, and its large, elongated head.

LATE TREVISO RED RADICCHIO IPG

A unique product, the result of a complex production technique. Perfect baked and in risotto. Also referred to as *fiore d'inverno* (winter flower).

RADICCHIO VARIEGATO DI CASTELFRANCO IGP

It has a beautiful head variegated with hues from light pink to red, and it has a sweet taste, with a pleasant, slightly bitter note.

VARIEGATED CHIOGGIA RADICCHIO

It has red leaves with white ribs. It is better suited to be used in salad raw, rather than cooked.

SPINACH

The best spinach is that which has not yet started to flower, as flowering makes the leaves tougher and more fibrous.

FENNEL AND ROOTS

Strongly aromatic and tasty, the only edible part of sweet fennel is the white bulb at its base, while in bitter fennel varieties the edible parts are the leaves and seeds. Turnip and celery are among edible roots: simple vegetables that can be used in many ways and offer varieties that can be consumed both raw and cooked.

ARTICHOKE THISTLE

Also known as a cardoon, it is highly regarded when it is ivory white. The bundle of stalks must be compact.

FLAT HEAD FENNEL

It is cultivated mainly in northern Italy and is characterized by compact and flattened white heads.

ROUND OR ELONGATED FENNEL

The shape is significant with round fennel better for dipping in oil, and the elongated one better suited to cooking.

TURNIP

Suitable for cooking, either boiled or stewed. It must be heavy and have a round shape, with a shiny skin without blemishes.

CELERIAC

It is a valued variety from the Trento province, with a delicate flavor. It is excellent raw, cut in strips, or cooked, served with fish.

CELERY FROM CHIOGGIA

This green variety is different from the white: it has a smaller head and an intense licorice scent. It is a very early variety.

PUMPKINS

There are countless varieties of pumpkin, different in shape (more or less rounded or elongated), size, or color. Used in traditional recipes, in particular in the Padana Plain, pumpkin is an ingredient that can be used for both sweet and savory dishes. It is also possible to consume its flowers and its seeds, toasted.

BELLOTTA PUMPKIN

It weighs 4½–6½ pounds (2–3 kg) on average and has a sweet taste. This variety can be stored for a long time.

BERRETTINA PIACENTINA PUMPKIN

It is a variety widespread in the Piacenza and Mantua areas, and it looks like the variety known as *marina di Chioggia*. It has a sweet and firm flesh.

CAPPELLO DEL PRETE PUMPKIN

Typical of the Parmense area, it has a firm flesh that is sweet and not very fibrous. It is therefore ideal for filling fresh pasta.

DELICA PUMPKIN

A hybrid variety, among the most commonly found in Italy. It is liked for its sweet taste and its firm, not very stringy flesh.

MANTUAN PUMPKIN

An ingredient of Mantuan *tortelli* and *gnocchi*. The flesh is very firm and sweet, with a rugged skin.

MUSCHIATA PUMPKIN

This pumpkin has a musk-scented floury flesh, and it is suited for cake making.

POTATOES

New or late, yellow or white-fleshed, white or red-skinned, there are countless varieties of potatoes, and they are never absent from both homely cooking and haute cuisine. They are unbeatable fried, tasty when baked, and their delicate flavor lends itself to infinite combinations, both traditional or experimental.

WHITE SWEET POTATOES

With a sweet taste, it is a traditional crop in Apulia and in Veneto. It can be boiled, fried, or baked.

AGATA POTATO

Widely used in the Viterbo area for the production of new potatoes. It is rich in starch, also ideal for purée and *gnocchi*.

FUCINO WHITE POTATO

This potato keeps well. Available over winter, it is very popular for its taste an look.

BLACK CANNELLINA POTATO

It has an irregular, slightly elongated shape with black sprouts. It is used for Ligurian stewed fish.

SILA POTATO IPG

With its very high starch content, its firm flesh needs a rather long cooking time.

BOLOGNA POTATO DOP

Its firm flesh and good appearance make it a versatile ingredient.

KENNEBEC POTATO
Widely available throughout Italy despite its American origins. It has very white, floury flesh.

SIRACUSA NEW POTATOES
This is a potato with a yellow, firm flesh, and a thin skin. It holds well during cooking and it can be used in all types of recipes.

PRIMURA POTATO
Historical variety within the DOP mark for the Bologna potato. Its flesh is slightly floury, and has a delicate flavor.

PRUGNONA OR PURPLE QUARANTINA POTATO
It has a delicate flavor, holds well during cooking, and is excellent in stews. The Genoese white *quarantina* belongs to the same family.

RED POTATO FROM COLFIORITO UMBRIA
It has red skin and yellow flesh. It is the variety used for the typical sweet ring-shaped potato cake.

MOUNTAIN POTATO FROM TRENTINO
It has a rich flavor, typical of mountain potatoes. This makes it perfect for simple recipes such as potato *tortel*.

VITELOTTE POTATO
Both its skin and flesh are of a deep purple color, due to the presence of high levels of anthocyanins. It smells of hazelnuts and it tastes a little like chestnuts.

JERUSALEM ARTICHOKE
Also known as a sunchoke, it is originally from North America. It is grown in Piedmont where it is often served with *bagna càuda*.

VARIETIES OF LEGUMES

Tasty, versatile, and available in countless varieties, legumes are a valuable source of vegetable proteins, as well as vitamins and trace elements. Fresh ones are available for only limited periods but, thanks to drying, beans, chickpeas, lentils, and peas can become the main ingredient of the most diverse range of recipes all year round.

TOASTED CHICKPEAS FROM CALABRIA
After being soaked in water and salt, in Calabria these chickpeas are then toasted in a frying pan under sand.

CHICKPEAS FROM MARCHE
They are small and rust colored and excellent for soups, purées, and croquettes, but can also be served in salads.

SMALL CHICKPEAS FROM VALDARNO
A variety grown in Valdarno, in Tuscany. They have thin skin and they are tender and tasty.

DRIED CHICKPEAS
They are excellent in soups, boiled and dressed in salads, combined with pasta and rice, or toasted and salted, and served as nibbles with aperitifs.

CHICKLING VETCH FROM UMBRIA
Used mainly as a flour, chickling vetch is only grown in Umbria and Marche. Also known as *cecine*.

GREEN BEANS
They are versatile and very filling, even though they have low levels of carbohydrates and proteins.

YELLOW POD BEANS

Less used than green ones, they include highly regarded varieties such as *meraviglia di Venezia* (Venice's wonder) and *corona d'oro* (golden crown).

SANT'ANNA BEANS

Very fine, they have this name because they are picked at the end of July on or around St. Anna's day. They have long, round, and fleshy pods.

AQUILA BEAN

White in color, with a dark stain that looks a little like an eagle (*Aquila*). They are grown on the plain in the province of Lucca.

CARNIA CRANBERRY (BORLOTTI) BEANS

Cultivated in Friuli Venezia Giulia, they have an oval shape and a light color, mottled or striated with red or purple.

DRY CRANBERRY (BORLOTTI) BEANS

They have the same characteristics of the fresh variety, but need to be soaked for at least 12 hours before cooking.

FRESH CRANBERRY (BORLOTTI) BEANS

These are very versitile beans: good in salads but they are also suited to soup.

MANGIA CRANBERRY (BORLOTTI) BEANS

A very ancient variety. They are consumed boiled and dressed with olive oil, or in stews with sausages.

CANNELLINI BEANS

It is advisable to cook them on a low heat in an earthenware container to ensure the beans are tender without becoming mushy.

ATINA CANNELLINI BEANS DOP

Variety grown in the Lazio region, they are different from other cannellini varieties because of their particular tenderness.

COCO NANO BEANS

An early dwarf variety. The seeds, with a rounded shape, are consumed boiled or baked.

CORONA BEANS

The beans are large and white, excellent in salads. Their cultivation is quite widespread in the Marche region.

BLACK-EYED PEAS (BEANS)

So called for the presence of a ring-shaped "eye" at the point where the seed is attached to the pod.

AQUILA DI PIGNONE BEANS

With a delicate taste and easy to digest, they are characterized by their color, part white and part mottled brownish-red.

CHRISTMAS LIMA BEANS

Also known as Pope's beans, they are large and flat and can be white or dark brown. Suitable for use in salads when boiled.

LAMON BEANS IPG

They have red or maroon streaks. The most highly regarded variety is the *spagnolet*, which has a very thin skin.

SORANA BEANS IPG

They are grown on the banks of the Pescia stream. They have a thin skin which disappears almost entirely with cooking.

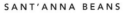

FRESH BROAD BEANS

They are available from early summer but they are at their best in midsummer. They can be consumed boiled or raw.

DRIED BROAD BEANS

They require to be soaked in water for a minimum of 24 hours before cooking, after which they can be cooked in the same way as fresh ones.

LENTILS

An ingredient extensively used for soups or side dishes. In Italy they are traditionally served with *zampone* or *cotechino*.

ALTAMURA (BA) LENTILS

Larger than average lentils, they come under a collective trade mark held by the Italian Patents and Trademarks Office.

USTICA LENTILS

They are characterized by their very small size. Their cultivation is almost entirely traditional, without machinery.

RED LENTILS

They tend to dissolve when cooked and are ideal to thicken soups, but also excellent in stews.

SALTED LUPINI BEANS

When prepared like this, *lupini* beans don't need to be soaked and are ready for consumption.

DRY LUPINI BEANS

They are normally commercially available in their dried state. They need to be soaked in water for one to two days before cooking.

FRESH PEAS

They are purchased in their pods and must be shelled. They need very little cooking and have a low caloric content.

DRIED PEAS

Less valued than when fresh, frozen, or canned. They need to be soaked for at least 12 hours.

SNOW PEA (MANGE TOUT)

They need to be firm when bought, and of a bright, light green color. They are trimmed like fresh green beans.

VARIETIES OF CEREALS

Sometimes skipped over for the much more popular rice, cereals are seeing a resurgence in popularity and are valued in all cuisines, where they are used in an infinity of rustic dishes—from soups to polenta—and also find excellent uses in countless types of salads.

OAT GRAINS

Dehusked grains are excellent for soups or salads. It is the richest cereal grain in both proteins and fatty acids.

OAT FLAKES

An essential ingredient for breakfast muesli and oatmeal, it can also be added to cereal soups.

COUSCOUS
Made with durum wheat semolina, a traditional preparation of cuisines in Trapani, Sardinia, Livorno, and Liguria.

DEHUSKED SPELT
Its internal chaff remains intact, retaining all its fiber and nutritional properties. It is suitable for soups that require a long cooking time.

SPELT FROM GARFAGNANA IPG
Excellent product obtained without the use of chemical fertilizers. Typically used for spelt soup.

SPELT IN ITS HUSK
Spelt is also called a hulled grain because, even after threshing, the grains are covered by a protective sheath.

PEARL SPELT
After dehusking, pearl spelt undertakes a further processing stage which bleaches the grain and reduces its cooking time.

SPELT
These days this is not very commonly found in Italy, but a variant from Campania, *speutone,* is recognized as a traditional product.

SPELT FROM TRIVENTO
An Italian cultivar of spelt, recently introduced in the Trivento area (in the province of Campobasso).

GRANO DEL MIRACOLO
The name given in the Parmense and surrounding areas to a durum wheat variety with exceptional fertility and yield.

DURUM WHEAT
It has large and heavy grains, which break cleanly, with sharp edges.All Sicilian durum wheat is classified as a traditional product.

SICILIAN AMEDEO DURUM WHEAT
A variety particularly suitable to bread making. It is used for some types of traditional bread.

SICILIAN MONGIBELLO DURUM WHEAT
It is a cross between the Trinakria and Valforte varieties, and it is used for the preparation of Sicilian *pagnotta del Dittaino* DOP.

SICILIAN SANT'AGATA DURUM WHEAT
It is a cross between the Adamello and Simeto varieties; it is particularly suited for bread and pasta making.

SENATORE CAPPELLI DURUM WHEAT
A highly regarded variety, rich in nutrients. Today it survives in a few areas of Central and Southern Italy.

BUCKWHEAT
It belongs to the Poligonacee family and is gluten free. Its grains can be used in soups among other uses.

RAW BUCKWHEAT
Before refining, the triangular shaped raw grains are protected by an inedible husk.

BUCKWHEAT FLAKES
On its own or with other types of flakes and dried fruit, it can be used for breakfast muesli.

SOFT WHEAT
It has elongated grains that break unevenly, with floury edges. It is grown in particular in the Padana Plain.

CORN
The most common variety is the yellow one, but there are also white, black, red, or bluish varieties of corn.

BIANCOPERLA CORN
Highly regarded corn variety with large and pearl-like grains, from which white polenta or Treviso polenta is obtained. It has a delicate flavor.

STORO CORN
According to tradition, in Storo, corn ears are hung outside houses and dried by the mountain winds.

OTTOFILE CORN
The ear of this ancient variety of Piedmont corn has eight rows of grains, hence its name, and it has a very sweet flavor.

DEHUSKED BARLEY
Also called *mondo*, this is whole grain barley, from which only the glumelle (inner scales) have been removed. It needs a long soaking and cooking time.

DEHUSKED ROCCAFORTE BARLEY
A variety obtained from a cross that is suitable for toasting, pearling, milling, and puffing.

TOASTED AND GROUND DEHUSKED BARLEY
Once dehusked, barley is toasted and then ground. Aniseed or other flavors may be added to it. The one from Marche is a typical variety.

PEARL BARLEY
It has undertaken a refining process that eliminates the husk. It can be cooked after thorough washing.

TOASTED BARLEY
Dehusked barley toasted at high temperature is the base for tisanes and coffee replacement beverages.

RYE
Ancient cereal used as flour, in particular for traditional breads and rustic cakes in Valle d'Aosta, Trentino.

BUCKWHEAT FLOUR
With a slightly bitter taste. Polenta, *pizzoccheri*, and *sciatt* are typical dishes from the Valtellina area prepared with this flour.

WHOLE GRAIN SOFT WHEAT FLOUR
Obtained by milling soft wheat grains. It is a uniform brown color, without impurities.

CORN FLOUR
Also called "yellow flour." Depending on the extent of sifting, it is used for polenta, bread, or cakes.

BREAD, NORTH AND SOUTH

There are countless varieties of breads in Italy. They vary on the basis of shape (from the simplest to the most imaginative), ingredients used in the dough, leavening, and processing techniques (traditional or innovative). Alongside the varieties widespread throughout the national territory, highly regarded niche products can also be found.

BAULETTO MANTOVANO
A bread with a long tradition, characterized by central cuts and lines along the top, which create ridge-like shapes.

BIGARANO FROM ROVIGO
It is prepared with the same dough used for *cioppa veneta*. Its shape is obtained by twisting long thin loaves.

BOZZA PRATESE
A Tuscan bread, without salt, with a rectangular shape and a dark brown color. It has a slightly acidic taste.

CASERECCIO
A definition that covers many different types of bread, all of them of a large size. Leftover bread was used over successive days.

DURUM WHEAT CIABATTINE
Typical of Sicily, they have a rectangular shape, with a crisp crust and limited crumb.

COPPIA FERRARESE IPG
The shape is given by two pieces of dough joined up as in a ribbon, with the outer extremities turned out to form four horns.

SESAME FILONCINI
Made with soft wheat, they are very soft and are characterized by sesame seeds on the top.

DURUM WHEAT FILONE
Widespread throughout Italy. The presence of durum wheat makes this a rich bread with a crisp crust.

FILONE RIMACINATO FROM SICILY
Made with re-milled durum wheat semolina, it has a characteristic yellow-amber color and crumb.

TYPICAL APULIAN FILONE
Typical bread from Andria (Bari). It is at its best when just cooled even though the crust remains crisp for several hours.

TUSCAN FILONE
Famous for being made entirely without salt. It has a crisp golden crust.

FRANCESINO
Bread of French origin that has quickly become widespread in Italy, in particular in many areas of Emilia Romagna.

MAFALDA
One of the most symbolic of Sicilian breads, its top surface is characteristically covered with sesame seeds.

MAGGIOLINO
A bread with a hard crust typical of Lombardy and other regions of the North. Its name (meaning "beetle") derives from its rounded shape.

MAROCCA FROM CASOLA

This is made with chestnut flour, which is plentiful in the Linigiana area, where wheat was once in short supply.

MICCA FROM PARMA

This bread stands out for having salt and lard added to the dough before shaping. It has a rather hard crust and a smooth crumb.

MICCONE PAVESE

Bread from the area of Oltrepò Pavese. Of large size, it is one of the ingredients of the typical *zuppa pavese*.

MICHETTA MILANESE

It is the bread roll used to make the typical Italian sandwich. The hollow inside is perfect for all types of fillings.

MONTASÙ VENETO

Well liked for its crumbliness, its name derives from its rather unusual shape, which looks a bit like a mountain.

NEAPOLITAN CASERECCIO

Baked in a wood oven, it is the classic Neapolitan loaf, also called *pane cafone*. It is typically used on the occasion of the feast of Sant'Anna.

PAGNOTTA DEL DITTAINO DPO

This Sicilian bread is produced between the provinces of Enna and Catania. It is made with different varieties of re-milled durum wheat semolina.

PAGNOTTA PUGLIESE

A smaller loaf than the *filone* from Andria but with similar characteristics. Its crust remains crisp for a long time.

PANCARRÉ

A sandwich bread that is very soft. To keep the slices soft, the loaf can be covered with a damp cloth until needed.

POTATO BREAD FROM ABRUZZO

Bread normally made with type "1" flour, semolina, and potatoes. It has a distinctive taste and a crisp golden crust.

MIXED SEED BREAD

A recently introduced product typical of Trentino Alto Adige. The dough includes milk and eggs as well as a variety of seeds.

SICILIAN OLIVE BREAD

It comes from the ancient peasant custom of eating bread with olives while working in the fields.

APULIAN PANE CASERECCIO

Made with durum wheat semolina, with some malt added to the dough. It is a rustic bread with a crisp crust.

SICILIAN PANE CASERECCIO

Called *vastedda*, it is a durum wheat bread with a crisp golden crust, which lasts a long time.

BREAD WITH TOASTED BRAN

Darker than ordinary bread, it is often made with starter yeast. It is made mainly in the Veneto region.

BREAD COOKED WITH EMBERS

Among the traditional cooking methods for bread there is also one that uses embers. The oven must be a wood oven, and it must not be too hot.

PANE DI GENZANO IPG

This naturally leavened bread is prepared in Genzano (near Rome). It has a thick crust and ivory-colored crumb.

PANE DI LARIANO

Bread from the Lazio region, made with partially refined flour, which gives both the crumb and the crust a unique firmness.

CORN BREAD

It is made in many Italian regions and it is characterized by a sweeter taste than that of wheat bread.

PANE DI MATERA

Made with re-milled durum wheat semolina from the Basilicata region, it is characterized by its warm color and the porosity of its crust.

MOUNTAIN BREAD

Rustic bread from the Apennines between Liguria and Emilia, it is traditionally cooked on chestnut leaves. It is excellent for at least three days.

RYE BREAD

It contains low levels of gluten because it is made with a mix that contains rye flour. It is typical of Alpine regions.

SENATORE BREAD

Long-lasting bread from Abruzzi, made with the wheat variety known as Senatore Cappelli and natural yeast.

BLACK BREAD FROM CASTELVETRANO

Prepared with local wheat flour, *tummini*, which gives it its rich color and intense taste.

APULIAN BREAD WITH POTATOES

Bread of ancient origins, it is made by adding mashed boiled potatoes to the flour. It has a golden and scented crust.

PANE SPIGA FROM ABRUZZO

Typical product from Vasto, widely available in the province of Chieti. It requires brewer's yeast to be added to the acidic dough.

POPPY SEEDS ROLL

Covered with poppy seeds, it is typical of Trentino Alto Adige and it is made in a wide variety of forms, using different types of dough.

MILK ROLLS

Of small size, they are soft and a little sweet because of the addition of milk or butter to the dough.

PUCCIA

Bread typical of the Belluno province, it is made with rye flour and, in the traditional version, with local wild oregano.

ROSETTA TRIESTINA

The "emperor's king," which reiterates that in the past white bread was used only by the aristocracy.

ROSETTA VENETA

This is the name used for *michetta* outside the Milano province. It is characterized by its five incisions and central "hat," giving it the shape of a rose.

SEMELLA

Unlike classic Tuscan breads, this bread has salt added to its dough. It is the typical roll used with *lampredotto*.

NEAPOLITAN SFILATINO

Made with soft wheat, it has a thin, elongated shape and a crisp crust. It is suitable for making sandwiches with soft and moist fillings.

SPACCATINA VENETA

Typical of the area of Padua and the rest of Veneto, it is made with a soft dough.

TARTARUGA

The characteristic diamond pattern on its top surface is made with a particular mold and is the reason for its name, which means "turtle." It is ideal for sandwiches.

ULIATE SALENTINE

The dough is made with a lot of water to make it softer, and black olives are added to it, with or without pits (stones).

ZOCCOLETTO VENETO

It is made with the same dough used for *ciabatta* but it is smaller. It is characterized by a very crisp crust.

HARD AND SEMI-HARD CHEESES

Seasoned for at least six months, hard cheeses are often of large size, with a hard rind, a compact and crumbly texture, and they keep for a long time. Semi-hard cheeses are seasoned for a period of two to six months.

ASIAGO DOP

There is a *mezzano* variety (seasoned for at least three months, with a sweet taste) and a *vecchio* variety (over nine months, spicy and grainy).

BAGÒSS

Produced with raw cow's milk, it has a dark rind, due to the use of flaxseed oil. It smells of hay and has a spicy final taste.

BASTARDO DEL GRAPPA

It has a strong, pleasant smell, and a full, sweet flavor, with a spicy note that becomes more intense over time.

BETTELMATT

A cooked or semi-cooked curd cheese, it is produced in the summer, when the scent and flavor of grass is at its strongest.

BITTO DOP

It has a cylindrical shape, with a white to straw-colored paste and a compact texture. It has a sweet and aromatic taste.

BRA DOP

It comes in soft, hard, and mountain pasture varieties. It has a moderately spicy and sweet taste in the soft variety.

CAPREL SARDO

It is produced in San Gavino Monreale using pasteurized goat milk. It has a soft, white porcelain paste.

CAPRINO CAVALESE

Goat cheese typical of Trentino, it is available fresh or seasoned. It is handcrafted and naturally seasoned.

CAPRINO SARDO
Hand crafted, mainly with whole fat goat milk. It has a spicy flavor that becomes more marked as the cheese ages.

CASTELMAGNO DOP
Cheese made with raw cow's milk, with small amounts of sheep or goat milk. It has a soft paste and a delicate flavor.

CRUCOLO TRENTINO
It has a slightly soft paste with obvious holes. It achieves its peculiar flavor through aging.

FIORE SICANO
Cheese made with raw cow's milk, superficially salted when dry. It is characterized by indigenous mold.

FONTAL
Name used to refer to all cheeses produced in the same way as *Fontina* but outside the DOP area.

FONTINA DOP
Depending on the aging period (at least eighty days), its taste gets more intense, and its rind darkens with age.

FORMAGGIO DI FOSSA
Produced in the Romagna-Marche Apennines (the one from Sogliano qualifies for the DOP mark). Its final taste turns from sweet to spicy.

FORMAI DE MUT DOP
Semi-cooked curd cheese produced in the mountain pasture area of the Bergamo region. If it is more than one year old, it can be grated.

GRANA PADANO DOP
Produced throughout the Po Valley right up to Trento. It has a fragrant, delicate, and pleasant taste, even after a long refining period.

LATTERIA FRESCO
Name given in the North to cow's milk cheese produced in the lowlands. Its taste depends on how cows are fed.

MAIORCHINO
Sicilian sheep milk hard cheese produced on the Peloritani Mountains. It is at its best after a long aging time.

MALGA OR UGOVIZZA
Summer pasture semi-cooked curd cheese produced from whole fat cheese in the Friuli region. It has minor cracks and cavities, and a sweet taste, spicier if seasoned.

MEZZANO DI CAPRA
Semi-seasoned cheese with a compact, semi-hard paste, aged for three months. Its taste is very delicate and sweet.

MONTASIO DOP
Produced in Friuli and part of Veneto. If fresh, it has a more delicate Alpine taste. It has a fuller flavor when semi-seasoned, and spicy when fully seasoned.

MORLACCO
Soft cheese from Veneto, low fat and salty. It is excellent with polenta, served with slices of *soppressa vicentina*.

MURAZZANO DOP
Handcrafted cheese from Piedmont, made with sheep or mixed milks, with a fine and delicate taste, and a grassy aftertaste.

PARMIGIANO REGGIANO DOP
Cheese for the table or to be grated, produced with milk from two successive milking runs. It is seasoned for a period of between 12 and 36 months.

PECORINO CANESTRATO PUGLIESE DOP
A sheep milk cheese, its rind bears the marks of the basket used as a mold. It is consumed fresh or seasoned.

PECORINO DI GROTTA
A sheep milk cheese. The one from the province of Viterbo is well known, seasoned in volcanic caves, which give it a very intense flavor.

PECORINO DI PIENZA
A sheep milk cheese produced in the province of Siena. It is sweet with spicy notes. The one seasoned in barrels is a traditional variety.

FIORE SARDO DOP
The industrial variety is made with different milks, while the handcrafted varieties use only raw sheep milk. Slightly smoked.

PECORINO PERLANERA SARDO
A sheep milk cheese, with a semi-hard, compact paste, and a slightly acidic flavor. It is can be identified by its dark rind that preserves the cheese.

PECORINO ROMANO DOP
A sheep milk cheese with a very white inside with an aromatic, slightly spicy taste. It can be grated, if sufficiently aged.

PECORINO SARDO DOP
A sheep milk cheese, with a white, soft inside. It has a slightly acidic taste. When mature, its inside becomes darker and its flavor spicier.

PECORINO SICILIANO DOP
A sheep milk cheese. If sold with the DOP mark, it has been seasoned for at least four months.

PECORINO TOSCANO DOP STAGIONATO
A sheep milk cheese that has been seasoned for longer than 180 days, which highlights its intense flavors and its slighly spicy notes.

PUZZONE DI MOENA
A cheese typical of Trentino. Washing its rind encourages the bacterial fermentation that gives it its intense aroma.

RASCHERA DOP
Produced in the province of Cuneo, it has a fine and delicate taste, with a moderately rich and spicy flavor if it has been seasoned.

SOLA DI CAPRA
A goat milk cheese from Piedmont, with a pungent aroma. It is soft, with small holes, and it has rounded corners.

SPEZIATO
Often made with cow's milk, flavored cheeses (with chives, chili pepper, or pepper) are widespread in Italy.

TOMA PIEMONTESE DOP
This cheese depends on the type of milk used—if whole milk, it has a fat, soft inside, if partially creamed, the inside is less fatty.

TRENTINGRANA
This cheese belongs to the Grana Padano DOP, but can assume the additional classification of *trentin* (from the Trentino region).

UBRIACO
Ubriaco translates as "drunk" and the purple staining from the grape marc makes rounds of *montasio*, *bra*, *asiago*, or *latteria* unique.

VALTELLINA CASERA DOP
This cheese has a compact texture and very fine holes. Its sweet taste becomes richer with aging.

SPUN-PASTE CHEESES

Mozzarella, *provolone*, and *caciocavallo* are all made by "spinning" the milk curds. *Pasta filata* cheeses can be seasoned more or less slowly, and *mozzarella* is different as it is left to rest for a short time in brine. They can be made with cow's or sheep milk, or a blend of milks.

BURRATA
Typical of Apulia, it is sweeter and more buttery than *mozzarella*, with a distinct milky taste. It is consumed as a course in itself.

MOZZARELLA DI BUFALA CAMPANA DOP
Made with buffalo milk, it uses a traditional production system that includes the use of a stick and a bowl. It is excellent fresh or baked.

MOZZARELLA FIOR DI LATTE
One of the best known cheeses in the world, it is made exclusively with cow's milk. It has a more compact texture than *bufala mozzarella*.

BUTIRRO
Called *burrino* in the Calabrian dialect, it is similar to *caciocavallo* but it conceals a core of soft butter.

CACETTI CAMPANI
Small, white, and smoked cheeses, shaped like a pear or like two spheres joined in the middle. They are made in Campania all year round.

CACIOCAVALLO
Typical throughout Southern Italy, it is one of the best *pasta filata* cheeses. If aged for a long time, it becomes quite spicy.

CACIOCAVALLO PUGLIESE
The *podolico* variety is very highly regarded. It can be aged for a long time, offering a wide range of complex flavors.

CACIOCAVALLO SILANO DOP
Very delicate and sweet if fresh, when seasoned its paste becomes quite flaky, with a slightly spicy taste.

PERETTA SARDA
With an enveloping flavor. If fresh, it is used as filling for the typical *seadas* (Sardinian fritters), and it is excellent broiled (grilled) if seasoned.

PROVOLA AFFUMICATA
Originally, this was the tester to be immersed in boiling water to see if the milk curds were ready.

PROVOLONE SARDO

It can reach 22 lbs (10 kg) in weight, and has a seasoning time of between three to six months. It has a compact texture, and its flavor can be sweet or spicy.

PROVOLONE VALPADANA DOP

It has a nearly white inside and it is produced in different types. Because it melts easily, it is ideal for cooking on a griddle.

RAGUSANO DOP

Typical Sicilian cheese, with a shape obtained though manual processing. It is at its best when seasoned.

FRESH OR SMOKED SCAMORZA

Produced with whole fat pasteurized milk. In the Neapolitan area, it is filled with olives and chili pepper.

TRECCIA DI SCAMORZA

A variant of plated *scamorza*. It can be white in color and sweet and light, or smoked, more aromatic, and darker.

SOFT CHEESES

Normally seasoned for only a short time, soft cheeses have a delicate taste, with a distinctive milky flavor. They can be fresh, like *caprini* and *tomini*, soft and without rind, like *pannerone*, or soft with a rind, seasoned for up to two months. It is a type of cheese that is often used in cooking.

BLUE DEL MONVISO

It has a creamy inside, veined with blue, with a white surface mold. It has a sweeter taste than other blue cheeses.

BRA TENERO DOP

If fresh, it has a soft inside, of a moderately uniform ivory white color. It has a sweet and milky taste.

BRIE

This cheese comes under the heading of raw milk cheeses, with a surface mold and a delicate, sweet, and rich flavor.

CACIOTTA ROCCAPONTINA

Produced with whole fat cow's milk, it is seasoned on wooden planks. It has a balanced taste, with milky tones.

CAPRINI AROMATIZZATI

Fresh, this cheese can be covered or mixed with spices, herbs, and dried fruit. Red or black pepper are common.

CAPRINI

Fresh cheeses of different shapes made with goat milk on its own, or mixed with cow's milk. Excellent for the table.

CASATELLA TREVIGIANA DOP

This cheese is without rind and has a shiny and creamy milky white inside. It has a fresh, slightly acidic taste.

CASATICA DI BUFALA

With the typical red-veined rind, it has a flavor that can go from sweet to rich, with a buffalo milk aftertaste.

FORMAGGELLA
This cheese is handcrafted in the hilly and mountainous areas of Lombardy. There are some very different varieties.

GIUNCATA
Cow's milk cheese from Calabria, with delicate taste and scent, similar to that of fresh raw milk.

GORGONZOLA PICCANTE
Its inside, which is firm and homogeneous, is less creamy than that of the sweet variety, with typical gray-green veining.

MARZOLINO DEL CHIANTI
Its compact texture, from white to light pink, and its thin red rind (from the inclusion of tomato) are its main characteristics.

PAGLIETTA
Cheese originally from the Cuneo province, it has a thin superficial layer of mold and a soft melting inside, with a slightly spicy taste.

PANNARELLO
Typical of Treviso and Pordenone, it is a cow's milk cheese to which cream is added, which makes it soft and sweet.

PECORINO A CROSTA FIORITA
Typical of the province of Florence, it takes its name from its rough rind, covered in grayish mold.

PRIMOSALE
Fresh cheese from a mix of milks. It is salted only on its surface, and it is consumed fresh. Excellent with arugula (rocket).

RICOTTA ROMANA DOP
Obtained from the whey of the sheep milk used for making *pecorino*. It has a typical sweetish taste.

ROBIOLA DI ROCCAVERANO DOP
Historical goat milk cheese from Piedmont. The flowers, grass, and bacterial flora of the stable it comes from give it an individual taste.

ROSA CAMUNA
With a shape reminiscent of the petal of a rose, it is produced in the Valcamonica area. It has a soft, compact, and scented inside.

SCIMUDIN
Handcrafted cheese from Lombardy. It is a raw paste cheese made with cow's milk. It has a fatty texture.

SQUACQUERONE
A fresh cheese made with cow's milk in Emilia Romagna. It has a soft inside and a sweet taste.

STRACCHINO
There are various types of this cheese in Lombardy. They all share the typical and unmistakable taste, which can be creamy or spicy.

TALEGGIO DOP
Fresh cheese whose seasoning continues until it is consumed. It needs to be carefully stored to allow good air circulation.

Page numbers in *italics* refer
to illustrations

Recipes preceded by an *
indicate a chef's recipe

Phaidon Press Limited
Regent's Wharf
All Saints Street
London N1 9PA

Phaidon Press Inc.
65 Bleecker Street
New York, NY 10012

phaidon.com

First published 2016
© 2016 Phaidon Press Limited
ISBN 978 0 7148 7279 7

Eataly: Contemporary Italian Cooking originates
from Le Ricette di Eataly series by Food Editore,
an imprint of Food S.r.l., Via Mazzini 6, 43121 Parma
© Food Editore, 2015

A CIP catalogue record for this book is available
from the British Library and the Library of Congress.

All rights reserved. No part of this publication
may be reproduced, stored in a retrieval system
or transmitted, in any form or by any means,
electronic, mechanical, photocopying, recording
or otherwise, without the prior written permission
of Phaidon Press Limited.

Commissioning Editor: Emilia Terragni
Project Editor: Ellie Smith
Production Controller: Amanda Mackie

Cover design by João Mota
Internal design by Sánchez / Lacasta
Recipe photography by Food Editore/Piermichele
    Borraccia
Artworked by Ana Rita Teodoro

The publisher would like to thank Theresa
Bebbington, Licia Cagnoni, Lucia Carletti, Clare
Churly, Valentina Coppo, Paolo Dalcò, Oscar
Farinetti, Jodie Gaudet, Emma Hipshon, Sophie
Hodgkin, Chris Lacey, Giulia Malerba, Cristiana
Mistrali, João Mota, Laura Nickoll, Margherita
Scorletti, Leon Smith, Tracey Smith, and Hans
Stofregen for their contributions to the book.

The publisher would also like to thank the following
Eataly chefs who contributed recipes to this book
and the original series: Lorenza Alcantara,
Ugo Alciati, Alberto Bettini, Antonio Bufi, Giorgio
Chiesa, Alessandro Coccia, Gianluca Esposito,
Fabio Greco, Luca Montersino, Enrico Panero,
Lucio Pompili, Fabio Nitti, Marta Pavera, Chiara
Testore, Pasquale Torrente, Elena Verzeroli, Viviana
Varese, Elena Vian, Anna Vicina, Claudio Vicina,
Elena Verzeroli, and Luca Zecchin.

The Eataly trademark is the property of Eataly and
used under licence by Phaidon Press Limited.

Printed in China

Recipe Notes

Butter should always be salted.

All herbs are fresh, unless otherwise specified.

Individual vegetables and fruits, such as onions
and apples, are assumed to be medium, unless
otherwise specified.

Eggs are assumed to be medium (US large),
unless otherwise specified.

Cooking times are for guidance only, as individual
ovens vary. If using a fan (convection) oven,
follow the manufacturer's instructions concerning
oven temperatures.

Exercise a high level of caution when following
recipes involving any potentially hazardous activity,
including the use of high temperatures, open
flames and when deep-frying. In particular, when
deep-frying, add food carefully to avoid splashing,
wear long sleeves and never leave
the pan unattended.

Some recipes include raw or very lightly cooked
eggs, meat or fish, and fermented products. The
elderly, infants, pregnant women, convalescents,
and anyone with an impaired immune system
should avoid these.

Exercise caution when making fermented products,
ensuring all equipment is spotlessly clean, and seek
expert advice if in any doubt.

All herbs, shoots, flowers and greens should be
picked fresh from a clean source. Exercise caution
when foraging for ingredients; any foraged
ingredients should only be eaten if an expert has
deemed them safe to eat.

When no quantity is specified, for example of oils,
salts and herbs used for finishing dishes, quantities
are discretionary and flexible.

Both metric and imperial measures are used in this
book. Follow one set of measurements throughout,
not a mixture, as they are not interchangeable.

All spoon and cup measurements are level,
unless otherwise stated. 1 teaspoon = 5 ml;
1 tablespoon = 15 ml.

Australian standard tablespoons are 20 ml,
so Australian readers are advised to use
3 teaspoons in place of 1 tablespoon when
measuring small quantities.